Today's Military Wife

Today's Military Wife

Meeting the Challenges of Service Life

6th Edition

Lydia Sloan Cline

STACKPOLE
BOOKS

Published by
Stackpole Books
5067 Ritter Road
Mechanicsburg, PA 17055
www.stackpolebooks.com

Printed in the United States of America

10 9 8 7 6 5 4 3 2 1

Cover design by Tessa Sweigert

Library of Congress Cataloging-in-Publication Data

Cline, Lydia Sloan.
    Today's military wife : meeting the challenges of service life / Lydia Sloan Cline.
      p. cm.
    Includes index.
    ISBN-13: 978-0-8117-3516-2
    ISBN-10: 0-8117-3516-8
    1. United States—Armed Forces—Military life. 2. Military spouses—United States—Handbooks, manuals, etc. I. Title.
    U766.C48 2008
    355.1'20973—dc22

                                                   2008030254

To all who serve, away and at home.

Recipe for a Military Wife

1$^1/_2$ cups patience
2 tablespoons elbow grease
1 pound courage
1 cup tolerance
dash of adventure

Marinate frequently with salty tears and pour off excess fat. Sprinkle ever so lightly with money, kneading dough well until payday. Season with international spices. Bake for twenty years or until done. Serve with pride!
—Author unknown

Contents

Introduction

The following questions were posted to message boards at various military communities.

"My husband just joined the Marine Corps. What will he be doing, will he be well, what about pay and ID cards?"

"My husband is considering joining the Air Force. He wants me and our baby to join him after Boot and Tech. But I'm currently working on a degree and have just started a new job. What should I do? I want to support him, but this is such a different lifestyle. Should I put my school life on hold until we move? Stay here until I'm finished? Can someone give me some insight?"

"My husband will deploy soon. What do you do to alleviate the stress when you know your loved ones are in danger? How do you busy yourselves to ease the anxiety?"

"I am about to be torn from my stable home, as my husband is going active duty soon. I know nothing about the military and am in a panic. I'm told they will pack up our home and send us to where he's stationed. What do I do? What do I keep or throw away? How much do we take? How well do the movers pack things, should I pack anything myself, should I feed them lunch? Please advise."

"How much should I tip the commissary bagger?"

"There is a 13-month wait list for housing at our new duty station. How will the movers ship our things when we don't know where we'll live? How do I find a place to rent and where the good areas are? We need to break our lease here, will we lose our deposit?"

"We're being transferred to Ft. Sill. What is their elementary school like? How hard will it be for me to find a decent job?"

"I am about to become a Navy wife. On top of planning a wedding I have to plan a move to New Orleans. I know nothing about that area. I'm particularly interested in housing, health care, nearby colleges, and anything else that I would find useful. Thank you in advance for any help."

"Does Germany have cable TV in English? Can I rent movies there soon after their release? I'm really into Days of Our Lives *and my son loves cartoons. Will we be able to continue watching them? Sorry if these sound like silly questions, but they're important to me."*

"Are any of the supports offered to military wives also offered to girlfriends/fiancées?"

If you're new to the military, these might be your own questions. Unless you grew up as a "brat" yourself, the military can be a perplexing place. There are strange customs, stranger acronyms, odd jobs, and odder duty hours.

Hence this book. It is written for the person who has married (or is about to marry) a member of the U.S. Armed Forces and wants to learn about the opportunities and challenges of service life. It is a reference of answers to frequently asked questions and issues unique to this lifestyle, such as moving, benefits, deployments, social affairs, and maintaining one's own career. Reasons behind customs and regulations are discussed on the premise that when they are understood they are easier to work with.

WHY READ THIS BOOK?

You may be wondering why, with the enormous amounts of information available on base and the World Wide Web, you should read an ink-and-paper book. That is a good question, but there is an equally good answer. This book's intent is to present the most relevant topics for those new to this lifestyle in one place and in an organized manner. In this current challenging climate, busy military wives have more productive things to do than wade through websites and visit offices seeking answers to questions they may not even know to ask. This book offers a starting point. Websites are referenced throughout each chapter so the reader can immediately find more information on topics that particularly interest her. For convenience, *she* is used for the spouse and *he* for the servicemember, as that is chiefly the makeup of the armed forces.

IMPORTANCE OF FAMILY MEMBERS

Modern military recruiting has a new focus: "deciders," as spouses and parents are called, are pitched with the benefits of military life almost as much as the potential servicemember is. This is an acknowledgment of the powerful role the family plays in the servicemember's job performance. Support programs are implemented and maintained on the premise that the military member whose family is satisfied with the lifestyle will be more likely to make the personal sacrifices necessary for a strong defense.

Military wives, not content to play the historic role of silent partners, communicate strongly with officials. Numerous studies and surveys record our wants and

There are more military family members than there are total uniformed servicemembers. Sixty percent of military personnel are married; over 80 percent of all career-status personnel are married. Many have minor children. Military families comprise diverse racial and ethnic backgrounds and family types. There are single parents, dual-income couples, families with a stay-at-home parent, and families that support elders who live with them.

needs, resulting in tangible programs and incentives such as family services, relocation centers, child-care centers, and civil service hiring preference.

Your direct influence on your spouse's career may not be great, but your influence on his morale is. Your attitude toward his job can greatly influence how well he does it, as well as his decision to remain in the service. In a volunteer force, where the retention of quality people is a priority, you can see how important that makes you.

THE MILITARY LIFESTYLE

If you are considering marrying a servicemember, this book may help you better understand the lifestyle and clarify misconceptions. For instance, some believe that this lifestyle is an automatic path to financial security, or that designer suits can be bought at the Exchange for pennies, or that military families don't pay taxes. Hmmm . . . not quite true. These and many other subjects are discussed in depth.

But there *are* huge advantages to this lifestyle. You may visit more places in ten years than many see in a lifetime. You have opportunities to make immediate friends at each duty station through Family Readiness Groups. Extraordinary benefits can stretch the paycheck. And while deployments and separations from friends and relatives can be stressful, many wives take pride in discovering how self-reliant they are.

You also have an unofficial partnership with the Department of Defense. It implements and advertises programs, but you must notice and participate in them. The spouse who declines to attend orientation briefings, is reluctant to participate in events because "she's not in the military," and otherwise distances herself from the community does herself a disservice. Life with the military is like anything else: what you get out reflects what you put in. The saying "Bloom where you're planted" is a way of life among the happiest, most successful military wives.

So, let's get going!

What Does Your Husband Do for a Living?

Everyone knows what teachers do. Few would have trouble describing the duties of construction workers or nurses. Most have an idea of what Web designers and video-game programmers do.

But what do airmen do? Do they all fly planes? Do all soldiers wear camouflage paint and drive tanks? Do sailors really swab decks? And the Marines and Coast Guard—what, exactly, do they do?

If your first contact with the service was when you met your husband, your idea of what he did might be hazy—part Hollywood, part stereotype. Now that you're married (or about to be), if your understanding isn't clearer, let's make it so.

Your husband is a member of the armed forces, the organization that protects the United States and its allies, that guards the way of life of the free world. Your husband is helping to ensure that our rights to vote, to free speech, to assemble peaceably, and to worship as we will are not taken away. He is helping to ensure that the flow of essential items to and from our allies is not impeded. Regardless of rank or job, every servicemember performs his duties for those reasons.

SOME BACKGROUND AND FIGURES

In 1789, as our founding fathers developed and refined the first military institutions, they determined that a civilian should head the military as part of a system of checks and balances. Therefore, the president of the United States is the commander in chief of the Armed Forces. Under the president is the Secretary of Defense, and under the Secretary of Defense are the Secretaries of the Army, Navy, and Air Force, all civilians. At the top level in the military chain of command are the Joint Chiefs of Staff—they are the heads of the Army, Navy, Marines, and Air Force, and they report directly to the Secretary of Defense.

The Army is America's oldest military service. The Continental Army was first established in June 1775 when the Continental Congress first authorized men to serve. The Navy came into existence in October 1775, and the Marine Corps was

The *armed services* are the Army, Navy, Air Force, Marines Corps, and Coast Guard. The *uniformed services* are the armed services plus the National Oceanic and Atmospheric Administration and the U.S. Public Health Service.

formed one month later. (The Marine Corps is technically a part of the Navy, but it has its own commandant.) The Coast Guard is the smallest service. Formed in 1915, it is part of the Department of Homeland Security in peacetime and part of the Navy when at war. The Air Force was originally part of the Army, but in 1947 the Army Air Corps, the General Headquarters Air Force, the Army Air Force, and the aeronautical division and aviation sections of the Army Signal Corps were combined into a new and separate service. Because of their shared history, many Army and Air Force customs and courtesies are identical.

Q: Why are marines called leathernecks?
A: The origins of this nickname are unclear. Some scholars claim it was applied to marines (probably by sailors) from the days when both American and British marines wore high, stiff leather collars, designed to either protect their necks from sword blows, keep them from slouching in uniform, or to steady the head when aiming firearms.

Each service has its specific mission: The Army defends on land, the Navy by sea, and the Air Force in the skies. The Marine Corps is a readiness force ("soldiers of the sea"), and the Coast Guard protects our coastal borders and conducts search-and-rescue operations.

As of December 2007, there were about 1.36 million active-duty military, 1 million guardsmen and reservists, 648,000 Department of Defense (DoD) civilian workers, and 1.9 million family members. The DoD's 2007 budget was slightly over $439 billion, about 4 percent of the nation's Gross Domestic Product (GDP; the total dollar value of all final goods and services produced in the country in a year). That figure includes the salaries, training, and health care of uniformed and civilian personnel, facilities and equipment maintenance, and operations. It doesn't include related items such as weapons research, the Department of Veterans Affairs, or the wars in Iraq and Afghanistan. The wars are funded via budget supplements; $600 billion was approved for 2008. To put military spending in context, see the pie chart on page 3.

NOT JUST ANOTHER JOB
The minimum requirements for entering the service are either U.S. citizenship or permanent residency (green card holders). Military members take an oath upon joining the service that asserts loyalty to those appointed over them and to the president. Hence, disobeying orders, not showing up for work, or even showing up late, can

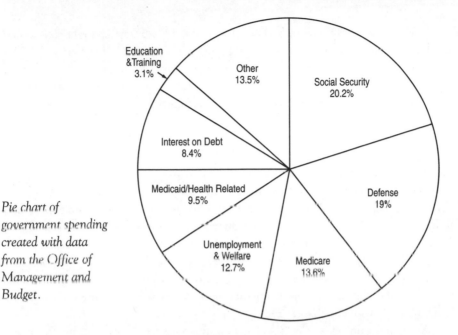

Pie chart of government spending created with data from the Office of Management and Budget.

have serious repercussions. The military cannot be quit at will; a servicemember is obliged to serve out the time specified on the enlistment contract he signed upon entering. Officers may resign, but even that typically takes several months to process, and if there is a "stop-loss" (a temporary hold on the ability of personnel to leave) in place, resignations are not accepted.

One day of active duty qualifies a noncitizen to apply for U.S. citizenship.

WHAT IS BASIC TRAINING?

Basic training is the initial process of transforming civilians into servicemembers. It involves intense physical activity and behavioral discipline.

When a new recruit reports for duty, he is "in-processed." In-processing includes receiving equipment and uniforms, a haircut, shots, dental exams, the ID card, and lots of paperwork. He must live in barracks (dormitories in the Air Force) on base, which are private or semiprivate rooms or suites.

Then basic training starts. It has two parts: everyone, regardless of his future field, attends the first part; the second part is job training in a specific field (e.g., infantry, food service, finance). In the Air Force the job training part is called Technical (Tech) School. In the Navy it's called A-School (advanced job training is C-School), and in the Army is called Advanced Individual Training (AIT). The second part may not be held at the same base as the first part.

The days are long for recruits. They get up at 4:30 or 5:00 A.M. for breakfast, and are done for the day after dinner around 8:00 P.M. Barracks lights-out is 10:00 or 11:00. Weekends off generally aren't given until near the end of training. Recruits have an opportunity to go to sick call each morning if they don't feel well. Transportation to religious services is provided on weekends. Hot meals are served in the mess hall, and Meals, Ready to Eat (MREs; packaged meals) are consumed when they're in the field.

Phone time is extremely limited—as little as five minutes on a Sunday is usual—and even that isn't granted until the recruit has "proven" himself. Letters are the best way for you to communicate—recruits live for mail call. However, know that your letters and packages are subject to being open and read. Don't send candy, chewing gum, cookies, soft drinks, or tobacco products, as these products are considered hindrances to the physical training process and will be confiscated. Unflavored cough drops are allowed and welcome. Many drill sergeants don't permit news clippings, so feel free to write about world events, but don't mail articles about them. If you need to contact your husband for an emergency, contact the Commanding Officer or the Red Cross (discussed in chapter 2).

After the training is over, there is a final exercise called the Crucible in the Marine Corps, the Battle Stations in the Navy, Victory Forge in the Army, and the Scorpion's Nest in the Air Force. Once the recruits pass this test they are official members of that service. They have a graduation ceremony, and a letter will be sent to you from the Commanding Officer with its specific date and time. You are encouraged to attend, as it's a major accomplishment. If an overnight stay is required, you'll need to arrange your own accommodations. Many servicemembers go on to more training, so getting leave (vacation) at this time isn't assured.

Officer basic training is different. Since so much of the physical and other training aspects were addressed during the Reserve Officer Training Corps (ROTC) or service academy education, officer recruits typically live in their own apartments during training, and the restriction on mail and communications doesn't apply.

RANK

"Rank" (or "rate" in the Coast Guard) is a relative standing or position, a hierarchical arrangement. It is the position each servicemember holds. Servicemembers are categorized as enlisted (voluntarily enrolled or drafted into military service), warrant officer (a person with a warrant—an official document bestowed by a military branch—to perform a specific task), or commissioned officer (a person who holds a commission—an official document bestowed by a sovereign government—to perform the duties and responsibilities of an office or position). Ranks have different names in the different services (see chart on page 5).

Pay Grade	Army	Navy	Marines	Air Force
Commissioned Officers				
O-1	Second Lieutenant	Ensign	Second Lieutenant	Second Lieutenant
O-2	First Lieutenant	Lieutenant Junior Grade	First Lieutenant	First Lieutenant
O-3	Captain	Lieutenant	Captain	Captain
O-4	Major	Lieutenant Commander	Major	Major
O-5	Lieutenant Colonel	Commander	Lieutenant Colonel	Lieutenant Colonel
O-6	Colonel	Captain	Colonel	Colonel
O-7	Brigadier General	Rear Admiral (L)	Brigadier General	Brigadier General
O-8	Major General	Rear Admiral	Major General	Major General
O-9	Lieutenant General	Vice Admiral	Lieutenant General	Lieutenant General
O-10	General	Admiral	General	General
Special Grades				
(5 Stars)	General of the Army	Fleet Admiral	(none)	General of the Air Force
Warrant Officers				
W-1	Warrant Officer. Grades W-2 to W-5 Chief Warrant Officer			
Enlisted Personnel				
E-1	Private	Seaman Recruit	Private	Airman Basic
E-2	Private	Seaman Apprentice	Private First Class	Airman
E-3	Private First Class	Seaman	Lance Corporal	Airman First Class
E-4	Corporal Specialist 4	Petty Officer, Third Class	Corporal	Sergeant Senior Airman
E-5	Sergeant Specialist 5	Petty Officer, Second Class	Sergeant	Staff Sergeant
E-6	Staff Sergeant Specialist 6	Petty Officer, First Class	Staff Sergeant	Technical Sergeant
E-7	Sergeant First Class Specialist 7	Chief Petty Officer	First Sergeant Master Sergeant	Senior Master Sergeant
E-8	First Sergeant Master Sergeant	Senior Chief Petty Officer	First Sergeant Master Sergeant	Senior Master Sergeant
E-9	Command Sergeant Major Sergeant Major	Master Chief Petty Officer	Sergeant Major Master Gunnery Sergeant	Chief Master Sergeant
Special Grades				
E-10	Sergeant Major of the Army	Master Chief Petty Officer of the Navy	Sergeant Major of the Marine Corps	Chief Master Sergeant of the Air Force

Within each rank there are subcategories called "pay grades," which are points on a graded pay structure where similar jobs are placed. Enlisted grades are E-1 through E-9, with E-1 being the lowest. Warrant Officer grades are W-1 through W-5, and officer grades are O-1 through O-10. In this hierarchical structure, all commissioned officers outrank all warrant officers and enlisted members. All warrant officers outrank all enlisted members.

Pages 7–9 show the insignia for each grade. This insignia is worn on the uniform.

Enlisted members who wish to become officers have several options. They may enroll in:

- The Reserve Officers' Training Corps (ROTC), which is a college leadership program that prepares students to enter the service as officers.
- Officer Candidate School (OCS), Officer Candidate Class (OCC) in the Marine Corps, or Officer Training School (OTS) in the Air Force, which are leadership programs in the military that prepare enlisted personnel to become officers.
- A service academy, which is a college whose mission is preparing its graduates to become military officers. The academies are the U.S. Military Academy at West Point, New York; the U.S. Naval Academy in Annapolis, Maryland; the U.S. Air Force Academy in Colorado Springs, Colorado; and the U.S. Coast Guard Academy in New London, Connecticut.

The Army and the Coast Guard permit enlisted members with ninety college credits to attend OCS, but they must complete a four-year college degree within one year of being commissioned or revert back to their enlisted rank. The other services require completion of a four-year college degree before attending OCS. Certain highly trained medical, legal, engineering, and religious professionals may receive a direct commission, which means they join the military without undergoing the standard training regimen. Direct commission officers typically make a standard four-year service commitment.

MILITARY JOBS

While there are many different occupations in the military, all fall into one of three categories: combat, combat support, or combat service support. Combat includes specialties such as infantry, artillery, and Special Forces teams. Servicemembers in these specialties use weapons and conduct their operations from aircraft, tanks, ships, and submarines. Combat support provides operational help such as military intelligence, security, and communications. Combat Service Support provides logistical help such as supply, transportation, health care, and payroll.

Enlisted Jobs

Enlisted personnel make up about 84 percent of the total armed forces and perform its daily operations. They are assigned specific jobs, called military occupational

ENLISTED INSIGNIA OF GRADE

AIR FORCE		ARMY		MARINES		NAVY
Chief Master Sergeant of the Air Force (CMSAF)		Sergeant Major of the Army (SMA)		Sergeant Major of the Marine Corps (SgtMajMC)		Master Chief Petty Officer of the Navy (MCPON)
Chief Master Sergeant (CMSgt)	Command Chief Master Sergeant	Command Sergeant Major (CSM)	Sergeant Major (SGM)	Sergeant Major (SgtMaj)	Master Gunnery Sergeant (MGySgt)	Fleet/Command Master Chief Petty Officer / Master Chief Petty Officer (MCPO)
Senior Master Sergeant (SMSgt)	First Sergeant (E-8)	First Sergeant (1SG)	Master Sergeant (MSG)	First Sergeant (1stSgt)	Master Sergeant (MSgt)	Senior Chief Petty Officer (SCPO)
Master Sergeant (MSgt)	First Sergeant (E-7)	Platoon Sergeant (PSG) or Sergeant First Class (SFC)		Gunnery Sergeant (GySgt)		Chief Petty Officer (CPO)
Technical Sergeant (TSgt)		Staff Sergeant (SSG)		Staff Sergeant (SSgt)		Petty Officer First Class (PO1)
Staff Sergeant (SSgt)		Sergeant (SGT)		Sergeant (Sgt)		Petty Officer Second Class (PO2)
Senior Airman (SrA)		Corporal (CPL)	Specialist (SPC)	Corporal (Cpl)		Petty Officer Third Class (PO3)
Airman First Class (A1C)		Private First Class (PFC)		Lance Corporal (LCpl)		Seaman (Seaman)
Airman (Amn)		Private E-2 (PV2)		Private First Class (PFC)		Seaman Apprentice (SA)
Airman Basic (AB) (no insignia)		Private E-1 (PV1) (no insignia)		Private (Pvt) (no insignia)		Seaman Recruit (SR)

Rank insignia.

OFFICER INSIGNIA OF GRADE

AIR FORCE	ARMY	MARINES	NAVY
General of the Air Force	General of the Army	(None)	Fleet Admiral
General	General	General	Admiral
Lieutenant General	Lieutenant General	Lieutenant General	Vice Admiral
Major General	Major General	Major General	Rear Admiral (Upper Half)
Brigadier General	Brigadier General	Brigadier General	Rear Admiral (Lower Half)
Colonel	Colonel	Colonel	Captain
Lieutenant Colonel	Lieutenant Colonel	Lieutenant Colonel	Commander
Major	Major	Major	Lieutenant Commander

Rank insignia.

OFFICER INSIGNIA OF GRADE

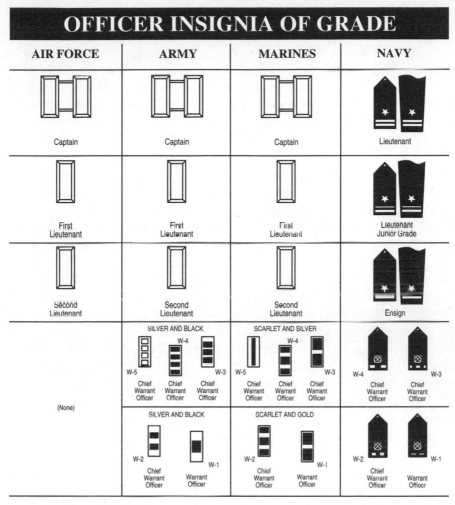

AIR FORCE	ARMY	MARINES	NAVY
Captain	Captain	Captain	Lieutenant
First Lieutenant	First Lieutenant	First Lieutenant	Lieutenant Junior Grade
Second Lieutenant	Second Lieutenant	Second Lieutenant	Ensign

COAST GUARD

Coast Guard officers use the same rank insignia as Navy officers. Coast Guard enlisted rating badges are the same as the Navy's for grades E-1 through E-9, but they have silver specialty marks, eagles and stars, and gold chevrons. The badge of the Master Chief Petty Officer of the Coast Guard has a gold chevron and specialty mark, a silver eagle, and gold stars. For all ranks, the gold Coast Guard shield on the uniform sleeve replaces the Navy star.

Rank insignia.

specialties (MOSs), in the Army and Marine Corps, ratings in the Navy and Coast Guard, and Air Force Specialty Codes (AFSCs) in the Air Force. These jobs are grouped into functional categories. Every position that is needed to staff a self-sustaining city can be found. There are construction workers, who build and repair the base buildings, airfields, and bridges. There are plumbers, electricians, and pipe fitters. There are electronic and electrical equipment repair personnel who maintain the weapons, navigational systems, and communications systems. There are intelligence gatherers who study photographs and monitor radar and surveillance systems.

Environmental health and safety specialists inspect facilities and food supplies to ensure their cleanliness. There are X-ray, eyeglass, and emergency medical technicians, recruiters, classroom trainers, language translators, bomb defusers, firefighters, cooks, truck drivers, and mechanics. There are record-keepers who keep track of it all. As an enlisted member progresses through his career field, he goes from worker/apprentice to supervisor/technician to leader/ manager.

Activities like artillery maneuvers cannot be practiced behind a desk, and naval maneuvers cannot be practiced on a chalkboard, so many military jobs require spending large amounts of time away from home. Separations due to deployment, unaccompanied tours, and training are a way of life (discussed further in chapter 9). Others may have nine-to-five jobs. Some military jobs have rigorous training requirements, such as the elite Navy SEALs or Army Rangers, which most applicants fail to complete, and who are assigned to other jobs instead. Many military jobs are identical to civilian ones, which is advantageous for after-service life; other jobs are unique to the military. Some are highly dangerous. And all services have their share of each. The dividing lines between services can get blurred; without the uniform, it's hard to tell a combat engineer in the Army from one in the Navy's construction battalion, or an Air Force control team member from an Army airborne trooper. A Coast Guard boatswain does the same work as a Navy boatswain, and both do the same job as a watercraft operator in the Army.

Every enlisted servicemember has at least one job; he may be assigned it, or he may request it. Whether he gets the one he wants depends on many things:

- The needs of the branch of service he's in.
- The current and projected number of people in that job (are there too many?).
- Physical limitations, such as colorblindness, the need for prescription eyewear, or the inability to lift heavy objects.
- Administrative limitations, such as the level of education required, the ability to receive security clearances, or training available at the time the servicemember is ready to take the job.
- Present requirements for that job—what experience from the civilian world is he bringing with him?
- Scores from the Armed Forces Vocational Aptitude Battery (ASVAB) tests he took upon enlisting.

If he wants to change his job, all of the above plus a few more criteria are considered:

- Budgetary and travel restrictions: Is the job needed at his current duty station? If not, approval of the new position would require assignment, something not usually done until he is eligible for reassignment.
- Commitments remaining on his current enlistment: For instance, if he received an enlistment bonus for his current job, a request of change probably wouldn't be approved until the commitment is satisfied.

- Time in service: If he won't have enough time remaining in the service after training for the job is completed, he probably won't be assigned it.

Jobs with shortages often offer bonuses for a renewed enlistment. That should not be the only consideration, though, when choosing a job or deciding to reenlist. Does the servicemember like the job? Because after the bonus money runs out, there's still that years-long commitment. Does good promotion potential exist? Can experience gained from the job be applied to the civilian world? What bases use that particular job, and are they located where you'd like to go? Is your husband unhappy with his present job? Help him research a new one. Surveys show that people with critical-skills jobs are often more confident and satisfied with their work and have easier transitions to civilian jobs.

Officer Jobs

Commissioned officers make up about 16 percent of the military. They are technically the only ones able to exercise command over a military unit. Most officers are assigned functional categories rather than specific jobs, as their duties require general administrative, leadership, and supervisory skills, not proficiency in one task. These categories are called "branches" in the Army, "groups" in the Navy and Coast Guard, "career fields" in the Marine Corps, and "career specialties" in the Air Force. There are combat specialty officers who plan and direct military operations. There are public relations personnel, recruitment managers, and food service managers. There are also specific professions, such as aerospace and computer engineers, doctors, nurses, pilots, physical therapists, lawyers, chaplains, and counselors. Officers can request a specific functional category, but whether they get it depends on the same factors as for enlisted servicemembers.

Warrant Officer Jobs

Warrant officers enter the service as enlisted members and, after special training and testing, assume greater responsibility and supervisory power within a narrow, focused range. Examples of warrant officer jobs include helicopter pilot and physician's assistant.

While there are still some military cooks, most dining facilities have been outsourced to private contractors. The military dining system is the largest employer of disabled people in the United States.

THE RESERVES

The military cannot rely only on the regular active-duty force for its missions. The reserves serve as a supplemental force that provides personnel ready and trained with critical skills needed to support the nation during peacetime, contingencies, and war. It enables the active-duty forces to expand and contract as needed. Reservists and National Guardsmen (for convenience's sake, both are referred to as reservists throughout this book) supplement and round out the active duty strength. Combined, they all are called the "Total Force."

The reserves were founded even before this country was: America's first militia regiments (the precursors of the Army National Guard) were organized by the Massachusetts Bay Colony in 1636 and are the militia referenced in the Constitution. Since then, the Guard has participated in every U.S. conflict from the Pequot War of 1637 to current deployments in Afghanistan and Iraq. Reservists are frequently called upon for combat, peacekeeping, reconstruction, and humanitarian missions. In recent years, reservists have, among other things, helped organize and advised the Iraqi army, distributed food and clothing in Pakistan, and built roads, schools, and clinics in Panama.

There are seven reserve components: the Army Reserve, the Naval Reserve, the Marine Corps Reserve, the Air Force Reserve, the Coast Guard Reserve, the Army National Guard, and the Air National Guard. There are three components of reservists: ready, standby, and retired.

Who Are Reservists?

Typical reservists are people who want to combine military and civilian life. They are job holders or students who may be called up at any time to supplement the active-duty component. The reserves are actively marketed to young people as a part-time job that teaches a skill and provides money for college or to help pay back student loans. Active-duty service is not required before joining.

Types of Reservists

The *Ready Reserve* is broken down into three subcategories: Selected Reserve, Individual Ready Reserve (IRR), and Inactive National Guard (ING). Selected reservists are available for immediate mobilization. They actively drill, are eligible for promotion, collect pay and benefits, and accumulate points toward retirement. IRR reservists have had military training, have some military obligation remaining, but are not affiliated with a drilling reserve unit. They are in a nondrilling status and are available only for national emergency; therefore, they generally do not collect checks or have access to military facilities. ING muster once a year with their unit.

Standby reservists are called when there are not enough qualified members in the Ready Reserve to fulfill mobilization requirements. The standby reserves are composed of selected reservists and individual ready reservists (IRRs). *Retired reservists* have already attained military retirement but have not yet reached age sixty, have not chosen to be discharged, and can be called to duty if there is a need and there are not enough ready reservists.

Active Guard and Reserve (AGR) personnel are full-time reservists. They are considered reservists on active duty, not "regular" active duty; that is, they don't transfer from their reserve unit to an active duty unit. Their pay and benefits are identical to those of the active-duty force.

Each state, as well as the District of Columbia, Puerto Rico, Guam, and the Virgin Islands, has an Army National Guard unit and an Air National Guard unit. A guard unit's purpose is twofold. As a state agency that swears allegiance to the governor, it can be activated to help with local emergencies, such as civil disorder or natural catastrophes (e.g., Hurricane Katrina). As a reserve component of the U.S. Army and Air Force, it can be activated into federal service to help with national emergencies. If the president decides the active-duty force needs to be supplemented for a non-domestic operational mission, up to 200,000 members of the Selected Reserve and 30,000 members of the IRR can be called to active duty for up to 365 days.

Reservist Training Requirements

Selected reservists are required to attend a minimum of forty-eight drills or assemblies (usually scheduled on evenings and weekends) each year, and must devote two weeks each summer to their units, to keep their skills up-to-date. They receive the same pay as active duty personnel except for certain allowances and incentive pays that are based on an agreement to serve on active duty for a specified length of time. Pay is received in the month after the training occurs. Reservists with certain critical skills are eligible for enlistment and reenlistment bonuses.

DELAYED ENLISTMENT PROGRAM (DEP)

Once an enlistment contract has been signed and the oath taken, a servicemember is usually put in the Delayed Enlistment Program. This is a holding status where he is officially in the military—the inactive reserves, to be exact—until his scheduled shipping date to basic training. It applies to active duty servicemembers only; a Guardsman is immediately a member of his National Guard unit. Some Guard units allow new recruits to participate in drills and receive pay before attending basic training. They may also use some MWR facilities (discussed in the Benefits and Services chapter). It is a long-standing DoD policy that he may change his mind about joining the service during this time, with no repercussions.

PROMOTIONS

The military has an "up-or-out" policy, officially called High Year of Tenure (HYT) or Retention Control Point (RCP). If a servicemember isn't regularly promoted within a set timetable, he is not allowed to stay in. Up to E-4, promotions are automatic and based mostly on time in grade, but after that, promotion criteria vary from service to service. Servicemembers within the same MOS, AFSC, or rating compete against each other for promotion. Congress sets the total number of military personnel and the number that each grade can have. Vacancies must occur in each grade and job before others can be let in. So even if a servicemember does everything right, if there are overages in that grade, he may still be denied a promotion. Zero promotions are often a direct result of a job's being overstrength. Some jobs have overages;

others have shortages. When a job is overstrength, the service must implement measures to manage the excess, such as voluntarily or involuntarily reclassifying people or raising the cutoff for test scores. Conversely, low cutoff scores in a specific job and rank result from a shortage in that area. One way to deal with the frustration that comes with waiting to be promoted is to reclassify to a shortage task that offers more immediate promotion opportunities.

All services have minimum standards for job performance and a timetable based on time in service and grade, but each considers items appropriate to its own mission. Being the most combat-oriented, the Marine Corps gives special consideration to combat time and conduct and relies more on meritorious promotions than do the other services (such promotions have minimal time-in-service requirements).

The Navy has a very formal promotion system with specific requirements in administrative and occupational ability and formal schooling. Candidates for promotion to grades E-4 through E-7 must perform satisfactorily on Navywide advancement exams.

The Air Force has the Weighted Airman Promotion System for personnel competing for promotion to grades E-5 through E-7. Factors such as time in service, time in grade, skill test scores, promotion test scores, performance reports, and awards and decorations are all considered, but each has a different weight.

The Army gives primary consideration to technical expertise in the MOS, but also considers personality traits such as professionalism and pride in service. Soldiers up for promotion to grades E-5 through E-8 come before a board. Separate lists are kept for each MOS, and the cutoff score goes up or down according to the Army's needs.

Coast Guard promotions to grades E-4 through E-9 are determined through servicewide exams, proficiency in assigned duties, on-the-job performance, recommendation of the commanding officer, and performance on written exams.

Officers whose dates of rank (dates they entered the service) are the same as, one year earlier than, or one year later than the date announced by the headquarters are considered for promotion at set intervals of time. During these intervals, called zones of consideration, a promotion board in Washington evaluates the officers' personnel records and compares them. Personal appearances before the board are not made.

There are three zones of consideration: below the zone, from which an exceptional few are promoted; the primary zone, from which most who are eligible are promoted; and above the zone, from which those who did not get pro-

Q: What does "Don't Ask, Don't Tell" mean?
A: It is a Clinton-era policy that requires homosexuals and bisexuals to neither engage in such activity on or off duty, nor discuss it. A servicemember may be discharged for not following this policy.

moted the first two times are given a third chance. The board members individually review each record, come to their own decisions, and vote. Performance appraisals, awards and decorations, schooling, and the exact nature of job duties are considered. Poor performance evaluations, judicial and nonjudicial punishments, and inadequate personal fitness levels (e.g., being overweight or failing physical training tests) are negatively considered by all services for both officers and enlisted personnel.

EDUCATION OPPORTUNITIES

Education is required to move ahead in today's military, and the military offers many opportunities for it. Classes are offered to servicemembers in everything from training in a specific job to military subjects in general to leadership skills. Many of these classes are required for promotion, are free, and the servicemember receives his full salary while taking them. If they're held on another base, his travel and per diem (daily) expenses are reimbursed up to a certain amount. Reservists are eligible for these classes, too.

High School Equivalency

Although a high school diploma is not necessary to enter the service, it is needed for advancement. If a servicemember does not have a high school diploma, he can take the test that leads to a General Equivalency Development (GED) diploma or certificate. The GED covers math, reading, writing, social studies, and science. Before beginning a GED course of study, know if the goal achieved will be a certificate or a diploma; the requirements for each vary. The diploma is closest to a high school diploma; the certificate is not recognized by many colleges.

Many people enroll in classes before taking the GED test. All services have a basic functional skills or continuing education program that offers classes in the GED subject areas.

College

College courses and degrees are highly desirable, and make the servicemember more competitive for promotion. Recognizing that servicemembers' schedules do not always allow for traditional routes of study, the military offers flexible, off-duty educational programs to help them achieve their educational goals.

The Defense Activity for Non-Traditional Education Support (DANTES)

This is a servicewide umbrella under which many educational programs operate. DANTES supports off-duty educational efforts ranging from high school degree completion to vocational certification to doctoral level college degrees. Its whole reason for being is to provide the flexibility that servicemembers and family members need to achieve their educational goals, given their erratic schedules and frequent moves.

With DANTES, servicemembers who are stationed aboard ships, who have moved two or three times during a semester, or who have even been deployed have achieved their educational goals.

Courses are taught via audiocassette, videotape, CD-ROM, e-mail, the Internet, PDA, podcast, print-based correspondence, and satellite TV. DANTES also has credit-by-examination programs, distance learning programs, college credit for service, career guidance materials, informational videos, certification programs, and the Troops to Teachers program.

DANTES maintains three online catalogs that list distance learning courses and programs. They are the Independent Study Catalog (this alone has over 6,200 offerings), the External Degree Catalog, and the Catalog of Nationally Accredited Distance Learning Programs. View these catalogs at *www.dantescatalogs.com*.

Servicemembers Opportunity Colleges (SOC)
Under the DANTES umbrella, the Servicemembers Opportunity Colleges (SOC) exist for servicemembers who want to pursue a college degree. It's a servicewide network of more than 1,750 accredited colleges and universities that contract with the Department of Defense to offer on-base (including overseas bases) associates and bachelor degree programs, individual classes, and distance learning classes. There is SOCAD for the Army, SOCNAV for the Navy, SOCMAR for the Marine Corps, SOCCOAST for the Coast Guard, and SOCGuard for the Army National Guard. There is no Air Force SOC because the Air Force actually issues its own accredited college degrees via its Community College of the Air Force (CCAF). However, the Air Force is a member of SOC's general program.

With SOC, a degree can be obtained without ever going to the main campus. Minimal residency requirements, the liberal acceptance of transfer credits (schools in the SOC network accept each other's credits), and the granting of credit for nontraditional learning such as military classes and training are examples of how SOC accommodates service families' special needs. Degrees can be job related; many servicemembers work on technical degrees to support their military jobs. SOC is open to family members and reservists.

SOC also operates the Concurrent Admissions Program (ConAP) for Army and Army Reservists. Upon enlisting, a servicemember selects from one of over 1,800 participating colleges. The school is sent a form stating the servicemember's intent to enroll during or after his enlistment.

Service-Specific College Degree Programs
Each service offers its own education opportunities:

The Air Force offers the Airman Education and Commissioning Program (AECP), in which active duty airmen may attend school full-time while earning full pay and allowances to earn a bachelor's degree, and then attend Officer Training School upon completion. It also offers the Airman Scholarship and Commissioning Program (ASCP), in which active duty airmen are discharged to become Air Force ROTC cadets, enabling them to complete a bachelor's degree and earn a commission. Then there is the Community College of the Air Force (CCAF), an accredited, degree-granting institution exclusively for active-duty enlisted airmen and reservists to earn an associate in applied science (AAS) degree designed for an Air Force specialty.

The Army operates the Army Continuing Education System (ACES). This worldwide program provides high school completion, college and vocational-technical classes, nontraditional study programs and testing services, and assistance with math, reading, writing, and computer skills. Within ACES is *eArmyU*, which offers eligible enlisted servicemembers and officers the opportunity to obtain professional and technical certifications, associate's, bachelor's, and master's degrees via online classes using Army-supplied laptop computers. Twenty-eight accredited colleges and universities participate in *eArmyU*, offering 145 certificates and degrees.

The Navy operates the Broadened Opportunity for Officer Selection and Training program for enlisted sailors and marines who want to attend a Navy ROTC university or the Naval Academy. The Navy also operates the United Services Military Apprenticeship Program (USMAP), a formal military training program that provides active duty Coast Guardsmen, marines, and sailors the opportunity to complete civilian apprenticeship requirements while on active duty. A completion certificate is provided by the U.S. Department of Labor. The Navy College Program (NCP) allows sailors to earn college degrees while on active duty by providing academic credit for Navy training, work experience, and off-duty education. The Navy College Program for Afloat College Education (NCPACE) is part of the NCP and offers tuition-free education to sailors on sea duty assignments. Its courses are offered by accredited colleges and universities and taught via technology or by an instructor who sails with the ship. Finally, there's the Seaman to Admiral (STA-21) program, which allows enlisted sailors to finish college and earn a Naval Officer commission.

Montgomery GI Bill

The Montgomery GI Bill is a popular means by which servicemembers pay for their education. It's actually a veteran's benefit, managed by the Department of Veterans Affairs (VA), not the Department of Defense (DoD). It grants $38,700 worth of education benefits in exchange for a military enlistment period of at least three years, along with a reduction in pay of $100 per month for the first year of service. The decision to participate must be made during basic training or time of enlistment into active duty. If a servicemember participates and later changes his mind, or if he is discharged before becoming eligible to use the benefits, he doesn't get reimbursed for what he's already paid. This is because the law words it as a reduction in pay, not a "contribution." In limited circumstances, unused GI Bill benefits may be transferred to family members.

Servicemembers can use their GI Bill benefits while on active duty, after discharge/retirement, or part during active duty and part after. But they must serve two continuous years of active duty first, before they can use them. Benefits automatically expire ten years after discharge or retirement. Because all the military branches now offer 100 percent Tuition Assistance while on active duty, and because the GI Bill pays more when going to school after military service than it does while on active duty, most servicemembers use tuition assistance while on active duty, and save their GI Bill benefits for afterward. Visit *www.gibill.va.gov/contact/contact.htm* or call 888-442-4551 for more information.

All bases have an Education Center. Here you'll find printed literature, applications for graduate exams, information on financial assistance, trained counselors, continuing education courses, and College Level Examination Program (CLEP) tests. A discussion of education and financial aid options available to family members is in chapter 6.

LEARN WHAT'S GOING ON

Knowing what jobs are available, what education and experience it takes to get them, and how to get promoted while in them are just a few of the ways to take control of your family's destiny in the military. Learn about, familiarize yourself with, and understand what's going on around you.

Many installations have museums with displays that are directly related to the mission of the installation. You'll see photographs and equipment comparing how the mission was carried out 100 years ago with how it is done today.

There are newspapers and magazines that center on each particular service, and reading them will give you a better idea of what the service is all about. A good place to start is the weekly newspaper published at most bases. There are the *Army Times*, the *Air Force Times*, and the *Navy Times*, weekly subscription papers that cover issues of interest to service families. Other subscription papers include *Military Spouse* and *The Stars and Stripes*. Online, there's *military.com*, which is free and has diverse content. There are also specialized publications, such as *Soldiers*, *All Hands*, *Leatherneck*, *Airman*, and *National Guard*, and ones with narrower focuses, such as magazines for infantrymen, retired naval personnel, and disabled veterans.

There are service-specific programs designed for spouses that cover subjects such as what is learned in basic training, acronyms, customs, socials, benefits, and places to go for help. These programs are called Army Family Team Building, Married to the Military (for Navy spouses), Welcome to the Military (for Air Force spouses), and LINKS (for Marine Corps spouses). They are held in homelike surroundings and are taught by experienced spouses who also serve as mentors. Sign up at the chaplain's office or the family services office. If you're not near a base you may be able to take these classes online.

Who knows, once you start learning about all these career and educational opportunities, touring the museums, and reading all the literature, you might get so interested you'll want to join the service yourself!

FURTHER READING

Books

Gordon, Debra, Dana Smith, and Sol Gordon, eds. *Uniformed Services Almanac, 50th edition*. Falls Church, VA: Uniformed Services Almanac, 2008.

Internet Resources

www.defenselink.mil/. Department of Defense website.

www.defenselink.mil/faq/questions.aspx. Search the DoD knowledge database and ask questions.

siadapp.dmdc.osd.mil/personnel/MMIDHOME.HTM. DoD personnel statistics.

www.todaysmilitary.com. General information about the military and its jobs.

www.soc.aascu.org/Default.html. SOC homepage with links to each service's SOC program.

www.dantes.doded.mil/Dantes_web/DANTESHOME.asp. The DANTES website.

estripes.osd.mil/. Downloadable editions of the *Stars and Stripes* newspaper.

www.milspouse.com/. *Military Spouse* magazine website.

www.military.com/spousecenter/index.html. Informational website that includes a blog written by and for military spouses.

www.whs.mil/library/. The Pentagon library.

www.bls.gov/oco/ocos249.htm. Job opportunities in the Armed Forces from the U.S. Department of Labor.

2

Benefits and Services

Here are some events showing the evolution of the armed forces' commitment to families.

1776–1847: Families considered a hindrance to military efficiency and operations.

1861: Wives of enlisted soldiers may be employed as laundresses.

1863: Conscription in Union Army; exemptions authorized for family or personal considerations.

1891: Congress reviews Army families' living and working conditions on the frontier. No record of action taken.

1896: Families of enlisted men recognized monetarily.

1913: Army regulations discourage marriage; marriage viewed in terms of its effect on efficiency to service.

1917: Congress enacts allotment system for families.

1942: Public Law 490—military family members' benefits granted.

1952: Study identifies lack of basic social services as a major problem.

1954: Family and soldier support programs enacted in an effort to improve retention.

1956: The Dependents Medical Care Act signed into law, entitling family members to military-provided medical care

1957: Serviceman's and Veteran's Survivor Act passed; family provided for when serviceman dies.

1960: Family members outnumber uniformed personnel.

1973: Supreme Court rule designates spouses of female servicemembers as "dependents."

1982: Public Law 97-252—retired pay may be treated as community property in divorce proceedings.

2007: Senior leaders signed the Army Family Covenant, a pledge to support soldiers' families with quality-of-life programs.

In the past twenty years, dozens more family-friendly policies have passed, such as increases in family separation pay and survivor benefits, and programs to help spouses find jobs. The bottom line is that things have changed for what used to be called "camp followers." These supports and services are proof of today's philosophy that happy, healthy service families make for a happy, healthy service.

Benefits like affordable health care, subsidized groceries, and free military flights for trips greatly stretch the dollar. In civilian life, most families pay a lot of money for programs we receive free or at a low cost. In this chapter we'll discuss the support system that exists for you.

DEERS AND THE IDENTIFICATION CARD

DEERS

To access your benefits, you must be enrolled in the Defense Enrollment Eligibility Reporting System (DEERS). Enrollment should be the first order of business after marrying, at which point your husband becomes your military sponsor. DEERS is a computer database that confirms and verifies all active duty personnel, retirees, family members, and reservists who are activated for more than thirty days. Service-members are automatically enrolled, and family members are enrolled by their sponsor via the sponsor's parent service. Retired servicemembers who receive retirement pay and their family members are automatically enrolled. Other eligible family members, including eligible surviving family members, can be enrolled, or can enroll themselves, at any Uniformed Service personnel office. To find the nearest one, go to *www.dmdc.osd.mil/rsl/owa/home*. You may verify your enrollment status with the base hospital or with DEERS. Its Beneficiary Telephone Center number is 800-334-4162 for California, 800-527-5602 for Alaska and Hawaii, and 800-538-9552 for all other states. You can also fax DEERS at 831-655-8317. Once your family retires or otherwise leaves the service with benefits, it will be your responsibility to inform DEERS of address changes.

Reservists enroll by submitting Form DD 1173-1 through a service center. Even if the reservist has not yet been mobilized, he should pre-enroll all eligible family members so they may be immediately enrolled upon his mobilization.

Memorize your spouse's Social Security Number. You will need it for all paperwork and forms that you fill out, at every office.

Keep your DEERS information updated, because if it's not, it can cause problems for Tricare claims (discussed later in this chapter). Updates include a change in the sponsor status, leaving active duty, change in service status, marriage or divorce, having a baby, moving, and becoming entitled to Medicare (you or a family member). Update in person by visiting a local ID card office or by phone (800-538-9552 or 866-363-2883 for TTY/TDD for the deaf).

The Identification Card

At the Pass and ID office you will be issued your ID card, a credit-card-sized piece of plastic with a digitized photo and barcode. This card is required for all military benefits and services. Military personnel may be issued a Common Access Card, which is an ID that has the dual purpose of allowing electronic commerce, mess hall access, and other capabilities. Everything from getting your medical records to checking out at the commissary to consigning clothes at the base thrift shop requires you to show your ID card. It's needed to get on base and sometimes even to move from building to building or to move within a building. So if you forget to bring it, go home.

Your husband must accompany you to the ID card facility to sign your ID card authorization papers, and this paperwork will be entered in RAPIDS, the Real-Time Automated Personnel Identification System. If he is not available, you will need a general power of attorney (this is discussed in chapter 9). Bring original copies of your birth certificate, marriage license, Social Security card, and photo identification. (Your birth certificate can be obtained from the vital records office in the state where you were born; the marriage license from the city or county clerk's office where the wedding took place.) As a courtesy, each service issues ID cards to eligible family members of other services as long as they have proper documentation. Children are not issued ID cards until they are ten years old (although they must be enrolled in DEERS).

Eligible ID card holders include lawful spouses, unremarried surviving spouses, and unmarried children under the age of twenty-one. Adopted children are eligible, as are stepchildren for whom the servicemember provides a household. Children who are wards of the servicemember for over twelve months are eligible. Children who are over twenty-one but incapable of self-support, or under twenty-three and a full-time student are eligible. Parents or parents-in-law dependent for over one-half of their support on the servicemember are eligible. (For medical care eligibility, the parent must also reside in the servicemember's home or in one maintained by the servicemember.) Certification of student status, adoption papers, medical statements, or other documentation of these situations are typically required to receive an ID card.

Additional eligible ID cardholders are unremarried former spouses who were married to the same military sponsor for at least twenty years of the time that he earned twenty years of creditable service (service applied to retirement pay). Spouses and children of servicemembers who died while on active duty, or of reservists who died while on active training, are eligible for ID cards. Family members of reservists who died while not on active training and before receiving the "twenty-year letter" (see chapter 11) are not eligible for ID cards. Widows and widowers lose their cards upon remarriage, but unlike divorcées, they can be reissued cards if that marriage ends. A remarried widow whose second marriage ends in divorce or death may receive commissary, theater, and exchange benefits but not medical benefits. Direct eligibility questions to your base Pass and ID office or to a recruiting office.

The ID card enables you to receive benefits on any base worldwide, no matter which service it belongs to. Its benefits flow directly to you from the Defense Department and cannot be taken away by your sponsor. However, the card is government property and must be surrendered if asked for by a commissioned officer, a noncommissioned officer, or a security/police officer while performing their duties. ID cards generally expire four years from the date of issue or expiration of the sponsor's service. Keep it current, as benefits are denied to holders of expired cards. If you lend your ID card to someone, even another cardholder, it can be permanently revoked.

After receiving your ID, it's a good idea to register your car on base, if you haven't already. You may receive a windshield sticker once it's registered, enabling easier access to the base. (Some bases have done away with these, preferring a 100 percent ID check instead.) If your car isn't registered, you may be subject to a search when you drive to the post gate. At that time you will be asked for your driver's license, car registration, and insurance.

If your husband is still in Basic Training, call his recruiter and ask for instructions on enrolling in DEERS and receiving an ID card.

THE EXCHANGE

The exchange system is a retailer that supports military readiness by supplying items that servicemembers and their families need, at locations around the world. Active duty, retired, and selected reservist families all have unlimited exchange access. The exchange operates everything from giant shopping malls to small stores aboard battleships. It has even operated tent stores in war zones and at the front lines. Exchanges have been around since 1895, when the War Department ordered post commanders to establish them at every post where practicable. This order set the standard for the concept and mission of today's Exchange Service.

The Army, Air Force, Navy, Marine Corps, and Coast Guard exchanges are administered separately and have separate headquarters. They are called the PX (post exchange) in the Army, BX (base exchange) in the Air Force, NEX (naval exchange) in the Navy (ship's store when afloat), MCX (Marine Corps exchange) in the Marine Corps, and CGX (Coast Guard exchange) in the

Not just another store. An AAFES sales manager restocks snacks in the base exchange at Kirkuk Air Base, Iraq. Photo courtesy of U.S. Army

Coast Guard. The exchanges have a twofold mission: to provide quality goods and services at reasonable prices and to generate profits to support the base morale, well-being, and recreation programs. All profits are returned to the customer in the form of libraries, swimming pools, and bowling centers, and fund youth activities, music programs, and unit functions.

Exchanges operate mostly with *nonappropriated funds*—money generated by their own profits and profits from base recreational activities. Because Congress doesn't control the money (as it does with appropriated funds), the manager of the store may run it pretty much as desired. As long as the volume of business justifies it, the manager can expand, hire more staff, and stay open longer. And speaking of staff, the exchange is a major source of employment for military family members; about 24 percent of its associates are family members, many of whom transfer to different locations as they move with their sponsor over the course of a career.

Brand-name clothing, makeup, house paint, jewelry, toys, tools, bread makers, refrigerators, video cameras, kitchen equipment, exercise machines, and major appliances are examples of the many items sold. Not all exchanges stock the same things, however. Regional interest has its effect, as does the base population. If you're at a place where there are a lot of single men, you'll find lots of electronics and flashy men's clothes. Places with many families stock a nice selection of baby items and children's clothes. A 1949 law restricts the type of merchandise that exchanges in the United States may sell, as well as their cost-price ratios, to ensure that they don't provide unfair competition to civilian businesses. Overseas there are no such limitations on stocking and special ordering items that stateside exchanges may not. These overseas locations have rules to prevent goods from spreading into the black market, such as limiting shoppers on how much they may spend on certain items. Appropriated funds (tax dollars) are used to ship goods to overseas exchanges, ensuring that shipping costs are not passed on to beneficiaries.

Surveys show the exchanges to feature consistently lower overall prices than civilian retail stores. Different items are marked up differently—necessities see the lowest markup, and luxury goods have the highest. Sales tax is not charged. With careful shopping, you may find better deals elsewhere, but the exchange should match local (but not online) prices on most items, even if the local item is on sale. The exchange also operates liquor stores, gas stations, and fast-food franchises, but prices in these are similar to off-base prices.

Overseas, the AAFES even sells cars! You can buy one for overseas use or stateside delivery. Eligible purchasers are those who are assigned to the country and those who are there on temporary duty for at least thirty days. Visit *www.encs.com/program.aspx?id=47* for details.

Exchanges do layaways, accept major credit cards, cash personal checks (including out-of-state or out-of-country checks), and accept returns on most items within ninety days. Returns can be made at any exchange, not just the one at which the item was purchased. If the exchange is running a sale but the sale items are gone when you show up, ask for a rain check, which is a written claim for the item at the sale price when it is restocked, even if the sale has ended.

If you live too far away from an exchange to shop there regularly, view the exchange online. (See the Internet reference section at the end of this chapter for Web addresses.). There's also the Exchange Mail Order Catalog, which carries many of the products found in the exchange plus other items from around the world. (Imported goods may require you to pay a customs tax upon arrival.) Specialty supplements, such as baby item catalogs, are issued several times a year, and these can also be found online, or you can call 1-800-527-2345 for a catalog.

Military Star Card
Although the exchange accepts major credit cards, it also offers its own Star card with a variable-interest plan. Credit limits are based on the applicant's disposable income, not rank. Spousal income can be used in figuring the limits, and family members with independent incomes may apply for their own Star card. The card can also be used for exchange purchases made online and through the catalog. It is generally not accepted at the ancillary shops, salons, and restaurants, as those are run by private contractors. Apply at the customer service desk at your local exchange, or call 877-891-STAR. Reservist families are also eligible for the card.

THE COMMISSARY
The commissary is an *appropriated-fund* operation, meaning it is paid for with tax dollars. It provides brand-name groceries for service families and is run separately from the exchange. The commissary and the exchange have different missions and are not in competition.

The Defense Commissary Agency (DeCa) operates 261 commissaries worldwide. DeCa makes no profit, selling its wares at the price it paid for them plus a 5 percent surcharge to cover operating costs (e.g., bags, utilities, shopping carts) and to pay for the construction and renovation of new and existing stores. No sales tax is charged. The DeCA system receives about $1 billion a year, and a set amount is provided to each store, which in turn, must operate within that budget. Thus, all decisions—operating hours, days of service, and so forth—are not motivated by profit. For instance, even if a commissary could ring up solid sales twenty-four hours a day, it could not stay open that long if the money to pay salaries and other operating costs is not in its budget. Typical operating hours are from 9 A.M. until 6 or 7 P.M., and noon to 5 P.M. on Sunday.

Because the commissary is nonprofit and subsidized, a shopping trip there will almost always be cheaper than the same trip in comparable off-base supermarkets.

(DeCa surveys show an average of 30 percent savings, even including prices from civilian supercenters.) Although space constraints and federal law restrict what is sold, if you want something you don't see stocked, such as kosher meat, ask the manager if it can be special-ordered. Many commissaries have fresh seafood, candy, plants, delicatessens, and bakeries that offer theme birthday cakes and specialty breads. Commissaries occasionally hold tent sales, where items are sold by case lots at even larger savings. Stock up at these events! When the commissary and the exchange carry the same item, that item will be cheaper at the commissary because of its different markup policy. Try to avoid shopping on payday, as it is very crowded then and the checkout lines are long. If you can time your trips a few days before or after payday, they will take less time.

Lines at the commissary are long on payday.

Commissaries accept WIC, food stamps, and manufacturers' coupons, and many take credit cards. Weekly flyers are also distributed there, with coupons for more savings. The baggers work for tips only. Some people tip $1 per $50 spent, or $5 per cart, perhaps adjusted up for weather conditions and distance to the car. Some tip $0.50 per bag. You may also bag your own groceries if that is your preference.

Both the commissary and the exchange are for use by authorized personnel only. You may purchase bona fide gifts for nonmilitary friends at the exchange (not the commissary), but buying products for resale, even if no profit is made. This can result in the loss of your shopping privileges and in disciplinary action against the military sponsor. All reservists (Ready, Selected, IRR, ING, retirees, including Gray Area retirees) and their authorized family members have unlimited commissary access, just as active-duty families do.

MEDICAL CARE

The primary mission of military treatment facilities is to serve active-duty personnel. Family members and retirees are treated on a space-available basis. However, military-provided medical care for the latter two groups has existed in some fashion since the late 1700s and has evolved into an elaborate system that utilizes military treatment facilities and contracted civilian providers.

Primary Care at Military Treatment Facilities

Primary (routine) care may be obtained at most base hospitals, where you are assigned a Primary Care Provider (PCP). Ask the base operator for the number of the central appointments desk. All hospitals and clinics are open to people from all branches of service.

Hospital staffing levels are set by Congress, which determines how many family member–related practitioners (such as pediatricians) may be hired. Medical personnel also participate in field exercises, take leave, and make permanent change-of-station moves like everyone else in the military. So there may be a wait for routine appointments.

Every hospital has a health benefits advisor (HBA), who will give you specifics on the care you may expect in a military facility, how to obtain civilian treatment under the government programs available to you, and how to file for reimbursement. The HBA will also discuss your specific situation and assist with problems.

When treated at the base hospital or dental clinic, you must arrive on time for your appointments. There are too few providers serving too many patients to allow them to wait for latecomers. Most clinics will cancel your appointment and fill your slot with an available patient, even if you're just ten minutes late. Two no-shows and you can lose your privilege of being treated at the base hospital for a year. If you want to ask lengthy questions during an appointment, mention that you'll need extra time when you book it. If you're unhappy with any care received at a military hospital, complain to the noncommissioned officer in charge (NCOIC) of that department. Com-

As a physician, people ask me why I practice in the military instead of privately. I answer that I believe there's more to a profession than pay. I enjoy the camaraderie, the field exercises, ministering to soldiers in need. I like wearing my uniform, and my wife and I enjoy the moving and the friends we've made. What keeps the brigade commander or combat officer in the Army? Does anyone ask them whether they're in because they can't do something else outside the service? I don't think so. It's the intangibles of military life that keep careerists in, no matter what the field. As for the quality of military medicine, people who enjoy their jobs do them well, no matter what they're paid.

plaining to the receptionist isn't helpful. You may also ask the patient representative to intervene. Finally, know that the emergency room is for just that—emergencies. Routine complaints will often be met at the emergency room with an hours-long wait because the more seriously ill will be taken ahead of you.

Medical Services Offered

Services offered at military hospitals vary drastically, depending on the size of the hospital, the size of the community it serves, and where it is located. Some are huge, glossy buildings that offer everything; others are tiny clinics that serve only basic needs. Generally, all of them offer the following:

- Treatment of medical and surgical conditions
- Treatment of nervous, mental, and emotional disorders
- Treatment of disease, including contagious diseases and chronic conditions
- Routine physicals and immunizations
- Prescription and nonprescription drugs
- Maternity and well-baby care
- Diagnostic services, lab tests, and X-rays
- Emergency and routine dental care
- Dental care as necessary to treat or prevent a medical problem
- Eye exams
- Ambulance service
- Artificial limbs and eyes
- Loan of wheelchairs and hospital beds
- Family-planning services and supplies
- Orthopedic braces, crutches, and other aids

If you need something that isn't offered, either you'll be sent via medevac—short for medical evacuation—to another military facility or, more likely, you'll use Tricare (discussed later in this chapter). In cases of catastrophic illness, you'll have access to world-renowned military hospitals, such as Walter Reed Army Medical Center in Washington, D.C.; Brook Army Medical Center in San Antonio, Texas; and the Naval Hospital in Bethesda, Maryland.

All services and medications you receive at military health-care facilities are free. If a hospital stay is required, family members are charged a small daily fee for meals. The law requires you to tell the military hospital if you have health insurance, such as insurance provided by your job. The hospital will then file with your insurer for the reasonable costs of the treatment. The insurance payment will be accepted as payment in full; no bill will be sent to you, even if your private policy requires a deductible and co-share of costs. Generally, services considered not medically necessary, inappropriate, or experimental are not covered. Also not covered are treatments that are not standard medical practice in the United States, such as chiropractic, homeopathy, Rolfing, and acupuncture. Surgery strictly for cosmetic reasons is not covered, nor is it provided in military hospitals. The military does employ cosmetic surgeons, but the work they do is reconstructive.

Reservists are entitled to medical care for any injuries that occur while traveling to, from, and during drills. If a reservist is activated for more than thirty consecutive days, his family is entitled to care at the base hospital facilities and Tricare. Using Tricare stateside is discussed here; using it overseas is discussed in chapter 8.

TRICARE

Tricare is a government-subsidized medical care system that currently serves about 5.5 million people. It combines the assets of all seven uniformed services to supplement military treatment facilities by using contracted civilian health-care providers. Tricare is not an insurance plan; it is a health-care entitlement. A regional contractor is not an insurance company; it is an administrator of the Tricare program. Enrollment is done by the sponsor, but a family member equipped with a general power of attorney may do the paperwork.

Tricare Regions

There are six Tricare regions, each operated by its own Tricare Service Center (TSC). A TSC's staff will help you enroll, explain benefits, file claims, and answer questions. Here are the regions and their contact numbers.

North Region
Maine, New Hampshire, Vermont, Massachusetts, Connecticut, Rhode Island, Delaware, Maryland, New Jersey, New York, Pennsylvania, Michigan, Wisconsin, Illinois, Indiana, Ohio, Kentucky, West Virginia, the District of Columbia, Virginia, and North Carolina.
1-877-TRICARE
https://www.hnfs.net/ common/home/

South Region
South Carolina, Georgia, Florida, Alabama, Mississippi, Tennessee, Oklahoma, Arkansas, Louisiana, Texas, excluding southwest corner.
1-800-444-5445
www.humana-military. com/

West Region
New Mexico, Arizona, Nevada, the southwest corner of Texas, Colorado, Utah, Wyoming, Montana, Idaho, North Dakota, South Dakota, Nebraska, Kansas, Minnesota, Iowa, Missouri, Hawaii, California, Washington, Oregon, and Alaska.
1-888-TRIWEST
www.triwest.com/

Puerto Rico, and Virgin Islands 1-888-777-8343

Europe Region
Europe, Africa, Middle East, Azores, and Iceland.
1-888-777-8343

Latin America and Canada
Canada, Mexico, Central America, and the Caribbean basin.
1-888-777-8343

Tricare Options

Tricare offers three major options from which family members and retirees can choose: *Prime, Extra,* and *Standard.* You may enroll in any of the three, or you may decline all and try to get all your care at a military treatment facility, where appointments are made on a space-available basis, and active-duty and Prime-enrolled patients are accommodated first. Federal law prohibits parents and parents-in-law from entitlement to Tricare benefits, even if they are the servicemember's official dependents. They may be seen at military health care facilities on a space-available basis.

Active-duty personnel and reservists are automatically enrolled in Prime, but they are still treated on base whenever possible. They don't use Tricare as a matter of routine, but when they do, they incur no out-of-pocket costs. If they cannot get to a military hospital for emergency care, the government will pay the bill. (If the bill must be paid up front, they should contact the treasurer of their own base hospital for reimbursement.) If they need non-emergency care but are assigned to an area without a military hospital, they should contact the health-care finder at the nearest military hospital for instructions on how to obtain civilian care at government expense.

Tricare Prime

This option is like a health maintenance organization. It requires users to enroll and to agree to get their health care from a specific list of health-care providers. They are assigned to a primary care manager at a nearby primary care site, which can be either a military hospital or a contract network clinic. PCMs can be physicians, physician assistants, or nurse practitioners, and be individuals or teams. When you make an appointment for primary care, you may ask for the manager or the manager team by name. To see a specialist, you must be referred by your PCM.

Prime has access standards that specify travel and wait time for getting an appointment. In general, their goal is for you not to have to travel more than thirty minutes to get to a facility or wait more than sixty minutes for a specialty appointment. Urgent-care appointments are supposed to be available within twenty-four hours, routine appointments within a week, and preventive care and specialty care in no longer than four weeks.

Enrollment in Prime is done annually with no "open season." Family members and retirees may enroll at any time, and their enrollment period will be the following twelve months. Contractor-issued cards are given, which list 800-numbers to call for appointments or for authorization of care. You typically have to be referred by your PCP to be reimbursed for medical care obtained from anyone other than your PCP. However, there is a point-of-service option in Prime that allows all enrollees except active-duty servicemembers to obtain non-emergency services from any Tricare-authorized provider without the PCM's referral. This option, and the services, costs extra.

Prime has an annual enrollment fee. (Active-duty personnel and their families do not pay it; retirees, retiree family members, and survivors do.) It also has cost-share fees which range from $12 to $30 that active-duty personnel do not pay, but all others do, for outpatient care. Fees are only charged at contractor hospitals, not military facilities. No refund is given for the annual enrollment fee if you decide to drop out during the year you enroll.

Tricare Standard

This is similar to indemnity insurance and is the cheapest selection for those who need frequent care. (It's not available for servicemembers.) The Standard option cost-shares civilian care with family members. There is no enrollment fee, but there are co-pays and deductibles. Patient costs are the highest of all three options, but Standard offers the most choices in provider selection; you can basically go to anyone who is licensed, accredited, and authorized. This is useful for patients who currently see providers that aren't in the Tricare network (but you will save money by using someone in the network). Standard patients may use a military treatment facility at no cost, but they are lower in priority for appointments than Prime patients.

There are no enrollment fees and no point-of-service charges. After an annual deductible is met, you pay a percentage of the total charges for any medical care you

To make your medical appointments most productive:

1. Stay on topic. You have a time allotment for each visit, so don't waste it on irrelevant chit chat.
2. Write down your symptoms, any medications you're taking, and other concerns before you arrive so that you don't forget to mention them.
3. Remind your doctor which tests you've had.
4. Write down the responses your doctor gives you. Make sure you understand what is told to you before you leave.
5. Know what tests you're being sent to the lab for.

For greatest efficiency:

1. Submit all claims separately; do not bundle multiple claims. Processors manage claims separately, so if you bundle multiple claims, a problem with one will delay payment on all.
2. Conduct business online whenever possible and call during nonpeak hours.
3. Make your PCM appointments online at *https://www.tricare online.com/portal.do.*

receive. Providers may bill you for up to 15 percent of the total charges for any medical care you receive. There is a catastrophic cap of $1,000 for active-duty families and a cap of $3,000 for all others. You may need to file your own claims; download the forms at *www.tricare.osd.mil/claims/default.htm.* There is no PCM, so you can self-refer to specialists. Standard enrollees may also use Tricare Extra.

Q: How do I find a doctor?

A: Lists of participating providers can be found at *www.mytricare.com*. A participating provider is one who accepts as full payment the amount Tricare pays. A doctor who does not accept Tricare payment in full is a nonparticipating provider. He or she may still be an authorized provider, which means that you may use their services and pay a higher out-of-pocket amount. Doctors who are not in Tricare networks are free to decide when or if they will participate in Tricare Standard, and they may participate on a case-by-case basis. The fact that doctors agree to accept Standard rates for one procedure does not obligate them to do so the next time the patient receives care.

Tricare Extra

This option offers more provider choices than Prime but less than Standard; you may go to any provider in the contractor's network. Extra is not available overseas or to active-duty servicemembers. Co-pays and deductibles apply, but your costs are between those of Prime and Standard. (The co-pay is 5 percent less than Standard's and there's no balance billing.) No enrollment is required, and there are no point-of-service charges. You don't have to file your own claims. You may use Extra on a case-by-case basis just by using the network providers and use Standard the rest of the time. There's no deductible when using the retail pharmacy network. There's no PCM. You can still seek space-available care in military hospital, but at low priority.

Prime Remote

As its name implies, this option provides civilian health care for servicemembers and family members permanently assigned to remote places. Active-duty servicemembers must enroll in it, and there are no out-of-pocket expenses for them. Enrollment for family members is optional. It is designed to have fewer out-of-pocket expenses for family members, and medically necessary travel may even be reimbursed. Generally, you don't have to file your own claims. Family members must live and work more than fifty miles or approximately one hour's drive time from the nearest military treatment facility. Prime Remote is offered in the fifty United States only. Reservists are eligible for Prime Remote if activated for more than thirty consecutive days, and their family members must reside with them in the same Prime Remote zip code to be eligible. The reservist does not have to be enrolled in Prime Remote for his family to enroll.

Tricare Plus

Tricare Plus is a military treatment facility access program, not a health plan; it provides primary care at selected local military treatment facilities. It doesn't guarantee access to specialty care at the military treatment facility. It's not portable; enrollment at one facility doesn't guarantee access at another.

Anyone eligible for care in military treatment facilities (except those enrolled in Prime, a civilian or Medicare HMO) can enroll and will have the same priority access as Prime enrollees. Your PCM at the military treatment facility is your principal health-care provider. You may still get care from civilian and/or Medicare providers. The rules for Standard, Extra, or Medicare apply, so you are not locked into an HMO-like program. There are no enrollment fees. However, know that it is not available at all military treatment facilities, and local commanders may discontinue it at their discretion if they feel it negatively impacts their capacities and mission.

Tricare Reserve Select

Reservists and their families are eligible for the same health benefits as the active duty component when the reservist is activated for more than thirty continuous days. Actually, health coverage is provided up to ninety days prior to activation for reservists who receive a "delayed-effective-date" order. Coverage lasts until 180 days following their activation. After the 180 days are up, reservists can purchase coverage under the Tricare Reserve Select program *if* they were activated for a contingency operation for ninety days or more on orders from the president, not the governor. Note that they cannot be eligible for, or enrolled in, the Federal Employees Health Benefits Program (FEHB), an insurance program for civilian government employees, to do this.

Reserve Select policies and coverage are similar to that of Standard and Extra, and enrollment may be done any time. Deductibles and co-pays apply. Log on to the Tricare website to select the type of coverage you want (servicemember only or servicemember and family) and the start date. Then print out the forms, fill them out, and mail or fax in with payment. Coverage type can be changed with a qualifying life event (e.g., marriage, divorce, birth) by submitting a form, also downloadable from the Tricare site, and submitting it to the regional contractor. Sponsors must report all qualifying life events to a military personnel office and DEERS.

Tricare Reserve Family Demonstration Project

This option's purpose is to facilitate health care access and limit out-of-pocket expenses for Reservists who are activated for more than thirty days to support a contingency operation. Such Reservists are eligible for Tricare as active duty servicemembers. Their care is provided at military treatment facilities or from network providers. When no longer on active duty orders, care may still be received in a military treatment facility for injuries or illnesses incurred while on active duty. Reservists may also be eligible for extended Tricare coverage through the Transitional Assistance Management Program (TAMP), discussed in chapter 9. Coverage extends to eligible family members.

In this program, Reservist family members who do not, or cannot, enroll in Tricare Prime may receive a waiver of the Tricare Standard and Extra annual deductible, and of the maximum allowable charge when they see nonparticipating providers who bill in excess of the Tricare maximum allowable charge. They may also receive a waiver of the Non-Availability Statement requirement (discussed later in this chapter).

Tricare ECHO

The Extended Care Health Option (ECHO) is a supplemental, not a stand-alone, program. It provides financial help to eligible beneficiaries who have specific, qualifying mental or physical disabilities: mental retardation, a serious physical disability, a psychological condition rendering the beneficiary homebound, or a diagnosis of a condition in an infant or toddler that is expected to precede a diagnosis of retardation or disability. It is available to active-duty family members and family members of activated reservists who live in the continental United States and its territories. It is not available overseas. ECHO provides:

- medical, assistive, and rehabilitative services
- training to use assistive devices
- transportation
- durable equipment
- home health care
- respite care
- special education
- institutional care

To enroll, talk to a case manager or your Exceptional Family Member Program (discussed later in this chapter), in which you must be enrolled. There is no enrollment fee. You pay a cost share for benefits (one cost share per sponsor, not beneficiary), and it is based on the sponsor's pay grade. After that cost share, Tricare will pay up to $2,500 per month. Available community and public services must be used before applying for ECHO benefits. If they don't exist, you must obtain a Public Facility Use Certificate, which is a letter from an appropriate public official explaining why public assistance is unavailable or insufficient for your needs.

Standard and Extra patients do not have to receive obstetric care at military hospitals and clinics. Prime enrollees need to coordinate any obstetric treatment not available at their military treatment facility with their PCP.

Non-Availability Statement (NAS): This is a certification from a military hospital stating that it cannot provide required care. It is needed only for non-emergency inpatient mental health care that is not provided by the military treatment facility. It is no longer required for anything else. Standard and Extra enrollees living in a military treatment facility catchment area must obtain an NAS from that facility before being admitted as an inpatient for mental health services. Of course, this is not needed at all if Medicare or another insurer will pay first.

Prescriptions

No matter which Tricare option you choose, you have four options for filling your prescriptions: at a military hospital (free), through a Tricare network civilian pharmacy, through a Tricare non-network civilian pharmacy (this will be more expensive than a network pharmacy), or through Express Scripts, a mail-order prescription program that sends maintenance drugs to your home. The network civilian pharmacy and Express Scripts charge the same amount, but with Express Scripts you can order up to a ninety-day supply of drugs. You also have 24/7 access to a pharmacist. Call 866-363-8667 to obtain mail-order envelopes and order forms. Express Scripts will contact your doctor for a new prescription.

Other Insurance

Federal law requires that Tricare be the last payer behind medical insurance from your own job, any other private medical insurance, or auto medical payment insurance. In double-coverage situations, Tricare pays either the patient's remaining obligation after the other plan has paid its maximum, or the amount it would have paid if there were no other coverage, whichever is less. If you have Medicaid (a government health care program for low-income and other qualifying groups), Tricare pays before Medicaid or before a policy that is specifically a Tricare supplemental. Tricare pays nothing if coverage by the first payer exceeds Tricare's maximum allowable charge. Claims for job-related illnesses and injuries are paid by workers' compensation programs and are not covered by Tricare Standard. When workers' compensation is exhausted, Tricare benefits can be used. Former spouses who normally are eligible for Tricare lose these benefits when they are covered by an employer-sponsored health plan.

Supplemental Policies

Tricare was never intended to cover all medical costs, and depending on your family's situation, your deductibles, co-payments, and cost shares can become substantial. If this is the case, you might consider a third-party supplemental insurance policy.

Tricare supplemental insurance policies are offered by military associations and private firms; some are listed in the appendix. They reimburse patients for out-of-pocket expenses incurred after Tricare pays its share. Each has its own rules about pre-existing conditions, family eligibility requirements, deductibles, mental health limitations, long-term illness, well-baby care, care provided to persons with disabilities, claims under the diagnosis-related group (DRG) payment system for inpatient hospital charges, and allowable charges. If you have insurance through your own job, make sure that any supplemental policy you buy isn't just a duplicate. For instance, since Tricare always pays after civilian insurance, it will probably pick up any costs above what your employer's insurance pays, making a supplemental policy unnecessary.

The Feres Doctrine

A 1950 Supreme Court ruling known as the Feres Doctrine claims that suits filed by subordinates against superiors would cause a breakdown in military discipline. Therefore, servicemembers cannot sue the government for damages that occur incidental to service. This includes suing for malpractice. Active-duty people can, however, receive compensation for malpractice in the form of a disability retirement or hospital care if they remain on active duty. If they're severely injured because of malpractice, they are also entitled to certain Social Security benefits and compensation from the Department of Veterans Affairs.

Family members and retirees can sue the government, but administrative claims must be exhausted before a person can go to court. To file a claim, fill out a form at your base claims office within two years of the alleged malpractice. Retirees can file only for malpractice that occurred after they retired. Legal representation, although recommended, is not required. Local lawyers for the military can settle claims for small amounts, but most claims are forwarded to the main claims offices of each of the services, and the military has six months to review the claim. Settlement may take place to avoid costly litigation.

Fisher Houses

Fisher Houses are lodges for families visiting servicemembers hospitalized for serious injuries, operations, or treatment. They are named after Elizabeth and the late Zachary Fisher, philanthropists who gave more than $40 million to the military, a sum that includes the money to build these lodges. At least one Fisher House can be found near every major military hospital. The cost to stay there is a small daily fee, and the surroundings are comfortable. All Fisher Houses are two-story, 5,000-square-foot homes, each containing five single bedrooms, two suites, a living room, a laundry room, and a fully equipped kitchen. Each bedroom has a phone and TV. You can cook, wash, iron, and have all the comforts of home while being near the person hospitalized. A house manager oversees the house's daily operation. There are thirty-seven Fisher Houses with more under construction; a list of locations is in the appendix. To request lodging at one, visit *www.fisherhouse.org* or call 888-294-8560.

DENTAL CARE

Dental care is available and free for active-duty servicemembers and activated reservists. However, dental care for family members is not as readily available at all duty stations as medical care is. Congress fixes the number of military dentists in proportion

Volunteers help decorate the Naval Medical Center Portsmouth Fisher House.
Photo courtesy U.S. Navy

to the number of active-duty personnel; family members don't enter into the equation.
If there's space available, they're treated. Some clinics that don't treat family members
do, however, provide fluoride treatments, X-rays, and cleanings for children.

Tricare Dental Plan: United Concordia
Dental care coverage, both CONUS (continental U.S.) and OCONUS (outside the
U.S.), is offered through United Concordia. It is for active-duty family members, not
servicemembers. It is also for nonactivated reservists to keep them dentally deploy-
able, but the government does not subsidize their (nor their families') premium cost.
Once a reservist becomes activated, he is no longer eligible for the dental program.
It is also not available for retired servicemembers and their families, former spouses,
or parents/parents-in-law.
    Covered services include:
- diagnostic (routine oral exams and X-rays)
- preventive (e.g., cleanings and fluoride treatments)
- sealants
- restorative (amalgam, resin, composite, prefabricated stainless steel crowns,
  inlays)
- endodontic
- oral surgery

- periodontal
- removable or fixed prosthodontics and repair (bridges, dentures)
- orthodontics (there is a $1,500 lifetime cap per eligible family member)

Premiums are deducted from the servicemember's pay, and cost shares are based on pay grade. To enroll, he must have at least twelve months remaining on his current contract and remain enrolled for a minimum of twelve months. As with medical coverage, greatest value is obtained by visiting participating dentists. They will also complete and submit claims on your behalf and accept payment directly from United Concordia.

The dental program is available worldwide, but some costs and processes OCONUS are different. For instance, OCONUS cost shares are the same for all pay grades, and premiums vary depending upon the specific enrollment plan and sponsor military status. The annual maximum and lifetime maximums for orthodontics are the same, but OCONUS accumulation of charges against the annual and lifetime orthodontic maximum is different. A nonavailability referral form from your Tricare Area Office (TAO) may be needed if there is no host nation provider list.

For more information, and to enroll in the dental program, call United Concordia, 800-866-8499, or enroll online at *www.ucci.com*.

LEGAL AID

Most installations have a legal office where you can get free legal advice and assistance. If your base doesn't have a legal office, go to the nearest office of another service. Any ID cardholder can obtain advice from any base's legal office. Many reserve lawyers also work weekends to help people from all services. Appointment procedures vary; some offices will see you on a walk-in basis, but others require you to have an appointment. If you have a quick question, you can usually just phone in and talk to a lawyer or paralegal. The following services are offered:

- landlord-tenant problems and interpretation of leases
- domestic relations (adoption, separation, nonsupport, and divorce)
- consumer problems (contract, product injury, and product failure)
- citizenship, immigration, and passports
- change of name, notarization, civil rights, depositions
- torts (civil wrongs for which you can receive monetary damages), contracts
- deployment readiness
- estate planning, including the drawing up of wills, powers of attorney, and bills of sale

Many offices provide arbitration service through which small-claims disputes between ID cardholders can be settled. Military lawyers can't advise you on personal business ventures or disputes with your employer. Nor can they represent you in court. Where appropriate, referrals to civilian resources will be made. The Army, Navy, and Marine Corps do have an Expanded Legal Assistance Program, however, wherein military lawyers will go to court with E-4s and below for personal cases (excluding criminal ones). The Staff Judge Advocate office will provide a lawyer for servicemembers of all ranks who are being court-martialed, going before an administrative board, or facing a nonjudicial punishment.

Military lawyers must meet the same requirements as civilian lawyers and must be members of the bar of at least one state.

SPACE-AVAILABLE TRAVEL

Most service families holding overseas permanent-change-of-station (PCS) orders travel to their new assignments via the Air Force's Air Mobility Command (AMC), which is based out of Scott Air Force Base in Illinois. When you're traveling on PCS orders, you reserve seats and your trip is a regular flight. However, AMC flights are available to you even if you're not PCS-ing, in which case you are flying space-available (Space-A) or, as it is commonly called, "taking a hop." The purpose of this privilege (it is not an entitlement or a right) is to enhance service families' quality of life.

Space-available means just that: After all the scheduled passengers and cargo are aboard, any remaining seats are offered to people who would like to go where the plane is going. AMC flights are scheduled on both military planes and civilian airliners; on the latter, the government buys all the seats. Hops are low-cost access to the world. With Space-A travel, military families can take holidays that many civilian families only dream about. Thanks to hops and low-cost lodging, you'll find military families enjoying some of the most expensive real estate in the world. Do you like sun? Hop to Hawaii and stay at the military's lovely Hale Koa Hotel, right on Waikiki Beach. Prefer snow? Hop to Germany and stay at the military lodge in Chiemsee and ski the Alps. There's hardly a place on this planet that you can't go using AMC as the principal means of transportation. To get anywhere from anywhere costs the same: nothing. (A head tax, transportation fee, or federal inspection fee is charged when you enter and leave commercial airports on commercial contract planes.)

How to Travel Space-A

Traveling Space-A is more complicated than booking a commercial flight, as Congress imposed rules to prevent unfair competition with domestic airlines. Here are some highlights. For more detailed information, visit *www.public.scott.af.mil/hqamc*.

There is no central booking phone number; you must contact each port to find out flights and flight times. A list of contacts is given in the appendix. Travel can be applied for in person, by fax, e-mail, or the Postal Service. When faxed, your sign-up time is based on the time listed on the fax data heading. For those applying in person, there is an optional self-registration program that allows passengers to sign up at a terminal without waiting in line. The entire family must have ID cards, additional photo IDs, passports, immunization records, and visas, if appropriate, when boarding.

All travelers remain on the register sixty days after registration, for the duration of their leave orders authorization, or until they are selected for travel, whichever occurs first. There is no need for revalidation. All legs of a flight are registered for at once, so if you make an intermediate stop, you keep the same place in line for all portions of your trip. Sign up for the return trip immediately upon reaching your destination.

The servicemember must be on official leave during all phases of the Space-A travel: the sign-in, the travel, and the return flight. And he must return when he said he would, regardless of whether a returning Space-A flight is available; to not return when scheduled is to risk a nonjudicial punishment.

Travel for business or personal gain is not permitted, nor to places where there are international restrictions. Conservative dress is required when flying Space-A: no open-toed sandals, shorts, tank/tube tops as outerwear, T-shirts with slogans or vulgarity, pictures of desecration of the flag, or revealing clothing. Servicemembers do not have to wear their uniforms.

Who May Fly
Family members can travel within CONUS and to, from, and between OCONUS locations. Except for certain cases, they must be accompanied by their sponsor and cannot travel with another military member in place of their sponsor. The exceptions are cases of environmental moral leave (EML), emergency travel, and command-sponsored Category 5. Spouses and dependent children may also travel unaccompanied in Category 4 when their sponsor is deployed for at least 120 consecutive days. During this deployment they may fly from CONUS and OCONUS locations, between CONUS locations, and within/between OCONUS locations. They may sign up ten days before deployment, travel on the first day of deployment, and the travel must be completed by the last day. A letter signed by the member's commander verifying the sponsor's deployment is required.

Children must be older than six weeks to fly, and pregnant women must be less than thirty-four weeks into their pregnancy. A physician's note is required otherwise. Pets may not be transported Space-A. They are permitted on military flights only during a permanent-change-of-station move.

Reservists may fly to, from, and between Alaska, Hawaii, Puerto Rico, the Virgin Islands, Guam, American Samoa, and CONUS. When on active duty, they may fly to any OCONUS destination where DoD flights operate. Reservists may fly Space-A within the United States, but without family members. Gray-area reservists may fly Space-A within the United States. Once they turn sixty and start drawing retirement pay, they and their family members are eligible for worldwide Space-A travel. Reservists must fax a copy of their current DD 1853 (proof of status for travel eligibility), a statement of border clearance documents, and a list of five possible destinations.

Priority Categories

Space-A flyers are assigned one of six priority categories and compete with other fliers within their categories based on date and time of registration. They may be bumped at any time to make room for scheduled passengers or cargo or category 1 flyers. If you are bumped, you'll be placed on the Space-A list at the location you were bumped, with the same sign-up time and date you received when you started your trip. The priority categories are:

1. DoD civilians or full-time, paid American Red Cross employees who have an emergency; servicemembers within the continental United States on emergency leave orders, who are traveling from their overseas duty station to the United States. Family members stateside may travel Space-A with their sponsors within the continental United States while on emergency leave.
2. Sponsors on environmental and morale leave, which is extra leave time granted to people stationed in what are considered adverse locations, and family members accompanying them; DoD teachers and accompanied family members on EML leave during nonsummer breaks.
3. Servicemembers on regular leave and family members accompanying them; servicemembers on permissive temporary duty for house hunting; active-duty family members traveling with their sponsors on house-hunting trips (only one family member may accompany the sponsor for this purpose).
4. Military family members traveling on emergency medical leave without their sponsor; DoD overseas schoolteachers on summer break.
5. Servicemembers on permissive temporary duty (other than house hunting) and their family members; active-duty family members living overseas on command-sponsored tours; students traveling without the military sponsor.
6. Retired military members and their families; active reservists; ROTC students.

Tips for Successful Space-A Flying

DoD Dependents Schools overseas are closed between December 20 and January 6. Many families try to fly Space-A during this time. Other peak travel months are December–January and June–July. Consider leaving and returning outside of those dates.

Nothing is guaranteed—flights, connecting flights, meals—anything. You can be bumped anywhere along your route. Plan accordingly. Most terminals close at night, and not all sell food. Thus, you might have to spend the night off base (on-base temporary lodging might be full). Money or a debit/credit card must be available. A stash of carry-on food is wise, too. Relief agencies have been contacted by people stranded longer than they thought in one place with insufficient money for expenses, and by military members who couldn't get a return Space-A flight before their leave ran out.

Travel light. Even though most planes allow seventy pounds of luggage per person, you may be switched en route to a plane that allows only thirty pounds per person. What will you do then? You cannot pay extra for excess luggage; only duty status passengers can do that, and not all terminals have lockers. You may bring only two suitcases and there are no porters. Golf clubs, ski equipment, or other bulky items count as one suitcase. Backpacks weighing up to twenty pounds are best. Hand-carried items must be able to fit under a seat or in an overhead compartment and are subject to 100 percent inspection. Checked bags are randomly inspected. Sharp objects must be placed in checked bags.

Carry extra prescriptions and medicines on your person, in case you get stuck somewhere. Also carry a blanket or a sweater, as cargo-type planes can get cold.

Flights are normally identified two to three hours prior to departure, but may be released as soon as thirty minutes prior. Flight schedules also frequently change. Scheduled flights get canceled; unexpected ones get added. Call the terminal for the latest information the day before you leave. Sometimes more seats are suddenly released after everyone has boarded. If your name is called at "show time" (the roll call for the departing flight) and you're not there, you won't lose your place in line, but you will have lost the opportunity to board that flight.

Space-A travelers can sign up for five places at once. If a flight to Portugal is booked, how about Spain or Germany? List the fifth place as "all" if you'll take an available seat on any flight. If the flights that go directly where you want to go are constantly booked, consider an indirect route via a less-traveled place. Places that AMC flies frequently, like Germany, are easier to get to than places flown infrequently, like Australia. Military ports offer more opportunities than commercial gateways. Almost every Air Force base offers worldwide Space-A flights. Call your air base, ask the operator for the passenger terminal number, then get flight information. If you live near a military airfield, ask if it offers hops. Hops are also available on Navy, Marine Corps, and Coast Guard flights and from Air National Guard and Air Force Reserve bases, and from various commercial airports. A list of Space-A locations and contact numbers is in the appendix. The easiest hubs to hop from are Dover AFB, Travis AFB, Norfolk NS, Baltimore/Washington International, Rhein Main, and RAF Mildenhall.

Exchange some U.S. currency for the currency of your destination before you go. Take foreign coins for phone calls and tips. Keep a pocket calculator handy to convert prices. Border towns usually accept either country's money. See chapter 8 for more information on traveling.

Make friends with your fellow Space-A travelers. Split unexpected cab and hotel bills with them. Exchanging tips and war stories makes the adventure more fun and the disappointments more bearable.

DoDEA SCHOOLS

The military has provided overseas schools for the children of its members since 1946, when the Navy built the first at Guantánamo Bay and American Samoa. Stateside schools were established well before that. These schools were first administered by the individual military branches, then by civilian managers, and they have evolved today into the Department of Defense Educational Activity (DoDEA). The DoDEA administers three separate systems: the Department of Defense Dependents Schools (DoDDS) Europe, DoDDS Pacific, and the Domestic Dependent Elementary and Secondary Schools (DDESS), which are stateside. Each of the three parts is further broken down into districts, with a superintendent for each district.

Altogether, there are 199 schools located throughout twelve foreign countries, seven states, Guam, and Puerto Rico. There are 8,700 educators and over 88,000 students who populate them. Preschool through twelfth grade is taught; DoDEA even runs a community college in Panama. All are fully accredited by U.S. agencies. DoDEA administration recognizes that military children face unique challenges, such as frequent moves. For that reason, a uniform curriculum is provided to help transition from one area to another. Providing an appropriate education to children with disabilities is also a mission.

Student progress is monitored through standardized tests. The Terra Nova Achievement Test is given to grades three through eleven. Every year, at every grade level tested, and in every subject area, DoDEA students score above the national average. DoDEA fourth and eighth grade students also take the National Assessment of Educational Progress (NAEP), "the Nation's Report Card," which compares student achievement in reading, writing, math, and science. DoDDS and DDESS student scores consistently rank at or near the top when compared with the scores of other participating states and jurisdictions. Minority students have been especially successful, scoring at or near the highest in the nation in mathematics. DoDEA schools graduate about 99 percent of their high school students.

Many DoD families live in foreign locations where there are no DoDEA schools in the commuting area, typically Central and South America, Mexico, Canada, and the Caribbean Islands. In these cases, the Non-DoD Schools Program (NDSP) supports and funds the education of children of authorized command-sponsored servicemembers and DoD civilian employees. Their options range from home-based schooling to private or public schools. Local NDSP liaisons assist with registration and funding.

DoDEA schools are currently located in these places:

DoDDS	DDESS
Bahrain	Alabama
Belgium	Georgia
England	Kentucky
Germany	New York
Guam	North Carolina
Italy	South Carolina
Japan	Virginia
Korea	Cuba
The Netherlands	Puerto Rico
Portugal	
Spain	

This chart shows how many children from each service use DoDEA schools:

Affiliation	DoDDS	DDESS
Army	35%	71%
Navy	14%	4%
Marine Corps	7%	18%
Air Force	31%	5%
Civilian	12%	1%
Coast Guard	0.1%	1%

The American Overseas Schools Historical Society is a museum in Wichita, Kansas, that collects, records, and preserves the history of educating American children abroad. It has historical records and memorabilia such as "Clarence," a medieval suit of armor that was the mascot for Bonn American High School in Germany. It has displays of student recollections of growing up overseas, including during crises such as the Tiananmen Square Massacre and U.S. Embassy bombings in Africa.

To register your children, you will need their birth certificates, Social Security numbers, previous school records, immunization records, and your husband's permanent-change-of-station orders.

CHILD DEVELOPMENT CENTERS

Half of all military families have at least one child under school age, and over half of those families are dual income. Many servicemembers themselves are single parents or dual-service couples. Therefore, Congress appropriates funds for Child Development Centers (CDC) to reduce lost duty time. CDCs care for children from six weeks to twelve years old. They have strict requirements for health and safety, curriculum, staff training, and qualifications, and most are accredited by the National Association for the Education of Young Children. Military CDCs are cheaper than private child-care centers because they are tax subsidized. Fees are calculated on a sliding scale for income. When figuring a family's income, quarters, and subsistence allowances are included.

Active duty, DoD civilian employees, reservists on active duty, and DoD contractors are eligible to use them; however, individual base policies on their usage vary. Some give priority to working parents over stay-at-home parents, so drop-in slots are limited. Other places operate centers solely for drop-ins. Most centers are open from 6 A.M. to 6:30 P.M. weekdays, year-round. Some have weekend hours. Bases with unique missions have centers open twenty-four hours. Some offer care for events and briefings.

Because demand for military CDCs is high and the need is not met 100 percent by the DoD, some have long waiting lists. Your position on the list depends on your status when you apply and on the date you apply, and will change if your status changes. Single parents and dual-military couples are always given priority over military-civilian couples on waiting lists because they must report for duty immediately after arriving at their new base.

An alternative to a center is in-home child care, also called family child care or child development homes. This is care provided in private homes, on base and off. Licensed providers meet the same standards for care and training as providers in the centers, and are also government subsidized. Nonlicensed providers generally aren't allowed to operate on base due to liability concerns. In-home providers may be more flexible than the centers in things like hours and transportation to after-school activities. It is

> To build or expand any facility, the military must prove a need to Congress. Although some funds are earmarked for specific projects, most must be prioritized. Barracks renovation, research and development, medical care, field operations, family housing, and civilian employee salaries all compete with daycare centers for funds.

important to discuss issues like late charges, providing diapers and food, backups for when the provider is unable to work, whether the provider is paid when you are on vacation and so forth. Better yet to put these issues in a written contract.

School-Age and Youth Programs
The military has school-age programs for before- and after-school care, holiday care, and summer camps for schoolchildren ages six to twelve. These programs may be in the base CDC, a youth center, or school. There are also partnerships with Boys & Girls Clubs of America and 4-H clubs, which allow for more activities. Then there are youth programs for children ages six to eighteen. These provide a place to go after school, evenings, weekends, holidays, and during summer vacation. Activities include supervised trips, lock-in slumber parties, arts-and-crafts classes, chess clubs, and team sports. Teenagers are allowed to come and go once they have permission to be home alone.

MORALE, WELFARE, AND RECREATION
Morale, Welfare, and Recreation (MWR) refers to nonappropriated fund facilities and activities. Their operating expenses are paid from user fees, not from taxes. Congress requires that most MWR facilities make a profit or at least break even, and to reimburse the government for utilities and maintenance/repairs. If a local commander wants to keep a money-losing MWR facility, its losses must be offset by a money-making one. The only MWR activities that are exempt from this are libraries and

fitness centers, as they are considered important enough to subsidize. Nevertheless, fees at military facilities are still cheaper than comparable civilian ones. Facilities vary, but you'll usually find the following on most bases:

Clubs

Most bases have an all-ranks club. They vary at each installation; at some places they're huge and elegant, and at others they're small and cozy. Many are themed, like sports bars. There is usually a good restaurant or bar. Clubs cash checks and provide meeting and party rooms, catering, restaurants, happy hours, pools, and even serving equipment, such as punch bowls and flatware, for loan. Some offer MasterCard and VISA credit cards. They can host social affairs too large to be held at home. On most Navy bases, everyone is considered a member of the club, and dues are not paid. In the Army and Air Force, this is not the case; facilities are available to members only, and dues are collected. Reciprocity—one club allowing members of another to use its facilities—isn't always granted.

Recreation Centers

Also called Community Centers or Community Activity Centers. These were originally lounges for the single sevicemembers. They often have a TV, pool and ping-pong tables, and a game room. Here you can buy discounted tickets (with no sales tax) to concerts, tours, and local and national attractions such as Disneyworld and Busch Gardens. You can also buy prepaid phone cards.

Reservists have unlimited access to most MWR facilities. But some base commanders restrict this access due to space constraints (often the case with golf courses), so call before making the trip.

Arts and craft centers are popular with spouses. They offer classes in photography, painting, drawing, sculpture, weaving, stained glass, leather working, lapidary, ceramics, woodworking, upholstery, matting/framing, sewing, wreath making, and flower arranging. Some sponsor contests in photography and fine arts.

Fitness Centers/Gyms

Base gyms can be anything from a single room with some weights to a huge fitness facility with a track, pool, weight machines, competitive sports teams, massages, and classes. Most services in base gyms are free to active-duty personnel. Classes may have a small cost. A few fitness centers charge a small membership fee for DoD civilians and family members.

Armed Forces Recreation Centers

The Department of Defense owns recreational properties all over the world. Examples are the Hale Koa beachfront hotel in Hawaii, the Shades of Green resort at Disneyworld, mountain ski chalets in Garmisch and Chiemsee, Germany, and the Dragon Hill Lodge in Seoul, Korea. Active-duty and reserve servicemembers, retired personnel, DoD employees, and delayed-entry recruits may enjoy them.

Check with the front desk at each place regarding policies. Some are very busy and require reservations a year in advance. Some accept reservations only for those traveling on official orders (e.g., temporary duty or change of station) and accommodate vacationers on a first-come, first-serve or standby basis. Some give particular guests priority over others. Some operate only during certain seasons. All have different policies on payment, pets, motorcycles and minibikes,

Need a cheap place to stay in New York City? The Soldiers', Sailors', and Airmen's Club houses military people in midtown Manhattan. It's a hotel at 283 Lexington Avenue, between 36th and 37th Streets. It offers safe, affordable rooms, compared with typical New York prices. Call 800-678-8413 for reservations.

quiet hours, cooking in cabins, open fires, check-in hours, limits on stays, and firearms. Some sites provide hookups for trailers; others don't. Some sites are near large cities, others are isolated. Amenities range from full support to nothing. Ask what amenities are available at a cabin, as some rooms are fully stocked and others require your own soap and towels. Fees are minimal or pegged to rank. For more information and to book reservations online, visit *www.armymwr.com/portal/travel/recreationcenters/*.

Other Facilities
Other MWR facilities you'll typically find on a large base include libraries; theaters; arts-and-crafts centers; thrift shops; fitness centers; playing and track fields; boats, motors, and fishing gear for rent; swimming pools; riding stables; campers, trailers, tents, and camping gear for rent; bowling alleys; eighteen-hole, nine-hole, and miniature golf courses; tennis courts; skating rinks; auto crafts shops; sports equipment for rent; photo labs; kennels; sports lodges; and various clubs such as aero, hunt, skeet, rod and gun, and chess.

EXCEPTIONAL FAMILY MEMBER PROGRAM (EFMP)
A family member who has a physical, developmental, educational, or intellectual disorder that requires special treatment, therapy, education, counseling, or medical care is eligible for a specific program called the Exceptional Family Member Program (EFMP). Participating members may be a spouse, child, stepchild, adopted child, foster child, or dependent parent who resides with the sponsor. This program assists with respite care, transportation, and treatment at medical facilities (military and civilian) and provides recreational and cultural activities, family support groups, and individual support.

If you have a special-needs family member, enrollment is mandatory. The aim of the program is to assist assignment monitors in assigning military families to areas where their family members' special needs can be met. Enrollment is for as long as necessary. Contact the coordinator at your base Family Services Center for the enrollment forms. Disenrollment requires a letter from a medical doctor stating that services are no longer needed, and it may be prompted by a change in marital status, change in dependency of the enrolled family member, or change in medical status of the enrolled family member.

Enrollment information is not given to promotion or school selection boards or put in the sponsor's records. It is not grounds for a sponsor's deferment or consideration for duties. It doesn't guarantee that the sponsor won't serve an unaccompanied tour or that he will always be able to travel with the family member during moves. Enrollment does not mean that a sponsor will not be deployed or assigned an overseas tour, or that he will get preferential treatment or be thought of as someone unable to carry out professional responsibilities. It simply prescribes an agreed-upon and systematic manner to communicate your family's special need when a random assignment is not suitable for you.

The program is interested primarily in ensuring that the special-needs family member isn't sent to a place with inadequate support facilities. This may involve the sponsor being in one place while the family is supported in another.

The special education office of every state Department of Education has an advocate for children with special educational needs. It can assist parents in finding services that their children need. Write to this office in care of the state capitol building.

FAMILY SERVICES

Services are in place to help with the unique needs and stresses of military life. Whatever name this organization takes where you are—Army Community Services, Navy Family Service Center, Airman and Family Readiness Center, Marine Corps Community Services, or Coast Guard Work-Life Center—the mission is to provide help in both everyday living and crisis situations. These services are open to reservist families, although reserve units have their own family support programs. Contact the reserve unit or the State Family Program coordinator for more information. They all have websites: *www.myarmylifetoo.com* (Army), *www.afcrossroads.com/* (Air Force), *www.nffsp.org.* (Navy), and *www.usmc-mccs.org* (Marine Corps).

The people who work in Family Services offices are trained civilians, military personnel, and volunteers. Following is a description of the core programs provided at most duty stations. You'll be given a referral to a local civilian resource for anything Family Services can't help with.

Social Work Services

Here you can find medical social services and community support, individual and group therapy, marital therapy, blended/step family therapy, substance abuse help, new parent assistance, women's groups, family, child and victim advocacy, stress management and parenting classes, foster care, crisis intervention, and grief counseling. If you feel in need, please contact these offices. The staff is trained and can offer insights and solutions you may not have thought about.

Crisis Line

A crisis line is manned by trained volunteers supervised by a social worker. You decide what kinds of problems to take to the crisis line. A crisis simply refers to something with which you have no experience.

Financial Readiness Program

Here you'll find one-on-one assistance with balancing your checkbook, making a budget, managing debt, consumer advocacy, Thrift Savings Plan information, and personal finance classes. You don't have to be command-referred to take advantage of this service.

Food Locker/Emergency Relief

The Community Food Locker will provide a free three-day supply of staples for emergency situations, such as money mismanagement, pay problems, or unplanned expenses. A referral from a social worker, commander, chaplain, financial counselor, or Family Services or Emergency Relief counselor is required before receiving food. If a locker isn't available, vouchers may be given to be redeemed at the commissary. There is also a program that provides emergency relief funds, which is discussed in chapter 5.

Other Family Services Resources

What else might you find at Family Services? Spouse employment assistance programs, thrift shop, parenting classes, conversational English classes, volunteering opportunities, outreach programs, information on voting registration and food stamp eligibility, programs for foreign-born spouses and bicultural families, and lists of quarters-cleaning teams. Air Force families will find the Airman's Attic, which gives donated clothes, kitchen utensils, furniture, and other items to married E-4s and below. The Air Force also has the Give Parents a Break Program, which provides free babysitting in situations of hardship, deployment, or special needs. Navy Family Service offices have additional services, such as ombudsmen, predeployment and deployment support services, hospitality kits, information about recreational facilities, child-care centers, Navy Lodges, information on how to get a passport before going overseas, legal aid, help with special needs children, and reference libraries about stateside and overseas duty stations.

Ombudsman/Key Volunteer Program

Called the Ombudsman Program in the Navy and Coast Guard and Key Volunteer in the Marine Corps, this program's purpose is to provide communication between Navy families and Navy officials. It is especially important in deploying commands. A volunteer ombudsman is usually the spouse of a high-ranking enlisted member and is appointed by, and guided by, the Commanding Officer (CO). She is the main link between families at home and the command during the deployment.

The program belongs to the command and is shaped by the commanding officer's (CO) perception of the command's needs. The ombudsman/key volunteer assists the CO in addressing the morale and concerns of its families. She also passes along complaints and suggestions by command family members and helps settle grievances. During deployment, the ombudsman helps families get their needs taken care of. If you don't know who your ombudsman is, ask the command.

MILITARY ONE SOURCE

At *www.militaryonesource.com* you'll find an amazing amount of resources for the military family. Unlike most websites, you can actually e-mail the people working it for help and they will research things for you and help you with suggestions tailored to your specific situation. Browse this site to see all that it has.

MILITARY CHAPLAINS

Military chaplains are accredited ministers who serve on active duty and perform the same spiritual services as civilian ministers. They are insulated from the chain of command and will protect your confidences. There also serve as marriage and family therapists.

SPOUSE ORIENTATIONS

Each service has programs that orient new spouses. They are called Heartlink in the Air Force, Army Family Team Building in the Army, LINKS (Lifestyle, Insights, Networking, Knowledge, and Skills) in the Marine Corps, and COMPASS in the Navy. These programs introduce spouses to the military lifestyle and give information about the base mission, customs, traditions, and resources. They are free, informal classes that last about ten hours spread over multiple days or evenings. The discussion leaders are military spouses and free child care is often provided to participants.

THE UNITED SERVICES ORGANIZATION (USO)

The USO is a private, nonprofit organization that provides entertainment to the troops and morale building services and activities to them and their families. It was formed in 1941 when President Franklin D. Roosevelt asked private organizations to provide leisure activities for the troops who were preparing for World War II. Five nonprofit agencies—the Salvation Army, the YMCA, the National Catholic Community Services, the National Traveler's Aid Association, and the National Jewish Welfare Board—pooled their resources and formed the USO. In 1979, it became an independent organization.

The USO operates over 130 stations all over the world. It provides services to the military community, such as arranging travel tours, hosting cultural understanding programs and operating airport lounges with amenities for service families to rest between flights. These lounges are located at the St. Louis; Charleston, South Carolina; Philadelphia; Seattle-Tacoma; Baltimore; Kennedy (in New York); San Diego; Los Angeles; Oakland; San Francisco; Dallas/Fort Worth; Raleigh/Durham; Denver; and Charlotte-Douglas airports. And, of course, there are the famous celebrity tours for servicemembers in remote locations and VA hospitals. For more information, visit its website at *www.uso.org*.

THE ARMED FORCES YMCA
The Armed Forces YMCA is a social service agency that focuses on junior enlisted families. It offers outreach programs in which trained volunteers visit families in civilian apartments, trailer parks, and other hard-to-reach areas. It offers Mom's Day Outs, kids' parties, help during deployments, emergency food supplies, and many other things. The YMCA supplements military services, so what it offers varies from base to base. Typical programs include shuttle buses to the commissary and exchange, English as a second language classes, and recreational activities for young, first-time servicemembers. Most programs are free. For more information, visit *www.asymca.org/index.html*.

AMERICAN RED CROSS
The Red Cross is a giant humanitarian organization that ministers to victims of natural calamity, poor health, and war. The American Red Cross, founded in 1881, has a long history of service to the military. It sends emergency communications on behalf of family members and provides financial assistance, counseling, and assistance to veterans. Red Cross workers on military installations brief departing servicemembers and their families regarding available support services and explain how the Red Cross may assist them during the deployment. If you need to contact a deployed servicemember in a hurry, the Red Cross will verify the emergency, which facilitates communication.

To contact the Red Cross for assistance, call 877-272-7337 (toll free) if you're a family member residing with an active-duty servicemember. Reservists and family members not residing in the servicemember's household should call the local Red Cross chapter. Find the nearest one at *www.redcross.org/where/where.html*. If you are a family member residing with a servicemember overseas, call the base operator or the Red Cross office at the overseas location. For more information, visit *www.redcross.org/index.html*.

Military installations are self-contained societies that operate virtually independently of their nearby civilian communities. They're towns in themselves. Take a walk around yours and see what's there. Use and benefit from their facilities. They are your facilities, there for you.

FURTHER READING

Books
Tomes, Jonathan P. *Servicemember's Legal Guide*, 5th edition. Mechanicsburg, PA: Stackpole Books, 2005.

Internet Resources
www.commissaries.com. Official site of the Defense Commissary Agency. Get sales and product information, recipes, and contact info/hours for local commissaries.
www.aafes.com. Official site of the Army and Air Force Exchange Service. Shop online.
www.navy-nex.com. Official site of the Navy Exchange. Shop online, book rooms at Navy Lodges, and more.
www.usmc-mccs.org. Official site of the Marine Corps Exchange. Shop online and access other services.
www.tricare.osd.mil/DEERS. Official DEERS website. You can enroll here.
www.tricare.osd.mil. OfficialTricare website. Schedule and view appointments, access health content and personal health information; use pharmacy tools, check food and drug interactions, and more.
www.tricare.osd.mil/reserve. Official Tricare website for reservists
www.defenselink.mil/ra/html/tricare.html. Points of contact for Tricare Reserve Select.
www.fisherhouse.org. Fisher House website.
www.tricaredentalprogram.com. Official Tricare Dental Program (United Concordia).
www.jagcnet.army.mil/legal. Army Judge Advocate General site. Has a lot of general information and useful links.
www.armymwr.com, *www.mwr.navy.mil*. Information on MWR facilities and activities.
www.takeahop.org. This private, noncommercial site provides an online signup for many Space-A gateways. It is operated by volunteers.
www.pepperd.com, *www.militaryhops.com*. Private Space-A site with a message board full of posts by frequent Space-A travelers.
www.uso.org. USO homepage.
www.am.dodea.edu. Department of Defense Education Activity website. Has links to DODDS Europe, Pacific, and DDESS.
aoshs.wichita.edu. American Overseas Schools Historical Society.
www.dmdc.osd.mil/rsl. Search for an locations to obtain an ID card at by city or state.
www.military-brats.com. Military children registry.
www.militaryhomefront.dod.mil/. DoD website that has quality of life information.

Tricare Phone Numbers

Phone hours are Monday through Friday 8:00 A.M. to 11:00 P.M., Saturday 9:00 A.M. to 8:00 P.M., and Sunday 10:00 A.M. to 5:30 P.M. (closed on holidays).

TRICARE For Life Program 1-888-DOD-LIFE (1-888-363-5433)

Pharmacy Program 1-877-DOD-MEDS (1-877-363-6337)

National Mail Order Pharmacy 1-800-903-4680 (1-888-DOD-CARE)

TRICARE Prime Remote 1-888-363-2273

TRICARE Dental Program 1-800-866-8499

Retiree Dental Program 1-888-838-8737

Active Duty Claims (Military Medical Support Office) 1-800-876-1131

1-(888)-4GO-WNAP. This number is for servicemembers in transition, reservists, and their families in Tricare's Southern Region only. It is an advocacy unit that offers free advice about finding a doctor, using the prescription-drug program or figuring out the Tricare co-pay system, VA health-care programs, and more.

For general information about TRICARE, call the toll-free TRICARE information line: 1-877-DoD-MEDS (1-877-363-6337). Hearing or speech-impaired beneficiaries may call TTY/TDD at 1-877-535-6778.

3

Socials, Customs, and Traditions

You're looking at an invitation for your first Hail and Farewell. What is it and why should you go? What should you do there? This chapter explains the military social functions you're likely to attend and the customs and traditions observed at them.

PURPOSE OF SOCIALS

Military people are a transient bunch. We spend a large portion of our lives separated from parents, siblings, and other family members. Consistently moving to new towns can be stressful. Through social gatherings, you are offered the chance to make "new" family and friends who are in the same situation and can empathize with your unique needs and stresses. They can help ease the isolation you feel when you arrive at a new duty station. Social gatherings are an easy way to make friends because the people attending are often there for just that purpose. The people you meet can offer tips on where to shop, leads on jobs, phone numbers for babysitters, and information on youth groups and church activities. Once you get to know them, you may feel more comfortable asking for help. This is particularly important when you're on your own during a long deployment. Social gatherings are also great opportunities to just dress up and have fun. Consider them a fringe benefit of military service.

Some social affairs are "command performances," meaning the servicemember is required to attend. These mandatory events have their roots in tradition. Such affairs are designed to promote camaraderie and esprit de corps. They enable servicemembers to get to know each other outside the workplace. A commander wants the people in his unit to know each other—to develop unity. If his unit is called upon to fight, that sense of unity will be critical. Although your attendance at such affairs is not mandatory, your presence will make the affair more fun and show your support for the unit and its mission. Social affairs are as lively and interesting as the people who attend them.

Some wives choose not to participate in military social affairs for personal reasons, and your involvement is your choice. But please don't let a lack of self-confidence keep you away. How else do you plan to develop that confidence? As the saying goes, "If you keep doing what you've always done, you'll keep getting what you've always gotten." Don't worry about making mistakes; the only people who don't make mistakes are people who don't do anything. Try not to let other people's negative experiences color yours; many of the people who disparage socials don't even attend them. Experience them yourself and make your own conclusions. Also, give the attendees the benefit of a doubt—people who seem standoffish may sim-

During my twenty years as a military wife, I have observed that wives who are actively involved in clubs and other civic activities seem to have the most successful military husbands. Shmoozing is an important skill, in both military and civilian life. Maybe it's a chicken-or-egg thing, or maybe it's just that successful people tend to marry each other. If you don't want to actively participate in coffees and family support group meetings, perhaps you could volunteer to make phone calls when necessary. Anything is better than nothing.

ply feel as awkward as you do. Others accuse all and sundry in a group of "wearing their husbands' rank," but this perception is often misguided. What you may be seeing is simply the confidence of someone who has successfully navigated deployments, socials, moving, and other challenges, or holds a responsible job herself.

SOME COMMON SOCIAL FUNCTIONS

Hails and Farewells

Before World War II, when the services were smaller, it was the custom for a new officer or NCO and his wife to pay a social call at the home of his superior. The superior and his wife would then later return the call. When the couple left, a social would be held for them.

In today's service, you can see how that would be impractical. So this custom has been replaced with the "hail and farewell," the modern equivalent of all calls made and received. It is held every two months or at whatever interval is necessary to accommodate the turnover of personnel. A hail and farewell usually takes the form of a dinner at a restaurant. Dress is informal. After dinner, speeches are made. People leaving receive going-away gifts, which usually are inscribed plaques, mugs, or souvenirs special to the unit. These are paid for out of a fund to which everyone contributes. Newcomers are then welcomed.

Attendance at such an affair shows respect for the people leaving and gives a warm welcome to those coming in. For this reason, the servicemember's attendance is usually required. These socials are good opportunities to see your friends and make a few new ones.

Receptions

In the old days, it was the custom for an officer or NCO new to a post to pay a social call to his superior on holidays, a call that was later returned. Like the hail and farewell, receptions now serve as the equivalent of all holiday calls. They are held at holidays, in honor of someone's promotion or retirement, or for special occasions, such as the christening or commissioning of a ship. Receptions can be held in the afternoon or evening and may be formal or informal. Those that start after 6:00 P.M. are always formal.

At the beginning of the reception, you will go through a receiving line. Its purpose is to permit the host to personally welcome the guests into the reception and is the official "calls made and received" portion of the event. Along with the host and hostess, you also may find important guests and visitors. The spouse goes first in the Army, Navy, and Marine Corps; in the Air Force, the servicemember goes first.

Receiving lines are not the place for any kind of conversation. When your turn comes, smile, extend your hand, greet the first person by name, introduce yourself, and say, "Nice to meet you." Then move on to the next. Sometimes the first person in line will be an adjutant (officer who acts as a military assistant) and that adjutant will introduce you to the receiving line people. When that's the case, the servicemember should introduce both you and your husband, using his title (e.g., Captain and Mrs. Smith). You don't shake hands with the adjutant. The person in line right after the adjutant will be the host or person of honor at the event (who is not necessarily the highest ranking one).

If you're wearing gloves, it's not necessary to remove them when you go through the line, and you can carry your handbag, but don't carry a cigarette or drink. There will be a table nearby to set drinks. While standing in line, if a very senior officer comes up and stands behind you, it is proper for your husband to offer to let him and his spouse precede you.

Receptions for individual units are held in the commander's home. The invitation to an affair of this nature often states a specific time frame. Punctuality is critical, since all units under that commander will arrive at and remain until their designated times. The reception line here consists of the commander and his wife, who stand at the doorway and greet everyone when the scheduled time for that unit arrives.

If you prefer to have a soft drink during the reception (or any event), do so. Don't feel obligated to drink alcohol at any affair. It's neither required nor encouraged.

Banquets

Banquets, or formal dinners, are held for special holidays such as Christmas or special occasions such as the field artillery's St. Barbara's Day Ball. They are often held in conjunction with receptions and present an opportunity to dress up in your finest, enjoy a nice meal, and dance afterward. The Posting of the Colors ceremony (described later in this chapter) is usually performed, and toasts are made. Seating is pre-arranged, with name cards to indicate locations. Look to the people at the head table for guidance about when you should toast and when you should stand, sit, eat, and anything else you might be wondering about. Etiquette and table manners are the same here as anywhere else. Talk to people around you. Do your part to make the evening a success.

After the meal, a waiter will probably come by to light the candle on your table. This is a remnant from the old tradition of lighting the after-dinner smoking lantern that indicated that it was now permissible to smoke. Here's a contemporary word about smoking at the table: don't. If you want a cigarette, go to the lobby.

Change-of-Command Ceremony

This ceremony is held to represent the passing of command from one commander to another. Depending on how large the unit and high-ranking the commander, the ceremony may be a large, elaborate affair with hundreds of people attending, or a small one with just a few dozen. The flag is passed from the outgoing commander to the incoming one, while the people under his command stand at attention. Visitors watch from chairs on the sidelines. Flowers are often presented to the commanders' spouses.

Coffees and Teas

These are socials primarily hosted and attended by officer spouses. They are intended just for spouses; children should be left home. Unless it's a potluck, the hostess typically provides food and might invite a speaker from the local community. Sometimes they are held to honor an incoming or outgoing spouse. If the spouse is incoming, be sure to introduce yourself to her. These events last one to two hours.

You're invited to a Coffee!

WHERE:
Miranda G.'s House
Anywhere Air Base

WHEN:
Thursday, Oct. 9, 7:30 P.M.

Sample coffee invitation.

Family Readiness Group (FRG)

These forums are the official conduit for command information. While they serve social and recreational purposes, their reason for existence is to answer unit-related questions and to provide support during a deployment. They differ from wives' or social groups in that they're open to anyone: the unit's single servicemembers, spouses, children, parents, friends, relatives, significant others, even retirees, and community members. FRGs may utilize unit office space, phones, copying equipment, and supplies needed to accomplish their goals. Meetings are usually held in someone's home or at a local restaurant, and each FRG decides its own goals and activities. Depending on the interests of the group, a meeting might include scrapbooking or a seminar on military child education. Some FRG members have specific positions, such as a leader, treasurer, newsletter reporter, activities coordinator, and fund-raiser chairperson. While they're all volunteer positions, the commander, as the FRG's ultimate leader, determines or approves an FRG's leadership.

When newly married, or new to a base, your husband needs to inform the FRG of your presence so that you can receive invitations to activities and information. Of course, feel free to make contact yourself. If the FRG doesn't know about you, it can't contact you. Try to attend your unit's FRG meetings and activities, since the volunteers who run them may get discouraged if no one shows up. FRGs depend on your participation. Some are dormant until there's a deployment. Others enjoy year-round activities. Don't complain that your FRG doesn't "do anything," while simultaneously ignoring any invitations extended. Better yet, volunteer to plan activities, edit a newsletter, or be a key caller (someone who passes information along a telephone chain). Answer your e-mails, make suggestions, and try to change things about it you don't like. Give it a chance; there may be a roomful of friends there.

There are also various online message boards where military spouses congregate; some people prefer them to other types of socials. The website *www.militaryspousesupport.net/boards/* is a good one. But while online forums are fun and informational, your local community needs you to participate, too.

Hosting an FRG or a Coffee

Here are some tips for hosting a Family Readiness Group or a Coffee.

- Distribute invitations at least two weeks before the meeting. Print up flyers on your computer and give them to your husband to distribute to his co-workers to take home. Include what kind of event you're throwing, the names of the hosts, the place, date, time, and where to RSVP. A map with directions is a nice touch; you can print one off from an online source such as Yahoo Maps, Google Maps, or Mapquest. Extend invitations to the women servicemembers in the unit, and to the male spouses. The latter may wish to attend but might need some encouragement. Make the event sound interesting, encourage people to participate, and let the ones who don't know they're missed. Ask people if they have transportation; if not, see if you can arrange it.

- Start the event no later than fifteen minutes after the stated time on the invitation.
- Feed your guests. It's a proven way to get people to come. Popular dishes are fresh fruit salads, a vegetable or cold-cut/cheese platter, chips and dip, hot wings, take-out pizza, or bowls of flavored popcorn. Iced tea and soft drinks go over well. Nice paper plates and utensils are fine.
- If there is no policy against it, some groups raffle off a door prize, something that costs about $10, with $1 tickets. Small plants or flowers work well, and it is a special surprise when the gift has been on the coffee table all evening and the hostess invites the winner to take it. Coffee mugs, picture frames, recipe boxes, and coupon holders are also well received.
- Ensure that everyone is mingling and having a good time and that newcomers are introduced around and drawn into a group. If the first forum a newcomer attends is a bad experience for her, she may not attend another.
- Try not to hold the event in conjunction with a baby shower. Both events make for an overly long evening, and the combination also pressures women who just want to attend the social to bring a present. Invite speakers. A financial planner, artist, a local cosmetician or hairdresser, CPR expert, interior designer, or a self-defense/home security expert (the local police department might provide someone for this) can make your event more interesting. Hold a jewelry-making, scrapbooking, cooking, candy-making, or crafts session. Ask a masseuse to give chair massages. Hold a pool party at someone's home or apartment. Hold a pajama party at a cabin at a military campground. Try a potluck, cookie or ornament exchange, or a mystery gift night where wrapped gifts are auctioned and the money goes toward a fund-raiser.

Other Socials

There are many more affairs common to all services, to only one service, and to a particular branch of that service. There are MASH parties for hospital staffs, all-hands parties, potlucks, promotion parties (or "wetting downs" in the Navy), retirement parties, commissioning ceremonies, the Marine Corps Birthday Ball, and the Coast Guard All Hand picnic. There are dinings-in and dinings-out, luncheons, brunches, and graduations. Customs vary from base to base, so when in doubt, just follow the lead of the senior people there. There are also wives' clubs. These vary by area; some have basewide clubs for officer wives, enlisted wives, or for all wives.

FUND-RAISERS

Fund-raisers are a means to raise money for a specific goal, such as children's egg hunts at Easter, chartering a bus to visit temporarily deployed husbands, or unit sports team shirts. Volunteers in a Family Readiness or coffee group coordinate fund-raisers. If you get a phone call from an active member asking for baked goods or other donation for a fund-raising effort, help if you can. They need all the support they can get so the fund-raiser—your fund-raiser—is a success. For the best results, hold a fund-raiser right after payday. Popular ideas include:

- baked goods, chili, or breakfast burrito sale held at the unit, area Walmart, the base hospital, or National Guard Armory; man a day and night shift at buildings open twenty-four hours
- silent auction of goods and services (e.g., babysitting, cooking) donated by local businesses or spouses
- cookbook of favorite recipes compiled by the spouses
- car wash near a busy store or gas station
- autograph show with a local celebrity or beauty queen
- sale of patriotic pins, potpourri bags, ornaments, or car flags
- used book, CD, or software sale
- gift-wrapping in December with supplies donated by the spouses (the exchange might sell supplies at cost)
- raffle

Know that there are rules governing fund-raising, such as allowable activities, accounting of funds, maximum amount allowed to be raised, and what the funds can be used for. Obtain guidance from the FRG leadership before doing a fund-raiser.

CUSTOMS AND TRADITIONS

Protocol

The military has a rich history of customs and traditions; many today are the same as they were over 100 years ago. Part of navigating these customs is knowing some basic protocols. Webster defines *protocol* as "a code that prescribes adherence to correct etiquette and precedence." The State Department defines it as a "rule book by which international relations are conducted." Its purpose is to create a cordial atmosphere in which the business of diplomacy may be conducted. Simply put, it's a plan that defines who does what, where, and when. As one diplomat observed, "We all can't go through the door at the same time." If you want to see an example of how formal protocol can be, view this precedence list at *www.usma.army.mil/Protocol/images/DA_precedence.pdf*.

While social affairs in today's military don't adhere to the kind of formality that may have been expected in the 1950s, the protocol and customs that do remain have the same purpose they have always had, which is to create order. Protocol is not designed to promote snobbery, but rather is a courtesy designed to recognize official status and give respect to those who, by their achievement, time in service, and experience, deserve it. This courtesy extends to spouses, as their support helps make that success possible. But don't stress over who you should introduce to whom first, what to serve, and when to stand up—know that it's better to do the wrong thing graciously than the right thing rudely or poorly. Protocol is as much about a good attitude as anything else. Here we'll discuss some common customs, traditions, and protocols.

The Flag

Flags that are carried on foot are called "colors" and are carried by a color guard. Flags mounted on vehicles are called "standards," and flags on ships are called "ensigns." When flying halfway up a pole, they are at "half mast" in the Navy and "half staff" in the other services.

Posting of the Colors

This is a tradition performed at certain events. The flags are carried by a color guard, which typically consists of four servicemembers. Two carry flags while the other two are "under arms," meaning that they're carrying rifles. Stand when the color guard is six paces before you, and remain standing until they are six paces behind you. Keep your eyes on the flag while it is passing by, but don't turn to follow it. Placing your right hand over your heart is optional, and if you do this, hold this position until the colors pass.

Reveille and Retreat

Reveille, or morning colors, is the name of the bugle call that accompanies the daily ritual of raising the American flag, signaling the start of the day. Retreat, or evening colors, is the lowering and folding of the flag into a star-topped triangle, signaling the end of the day. It is accompanied by the bugle call "To the Colors." Both are played over the amplifier system that has replaced the lone bugler of old.

If you're outdoors on a military base during retreat, stand quietly facing the direction of the music, hold your right hand over your heart (military members hold a salute), and wait for the call to be finished. If you're driving, get out and stand the same way. If you're on a ship, stand facing the flag.

The Salute

A salute is a form of greeting between servicemembers. Enlisted personnel salute warrant and commissioned officers. Officers salute senior officers. All servicemembers salute a person wearing a Medal of Honor. The salute may be a greeting such as, "Good day, Sir" or it may include the unit motto, "Always Forward, Sir!" The officer then returns the salute and greeting. Saluting is not done indoors unless a servicemember is reporting to a superior.

Scholars differ on its origins; some say that during the Middle Ages, when two knights met, they raised their visors to expose their faces, thus making them recognizable as ally or enemy. This raising was performed with the right hand. Others say that when men wore heavy capes to conceal their swords, two men greeting each other would raise their right arm to show it was not on the sword hilt. Neglecting to raise the arm could signal an attack.

A cannon salute is given to visiting flag officers (admirals and generals) and dignitaries, on special occasions such as Memorial and Independence Days, and at military funerals. The number of times it is fired varies with the occasion. If you are outdoors on a military installation during this ceremony, stop what you are doing and face in the direction of the national flag. Stay this way until last gun is fired.

Proper Dress for Spouses

While it's common these days to hear, "People should be happy to see me no matter what I'm wearing," part of good manners is dressing appropriately out of respect for the event and people it honors. Here are some guidelines.

Event	Dress
Coffees/FRG	Casual
Teas	Informal or Casual
Hail and Farewell	Informal or Casual
Reception	Informal
Banquet	Formal
Cocktail party	Informal
BBQ, other outdoor affair	Casual or very casual
Open House (before 6 P.M.)	Informal
Parade, Change of Command	Informal
Graduation, Promotion Party	Informal

Type of Occasion	Women	Men
Formal	Long gown, tea-length dress, cocktail dress; luxury coat	Dinner jacket or tuxedo; mess uniform; black tie
Semiformal (If an event is designated as semiformal, follow the guidelines for informal dress.)		

(continued)

Type of Occasion	Women	Men
Informal	Something you'd wear to a nice restaurant or afternoon wedding. Ramp up the dressiness if after 6:00 P.M.	Business suit and necktie after 6:00 P.M, sport jacket and dress trousers before 6:00 P.M.
Casual	Slacks, shirt that covers shoulders. No sweat pants, halter or tube tops.	Sweater, sport coat (no tie), sport shirt, slacks (no jeans). Street shoes, no running shoes.
Very Casual	Picnic-type clothes	Shorts, jeans

If unsure, call the hostess and ask what you should wear. Protocol is flexible; what's appropriate for D.C. may not be so for the Deep South. And, if you can't find the perfect outfit, put on something less than perfect and go anyway. Your hosts are less concerned with what you wear than with your showing up.

How to Address Military Personnel

Army, Air Force, Marine Corps

Title	In Person	In Writing
General	General	Gen.
Lieutenant General	General	Lt. Gen.
Major General	General	Maj. Gen.
Brigadier General	General	Brig. Gen.
Colonel	Colonel	Col.
Lieutenant Colonel	Colonel	Lt. Col.
Major	Major	Maj.
Captain	Captain	Capt.
First Lieutenant	Lieutenant	1 Lt.
Second Lieutenant	Lieutenant	2 Lt.
Chief Warrant Officer	Chief, Mr., or Ms.	CWO
Warrant Officer	Mr. or Ms.	WO
Cadet	Cadet	Mr. or Ms.
Chaplain	Chaplain	Rank (Ch.)
Doctor	Doctor	Rank (Dr.)
Sergeant Major	Sergeant Major	Sgt. Maj.

Army, Air Force, Marine Corps (*continued*)

Title	In Person	In Writing
Chief Master Sergeant	Chief	Chief MSgt.
First Sergeant	First Sergeant	1 Sgt.
Master Sergeant	Master Sergeant	MSgt.
Gunnery Sergeant	Gunnery Sergeant	GySgt.
Sergeant First Class	Sergeant	Sfc.
Staff Sergeant	Sergeant	SSgt.
Technical Sergeant	Sergeant	TSgt.
Sergeant	Sergeant	Sgt.
Specialist	Specialist	Spec.
Corporal	Corporal	Cpl.
Private First Class	Private	Pfc.
Private	Private	Pvt.
Airman First Class	Airman	A1C
Airman	Airman	Airman

Note: Officers are addressed by their titles and last names. Doctors and chaplains are "doctor" and "chaplain" unless a lieutenant colonel or above; then refer to them by military rank.

Navy and Coast Guard

Title	In Person	In Writing
Fleet Admiral (Navy only)	Admiral	Fleet Adm.
Admiral	Admiral	Adm.
Vice Admiral	Admiral	Vice Adm.
Rear Admiral	Admiral	Rear Adm.
Commodore	Commodore	Como.
Captain	Captain	Capt.
Commander	Commander	Cmdr.
Lieutenant Commander	Mr. or Ms.	LtCmdr.
Lieutenant	Mr. or Ms.	Lt.
Lieutenant Junior Grade	Mr. or Ms.	LtJG

Navy and Coast Guard (*continued*)

Title	In Person	In Writing
Ensign	Mr. or Ms.	Ens.
Chief Warrant Officer	Mr. or Ms.	CWO
Warrant Officer	Mr. or Ms.	WO
Doctor	Doctor	Rank (Dr.)
Chaplain	Chaplain	Rank (Ch.)
Cadet	Cadet	Mr. or Ms.
Midshipman	Mr. or Ms.	Mr. or Ms.
Master Chief Petty Officer	Master Chief	MCPO
Senior Chief Petty Officer	Senior Chief	SCPO
Chief Petty Officer	Chief	CPO
Petty Officer First Class	Petty Officer	PO-1
Petty Officer Second Class	Petty Officer	PO-2
Petty Officer Third Class	Petty Officer	PO-3
General Apprentice	Seaman	
Recruit	Seaman	

Note: Officers and petty officers are addressed by their titles and last names. Doctors and chaplains are addressed as "doctor" and "chaplain" unless a captain or above; then refer to them by military rank. A general apprentice is addressed as "seaman," "fireman," "airman," "stewardsman," and so on, as appropriate.

Addressing Invitations

When addressing an envelope and invitation, write the guests' names, titles, and ranks in full on the invitation (abbreviated exceptions are Mr., Mrs., Dr., and a middle initial). On the envelope, address the guests by rank first, and then last name.

- Captain Lamar Boyd and Gail Russell (different last names)
- Sergeant-Major (RET) Robert Lynn (RET is the abbreviation for Retired)
- Captain Maria Molina and Mike Molina (civilian husband)

Write dates and hours in full. Only capitalize the day and month. The year isn't necessary.

- "Saturday, the twenty-fourth of May, six-o-clock"
- "Monday, the twenty-fifth of February, seven-thirty"

Close the invitation with, "Sincerely yours."

MAJ & Mrs. Terrence Thomas
Request the honor of
the company of
Captain and Mrs. Valdez

---

at a Christmas reception
Saturday, the fifth of December
At six-thirty P.M.

The Base Officer's Club

Please R.S.V.P. no later than Oct. 9.
Dress: business casual

A hand-written invitation to a unit function.

Sergeant and Mrs. Jay Jones
request the pleasure of
First Sergeant Leon Wilke's
company at dinner

Friday the twentieth of May
at six o'clock

1820 Pheasant Trail
Apt. 112

RSVP 555-1212

A hand-written invitation to a personal event.

General Etiquette Tips

- Don't call an older woman by her first name until she invites you to do so. Likewise, when speaking directly to her husband, use his title until invited otherwise, no matter how informal the occasion.
- Don't discuss your medical problems with doctors, your legal problems with lawyers, or your quarters problems with the head of the housing office at

social affairs. Discuss these things in the proper places and during office hours.

- Don't refer to yourself and your husband collectively as "we're sergeants" or "we're lieutenants" unless you both really are sergeants or lieutenants. Don't refer to your husband by rank.
- Bring a hostess gift when you attend a party or dinner at someone's house. Appropriate gifts are fresh-cut flowers, flavored coffee, a box of chocolates, or a tin of homemade goods. Include a label identifying who it's from.
- Don't discuss controversial or sensitive subjects at socials. Gossiping and giving out too much personal information is not prudent, either.
- Stand when a senior official walks into a room at an awards or promotion ceremony and is announced; when the "attention to orders" announcement is made; and when dining out, during a toast. When toasting, take your cues from the toastmaster. Stand if he or she stands; sit when told. Ladies join in on all toasts that are not to the ladies. Don't drink a toast to yourself. The printed program may list all toasts offered that evening and responses expected of the guests. Also, don't feel obliged to drink alcohol; lifting the glass to your lips is sufficient.
- When arriving at your seat during a formal dinner, don't immediately sit down. Look to the head table for cues. A man should assist the woman to his right with her chair. Don't talk or leave your seat during a speech, and remain quiet through the Retiring of the Colors.
- At any affair, make a point of introducing yourself to the senior people there. It's a nice courtesy, protocol at its finest. So often luncheons and welcome coffees are great successes in terms of attendees, food, and gaiety, but failures in that most guests never meet the people the event was intended for. Introduce yourself to the senior woman and her husband, if he is there. Both will be pleased. Before you leave any social affair, seek out the host or hosts.
- Stand when someone older or more senior comes over to talk to you.
- Don't discuss anyone's military evaluations.

Introductions
You're going to be introducing people to each other for the rest of your life. Etiquette experts have laid out this protocol for doing so:

- A man is presented to a woman (but junior female servicemembers are presented to senior male servicemembers, as rank precedes gender).
- The honored or higher-ranking person's name is stated first, then the name of the person being presented.
- Young people are presented to older people of the same sex.
- A single person is introduced to a group.

- A man rises if seated. A woman doesn't, unless she's being presented to an older woman or the wife of a senior official. She should remain standing until the other is seated. She doesn't rise if being presented to another woman about her own age.
- A woman should extend her hand to a man.

Here are some examples of introductory conversation:

- "Major Hughes, this is my sister Sue."
- "Mrs. Awana, may I present Tae-Won."
- "Everyone . . . I'd like you to meet Jennifer Long. Why don't you all go around and introduce yourselves?"
- "First Sergeant, this is Specialist Langley. Specialist Johnson, First Sergeant Davis."

If you feel uneasy about military etiquette, read some of the books listed at the end of this chapter. Also, study the people around you. Whose mannerisms do you admire? Who seems especially poised? Eventually your own style will develop as your familiarity with social affairs grows. And if all this seems overkill, know that as your husband goes up the ladder, newcomers will look to *you* for cues and guidance.

Calling Cards

Calling cards were introduced into this country after the Civil War and were used for the numerous official and social calls that officers made. Traditionally, an officer would leave his card on his first social call. If the people on whom he was calling weren't home, he would leave his card with the servants and receive "credit" for the call. Although the servants are long gone, you may see a silver tray at the entrance for leaving a card at certain officers' receptions that take place in the home of a higher-ranking officer. Note that today's "calling card" refers to a person's business card. It's called a calling card when used for social visits. While cards are mostly used by officers and high-ranking NCOs, these days they are also popular with stay-at-home moms as a convenient means to exchange contact information. They're also useful for gift enclosures. You can order cards through the exchange.

Invitations

When an invitation includes RSVP (French for "Respondez, s'il vous plait"), it means "please respond." The hostess needs to know how much food to buy and how many chairs to borrow. No one is so busy she can't find three minutes to do this. "Regrets only" assumes you will attend unless you notify otherwise. RSVP via a phone call, text message, or e-mail. Don't do it in person because it's too easy for the hostess to forget your response. When people are at social affairs or just out and about, they have other things on their mind.

Sometimes spur-of-the-moment parties have phone invitations. If your invitation arrives this way, don't engage the person in a long conversation. Likewise, some formal events don't have an RSVP phone number because a written response is required. Finally, if you RSVP to an event held at a place where advance payment is needed, please honor your obligation even if you later can't attend. The organizers obligate themselves for a certain number of people and must pay for no-shows.

If only one of you is able to attend an event, the type of event must be considered before you RSVP. Social events in the home can be declined if you or your husband is unavailable, with the notable exception of the commander's New Year Reception. The servicemember is expected to attend the New Year Reception even if the spouse can't. Otherwise, the spouse may attend most functions if the servicemember is unavailable.

Thank-you Notes

Send a written thank-you note addressed to the hostess after attending an affair in her home. This is in addition to the thanks you give as you leave. The note can be written on a preprinted thank-you card or personal stationery. You should also send written thank-you notes to anyone who gives you baby shower or birthday presents, invites you to dinner, or does something special for you.

ABOARD SHIP

The Navy offers a lifestyle unique in many ways from that of its sister services. One of the things that sets it apart is the custom of having some social affairs aboard ship. Although the same rules of dress—casual, informal, and formal—that apply to socials ashore apply here, know that you'll be climbing steep ladders, walking drafty passageways, and stooping to get through short hatches to get to your final destination. So don't wear short dresses or high heels. Slacks are best, with low-heeled or rubber-soled shoes. Don't wear flimsy shoes, since in summertime the metal decks get very hot. Carry a handbag with a shoulder strap, and keep sunblock, sunglasses, and perhaps some seasickness medicine in it.

If the ship is moored, you'll enter it by walking down the pier and along the gangway, in front of your husband. But if it's anchored in the harbor, you'll ride a motorboat to it. Motorboats leave on a regular schedule from the fleet landing. The stern seat, considered the "seat of honor," should be left for the senior woman. When you step onto the quarterdeck, introduce yourself to the officer of

Q: Why are Navy promotion parties called "wetting downs"?

A: Wetting downs got their name from the tradition of pouring salt water over the new stripe to make it match the old, tarnished ones. Today a whole new set is sewn on, however, as tarnished stripes are considered shabby.

the deck. If your husband has not accompanied you aboard and is unable to meet you, an escort to the wardroom (dining area) will be provided.

You'll probably visit your husband aboard ship sometime when he has duty or when spouses are invited to dinner. Every rule regarding manners and propriety that applies to shore applies here, plus a few more. Don't come aboard ship without an invitation, and when you do come, leave pets at home. When you are aboard, remember that you are in the single sailors' home and act accordingly. Don't wander about unescorted; many areas are restricted. Do not take photos unless given permission. Remove your hat if you're wearing one, and don't smoke unless you specifically ask and are granted permission. Alcohol is not served aboard ship, being against Navy regulations.

The quarterdeck is the area of the ship where official and ceremonial functions are held while the ship is in port. It is considered the ship's "seat of authority." The OOD (Officer of the Deck) is located on the quarterdeck, and he or she represents the captain. The commanding officer of a ship is always referred to as "Captain" regardless of their rank. If you're invited to the bridge, don't touch anything or sit in the commanding officer's chair. Don't remain on board after taps, and don't miss the last boat back to shore.

MILITARY WEDDINGS

There isn't much difference between a military and a civilian wedding, as the military wedding, like most civilian weddings, is held in a chapel, and the ceremony is

A wedding held in a military chapel.

performed by clergy. But a military wedding has some additional service traditions. The following are general; direct specific questions to your chaplain or base protocol office.

Prerequisites

As with a civilian wedding, a military one requires a civil marriage license and could require a blood test and religious counseling or classes. As a courtesy, most base hospitals will give you the blood test at no charge. And the Exchange sells diamond engagement and wedding rings.

An engagement tradition for a midshipman or cadet is to give his fianceé a miniature of his class ring as an engagement ring. ROTC personnel may give miniatures of their fraternity rings to their fiancées. During the wedding ceremony, a simple band is exchanged to complete the set.

Know that the chances of success in marriage are statistically higher among couples who participate in marriage preparation and enrichment programs. Studies show that couples who enroll decrease their chances of divorce and increase their chances of happiness. These programs help couples examine their strengths and weaknesses in critical areas of married life, such as finances, relatives, religion, sexuality, and desire for children. Ask your chaplain or Family Services Center about registering for such classes.

Attire

The uniforms that the military groomsmen and saber-bearers wear depend on how formal your wedding is. At an informal ceremony, where the bride wears a short dress or simple gown, the servicemembers wear service or dress uniforms with long (four-in-hand) ties. At a formal wedding, where the bride wears a long gown with a veil and train, dress or mess uniforms with bow ties are worn. The best man and ushers wear the same uniform as the groom. Civilian wedding party members wear business suits or tuxedos, whichever are more appropriate. A ceremonial belt may be worn with the uniform, but a boutonniere is never worn with it. Military guests make their own choice whether to attend in uniform.

Location

If your wedding is held in a military chapel, contact the chaplain's office. Most chaplains schedule weddings on a first-come, first-served basis. Some chapels, such as the historic Fort Myer, Virginia, chapel, are in such demand that you may need to make reservations a year in advance. Service academy chapels have their own scheduling system to accommodate the many weddings they have after graduation. A military wedding may be held at a civilian church as well, but the people there must be instructed in military protocol.

There is usually no fee for a military chaplain to perform the service, but all service providers (e.g., organist, photographer, caterer) will charge a fee. Consult with the chaplain for rules that the photographer and other service providers must follow. Some do not allow petal or rice throwing (guests can blow bubbles instead), aisle runners, candelabras, or lit candles.

Invitations

Invitations may include the parents' military rank. If the parent is retired, "(Ret.)" follows the name. As a courtesy, you should send invitations to the servicemember's commander and spouse and all the people in the unit and their spouses. This is true even if you're not getting married where your fiancée is assigned. Military tradition calls for the chaplain and spouse to be formally invited to the reception. The servicemember's commanding officer and spouse should also be invited and, if they attend, seated in the front pew.

Saber Arch

This ceremony is authorized for commissioned, noncommissioned, and warrant officers only. It is an old English and American custom that displays a symbolic pledge of loyalty to the newly married couple from their military family. An honor guard of servicemembers will make an arch of drawn sabers after the ceremony, under which you and the groom will walk. Rifles may be substituted for sabers. The honor guard must wear white gloves. The arch takes place outside of the church, or in its foyer in case of rain. Borrow sabers from the base chapel, an ROTC detachment, a military preparatory school, or a service academy. If saber-bearers are needed, cadets are often willing to assist. It is important that you consult with the chaplain about a saber arch first, though, as some do not permit weaponry, even ceremonial, on church or synagogue grounds and will request the arch be performed at the reception.

Only the newly married couple should pass under the arch. Your passing is culminated with a "sword swat," where one of the saber-bearers will whack your rear end with the flat side of a saber and say, "Welcome to the U.S. Army/Navy/Air Force/Marines!"

Cake Cutting

At a military wedding reception, it is customary to use an officer or NCO's sword to cut the wedding cake. (This is also customary during birthday celebrations.) The groom then hands the bride his unsheathed saber and with his hands over hers, their first piece is cut.

A more formal tradition is to have the saber-bearers enter the reception room on command, and line up in front of the wedding cake, facing each other. The bride and groom leave the receiving line, then pass beneath the arch. They may pause and kiss, then proceed to cut the cake. As an aside, a really special cake topper is one that shows the groom in uniform. You can buy this in the exchange catalog.

MILITARY FUNERAL

Military funerals resemble civilian funerals with some additional traditions conducted regardless of the deceased's rank. These traditions may vary slightly from base to base, but generally, the ceremony will start with a flag-draped casket loaded onto a hearse. (Caissons, which are horse-drawn carts, are used at Arlington National Cemetery.) The hearse is driven to the burial site where six military pallbearers will remove the casket from the hearse and carry it to the grave site. The flag is held waist-high over the casket by the pallbearers. The Committal service is read by the chaplain, followed by three-volleys from an honor guard's rifle. These are volleys, not a salute, and derive from an old battlefield custom where the warring sides would stop to clear their dead from the battlefield. The firing of three volleys meant that the dead had been properly cared for and that side was ready to resume fighting. A bugler will play "Taps," and the flag is then carefully folded and presented to the next of kin. Sometimes three shell casings will be placed into the folded flag before it is presented, each casing representing one volley.

As you can see, military life has many traditions, and you will have many opportunities to participate in them. They are a large part of what makes this lifestyle so unique.

FURTHER READING

Books

Baldrige, Letitia. *New Complete Guide to Executive Manners*. New York: Macmillan, 1993.

Swartz, Oretha. *Service Etiquette*. Annapolis, MD: Naval Institute Press, 1988.

Social Customs and Traditions of the Sea Services. FamilyLine Guideline Series. E-mail nsfamline@aol.com.

Internet Resources

www.wilderdom.com/games/Icebreakers.html. Ideas for icebreakers at a coffee or FRG.

www.armyfrg.org. Army Family Readiness Group online. Find Command information for your unit.

navywivesclubsofamerica.org. National club for wives of enlisted Navy personnel.

www.lifelines.navy.mil/FamilyLine/GetOurPublications/index.htm. Download pamphlets about launching clubs and FRGs, about social customs and traditions, and other subjects.

www.armyfrg.org. Army virtual FRG site.

www.bartleby.com/95/11.html. Find examples of written invitations here.

4

Your Education and Career

Many military wives work or attend college. A move may disrupt your career and educational goals, but it doesn't have to completely derail them. Programs and strategies have been specifically designed to counter disruptions. Some are available to all branches; some are service-specific. We'll discuss them here. Education assistance specifically for widows of active duty servicemembers is discussed in chapter 12.

EDUCATION

Servicemembers Opportunity Colleges
The network of SOCAD, SOC, SOCNAV, SOCMAR, and SOCCOAST schools discussed in chapter 1 are available to you as well as to servicemembers. They have flexible learning programs and liberal acceptance of each other's credits. The SOC program will make your transition from one city to another as seamless as possible.

Army
Army Emergency Relief's Spouse Education Assistance Program. If you are assigned in Europe, Korea, Japan, or Okinawa, you can apply for an education grant from AER, up to a maximum of $350 per term.

GI Bill Transferability. The Army allows servicemembers in certain military occupational specialties (MOS) to transfer up to eighteen months of their GI Bill benefits to their spouses and children. The following conditions must be met:
- Children are eligible between the ages of eighteen and twenty-six (or ten years from the soldier's date of discharge, whichever comes first) and must have a secondary school diploma or equivalent.
- The soldier must have elected the GI Bill upon enlistment.
- The soldier must have at least six years of active duty upon reenlistment (ten years for transfer to children).

- The soldier must reenlist for at least four years.
- The soldier must be serving an MOS specific SRB zone B or C.

Once the paperwork is completed, the Department of Veterans Affairs will administer the benefit payments. Family members have ten years from the soldier's date of discharge to utilize these benefits. Visit *www.gibill.va.gov/documents/Army_Transferability_to_Dependents.pdf* for details.

Overseas Spouse Education Assistance Program (OSEAP). This program is available to spouses of active-duty soldiers who reside with their sponsor in their assigned overseas command. It is only offered for the first undergraduate degree and not for any graduate-level degrees. If you wish to use it to take online classes at schools in the United States, they must be approved schools listed in the DANTES catalogs. Visit *www.aerhq.org/* for details.

Stateside Spouse Education Assistance Program (SSEAP). This is a need-based education assistance program designed to provide spouses of active-duty and retired soldiers, and widow(er)s of soldiers who died either on active duty or in a retired status, and residing in the United States, with financial assistance to pursue educational goals. Its intent is to assist spouses and widow(er)s to acquire the education needed to increase their job opportunities. Visit *www.aerhq.org/Education_Spouse_Stateside_ProgramDescription.asp* for details.

MG James Ursano Scholarship. This scholarship is for dependent children of soldiers on federal active duty, retired, or deceased while in active or retired status. For more information, visit *www.aerhq.org/education_dependentchildren_mgjames.asp*.

Air Force

Air Force Aid Society's Spouse Tuition Assistance Program (STAP). This program is for spouses of active-duty airmen and officers stationed overseas who are attending high school or college. STAP provides 50 percent of course tuition with a maximum of $1,500 per academic year. Visit *www.afas.org/index.cfm* for details.

General Henry H. Arnold Education Grant Program. This program provides $1,500 grants to selected sons and daughters of active-duty servicemembers. Visit *www.afas.org/Education/body_instructions.cfm* for details.

Navy and Marine Corps

The Navy Marine Corps Relief Society's Spouse Tuition Aid Program (STAP). This program is for spouses of active-duty personnel stationed overseas. You may be a full- or part-time student, working on a vocational certificate, undergraduate, or graduate degree. A maximum of $300 per semester and $1,500 per year is available for undergraduate studies, and $350 per semester and $1,750 per year for graduate studies. Visit *www.nmcrs.org/stap.html* for details.

VADM E. P. Travers Scholarship and Loan Program. This program is for spouses and dependent children of active-duty personnel or dependent children of a retired member of the Navy or Marine Corps. You must also be a full-time undergraduate student at an accredited college or university. Grants of $2,000 and interest-free student loans of up to $3,000 are available. Visit *www.nmcrs.org/travers.html* for details.

Coast Guard

Coast Guard Mutual Assistance (CGMA). This program offers a supplemental education grant of up to $150 per year that can be used for any family member's education expenses. This assistance is not for tuition; it is for supplemental items such as the College Level Examination Program (CLEP), the Scholastic Aptitude Test (SAT), and study programs. CGMA also offers education-related loans.

Dependents Educational Assistance Program

The Department of Veterans Affairs has a program for spouses and children of specific hero and veteran groups. If your sponsor:

- suffered an injury that resulted in complete service-related disability;
- was interned, captured, or detained in the line of duty by a hostile force or foreign government;
- was killed or is permanently Missing in Action; or
- is still on active duty but has been injured and is disabled and headed toward permanent and total separation from the Armed Forces on grounds of physical disability,

. . . then you and your children may be eligible for up to forty-five months of educational funding to work on qualified educational goals, including going back to school or college for a degree, attending college part time, or taking certain vocational classes.

Spouses to Teachers

This is a Department of Defense project that helps spouses of active duty and reservists become public school teachers. It's not available in every state yet. Visit *www.spousestoteachers.com/* for details.

Accredited Financial Counselor Fellowship Program

The FINRA (Financial Industry Regulatory Authority) Investor Education Foundation funds a program for military spouses that provides a limited number of fellowships (money for working in a specific field) in a distance-learning financial counselor program. Successful completion of the program and practicum will enable you to become an accredited financial counselor. The fellowship covers the costs associated with completing the training and testing. As part of the program, you are required to offer financial counseling and financial education to the military community. For details visit *www.nmfa.org*.

Miscellaneous Financial Aid

National Military Family Association Scholarship. The NMFA's Joanne Holbrook Patton Military Spouse Scholarship is for spouses of active-duty personnel, reservists, retirees, and survivors. Its purpose is to obtain professional certification or to attend post-secondary or graduate school. Scholarships are typically $1,000 each and may be used for tuition, fees, books, and school room and board. Visit *www.nmfa.org* for details.

Scholarships for Military Children Program. These scholarships are available to unmarried children under the age of twenty-one (twenty-three if enrolled in school) of military active-duty, reservist, and retired personnel. Applicants must be planning to attend an accredited college or university full time or be enrolled in a program designed to transfer directly into a four-year program. At least one $1,500 scholarship is awarded at every commissary location with qualified applicants. Scholarship applications are available at commissaries or can be downloaded from *www.commissaries.com* or *www.militaryscholar.org*.

Local spouses' club and Thrift Shop. Many offer annual scholarships to spouses and children.

Pell Grants. These are need-based federal grants typically awarded to undergraduate students who haven't earned a bachelor's or graduate degree or who are enrolled in a post-baccalaureate teacher certification program. The Free Application for Federal Student Aid (FAFSA) form is used to determine your eligibility. To learn more about Pell and other federal grants, visit *studentaid.ed.gov/PORTALSWebApp/students/english/index.jsp*.

In-State Tuition

Most states have laws that give in-state (resident status) tuition to servicemembers and their families. The following table outlines this information.

	Tuition charge for nonresident active-duty military personnel stationed in the state.			Military family members charged the same rate as military?		
State	In-State	Out of State	Determined by Individual Institution	Yes	No	Varies
Alabama			X	X		
Alaska	X			X		
Arizona	X			X		
Arkansas	X			X		
California	X					X

(continued)

| State | Tuition charge for nonresident active-duty military personnel stationed in the state. | | | Military family members charged the same rate as military? | | |
	In-State	Out of State	Determined by Individual Institution	Yes	No	Varies
Colorado	X			X		
Connecticut			X		X	
Delaware	X			X		
District of Columbia	X			X		
Florida	X			X		
Georgia	X			X		
Hawaii	X			X		
Idaho		X			X	
Illinois	X			X		
Indiana	X			X		
Iowa	X			X		
Kansas	X			X		
Kentucky	X			X		
Louisiana	X			X		
Maine	X			X		
Maryland	X			X		
Massachusetts	X			X		
Michigan		X			X	
Minnesota	X			X		
Mississippi	X			X		
Missouri	X			X		
Montana	X			X		
Nebraska	X			X		
Nevada	X			X		
New Hampshire	X		X			
New Jersey	X			X		
New Mexico	X			X		
New York	X			X		
North Carolina	X			X		
North Dakota	X			X		
Ohio	X			X		
Oklahoma	X			X		
Oregon	X			X		
Pennsylvania	X			X		
Puerto Rico	X			X		
Rhode Island	X			X		
South Carolina		X	X			
South Dakota		X			X	
Tennessee	X			X		
Texas	X			X		
Utah	X			X		
Vermont		X		X		
Virginia	X			X		
Washington	X			X		
West Virginia	X			X		
Wisconsin	X			X		
Wyoming	X			X		

UNEMPLOYMENT BENEFITS

Twenty-one states allow military spouses to receive unemployment benefits when they quit their jobs to follow their sponsors to new duty stations. These monetary payments extend for a specific period of time or until the worker finds a new job. Eight states deny such benefits outright; the rest consider them on a case-by-case basis. If you are eligible, benefits can help ease the stress of relocation and job hunting. Contact your state unemployment office for details.

EMPLOYMENT

Many wives believe that employment is impossible to find because employers don't want to hire military spouses. DoD surveys on spousal employment show that over half the people married to active-duty servicemembers work. Obviously, someone is hiring them. There isn't much difference between the average

When searching for a school, avoid diploma mills. A diploma mill is an institution of higher education that operates without supervision of a state or professional agency. It grants diplomas that are either fraudulent or worthless because of this lack of supervision and standards. Tip offs to a diploma mill include:

- not licensed to operate in any states
- not authorized for tuition assistance, the GI Bill, or federal financial aid
- not accredited by any legitimate education agencies or the U.S. Department of Education.

three-year tour of duty and the average three and a half years spent by people in the same civilian workplace. When there are jobs to be had, qualified people who know how to market themselves get them. Furthermore, the DoD has programs to help military wives maintain continuity in a career, or to just find a job. Here we'll discuss strategies for finding a job stateside. Overseas employment is discussed in chapter 8.

One-Stop Career Center

This Department of Labor–sponsored website offers career resources and workforce information to job seekers, students, businesses, and workforce professionals. Here you'll find counselors who can offer insights about the local job market. They're also in touch with the base Civilian Personnel Office and the exchange. At *www.servicelocator.org* you can enter your zip code to find the closest One-Stop center; there are over 3,000 located across the country. The ones near military installations partner with the base Education Center and Family Support Centers. They offer various services to the job hunter: seminars, informational pamphlets, and help in filling out applications. Many have workshops on interviewing and resume writing, as well as tips on finding a private-sector job. Make an appointment with a counselor there to review your application materials. Sometimes people who were initially passed over for a job might receive advice on how to make an application more accurately reflect their qualifications and be more successful the next time.

There is also the Transition Assistance Program (see chapter 11), which conducts workshops on the job search process and is available to spouses, reservists, and civilians who are subject to a reduction in force.

The Career Advancement Initiative

The Departments of Defense and Labor formed this program to help military spouses develop portable careers. Career Advancement Accounts (CAA) is a demonstration project that helps military spouses gain the skills and credentials necessary to begin or advance their careers. CAAs offer grants of up to $3,000 (renewable once) for training and education, enabling participants to earn a degree or credential in portable, in-demand fields in almost any community across the country. You are eligible for a Career Advancement Account if you:

- have a high school diploma or GED
- are not currently receiving training assistance funded by the U.S. Department of Labor
- are married to an active-duty servicemember/sponsor who:
  — is an E-1 through E-5, or O-1 through O-3;
  — is assigned to one of the installations participating in the pilot site or is deployed or on an unaccompanied military tour from the participating installation; and,
  — has a minimum of one year remaining at the current installation duty assignment (unless affected by a BRAC closure).

Career Advancement Accounts can be used to receive training or education in one of these fields:

- Health Care (e.g., nurse, radiologic technician, dental hygienist, pharmacy technician)
- Education (e.g., teacher, child-care worker, teacher's assistant)
- Financial Services (e.g., claims adjuster, real estate sales agent, credit analyst, bookkeeping clerk, bank teller)
- Information Technology (e.g., computer support specialist, network analyst, database administrator)
- Skilled Trades (e.g., carpenter, electrician, plumber)

Currently, the participating bases in this program are: Camp Pendleton Marine Corps Base, California; Eglin Air Force Base, Florida; Fort Benning Army Installation, Georgia; Fort Bragg Army Installation, North Carolina; Fort Carson Army Installation, Colorado; Fort Lewis Army Installation, Washington; Hickham Air Force Base, Hawaii; Hurlburt Field Air Force Base, Florida; Marine Corps Base Kaneohe Bay, Hawaii; McChord Air Force Base, Washington; Naval Air Station Brunswick, Maine; Naval Air Station Jacksonville, Florida; Naval Station Kitsap,

Washington; Naval Station Pearl Harbor, Hawaii; Peterson Air Force Base, Colorado; Pope Air Force Base, North Carolina; San Diego Naval Station, California; and Schofield Barracks Army Installation, Hawaii. Visit *caa.milspouse.org/* or your base Education Center for more information.

Department of Labor (DoL) Business Partners

The DoL promotes the hiring of military spouses and transitioning servicemembers with national business partners. The Army Spouse Employment Partnership does the same thing. Their combined business partners include AT&T, Allstate, Aramark Corporation, Bank of America, Citigroup, CVS Pharmacy, First Data Corp., Good Samaritan Society, IICA, Home Depot, IBM, Intercontinental Hotels, Kelly, Manpower, PETCO, Saks Inc., Shell Oil, Starbucks, Toys "R" Us, and Verizon. Visit the Military Spouse Resource Center at *www.milspouse.org* and *www.myarmylifetoo.com* for more information.

Spouse Telework Employment Program (STEP)

STEP is a partnership among six federal agencies (the Departments of State; Defense; Labor; Homeland Security; the Coast Guard; the National Guard Bureau; and the General Services Administration) to improve military spouses' access to remote training and private sector telework opportunities. The STEP partners are currently developing a pilot program called "Jobs Without Borders" that will connect approximately fifty military and Foreign Service spouses with private-sector telework opportunities. When completely up and running, its goal is to provide opportunities for career continuity and development no matter where spouses are located. Additionally, the DoL is exploring opportunities for expanding military spouse participation in existing employment and training programs, such as apprenticeship and the Workforce Investment Act (WIA) Dislocated Worker program.

Develop a Portable Career

All job hunters must work to make themselves marketable, and job hunters who move a lot must work even harder. Some people feel that just because they have a college degree they are entitled to or guaranteed a college-level job and a certain pay. The reality is that a college degree by itself guarantees nothing, and it's easier to find work in some degree fields than in others. Being bilingual is required in a lot of places within the United States. If you are currently unemployed, spend some time learning Spanish or perhaps even Mandarin Chinese. If it isn't useful at this duty station, it might be at the next.

Having a degree or certification in a portable career field will help continuity. The following are fields that the Departments of Labor and Defense have identified as high-growth industries. It's not a comprehensive list, but it's a start if you are contemplating what type of career you would like to have and what might work well for your lifestyle.

Financial Services
- Bookkeeping, Accounting, and Auditing Clerks
- Credit Analyst
- Payroll and Time-Keeping Clerks
- Claims Adjusters, Examiners, and Investigators
- Real Estate Sales Agent
- Bank Teller
- Tax Preparer

Health Care
- Practical/Vocational Nurse
- Surgical Technologist
- Dental Hygienist
- Radiologic Technician
- Emergency Medical Technician (EMT)
- Medical Records and Health Information Technicians
- Pharmacy Technician

Information Technology
- Network and Data Communications Analysts
- Database Administrator
- Computer Support Specialist

Additionally, tradespeople (e.g., carpenters, plumbers, electricians) are frequently in demand, as are hairdressers, aestheticians, nail technicians, and massage therapists.

Show your flexibility. When interviewing, play your transience to your advantage. Show that you can apply old skills to new jobs, build on your storehouse of knowledge with each job, and bring this knowledge successfully to the next. Your experience and adaptability will work in your favor. Make a case for how your transfers have given you a more worldly perspective.

Child-Care Provider

Many spouses become licensed in-home child-care providers. There is always a demand for this service. It provides the additional benefits of allowing you to:
- work at home.
- transfer your certification to your spouse's next duty station.
- receive military-provided insurance and food subsidies.
- set your own hours with a minimum of ten per week.
- receive referrals from Child Development Services, free training, and child-care resources.

A background check is required, which can take up to three months to complete.

Commute

Many duty stations are in small communities. Since there isn't much commerce in small towns, job opportunities are limited. But many of these small communities are a short drive from large communities where lots of opportunities exist. If you want to work and can't find anything outside Gate 1, you may have to commute. If your car gets poor mileage, sell it for a more efficient one or carpool to split expenses. Put an ad in the paper for other commuters. Surely you're not the only one wants to work in the city.

Temporary Employment Agencies

Temporary agencies can be good resources. Larger ones even offer training and benefits. Some temporary jobs have turned into permanent ones for employees who have proven themselves. Temporary agencies place everyone from secretarial, clerical, and factory workers to highly skilled professionals. If you use an agency, try to use a fee-paid one, meaning the hiring company pays the fee. Or use an agency that only collects a fee after it finds you a job. Don't go with agencies that ask for payment up front whether they find you a job or not.

Adecco

Adecco is a temporary employment agency that has partnerships with the services. They have branches nationwide and have connected tens of thousands of military spouses with temporary and permanent jobs, full-time and part-time. Adecco is also part of the Army's Spouse Employment Partnership, which includes twenty-six national civilian companies as well as military and federal employers ranging from the Exchange to Starbucks. These employers have hired thousands of military spouses. Adecco has worked with more than 20,000 spouses through seminars, job fairs, and other outreach programs. Its Career Connections program offers career counseling, resume enhancement,

Some states give unemployment benefits to spouses who quit jobs due to PCS moves.

When Attending a Job Fair
- Learn which companies will be there and research them beforehand.
- Have high-quality copies of your resume available to hand out.
- Dress professionally and be well-groomed. It doesn't matter if the job won't require that level of attire.
- Don't bring family and friends. This isn't a social affair.
- Visit booths you're not interested in first, for interviewing practice.
- When approaching the booth, smile and extend your hand.
- Follow up your interview with a brief thank-you e-mail or note expressing your interest in the position.

interview training, and online skills training. Contact Adecco before you move, so they can have something lined up for you when you arrive.

The Federal Civil Service

"Civil service" refers to public sector (tax-funded) employment. The Federal Civil Service is funded by our central, sovereign government as opposed to state or local governments. A civil, or public, servant works for a government department or agency. The term "civil" derives from *civilian*, which explicitly excludes the military sector (although civilian employees work in it).

The Federal Civil Service is a family-friendly employer with good pay and benefits. Military spouses profit from priority placement (discussed later in this section) within the service, but you must learn its complex hiring system. There are many rules and regulations on how, where, when, and for what you can apply. Management can't pick the person they want as easily as they might in the private sector.

The reason it's so complicated is due to accountability. The taxpayer pays federal salaries, and the taxpayer wants a fair system of hiring. Without regulations, jobs might be given to friends and relatives, and promotions could be made on popularity, not merit. So the complex system of regulations exists to protect everyone. Bureaucracy is the result of this need for accountability. An overview on applying for civil service jobs, and the search process in general, is at *www.bls.gov/opub/ooq/2004/summer/art01.pdf*.

Types of Federal Jobs

There are many different government job appointments, but the ones relevant to most military spouses are the General Schedule (GS) and Nonappropriated Funds (NAF) jobs. Congress appropriates tax dollars to pay GS salaries, but NAF salaries are paid from the locally generated proceeds of Morale, Welfare, and Recreation (MWR) activities and the exchange. NAF jobs are not civil service positions; they're governed by Department of Defense policies.

GS jobs are assigned grade levels ranging from 1 to 18. Levels 1 through 4 are clerical; 5 through 8, clerical supervisor; 9 through 12, midlevel administrative; and 13 through 15, senior positions. Levels 16 through 18 are held by appointees. A federal employee's pay is determined by the level of the job, not by the person's qualifications. Though you may have qualified for a GS-7, if you occupy a GS-5 slot, you are paid a GS-5 salary. GS jobs run the occupational gamut from custodial worker to nuclear physicist.

NAF jobs are usually of an MWR nature, as almost all NAF money an installation receives is for quality-of-life projects. They are graded 1–15, with 1–10 being the most common. Typical NAF jobs held by military spouses are club manager, childcare worker, cashier, cook, bartender, and daycare worker. (Incidentally, base facilities such as the clubs, shoppettes, commissaries, and exchanges are huge employers of military spouses.) Office positions, such as clerical and accounting, that support these activities fall under the NAF universal annual category; workers receive the same pay rates as GS rates, and they're the same worldwide. Other NAF rates are based on local wage surveys. NAF facility managers have direct hiring ability. The chart below shows some NAF positions and grades.

NAF Job Title	Grade
Laundry Worker	1
Janitor (Light)	1
Service Station Attendant	1
Janitor	2
Food Service Worker	2
Laborer (Light)	2
Service Station Attendant	3
Waiter/Waitress	3
Stock Handler	4
Bartender	5
Fork Lift Operator	5
Warehouseman	5
Helper (Trades)	5
Service Station Attendant	5
Truck Driver (Light)	5
Truck Driver (Medium)	6
Sewing Machine Operator	6
Barber	7
Beautician	7
Bowling Equipment Mechanic	7
Small Appliance Repairer	7
Building Maintenance Worker	7
Truck Driver (Heavy)	7
Building Maintenance Worker	8
Cook	8
Truck Driver (Trailer)	8
Carpenter	9
Painter	9
Plumber	9
Auto Mechanic	10
Electrician	10

Familiarize yourself with the *Handbook of Occupational Groups and Series*, which describes in great detail all the education, experience, and combinations thereof needed for the job. You can find it at *www.opm.gov/fedclass/text/HdBkToC.htm*. These standards, which are written in Washington, are a fact of law and cannot be downgraded or waived.

To be considered for a job, your qualifications as described on your application materials must match the qualifications of the job you're applying for. You cannot successfully apply for any federal job that interests or intrigues you. After you're hired, the government will often pay for courses to improve your knowledge in the field. But if your background doesn't qualify you in the first place, the government will not train you. In fact, the Civilian Personnel Office (CPO) keeps a list of classes allowed for each job category, and once you're working and register for a class, the list is checked to ensure the course is appropriate for your field.

The Application Process

Start by visiting your base CPO or One-Stop Career Center. They'll have a list of current NAF and GS job vacancies. You can also visit federal agencies directly, or go to USAJobs at *www.usajobs.opm.gov*, the official government jobs website. At this site you can register, fill out a resume, and post it for federal recruiters to see. Know that many agencies with direct hiring authority post vacancies on their own websites, so frequently check ones you're interested in.

Application Forms

Most federal jobs require a resume, which is a document that enables an employer to evaluate the applicant's suitability for a specific job, and a Knowledge, Skills, and Ability (KSA) form, which is a questionnaire that supplements the resume. Different agencies may require additional forms. The exchange has its own form.

Creating a Resume. Use the online resume builder at the USAJobs. It allows you to create one uniform resume that provides all of the information required by government agencies. Alternatively, you may submit Optional Form OP-612. You may mail in or fax your application, as well as submit it online. Know that all resume builders are different, and each agency has a different one. Therefore, due to character lengths and resume field restrictions, you have to create multiple resumes. Prepare your resume in a Microsoft Word document on your own computer so you can check for grammar and spelling, and then import it into the online field. Be sure to submit it by the cutoff date for your application to be considered.

Filling out the KSA. The Knowledge, Skills, and Abilities form has questions that vary depending on the job for which you're applying. Respond with narrative statements in the first person. You must describe in detail how you fit the requirements of the job opening. It is rated on a point system from 1 to 10, with points given for experience, education, and veteran status. Points may be given for other preferential status, such as certain groups under the Equal Employment Opportunity laws or displaced career civil servants.

Optional Form OF-612.
This can be used in lieu of a resume when applying for a Federal Civil Service job.

General Information
Optional Application for Federal Employment – OF 612

You may apply for most Federal jobs with a résumé, an Optional Application for Federal Employment (OF 612), or other written format. If your résumé or application does not provide all the information requested on this form and in the job vacancy announcement, you may lose consideration for a job. Type or print clearly in black ink. Help speed the selection process by keeping your application brief and sending only the requested information. If essential to attach additional pages, include your name and job announcement number on each page.

- Information on Federal employment and the latest information about educational and training provisions are available at www.usajobs.gov or via interactive voice response system: (703) 724-1850 or TDD (978) 461-8404.

- Upon request from the employing Federal agency, you must provide documentation or proof that your degree(s) is from a school accredited by an accrediting body recognized by the Secretary, U.S. Department of Education, or that your education meets the other provisions outlined in the OPM Operating Manual. It will be your responsibility to secure the documentation that verifies that you attended and earned your degree(s) from this accredited institution(s) (e.g., official transcript). Federal agencies will verify your documentation.

  For a list of postsecondary educational institutions and programs accredited by accrediting agencies and state approval agencies recognized by the U.S. Secretary of Education, refer to the U.S. Department of Education Office of Postsecondary Education website at http://www.ope.ed.gov/accreditation/.

  For information on Educational and Training Provisions or Requirements, refer to the OPM Operating Manual available at http://www.opm.gov/qualifications/SEC-II/s2-e4.asp.

- If you served on active duty in the United States Military and were discharged or released from active duty in the armed forces under honorable conditions, you may be eligible for veterans' preference. To receive preference, if your service began after October 15, 1976, you must have a Campaign Badge, Expeditionary Medal, or a service-connected disability. Veterans' preference is not a factor for Senior Executive Service jobs or when competition is limited to status candidates (current or former career or career-conditional Federal employees).

- Most Federal jobs require United States citizenship and men that males over age 18 born after December 31, 1959, have registered with the Selective Service System or have an exemption.

- The law generally prohibits public officials from appointing, promoting, or recommending their relatives.

- Federal annuitants (military and civilian) may have their salaries or annuities reduced. Every employee must pay any valid delinquent debt or the agency may garnish their salary.

- Send your application to the office announcing the vacancy. If you have questions, contact the office identified in the announcement.

How to Apply

1. **Review** the listing of current vacancies.
2. **Decide** which jobs, pay range, and locations interest you.
3. **Follow instructions** provided in the vacancy announcement including any additional forms that are required.
   - You may apply for most jobs with a resume, this form, or any other written format; **all applications must include the information requested in the vacancy announcement as well as information required for all applications for Federal employment** (see below):
   - The USAJOBS website features an online résumé builder. This is a free service that allows you to create a résumé, submit it electronically (for some vacancy announcements), and save it online for use in the future.

Certain information is required to evaluate your qualifications and determine if you meet legal requirements for Federal employment. If your resume or application does not include all the required information as specified below, the agency may not consider you for the vacancy. Help speed the selection process - submit a concise resume' or application and send only the required material.

Information required for all applications for Federal employment:

Job Vacancy Specifics
- Announcement number, title and grade(s) of the job you are applying for

Personal Information
- Full name, mailing address (with zip code) and day and evening phone numbers (with area code) and email address, if applicable
- Social Security Number
- Country of citizenship (most Federal jobs require U.S. citizenship)
- Veterans' preference
- Reinstatement eligibility (for former Federal employees)
- Highest Federal civilian grade held (including job series and dates held)
- Selective Service (if applicable)

Work Experience
- Provide the following information for your paid and volunteer work experience related to the job you are applying for:
  ▶ job title (include job series and grade if Federal)
  ▶ duties and accomplishments
  ▶ employer's name and address
  ▶ supervisor's name and telephone number - indicate if supervisor may be contacted
  ▶ starting and ending dates (month and year)
  ▶ hours per week
  ▶ salary

U.S. Office of Personnel Management
Previous edition usable

NSN 7540-01-351-9178
50612-101

OF 612
Revised June 2006

Page 1 of 4

How to Apply (continued)

Education

- High School
  - ▶ Name, city, and State (Zip code if known)
  - ▶ Date of diploma or GED
- Colleges or universities
  - ▶ Name, city, and State (Zip code if known)
  - ▶ Majors
  - ▶ Type and year of degrees received. (If no degree, show total credits earned and indicate whether semester or quarter hours.)
- Do not attach a copy of your transcript unless requested
- Do not list degrees received based solely on life experience or obtained from schools with little or no academic standards

Upon request from the employing Federal agency, you must provide documentation or proof that your degree(s) is from a school accredited by an accrediting body recognized by the Secretary, U.S. Department of Education, or that your education meets the other provisions outlined in the OPM Operating Manual. It will be your responsibility to secure the documentation that verifies that you attended and earned your degree(s) from this accredited institution(s) (e.g., official transcript). Federal agencies will verify your documentation.

For a list of postsecondary educational institutions and programs accredited by accrediting agencies and state approval agencies recognized by the U.S. Secretary of Education, refer to the U.S. Department of Education Office of Postsecondary Education website at http://www.ope.ed.gov/accreditation/.

For information on Educational and Training Provisions or Requirements, refer to the OPM Operating Manual available at http://www.opm.gov/qualifications/SEC-II/s2-e4.asp.

Other Education Completed

- School name, city, and State (Zip code if known)
  - ▶ Credits earned and Majors
  - ▶ Type and year of degrees received. (If no degree, show total credits earned and indicate whether semester or quarter hours.)
- Do not list degrees received based solely on life experience or obtained from schools with little or no academic standards

Other Qualifications

- Job-related:
  - ▶ Training (title of course and year)
  - ▶ Skills (e.g., other languages, computer software/hardware, tools, machinery, typing speed, etc.)
  - ▶ Certificates or licenses (current only). Include type of license or certificate, date of latest license, and State or other licensing agency
  - ▶ Honors, awards, and special accomplishments, (e.g., publications, memberships in professional honor societies, leadership activities, public speaking and performance awards) (Give dates but do not send documents unless requested)

Any Other Information Specified in the Vacancy Announcement

Privacy Act Statement

The U.S. Office of Personnel Management and other Federal agencies rate applicants for Federal jobs under the authority of sections 1104, 1302, 3301, 3304, 3320, 3361, 3393, and 3394 of title 5 of the United States Code. We need the information requested in this form and in the associated vacancy announcements to evaluate your qualifications. Other laws require us to ask about citizenship, military service, etc. In order to keep your records in order, we request your Social Security Number (SSN) under the authority of Executive Order 9397 which requires the SSN for the purpose of uniform, orderly administration of personnel records. Failure to furnish the requested information may delay or prevent action on your application. We use your SSN to seek information about you from employers, schools, banks, and others who know you. We may use your SSN in studies and computer matching with other Government files. If you do not give us your SSN or any other information requested, we cannot process your application. Also, incomplete addresses and ZIP Codes will slow processing. We may confirm information from your records with prospective nonfederal employers concerning tenure of employment, civil service status, length of service, and date and nature of action for separation as shown on personnel action forms of specifically identified individuals.

Public Burden Statement

We estimate the public reporting burden for this collection will vary from 20 to 240 minutes with an average of 90 minutes per response, including time for reviewing instructions, searching existing data sources, gathering data, and completing and reviewing the information. Send comments regarding the burden statement or any other aspect of the collection of information, including suggestions for reducing this burden to the U.S. Office of Personnel Management (OPM), OPM Forms Officer, Washington, DC 20415-7900. The OMB number, 3206-0219, is currently valid. OPM may not collect this information and you are not required to respond, unless this number is displayed. Do not send completed application forms to this address; follow directions provided in the vacancy announcement(s).

THE FEDERAL GOVERNMENT IS AN EQUAL OPPORTUNITY EMPLOYER

U.S. Office of Personnel Management
Previous edition usable

NSN 7540-01-351-9178
50612-101

OF 612
Revised June 2006

Page 2 of 4

OPTIONAL APPLICATION FOR FEDERAL EMPLOYMENT - OF 612

Form Approved
OMB No. 3206-0219

Section A - Applicant Information

Use Standard State Postal Codes (abbreviations). If outside the United States of America, and you do not have a military address, type or print "OV" in the State field (Block 6c) and fill in the Country field (Block 6e) below, leaving the Zip Code field (Block 6d) blank.

1. Job title in announcement

2. Grade(s) applying for

3. Announcement number

4a. Last name

4b. First and middle names

5. Social Security Number

6a. Mailing address

7. Phone numbers (include area code if within the United States of America)

7a. Daytime

6b. City

6c. State

6d. Zip Code

7b. Evening

6e. Country (if not within the United States of America)

8. Email address (if available)

Section B - Work Experience

Describe your paid and non-paid work experience related to the job for which you are applying. Do not attach job description.

1. Job title (if Federal, include series and grade)

2. From (mm/yyyy)

3. To (mm/yyyy)

4. Salary   per
$

5. Hours per week

6. Employer's name and address

7. Supervisor's name and phone number

7a. Name

7b. Phone

8. May we contact your current supervisor?   Yes ☐   No ☐
If we need to contact your current supervisor before making an offer, we will contact you first.

9. Describe your duties, accomplishments and related skills (if you need to attach additional pages, include your name, address, and job announcement number)

Section C - Additional Work Experience

1. Job title (if Federal, include series and grade)

2. From (mm/yyyy)

3. To (mm/yyyy)

4. Salary   per
$

5. Hours per week

6. Employer's name and address

7. Supervisor's name and phone number

7a. Name

7b. Phone

8. May we contact your current supervisor?   Yes ☐   No ☐
If we need to contact your current supervisor before making an offer, we will contact you first.

9. Describe your duties, accomplishments and related skills (if you need to attach additional pages, include your name, address, and job announcement number)

U.S. Office of Personnel Management
Previous edition usable

NSN 7540-01-351-9178
50612-10
Page 3 of 4

OF 612
Revised June 2006

Section D - Education

Upon request from the employing Federal agency, you must provide documentation or proof that your degree(s) is from a school accredited by an accrediting body recognized by the Secretary, U. S. Department of Education, or that your education meets the other provisions outlined in the OPM Operating Manual. It will be your responsibility to secure the documentation that verifies that you attended and earned your degree(s) from this accredited institution(s) (e.g., official transcript). Federal agencies will verify your documentation.

For a list of postsecondary educational institutions and programs accredited by accrediting agencies and state approval agencies recognized by the U.S. Secretary of Education, refer to the U.S. Department of Education Office of Postsecondary Education website at http://www.ope.ed.gov/accreditation/.

For information on Educational and Training Provisions or Requirements, refer to the OPM Operating Manual available at http://www.opm.gov/qualifications/SEC-II/s2-e4.asp.

Do not list degrees received based solely on life experience or obtained from schools with little or no academic standards.

1. Last High School (HS)/GED school. Give the school's name, city, state, ZIP Code (if known), and year diploma or GED received:

2. Mark highest level completed: Some HS ☐   HS/GED ☐   Associate ☐   Bachelor ☐   Master ☐   Doctoral ☐

3. Colleges and universities attended. Do not attach a copy of your transcript unless requested.

			Total Credits Earned		Major(s)	Degree (if any), Year Received
			Semester	Quarter		
3a. Name						
City	State	Zip Code				
3b. Name						
City	State	Zip Code				
3c. Name						
City	State	Zip Code				

Section E - Other Education Completed

Do not list degrees received based solely on life experience or obtained from schools with little or no academic standards.

Section F - Other Qualifications

License or Certificate	Date of Latest License or Certificate	State or Other Licensing Agency
1f.		
2f.		

Section G - Other Qualifications

Job-related training courses (give title and year). Job-related skills (other languages, computer software/hardware, tools, machinery, typing speed, etc.). Job-related honors, awards, and special accomplishments (publications, memberships in professional/honor societies, leadership activities, public speaking, and performance awards). Give dates, but do not send documents unless requested.

Section H - General

1a. Are you a U.S. citizen?   Yes ☐   No ☐   →   1b. If no, give the Country of your citizenship

2a. Do you claim veterans' preference?   Yes ☐   No ☐   →   If yes, mark your claim of 5 or 10 points below.

2b. 5 points ☐ →   Attach your Report of Separation from Active Duty (DD 214) or other proof.

2c. 10 points ☐ →   Attach an Application for 10-Point Veterans' Preference (SF 15) and proof required.

3. Check this box if you are an adult male born on or after January 1st 1960, and you registered for Selective Service between the ages of 18 through 25 → ☐

4. Were you ever a Federal civilian employee?   Yes ☐   No ☐   →   If yes, list highest civilian grade for the following:

4a. Series	4b. Grade	4c. From (mm/yyyy)	4d. To (mm/yyyy)

5a. Are you eligible for reinstatement based on career or career-conditional Federal status?   Yes ☐   No ☐
If requested in the vacancy announcement, attach Notification of Personnel Action (SF 50), as proof.

5b. Are you eligible under the ICTAP*?   Yes ☐   No ☐
*ICTAP (Interagency Career Transition Assistance Plan): A participant in this plan is a current or former federal employee displaced from a Federal agency. To be eligible, you must have received a formal notice of separation such as a RIF separation notice. If you are an ICTAP eligible, normally you will be provided priority consideration for vacancies within your commuting area for which you apply and are well qualified.

Section I - Applicant Certification

I certify that, to the best of my knowledge and belief, all of the information on and attached to this application is true, correct, complete, and made in good faith. I understand that false or fraudulent information on or attached to this application may be grounds for not hiring me or for firing me after I begin work, and may be punishable by fine or imprisonment. I understand that any information I give may be investigated.

1a. Signature	1b. Date (mm/dd/yyyy)

Previous edition usable
U.S. Office of Personnel Management

NSN 7540-01-351-9178
50612-10
Page 4 of 4

OF 612
Revised June 2006

Many applications are run through Resumix, an automated resume-scanning system that reads with optical character recognition software, imaging technologies, and a skill-extraction system. Resumix creates skill sets for every applicant, based on keywords. Therefore, it is critical that your resume and KSA contain keywords/skills that match the precise language of the vacancy announcement. If they don't, you won't be selected. If the vacancy announcement doesn't list many skills, research similar announcements and use their most frequently mentioned skills.

Even if a human recruiter gives a first pass to the applications, it will be a fast skim, since they receive so many. Make your application pass the skim test. Your main credentials must be seen within ten seconds, so put them at the top of the first page. Answer each question in the KSA section briefly and directly. If a master's degree is important for the job, don't put it at the end of the second page. If a KSA question asks about a specific ability, discuss your experience with it, not your enjoyment of it. Only address what is asked; don't wander off on tangents. Quantify your accomplishments; for instance, saying that you managed ten people is more informative than simply saying that you managed people. If something on your application is ambiguous, nobody has the time to call you to clarify, nor the authority to assume what you mean. You'll just be passed over.

Finally, follow up. Leave a voicemail message expressing your interest about thirty days after submitting your application. Along with showing that you are strongly interested in it, job announcements are sometimes canceled and reissued. If you don't check on this, you won't know to reapply.

Reading some of the many career advice books on the market will make you a stronger job candidate.

If you are selected for an interview, it may take place over the phone, in person, or before a panel. Dress well and read some of the many interviewing books on the market; they discuss common questions applicants are asked to answer and give other tips.

Military Spouse Hiring Preference

The Spouse Hiring Preference of the Military Family Act (Public Law 99-661) gives worldwide employment preference to spouses of active-duty servicemembers, including Coast Guard and full-time National Guard, who are relocating to accompany their military sponsor on a permanent-change-of-station move. The intent is to lessen the employment and career interruptions of spouses who relocate with their military sponsors. Note that this act does not mean that you can walk into your old job at the new duty station. For priority consideration to have any effect, a vacancy for which you're qualified must already exist. The government will not create a job for you. There is no guarantee that the job you held at the last station will be available at the new one. But when it is, the following criteria apply.

Requirements. The move must be to an active-duty assignment (the sponsor cannot be separating or retiring), and the spouse must have been married to the sponsor prior to the reporting date to the new assignment. The spouse must be ranked among "best qualified," and the job must be in the same commuting area as the servicemember's duty station. Additionally, the spouse must fall under one of the following categories: a current federal career/career-conditional employee; an NAF employee; a Veterans Recruitment Act (see chapter 11) or Schedule A handicapped appointment (see glossary); have reinstatement eligibility; have eligibility under Executive Order (E.O.) 12721 (see glossary); or have competitive service eligibility based on employment under other merit systems. Overseas, military spouses are given preference in accordance with local hiring procedures.

Time Limits. Spouse preference eligibility begins thirty days prior to the sponsor's reporting date to the new duty station and continues throughout the tour until you accept or decline a permanent appropriated or nonappropriated fund position from any federal agency in the commuting area. There is no limit to the number of times spouse preference may be exercised when applying for temporary jobs.

You may be simultaneously referred for permanent and temporary positions until you accept or decline a continuing position. However, if you are placed into a temporary position, preference eligibility for other temporary jobs is suspended until sixty days prior to the expiration of the temporary job you accepted. Overseas, you do not receive preference until you actually arrive at the location.

Applicable Jobs. The jobs to which this preference applies are federal civilian positions GS-2 through 15, comparable Wage System jobs (see glossary); and NAF jobs level 3 and below. Spouses who teach in Department of Defense Dependents Schools are also included. Positions that require mandatory mobility agreements and positions in intelligence-related activities are excluded. The preference applies only to external recruitments, not noncompetitive ones. If the choice is made to select from a list of noncompetitive candidates, or from an alternative recruitment source, spouse preference does not apply. The alternative recruitment sources are: a 30 percent disabled veteran; VRA appointment; transfer at the same or lower grade, reassignment or change to lower grade; placement to correct an Equal Employment Opportunity deficiency; placement of a handicapped individual; or placement of an employee returning from an overseas tour or duty with return rights.

You may register at a grade no higher than what you were at your previous permanent job. If your only federal service was overseas under a time-limited appointment, you may register for the highest grade held if you have appointment eligibility under E.O. 12721. If you are not a current federal employee who has E.O. 12721 and reinstatement eligibility, you may register under either option, whichever is more beneficial.

If you have no prior federal employment, your preference eligibility will be at the grade for which you qualified on an employment register. You may register for the lowest grade for which you are qualified and available.

Documents Needed. When registering for spouse preference, bring these documents with you:

- application or resume
- statement requesting military spouse preference
- copy of PCS orders

If you are a current federal employee, you should additionally bring:

- copy of Notification of Personnel Action (NPA, formerly the SF-50), which documents your appointments
- copy of last performance appraisal

CAREER FAIRS

Career fairs are events where representatives from government agencies, private companies, and schools set up booths and interview candidates on the spot. Colleges and different organizations sponsor them. Dress well and bring copies of your resume. Visit

If you leave a federal civil service job because of a transfer, try to get leave without pay (LWOP) if you intend to seek another civil service job. If you find one before your LWOP runs out, you'll maintain your career status as well as vacation and sick leave.

Employers routinely Google prospective applicants. Candidates who might have gotten the job have been rejected due to photos or blogs they've posted. Nothing posted on the Web ever goes away, even when deleted. Google's "Wayback Machine" is found at *www.archive.org/index.php*. This tool takes snapshots of every website at different points in time and stores them. So items you may have posted a year ago and are no longer on your current site may still be accessed.

If your teen needs pocket money, ask the base Family Services office if it has a "Hire a Teen" program, which matches teens with adults who will hire them.

www.nationalcareerfairs.com/monster to search for career fairs by area.

JOB HUNTING ON THE INTERNET

There are many websites devoted to job hunting. You can look for jobs in newspaper classifieds online, on corporate websites, and on sites that allow job seekers to post resumes. You can also use the Internet to research companies and thus be more knowledgeable during the interview.

Some popular career-related websites are: *www.monster.com*; *www.careerbuilder.com*; *www.snagajob.com*; *www.theladders.com*; and *www.militaryspousejobsearch.org*.

SELF-EMPLOYMENT

Some military wives with transportable skills set up home offices. This is popular in the civilian sector, as more people attempt to maintain careers while staying home with children or just because they prefer a more flexible routine. Many people set up shop as virtual assistants; visit *www.staffcentrix.com* for details on this. Others find work through *www.ifreelance.com* or become online tutors through places like *www.tutorvista.com*. Some teach at online universities.

PATRIOT EXPRESS

This is a pilot program run by the Small Business Administration. It provides loans of up to $500,000 and guarantees of loans up to $150,000 to start or expand a small business. Groups eligible for this loan are:

- veterans
- service-disabled veterans
- active-duty servicemembers eligible for the military's Transition Assistance Program
- reservists and National Guard members
- current spouses of any of the above
- the widowed spouse of a servicemember or veteran who died during service or of a service-connected disability

For more information, visit *www.sba.gov/patriotexpress/index.html* for details.

SELF-EMPLOYMENT SUCCESS STORIES

An Army wife turned her love and knowledge of oriental rugs into a business. She found a wholesaler and exhibited her rugs at coffee groups, officers' clubs, and the local merchandise mart. Because her overhead was minimal, her prices were cheaper than those of oriental rug stores. Word-of-mouth advertising spread, and her business thrived.

An Air Force wife located clothing wholesalers and is a Powerseller on eBay.

A Navy wife who had given up her job as a second-grade teacher when she moved launched a business teaching etiquette classes to little girls.

Another Navy wife provides child care, and cleans offices and houses on weekends. She generates so much business that she hired four helpers.

An Army wife has a party-planning service. She coordinates with local talent to perform at kids' birthday parties and corporate events.

An Air Force wife uses her degree in fine arts to make a brisk business selling her handmade beaded jewelry at *www.cafepress.com*. Another sells baked goods on *www.etsy.com*, a busy site for handmade items.

A Marine Corps wife who spent much time online decided to be productive with it. She took some Web design classes, started a website, and enrolled in the Google AdSense program, bringing in spending money.

One Army wife turned her hour-long commute into a business. She bought a used forty-seat commuter van, got a chauffeur's license and insurance, and distributed flyers in mall and discount store parking lots. In two weeks she was in business. She picked everyone up at a common point, dropped them off along a route she devised, and then went to her own job. At 5:00 P.M. she picked them all up and drove home. Within a month she had her entire van filled and a waiting list so long she bought a second van and hired a rider to drive it. When it came time to move, she sold the service to a local businessman.

Defense Department regulations permit spouses to operate nonprofessional businesses from government quarters. If you live off base, research if local zoning laws permit home businesses and if a license or permit is needed. Consider liability coverage. Your present homeowner's or renter's policy might provide some. Obtain a state sales tax number, keep good tax records, and talk to a lawyer or accountant about legitimate deductions. A small business course at the community college might be in order, as well as a membership in a professional association in your field.

Do your due diligence when investigating home businesses. Ignore unsolicited e-mails. Don't send money for equipment, fees, information, or for the ability to contact an employer. Unsolicited opportunities for medical billing, stuffing envelopes, and product assembly are always fraudulent. Finally, real employers will require a resume, interview, and references, whether the job is work-at-home or not.

Useful references for this purpose are the *Associations Yellow Book* and the *Encyclopedia of Associations*.

VOLUNTEER

Volunteerism has dual benefits—keeping skills sharp and making contacts. You might have the opportunity to attend workshops and seminars and meet people who hire. If something opens at the place where you're volunteering, you'll be a known quantity. You don't need to volunteer forty hours a week; just a few hours a week may prove fruitful. Market your volunteer experience as you would any paying job. Don't treat it as "just volunteering." It's work, and describe it as precisely as paid employment.

Maintaining a career when moving constantly is difficult, but people do it. It simply takes more assertion and effort. Make that effort, present yourself well, and eventually you'll hear, "When can you start?"

> Follow up your resume with a phone call, or better yet, write in your cover letter that you'll call. Few people do this, so that alone will give you an edge. Keep a professional message on your voicemail or answering machine. Don't answer the phone if you're not immediately ready to be interviewed. Develop a firm, confident handshake, not a limp "ladies" handshake. Don't overshare during an interview, and pay attention to the interviewer's body language.

FURTHER READING

Books

Bolles, Richard Nelson, and Mark Emery Bolles. *Job Hunting Online: A Guide to Using Job Listings, Message Boards, Research Sites, the Underweb, Counseling, Networking, Self-Assessment Tools, Niche Sites*. Berkeley, CA: Ten Speed Press, 5th edition, 2008.

Canfield, Jack, with Janet Switzer. *The Success Principles: How to Get from Where You Are to Where You Want to Be*. New York: Collins Living, 2006.

Damp, Dennis. *The Book of U.S. Government Jobs: Where They Are, What's Available and How to Get One*. Moon Township, PA: Bookhaven Press, 2008.

Farly, Janet. *The Military Spouse's Complete Guide to Career Success: Finding Meaningful Employment in Today's New Global Marketplace*. Manassas Park, VA: Impact Publications, 2008.

Henderson, David G. *Job Search: Marketing Your Military Experience*. Mechanicsburg, PA: Stackpole Books, 2004.

Jones, Katina. *The 200 Best Home Businesses: Easy to Start, Fun to Run, Highly Profitable*. Avon, MA: Adams Media Corporation, 2005.

Internet Resources

www.mscn.org. Military Spouses Career Network website. Has information on maintaining a career, including state-by-state unemployment benefits.

www.careerkey.org. Helps you evaluate the types of jobs suited for your personality and capabilities.

www.military.com/spouse/ca. Military.com's Spouse Career Center.

schools.military.com/schoolfinder. Military.com's School Finder.

aid.military.com/scholarship/search-for-scholarships.do. Military.com's Scholarship finder.

caa.milspouse.org. Info on military spouse career advancement accounts.

www.sba.gov. Small Business Administration.

trsinstitute.com/about_us/military_spouse_program.asp. TRS (Transcription Relief Services) has an online medical transcription education program for military spouses, as well as a scholarship for which you can apply.

5

Money Matters

Money! It fascinates and frustrates us. How to earn it, save it, and spend it is the subject of endless books, magazines, and fights. This chapter discusses the money that comes into your household and ways to manage it.

YOUR PERSONAL FINANCES AND THE MILITARY

While managing money well is important for everyone, it's especially important to servicemembers. Financial fitness is as important as physical fitness. Money troubles affect productivity, deployability, and military readiness. Poor money management may cause a servicemember to lose a security clearance, career opportunities, promotions, and even face sanctions. Bounced checks and other bad debts are brought to the attention of commanders. An excessive amount of such notices can break a career; indeed, hundreds of people are involuntarily separated each year for their inability to manage money.

Why should something as personal as our finances have any relevance to the job? Isn't that an invasion of privacy? What business is it of anyone but our own if we have excessive debts or write bad checks?

As we know, being a servicemember is not an ordinary office job. There are unique risks and responsibilities. Many jobs involve classified knowledge. Most jobs involve, to some extent, sensitive information or access to areas where it's kept. Because of this, servicemembers and their families can be targets of those who would like this information. Thus the service must be concerned with potential vulnerabilities to exploitative situations, such as severe indebtedness, mental or emotional problems, substance abuse, or criminal or sexual misconduct. Such concern is not intended to pry but rather to protect.

The ability to manage money is also considered critical to good leadership. If a person cannot manage his own money, how is he to manage other people? How can any NCO or officer properly do his job with money troubles on his mind?

Finally, each of us represents the service as a whole. Many civilians judge the whole military on the conduct of the two or three they might know. Notice the way many local papers report traffic accidents involving servicemembers: "There was an accident on I-40 involving a Fort Campbell soldier and a Clarkesville resident." Why the Clarkesville resident's occupation is left out but the servicemember's—who is also a Clarkesville resident—is noted demonstrates the high visibility in the local community.

PAY GAP?

For a long time, military pay scales lagged behind civilian ones. However, in 2008, the 10th Quadrennial Review of Military Compensation (QRMC) showed that the pay gap has basically closed. The data includes pay, allowances, and the tax-free nature of some military pay. Lower-ranking members, such as those enlisting right out of high school, actually make more than their civilian counterparts, while those who rank higher and or have specialized skills, may make less. Plus, with so many spouses in the workforce now, there are quite a few mid-level dual-income service families earning six-figure incomes. You can find military pay scale charts at *www.defenselink.mil/militarypay*. For comparison purposes, the median annual household income in 2006 was $48,201, according to the U.S. Census Bureau data. Remember that medical, exchange, and commissary benefits, and any others used, such as Space-A, are valuable noncash compensations.

PAY

Before you can manage your money, you need to know how much you have to manage. For most active-duty families, the primary source of income is the servicemember's paycheck. It can be received once or twice a month. Direct deposit is required. Servicemembers on unaccompanied tours have a split-deposit option where part of the paycheck can go to him and the rest to the family.

The Leave and Earnings Statement

Each paycheck is accompanied by a Leave and Earnings Statement (LES), which is the pay stub. If the servicemember is paid twice a month, the pay stub will be an Advice of Payment that has a brief explanation of the pay. Full details are shown at the end of the month. The LES has three main parts: pay/allowances, allotments, and deductions. It also contains information about leave (vacation). Reservists will see drill and retirement information. Sample LESs are in the appendix.

myPay

The LES is not mailed. A copy can be requested at the base Finance office. However, the most convenient way to access it is online at *https://mypay.dfas.mil/mypay.aspx*, by logging into a feature called "myPay." A personal identification number (PIN) is needed. Active-duty personnel can view and print their LES for the past twelve months one week before payday; reservists can view it for the past three months. Servicemembers can allow spouses to access their LES in a read-only mode with their own PIN, as by law, spouses are not authorized to have the servicemember's PIN. If you need access to the LES and have a power of attorney, you can request access from the unit's rear detachment commander or the Noncommissioned Officer in Charge (NCOIC).

At myPay, sevicemembers can also:

- start, stop, and change military TSP contributions and mailing address
- change direct deposit bank account
- print last five W-2s and change W-4 tax withholdings
- change mailing address for home and the Thrift Savings Plan
- purchase U.S. Savings Bonds
- start, stop, and change pay allotments to financial institutions

Types of Pay

Basic Pay. Since 1790, every servicemember has received basic pay, a simple wage that covers a twenty-four-hour, seven-day workweek. Whether the servicemember is in a combat unit or escorting civilian contractors that provide water to the unit, all jobs are needed and important. This is why everyone with the same rank and time in service gets the same basic pay. Income is taxable except when the servicemember is deployed to certain combat zones. Some states don't tax military pay, and some don't tax it unless you are stationed within the state. The state that a servicemember lists as his official residence with the finance office determines which tax rules apply.

Reservists receive the same pay as active-duty members during basic training and job school, or any other time performing full-time duty (such as the two-weeks annual active-duty training, or if mobilized). The pay scale is different for weekend drills, however. Guard/reserve members receive four days' worth of pay for each weekend drill.

Special Pay. Special pay recognizes critical skills, helps compensate for unique hardships, and persuades people to reenlist. Most special pays range from $600 per year to $12,000 per year (more for certain dental and medical specialties) and take the form of pay for submarine duty, nuclear duty, foreign duty, or demolition duty. It shows up as flight pay, sea pay, pay for proficiency in foreign languages, and pay for jobs with chronic manpower shortages. Medical professionals, divers, engineering and scientific officers, and people who serve in hostile-fire/imminent-danger and combat zones get special pay. It is also given to people in some overseas areas if they remain there, and reservists may get incapacitation pay if injured while drilling. Some pays are nontaxable, such as hostile-fire/imminent-danger pay (HF/IDP).

Combat-related Injury and Rehabilitation Pay (CIP). Servicemembers earn this type of pay for the time they spend in rehabilitation for wounds, injuries, and illness incurred from being in a combat operation or combat zone. Its purpose is to help soften the future reduction of HF/IDP pay. Currently, CIP pay is $430 per month minus any hostile-fire/imminent-danger pay accrued that month. HF/IDP continues for up to three months for servicemembers hospitalized for the treatment of an injury, wound, or illness incurred in a combat zone or operation.

Advance Pay. This type of pay may be granted up to thirty days before a permanent-change-of-station (PCS) move and up to sixty days after it. Its purpose is to help with moving expenses. The maximum amount is three months' base pay minus deductions, repaid over twelve months. In cases of financial hardship, the repayment can be extended up to twenty-four months.

Reenlistment and Selective Reenlistment Bonuses. The purpose of this money is to encourage people to reenlist into jobs that have shortages. Currently, the Army gives up to $40,000, the Air Force and Navy give up to $60,000, and the Marine Corps gives up to $35,000. Higher sums are commensurate with jobs that pay well in the civilian world or are considered very difficult. Generally, half of the bonus is paid at reenlistment time and the remainder paid in equal installments annually over the term of the enlistment. Sometimes they're paid in a lump sum at reenlistment. If the member doesn't serve in the job for the entire reenlistment period, a prorated portion of the reenlistment bonus must be repaid. Bonuses are taxable unless received while the servicemember is deployed to a combat zone.

Allowances

Allowances are moneys for food and housing. They're not intended to completely cover such expenses; it's up to you to maintain a standard of living that your allowances and basic pay can support. Don't view allowances as money that is as steady as basic pay; some, like BAS, can decrease month to month, depending on the circumstances under which the allowance is granted. Wait until you actually see the money before spending it. If extra money is accidentally credited, it will be debited as soon as the mistake is discovered.

You might find the following allowances on your husband's LES:

Basic Allowance for Subsistence (BAS). In the early days, three meals a day came with a military paycheck. Where mess halls weren't available, servicemembers were given money to buy food—or "subsistence." This evolved into the basic allowance for subsistence, an allowance for food. It is for the servicemember, not the family. If a servicemember is in basic training, assigned to an unaccompanied tour, or moves into the barracks/dormitory, he does not receive a BAS, since the government feeds him. BAS is not suspended, however, when he is temporarily away from the home station, such as a deployment or field duty, nor when he's on an unaccompanied assignment overseas. Enlisted personnel receive more BAS than officers, a long-standing tradition dating from an early congressional decision that the government should pay the entire cost of feeding enlistment members, but not for officers. This allowance is nontaxable.

Family Subsistence Supplemental Allowance (FSSA). This allowance increases the BAS for qualifying servicemembers, typically those with very large families. It provides a supplemental allowance of up to $500 per month and is designed to raise household income to 130 percent of the federal poverty line, thus removing them from food stamp eligibility. Recipients must recertify annually as well as upon a promotion, permanent-change-of-station move, an increase in household income of $100 dollars or more, or change in family size.

Basic Allowance for Housing (BAH). This money helps pay housing and living costs. The amount given is based on rank, location, and whether or not you have dependents. For the latter, an amount is given based on *one* dependent; it is not increased with additional ones. Each year the DoD hires an independent agency to survey average, acceptable-quality housing costs in all areas where large amounts of servicemembers live. This data is used to compute the amount of BAH given. It's designed to cover 100 percent of *average* housing costs. BAH is paid only to families who don't live in government quarters and is recalculated upon a move. Families who live in quarters "pay" for them by forfeiting BAH. If a servicemember is on an unaccompanied tour overseas, his family may still collect BAH even if the servicemember lives on base. BAH is nontaxable.

Reservists who are entitled to a housing allowance receive a special reduced one called BAH Type II. It is granted when they are on active duty for less than thirty days. If they are on orders to serve on active duty for thirty days or more, they receive the same full housing allowance rate as active-duty members.

Overseas Housing Allowance (OHA). This is money given to help with off-base living costs overseas. The amount depends on location, and it's calculated every two weeks to compensate for fluctuating currency exchange rates. Money to help with move-in expenses and reimbursement for costs to improve the security of the off-base residence is also given.

Family Separation Housing Allowance. This provides a dual housing allowance for servicemembers on unaccompanied tours overseas who are unable to get into government quarters but are still supporting a family stateside. It's equal to the OHA and BAH at the "with-dependents" rate for their family.

Family Separation Allowance. This is money paid at a daily rate to defray minor expenses incurred when the servicemember is involuntarily stationed someplace where his family isn't sent. Servicemembers deployed on ships away from home port or on temporary duty more than thirty days also get it.

Clothing Allowance. Officers receive a one-time clothing allowance payment after they are commissioned to purchase uniforms and insignia. Enlisted members are issued items when they come on active duty if the service is unable to issue them an initial allotment of uniforms, and are given lump-sum maintenance allowances thereafter. The exact amount is based on retail costs. There are also supplemental clothing allowances for special duties (e.g., band) or for those who are required to wear civilian clothing on duty.

Continental U.S. Cost-of-Living Allowance (CONUS COLA). This money is given to people living in areas where the cost of living is 8 percent or more above the national cost of living. Currently, fifty-two areas qualify. The exact amount is pegged to rank, presence of a family member, and the area. Servicemembers on unaccompanied overseas tours whose primary family member lives in a high-cost area may also receive it. CONUS COLA is taxable.

Cost-of-Living Allowance (COLA). This is a supplement given to people living overseas OCONUS (outside the continental U.S.) to help compensate for higher prices. COLA payments are given regardless of whether you're living in quarters or on the economy, vary with location and rank, and are pegged to local currency exchange rates.

Per Diem. This is a daily allotment for food and lodging while on government business.

Hardship Duty. This type of payment is for servicemembers assigned to areas considered hardship or hazardous locations and varies greatly depending on the area.

LEAVE

Leave is requested through supervisors or commanders. For any kind of leave, Saturdays and Sundays are counted; a vacation from Wednesday to Wednesday is counted as seven days off, not five. Military regulations require leave to start and end in the local area. So, if leave is begun on Monday, the servicemember cannot leave the local area until Monday, even if he is off duty on Saturday and Sunday. Likewise, if his leave ends on Friday, he must return to the local area on that Friday, even if he's not scheduled to work until the following Monday. Thirty days of paid leave per year are given each year, two and a half days per month. Up to sixty days of unused leave may be sold back at separation or reenlistment at the rate of a day of taxable base pay for each day of leave.

Types of Leave

Annual Leave. Vacation time is accrued at the rate of two and a half days for each month of active duty. Up to sixty days may be accumulated; after that, a servicemember must "use or lose."

Advance Leave. Servicemembers who need to take leave but don't have enough can have time "loaned" to them.

Excess Leave. When the servicemember doesn't have enough leave accrued but is unable to pay back borrowed leave, they can use this leave without pay for emergency situations.

Emergency Leave. This type of leave counts as annual leave when taken but can be used only for a family emergency. It's usually given for up to fifteen days but can be approved for thirty. The Red Cross must verify the emergency before emergency leave can be granted.

Convalescent (Sick) Leave. Sick leave is given if a servicemember is under special medical care or recovering from an operation.

Environmental and Morale Leave. This type of leave is offered to servicemembers in remote, isolated locations where transportation is not easily available.

Terminal Leave. When discharged or retiring, a servicemember can start leave for as many days as he has saved up and receive full pay, housing and food allowances, and any special pays, until the official date of separation.

Permissive Temporary Duty Assignment (PTDY). PTDY may be granted when a servicemember wants to attend a conference or class that the military won't pay for but which benefits him professionally, which benefits the military. An example is a computer specialist attending a Microsoft certification course. Recipients do not receive any travel pay or reimbursement, but their leave isn't charged.

Special-Leave Accrual (SLA). This is leave that accrues when a servicemember is stationed in an area that entitles him to hostile-fire/imminent-danger pay for at least 120 continuous days. Up to ninety days of leave may be carried at the end of a fiscal year, and then must be used before the end of the third fiscal year after the fiscal year in which the service ended. Unused leave accrued while serving in a combat zone is tax exempt if sold back when separating from the service.

There are also leaves for special situations such as maternity or adoption, R&R (rest and recuperation), rehabilitation, delay en route, and sick-in-quarters. There is leave awaiting orders, military academy leave, and proceed time. *Passes* or liberties are nonchargeable short amounts of time that do not require annual leave and are usually less than seventy-two hours.

Servicemembers may carry over 120 days of leave across fiscal years. Personnel who accumulate this much leave (common for those deployed for long times) and want to carry it to the next fiscal year must request it from their command. This has to be proactively requested; otherwise leave is subject to the "use or lose" default.

ALLOTMENTS

Allotments are moneys sent directly from the paycheck to specific places and people to care for financial responsibilities. Typical allotments are for child support, alimony, SGLI (life insurance, discussed later in this chapter) premiums, the GI Bill, to pay debts, contribute to the Thrift Savings Plan or other savings accounts, and to buy U.S. Savings Bonds. The LES also shows withholdings for FICA (Social Security), federal and state income taxes, and any other amounts owed to the government, as well as for advances in pay. There is a deduction for Tricare and the dental plan. A small deduction is made from enlisted paychecks to support the military's retirement homes.

SAVINGS DEPOSIT PROGRAM (SDP)

All servicemembers deployed at least thirty consecutive days may participate in this program. Each month an amount no greater than their total monthly pay and allowances can be allotted to an account that pays 10 percent interest. The money must be withdrawn within ninety days of returning from the deployment region. Servicemembers make the deposits with their deployed finance unit.

WAGE GARNISHMENT

A court-ordered garnishment may be applied to servicemembers' paychecks for spousal or child support. Garnishments are not considered allotments, as they are a separate legal procedure. Upon proper notification from an authorized person, the finance office will start a statutorily required child or child and spousal support allotment from the pay and allowances of a member on extended active duty when the member has failed to make periodic payments under a support order. Some states do not allow garnisheeing the wages of the head of a household for nonsupport of family members. However, in those states not allowing it, federal law allows garnishment for past and current amounts owed. So, if a servicemember has not paid court-ordered support for years and is called to active duty, the person owed support can have his pay garnished. The Legal office can advise in such a situation, but cannot represent military personnel.

There are other pays, allowances, and leave that are specific to moving, and they are discussed in chapter 7.

PAY AND LEAVE DURING BASIC TRAINING

Pay

The first paycheck will arrive about six weeks after being inducted and will contain base pay for the recruit's rank, plus housing (BAH) and family separation (FSA) allowances. It will be prorated to the number of days on active duty. Taxes and deductions for nonissue items such as running shoes, soap, shampoo, and laundry will be taken out. BAH is given even when the recruit is living on base during boot camp and training, because by law, families must be provided for. It is based on where a new recruit's family currently lives, not on where the recruit is assigned.

Since direct deposit is mandatory for military pay, new recruits should have a bank account set up before leaving for basic training. If an account is set up at the base credit union or bank, it may take several weeks to receive a debit card (which may impact your ability to access the pay).

Leave

After boot camp, the Marine Corps and the Coast Guard allow their recruits to take ten days of leave. Otherwise, servicemembers typically don't get their first leave until job training graduation, at which time they can take ten days of leave, if their first assignment is CONUS, and fifteen days of leave if it's OCONUS. At Christmas recruits are usually allowed to take leave even if they haven't saved any yet. Recruits may also be authorized a permissive TDY to return to their hometown and assist the recruiter for up to twenty days, so some time can be spent working with the recruiter, and some of their time at home on leave.

In general, if the school is longer than twenty weeks at a single location, family members may travel to it and set up a household at government expense. If the school lasts less than twenty weeks, government-reimbursed transportation is usually not authorized. Family members who wish to relocate to the school's location do so at their own expense. In either case, servicemembers in job school receive a housing allowance, based on the actual location of their dependents. Know that since your husband is probably going to be restricted to base during the first part of their training (usually, the first thirty days or so), you may have to find a place to live on your own.

In December, most bases have a "Christmas Exodus," at which time many recruits may go home for a few days.

SET GOALS

Now that you know what to expect financially, set some goals for your household. All those that are well run have financial goals and plans for managing their money. As an ancient Roman put it, "You won't reach port if you don't know where it is." Goals give you something to look forward to. They're also a powerful reminder for saving. Nobody likes passing something up because they can't afford it, but to pass it up because you're saving for something better can make saving easier.

Where do you want to be in five years? In ten? In twenty? What sort of retirement do you envision? What do you want to do for your children? What do you want to buy? Write down your goals and dreams, and tape them on your refrigerator, maybe along with photos of the things you want. Having usual reminders like this to look at helps keep us on track. Design a budget to help you achieve these goals. Know how much you spend, and on what, each month. Following is an example of a goals sheet you might lay out.

Goal	Achievement Date	Time Frame	Cost	Monthly Savings Needed

At this point, it's also useful to develop a spending philosophy. This can be part of a larger "life mission statement," where you clarify priorities and what's important to you. One philosophy is to achieve financial goals by cutting back lesser priority items to concentrate on the greater ones. Another philosophy strives to increase income so that small enjoyments don't have to be sacrificed for larger ones. References for books with each philosophy are given at the end of this chapter.

A SPENDING JOURNAL

If you are just beginning to get your financial affairs in order, the importance of a spending journal cannot be overemphasized. This is a small notebook in which each and *every* purchase you make is recorded: vending machine chips, dry cleaning, movie rentals, lattes, groceries, iTunes downloads. Yes, it is a nuisance to record every cent, but it is critical in showing precisely where your money is going. You may think that you know where it's going. But things bought at the beginning of the month are easily forgotten by the end. A spending journal will show you what your spending priorities are—which may be different from what you think they are. Keep it for at least four months. It may prove to be an eye opener.

DESIGN A BUDGET

After you've kept a journal for four months, use the information in it to design a spending plan. This plan should outline how you will allocate, or budget, money toward your goals or obligations. Such information will make your budget realistic, not a pie-in-the-sky exercise you'll never stick to. It will show you where you can make cuts, and maybe even where you should make increases. Budgets are analogous to diets. They're hard to stick to at first, but the longer you do, the easier it gets. And you'll enjoy the results.

If you need help, visit your Family Services office. There you can get help with all sorts of financial matters: reading the LES, balancing a checkbook, saving, managing money, using credit, and combining a newlywed couple's two separate households and spending styles into one. When couples bicker over money, the lack of it is often less of a factor than differing ideas on how to manage it. It's unfortunate that most of the servicemembers who get help are command-referred, not there of their own free will. Use this resource if for no other reason than to confirm your good judgment. Moving, the birth of a child, even spousal employment can wreak havoc on your financial situation. Nobody plans to fail; they fail to plan. Look at the following sample budget for ideas on setting up your own. Or use it to record your expenses and see if your monthly outgo exceeds your income.

Month of _____

Category	Monthly Budget Amount	Actual Amount	Difference
INCOME:			
Military Income			
Spouse Income			
Moonlighting Income			
Child Support			
INCOME SUBTOTAL			
EXPENSES:			
Mortgage/Rent			
Electric			
Water			
Natural Gas			
Firewood			
Garbage/sewer			
Internet			
Cable TV			
Cell phone			
Landline			
Gasoline			
Groceries			
Eating Out			
Adult Clothing			
Children's Clothing			
Entertainment			
Car Insurance			
Renter's/Homeowner's Insurance			
Personal Property Insurance			
Yard/Garden			
Cleaning Service			
Car Payment			
Parking/Tolls			
Alcohol/Tobacco			
Medical/Dental			

Category	Monthly Budget Amount	Actual Amount	Difference
Health/Beauty			
Daycare			
Subscriptions			
Alimony/Child Support			
Subscriptions			
Credit Card Payments			
Tuition Payments			
Pets			
Charity			
Savings Contributions			
Vacation Account			
Gym Membership			
Sports Activities			
Garage Sales/Auctions			
Misc			
Pocket Money			
Expenses Subtotal			
Net Income (Income-Expenses)			

DEVELOP AN ORGANIZATION SYSTEM

All of the paperwork generated by the items in your budget needs to be stored somewhere. Good money management requires the ability to find receipts, warranties, and other important documents when necessary. Otherwise, you'll spend money duplicating what you have but can't find, won't be able to claim needed benefits because you lack documentation, and will pay late fees. Being organized will also enable you to be more productive, as you won't waste time looking for things. Create an easy, portable filing system by labeling separate hanging folders for all your different needs, and put them in a sturdy box. Choose a size that will fit under the desk or table where you pay your bills. You can also use a filing cabinet, a plastic crate, or an expandable accordion type paper holder. Visit an office supply store for ideas.

In these file folders you should keep official birth, marriage, divorce, adoption, or death certificates; naturalization or adoption papers; custody and visitation papers; immunization records; wills; Social Security cards; car titles; property deeds; safety-deposit box locations and keys; extra house and car keys; passports; savings bonds; computer passwords; creditor phone numbers and addresses; copies of TAD, TDY, or

A plastic box with hanging file folders can be stashed anywhere, and will keep your important documents organized and easy to find.

PCS orders; checking, savings, and brokerage account statements; item receipts; storage/warehouse receipts; documentation of work history; school records; club papers (e.g., soccer, Scouts); "keeper" children's artwork; phone company statements; magazine subscriptions; bills; old check registers; bank statements; product literature (warranties, instruction books); business correspondence; car and house maintenance papers; car, life, and health insurance papers; tax deduction receipts; powers of attorney; property deeds; car titles; and pet records. Record your wallet contents by laying them on a photocopy machine, and place the paper in its own file. All of this has the added benefit of making your household always deployment ready.

INVENTORY YOUR POSSESSIONS

An important item for your organization box is an inventory of your household goods. If they are lost or stolen, it is difficult to claim anything, or even remember what they all were, without records. Take digital photos of everything you own, including the inside of closets and drawers. Photograph the make, model, and serial numbers. Then copy it all onto a CD. Get professional, written appraisals for valuables. This evidence will facilitate any insurance claims you may need to make. Keep them, and receipts, in their own file folder.

SAVING

Develop the habit of depositing something—anything—into a savings account each pay period. Have it withdrawn automatically so you don't set your standard of living to the full paycheck amount, and consider putting it somewhere not readily available with your ATM card. Soon you'll start looking forward to paydays for the sheer pleasure of watching your savings grow. Treat a monthly contribution as a bill instead of an afterthought made if there's anything left over. Build up one month's pay as a buffer against unexpected car repairs, travel expenses, medical cost-shares, and all the other curveballs life throws. Curveballs really shouldn't be a surprise. When people blame them for causing their financial downfall, they are misguided. It's usually the lack of foresight and cushion-building that caused the curveball to send them over the edge.

Emergencies can take a big chunk out of a healthy savings, and if you have no savings, you create stress on your family and start to pile up hard-to-eliminate debt. Once you establish your emergency account, start another for splurging and taking advantage of great sales. Lost opportunities have their cost, too. Let's discuss some simple saving instruments—savings and checking accounts, the Thrift Savings Plan, Treasuries, CDs, and money market accounts—and where to open them.

Save money in a hard-to-access place so you won't be tempted to withdraw it for impulse buys. When you learn that you can live without those buys, your balance will grow.

Before spending, analyze the item on a value continuum. Houses appreciate, cars depreciate, and vacations disappear altogether. A $60 dress will bring $2 at a yard sale. Used furniture has to be practically given away. Anyone who has ever tried to pawn something will testify to the poor resale value of most household goods and jewelry.

The cultural ethic that sums up our lives as "we are what we drive" is created by advertisers—people who want us to feel that whatever we have is not enough. Before taking out a loan, ask yourself if you really want to finance this depreciating asset. Wouldn't you prefer to have that money working for you instead?

BANK ACCOUNTS

There are two main types of bank accounts: checking and savings. They are opened at banks, savings and loans (see glossary), and credit unions. Joint accounts allow two or more people equal access. A popular bank and insurance company with service families is *www.usaa.com*.

Checking Account

This is a service that allows you to deposit money and access it via paper checks, ATM (automated teller machine) cards, or electronic debit cards.

A minimal initial deposit is needed to open a checking account. Fees vary, and many banks offer no-fee, no-frill accounts. Some banks even pay interest when a minimum balance is maintained. If checks are stolen, you can report them to the bank to stop charges to your account. You can also stop payment on a check before it clears. Many people pay their bills online from their accounts, saving postage and practically eliminating the need for paper checks. Some banks even allow you to deposit the check electronically from your home by scanning and uploading it to them.

When a check is written, it is the same as cash and should be considered immediately withdrawn from the account. A "float," that is, the time between deposit and when the funds actually clear is short or nonexistent, as some merchants electronically withdraw the funds immediately. If a check is presented to the bank and there are insufficient funds to honor it, it may "bounce," which means it is returned unpaid to the recipient. You are assessed fees from both the recipient and bank when this happens. So keep a ledger that records all deposits and withdrawals. This information can also be viewed online and on an ATM receipt. You may be able to download this information to Quicken, a popular personal finance software program, or enter it at *www.mint.com*.

Checks are sold by the bank, but independent printers usually sell them cheaper. Two popular ones are at *www.checksunlimited.com* and *www.checksinthemail.com*. But ask your bank if it will accept them first. Not all banks will.

A debit card looks like a credit card and is accepted where credit cards are, but it is not a credit card. When you "charge" with it, the amount is debited directly from your checking account. Know that purchases made with debit cards don't carry the same protections as purchases made with credit cards.

Savings Account
Also called a passbook account, this is a liquid account that provides insurance in case of bank insolvency up to $100,000 per person and $250,000 on retirement accounts. It typically has low or no minimum balance requirements, few fees, and a low interest rate. Savings accounts may have restrictions on number of transactions and provide the owner with a booklet that has each deposit and withdrawal stamped inside it at the time of each in-branch transaction, hence the name passbook.

THRIFT SAVINGS PLAN
To help you save for retirement, the federal government offers the voluntary Thrift Savings Plan (TSP). It offers the same savings and tax benefits that private sector 401(K) plans offer. Unlike the military pension plan, the money in it belongs to the participant no matter how much time is served. It's a defined contribution plan, meaning that the amount of retirement income received depends on how much was contributed over the working years and the return (earnings) those contributions earned. Participants choose from five funds in which to put their money, some being more aggressive and higher risk (with potentially higher reward) than others. A life-cycle fund can also be chosen, which automatically adjusts the risk/ratio of the funds to the age of the participant. Servicemembers in certain specialties who agree to serve on active duty for six years may be eligible for matching contributions during that six-year active-duty obligation.

Any percentage of basic pay can be contributed, but the Internal Revenue Service limits total yearly contributions to $15,500. Contributions are made with before-tax income, which lowers your income for tax purposes. Taxes are deferred on those contributions until withdrawal.

Servicemembers can contribute to the TSP within sixty days of joining the service. After that time, enrollment is done during an annual "open season." However, you can start, stop, or change the amount of your TSP contributions at any time. You can also roll other qualified retirement accounts in which you're already invested into it, and when you leave the service, you can roll the TSP into an eligible retirement account if you want. Since the TSP is for long-term retirement savings, there are penalties for early withdrawal. Visit *www.tsp.gov* for details.

U.S. TREASURY SECURITIES
For short- or long-term savings, U.S. Savings bonds, also called Treasury bonds, are popular. They're debt obligations of the U.S. government, a low-risk savings product that earns competitive interest while protecting you from inflation. There are three kinds:

- *Series EE Bonds*. These are purchased at half their face value. You cannot buy more than $5,000 (face value) during any calendar year. EE bonds increase in value as the interest accrues or accumulates and pay interest for thirty years. When EE bonds "mature," or come due, you are paid your original investment plus all of the interest. They're available in denominations of $100, $200, $500, and $1,000.
- *Series HH Bonds*. You can only purchase these in exchange for Series EE or E bonds and Savings Notes, or with the proceeds from a matured Series HH bond. They are purchased at their face amount in $500 to $10,000 denominations, but there is no limit on the amount you can purchase. These bonds don't increase in value and have a maturity of twenty years.
- *Series I Bonds*. These bonds are sold at face value and grow with inflation-indexed earnings for up to thirty years. You can buy up to $5,000 in any calendar year. They're available in denominations of $50, $75, $100, $200, $500, and $1,000.

Interest earned from bonds is exempt from state or local income taxes, and federal tax can be deferred until the bond is cashed or reaches the end of its interest-bearing life. There are no fees or commissions when you buy them directly from the government. Bonds are mailed to the bondholder and can be replaced if is lost, stolen, or destroyed. Active-duty military can arrange to have their bonds held for safekeeping. You can buy bonds through payroll deduction or at *www.savingsbonds.gov*.

CERTIFICATES OF DEPOSIT (CDS)

A CD is a time deposit with a bank. It can be bought in any denomination, with maturity dates from three months to five years. The interest rate paid is usually slightly higher than the yield for T-bills and varies with the maturity date. Compare interest rates at *www.bankrate.com*. Like all time deposits, the funds may not be withdrawn on demand like those in a checking account without penalty.

MONEY-MARKET ACCOUNTS

In a money-market account, your money is merged with millions of dollars of other people's money. The institution with which you deposited your money uses this large pool to buy short-term government and corporation debt notes, such as certificates of deposit (CDs), treasury bills, and government agency bonds.

Money-market accounts compete with passbook accounts for people's savings funds. The idea behind both is the same: You get back the amount of money you put in plus interest. Money-market accounts, however, also offer a check-writing feature and slightly higher interest, and your share of this interest is credited to your account daily. Unlike bank deposits, money-market accounts aren't federally insured, but the notes they buy have little risk of default.

CREDIT UNION

As an alternative to a bank, most bases have a credit union you can join. The main difference between a bank and a credit union is that anyone can open an account at a bank, but only a select group of people, typically those who share an affiliation (e.g., military, teachers, people who work at a specific employer) can join a credit union. There are credit unions for many different groups of people who share an interest or profession.

A credit union pools deposit money to pay monthly dividends and make loans to its members. The interest on these loans is usually lower than interest on bank loans. Monthly service charges are also lower; in fact, because you receive dividends, you usually earn money on your checking or "share" account each month. Some credit unions offer individual retirement accounts (see glossary) and certificates of deposit, and many service credit unions allow you to remain a member even after you move or leave the service. Popular credit unions with military families are the Pentagon Federal Credit Union, *https://www.penfed.org*, and the Navy Federal Credit Union, *www.navyfcu.org*.

CREDIT

Credit is a loan, a method of purchase that enables you to buy now and pay later. Access to credit is essential in today's economy. Most people cannot afford to buy their homes or cars outright, and possession of a credit card is required for many tasks such as renting cars, booking motel rooms, and cashing checks. Used judiciously, credit can let you avoid carrying large amounts of cash, help out in an emergency, order items over the phone or Internet, take advantage of bargains when you don't have the cash, and pay for multiple purchases with just one check.

There are two major types or credit: installment loans and revolving loans.

Installment Loan

This type of loan is repaid in equal payments, called installments. It's referred to as "buying on time." When you finance goods through the store (the "easy payment plan") you are receiving installment credit. You typically sign a contract, make a down payment, and agree to pay the balance with a specified number of installments, in which finance charges, the costs for granting you the loan, are included. These loans are for single, specific, and expensive purchases. You can use the item while you pay it off over a specified time period, usually several years. The item legally belongs to the lender until the loan is paid off. For example, when you buy a car, the lender holds the title until the last payment is made. The car is the lender's collateral, or security against you defaulting (not paying).

Revolving Loan

You can get access to a noncollateralized, limited amount of money with a revolving loan that you can spend on whatever you want. The most common source of it is the credit card, a financial instrument issued by retailers, banks, and businesses. The major cards are Visa, MasterCard, American Express, and Discover, and they're accepted worldwide, by all sorts of businesses. Nonmajor credit cards are issued and accepted by just one merchant, such as the military STAR card or Sears.

If you're the last person in America who hasn't received an unsolicited application for a major credit card in your mailbox, call any bank and you'll be sent one. You don't need an account there to apply. The local bank doesn't issue the card, it just handles the application. The issuer is a huge bank such as Chase Manhattan or Citibank.

SELECTING A CREDIT CARD

Competition among issuers is intense, and consumers with good credit records can find attractive incentives such as low introductory rates, waived annual fees, annual rebates of a percentage of the total amount spent, or points good for things like Disney vacations, hotel stays, airline tickets, and car purchases. Browse different offers at *www.creditcardguide.com*.

YOUR CREDIT RECORD

Your use of credit will ultimately become an ongoing record with the major U.S. credit-reporting agencies: *www.experian.com*, *www.transunion.com*, and *www.equifax.com*. These agencies document what type of credit you have, how long you've had it, if you're seeking new credit, and how you pay your current credit. Any derogatory notes made about your payment record are included. You'll also find court judgments, spousal employment, and a list of businesses to which you have applied for (and been denied) credit. Based on all this, you'll be assigned a credit score, a number that creditors use when assessing if they want to do business with you. Most lenders use what's called the FICO score, named after the Fair Issac Corp. of San Rafael, California, which developed it. Gender, race, religion, nationality, and marital status are not considered in credit scoring. Eventually bad reports drop off, but it takes about seven years. Credit accounts held jointly with your husband are listed under both names.

Good credit is established by paying your bills on time and not having maxed-out credit cards or debt levels out of proportion to your income. Bill paying must be current—that is, paid each month. Skipping a month and paying double the next month is not the same thing. If you have no credit history and need a loan, you might ask a relative to cosign a debt for you. This means that you make the payments but the cosigner is ultimately responsible in case you default (stop paying). On the flip side, if you are asked to cosign a loan, know that you will be responsible if the person defaults and that the amount will be considered part of your total debt load if you later apply for a mortgage, car, or other loan.

Guard your credit rating. A good one is rewarded with the best offers and terms. A poor one makes life difficult. You may be rejected for a mortgage loan or any other loan at a reasonable rate, landlords may not rent to you, and employers may shun you. (It is legal and common for employers to check the credit records of potential employees. Some check driving records, too.) Know that any company that promises to repair a bad credit rating for a fee is lying. No one can remove bad credit reports that are accurate from your file.

> To calculate your debt-to-income ratio, divide your total monthly debt payments (excluding your mortgage) by your monthly after-tax income. The subsequent percentage is your debt-to-income ratio. If it is under 15 percent, you are managing your credit well. If it's over 20 percent, financial counselors advise getting your spending under control.

What can be done—and you don't have to hire anyone to do it—is to obtain a copy of your credit history and contest derogatory reports that you feel are erroneous. If the report is in error, it is deleted. If not, it stays. Included in your credit history is a record of your employment, debts, and payments.

Review your credit record annually, especially if you have a common name, and at least six months before making a major purchase such as a house. You can get a free annual report from the three bureaus listed earlier at *www.annualcreditreport.com*, phone number 877-322-8228 (it doesn't include your FICO score; a fee is charged for that). If you are turned down for credit, you are entitled to a free report from the agency that supplied the would-be creditor with that information.

> Studies show that people who use credit cards regularly instead of cash spend more on impulse buys as well as on planned items. It's easy to amass credit card debt but it's not so easy to pay it off. If you're just making minimum payments on a high-interest balance, you're making the bank rich but not doing much for yourself.

SECURED CREDIT CARDS

If your credit record makes you ineligible for a regular credit card, you can obtain a secured one. A secured, also called prepaid, credit card account is opened by depositing money into that account, the same way a deposit is made to a bank account. You can use prepaid cards to rent cars and book hotels, although they are often rejected for time payments due to retailer concerns that the money will not be there when the bill arrives. There is no interest charged or monthly bill, but there are fees to set the account up and additional fees each time you deposit more cash into it.

MONEY ORDERS AND CASHIER'S CHECKS

If you want to pay for a purchase via the postal service and a personal check isn't accepted, buy a money order or cashier's check. A money order is a paper that orders a sum of money to be paid to someone else. It's bought for face value plus a fee. Buy money orders cheapest at the U.S. Post Office. They're also available at Western Union, grocery stores, and convenience stores. Because the money order must be paid for in full at the time of purchase, the payee is guaranteed the money will be paid to him.

Most stores have limits for how much someone can make a money order, so for larger amounts, typically $500 or more, buy a cashier's check from a bank. These also have purchase fees. Have cash ready for the full amount, as checks and credit cards are not accepted as payment.

Be careful of who you accept money orders and cashier's checks from. Fakes are favored by scammers who seek to fraudulently purchase items from you. Scammers also relentlessly send out e-mails hoping to find people who will send them cash via Western Union for some phony scheme in return for fake money orders and cashier's checks returned as "payment."

THINGS TO AVOID

Speaking of scams, part of acquiring wealth is knowing how not to get tricked out of it. Here are some things to avoid.

Phishing

Derived from the words *fishing* and *phreaking*, this is an attempt to fraudulently acquire personal data, such as usernames, passwords, and credit card numbers, by pretending to be a trustworthy, well-known company. Phishing is done with messages sent via e-mail, instant messaging and phone texting. The message directs the recipients to websites asking for data. These resemble real merchant and bank sites but are really frauds, down to the faked security lock in the lower right-hand corner.

No legitimate company will ever send you an e-mail soliciting your personal information. Nor are Dutch lotteries and Nigerian oil ministers really seeking to share fortunes with you. Just delete these messages. Don't click on embedded links because they'll take you to sites where malware such as keyloggers and spyware (see glossary) will automatically install on your computer. Malware may also install when you click on pop-up ads, visit fake websites, or download free software. Don't enter personal information in any site you're not 100 percent familiar with. If you're unsure of the website's validity, enter its known address into a new browser window, not the link provided in the e-mail.

Credit Assistance Companies

These promise to repair bad credit ratings or help people with poor credit histories obtain bank loans and major credit cards. Although it isn't against the law for independent companies to charge consumers a fee for putting them in touch with banks that offer Visas and MasterCards or loans, they don't have an inside track on getting them. They just know how to develop mailing lists of consumers who have problems getting credit cards or loans and how to write convincing ads. Once you pay your fee, these companies simply contact a few banks and ask them to send you a credit card or loan application. That doesn't mean that the bank will approve it.

1-900 Phone Numbers

You may have received notices saying that you have won a valuable cash prize or free gift and instructing you to call a 900 number for more information. These are calls that you pay for. Don't confuse them with 800, 877, or 888 numbers, which are toll free. You'll be charged high fees for calls to 900 numbers, or they charge per minute. On the per-minute calls, you'll find yourself on hold, and then be given a lengthy recorded message. Don't expect much of a prize for your trouble.

Phone Solicitors

These "cold-callers" are people who obtain your number from a list they bought, or from a computer that randomly generates numbers, and try to sell you goods or services. Never give your credit card or bank account number to an unsolicited caller, and be wary of solicitors who don't want you to send money via U.S. mail. Scammers don't like the U.S. Postal Service, because mail fraud carries stiff penalties. Thus, they'll often ask you to use Federal Express or another private carrier. One phone scam involves the caller obtaining the numbers of people with a deployed family member and pretends that the family member needs money. These scams prey on public goodwill and a desire to support the troops. Again, don't provide personal or financial information to anyone over the phone, and verify with the family member or the Red Cross if such help is really needed.

Door-to-Door Sales

If you live in an apartment or government quarters, you are probably familiar with door-to-door solicitors, people who sell everything from restaurant discount coupons to auto services. Soliciting is actually prohibited in government quarters, and solicitors should be there by appointment only. They may approach people in common public areas such as the exchange or commissary parking lot; however, soliciting appointments in areas used for processing and housing transient personnel is not permitted.

If you do make an appointment, ask to see the solicitor's permit. Solicitors must be authorized to operate on base. To get this authorization, they undergo a background check. But standards vary for these checks, so final "authorization" really rests with you. Know what you're buying and give yourself a few days to cost-compare. If you're told it's a "one-time only" special, that's often a tip-off to an undesirable product. Good stuff doesn't have to sell this way.

Payday Loans

These short-term loans are for small amounts only, typically $100 to $1,000, due at the next paycheck. No collateral is required, just a steady job, bank account, and ID. The interest rate is unusually high—typically 400 percent to 1,000 percent annualized—and compounds quickly, resulting in you paying back far more than you borrowed. Most people end up taking longer to pay it back, resulting in the original sum plus interest being rolled over into new loans with new charges and interest. Successful payback of the loan isn't reported to credit agencies, and collections are highly aggressive. Payday lenders are outside every base's front gate and online, often advertising themselves as "check cashers," even though they don't cash personal checks. A DoD study found that servicemembers use payday lenders three times as much as civilians. There's no good reason for this. When in need, go to one of the military emergency aid organizations discussed later in this chapter.

Rent-to-Own (RTO)

This type of business rents items, typically furniture, electronics, and appliances, that will eventually be owned by the renter when the rental period is over. No up-front payment is required, but the renter will easily pay four times the product price under such an agreement over a two-year period. As with payday loans, the annualized interest and other fees make this a poor way to purchase a product. If you miss a payment, rent-to-own stores are quick to repossess, leaving you out both the product and money.

Pawn Shops

These business take your personal property as collateral against a small loan. The loan is based on the pawnbroker's appraisal of the property's value. A fee is added to the loan amount, and it's usually due in two weeks. If the loan is not paid back, then the item can be sold by the pawn shop. Or you can renew the loan and pay another fee. Interest rates annualize from 200 to 500 percent, so it's best to avoid them.

Identity Theft

This is the practice of fraudulently obtaining your personal and financial information (birth date, Social Security number, address, name, bank account number). Identity thieves open credit cards, make purchases, obtain jobs, even take out mortgage loans, collect tax returns, and commit crimes in other people's names. We can't make ourselves completely immune to ID theft because, even if we do everything right, personal data can be and has been obtained by hackers who gain access to corporate servers, by dishonest employees who sell it or by "tumblers" who use computers to generate random numbers some of which will work. There have been high-profile examples of government agencies and corporations being victimized. Nevertheless, there are things you can do to minimize identity theft.

- Practice OPSEC (Operational Security) on yourself. Don't carry your Social Security card, birth certificate, or seldom-used credit cards in your wallet. Cover credit cards, checks, and IDs when out to avoid their information being surreptitiously written down or photographed. Don't let a clerk walk away with your ID or credit card for any reason.
- Don't put outgoing mail in a residential box.
- Place fraud alerts on your credit accounts. This requires creditors to follow certain procedures before they open new accounts in your name or make changes to existing ones. Check your credit accounts at least annually to ensure all is in order.
- Be prudent with your information on the Internet. Many people put large amounts of photos and personal data on social networking sites. This, combined with information that is easily obtained from intelligence-gathering sites like *www.intelius.com, www.ussearch.com, or www.pipl.com,* makes you vulnerable. Run your own name through those sites; see what comes up.
- Shred documents with personal information, including preapproved offers for credit, before throwing them out. Shredders can be bought at office supply stores. To remove your name from preapproved credit and insurance offers from the major companies, visit *www.optoutprescreen.com.*
- Never give your Social Security number to anyone except those who have a strict need to know—like the office that signs your paychecks. Some places, like medical offices, don't need it even though they ask for it. Question their need to know.

- Keep current spyware and virus protection on your computer. Use a combination of upper and lowercase letters and numbers for passwords, and change them monthly.
- Don't print your driver's license or Social Security numbers on your checks. Have your first initial instead of your full first name printed.
- Avoid accessing sensitive or password-protected accounts in Internet cafés, especially overseas, since those computers are often infested with keyloggers.

Shred unwanted credit card offers and other sensitive documents before throwing them out, so they can't be found and used.

If you fall victim to identity theft, contact the Federal Trade Commission (FTC) at 877-438-4338. You'll be referred to agencies that can assist you. For example, if your Social Security number has been obtained, you will be directed to the Social Security Administration. Similarly, you may need to contact the United States Postal Service if you suspect your address is being used fraudulently to obtain your mail. Then file a report with your local police. You'll need the police report and the FTC complaint to resolve disputes with creditors.

Military-Affiliated Emergency Aid Organizations

Army Emergency Relief, Air Force Aid, the Navy Relief Society, and Coast Guard Mutual Assistance are private organizations closely connected with the services but not officially part of them. The services give office space and pay salaries for one or two employees, but the money used for aid comes strictly from donations. The mission of these organizations is to provide financial assistance to servicemembers and families in special times of need. Navy Relief provides even more for sailors and marines: It has nursing services for new mothers and homebound retirees; budget counseling; assistance with transportation and housing; and information on benefits, allowances, pensions, and government insurance. It also sponsors thrift shops, distributes infant layettes to needy families, and has waiting rooms where you can leave your children while at a doctor's appointment.

Aid offices will help family members directly as long as the family member has a general power of attorney. (The Navy Relief Society does not require this to help family members.) When you visit one, bring all supporting evidence of need—leave papers, Leave and Earnings Statements, payment books, auto repair estimates, and dental or medical bills. Each case is considered on its own merits, without publicity. When a need is proved, interest-free loans, loan and grant combinations, or outright grants are given. Loans are repaid via paycheck deduction.

Family members of prisoners and deserters are also eligible for assistance, but aid is limited strictly to what is needed to avoid immediate privation, and available only until the servicemember is either given a discharge sentence or dropped from the rolls.

Emergency aid can be given for:

- personal needs in case of nonreceipt or loss of pay
- emergency medical expenses
- travel expenses when emergency leave has been authorized
- expenses in meeting authorized port calls
- initial rent payments or payments to prevent eviction
- purchase of food if you have none and payday is a long way off
- utility deposits or payments to prevent service from being cut off
- expenses for a parent's funeral that the servicemember is required to pay or to help pay

- repairs to a servicemember's private vehicle, or transportation costs when the vehicle is essential for the unit mission
- essential medical or dental bills
- sudden expenses of an unexpected move

Money is not provided for ordinary leave, liberty, or vacations. It is not provided for divorce or marriage fees, civilian court fees, fines, bail, legal fees, bad-check fees, income taxes, or any other outstanding debts. Nor does car insurance or auto licensing count as an emergency. Finally, assistance will not be given on a continuing basis.

If you're in need after hours, try the Red Cross. If there's no relief office from your branch of service nearby, apply with the relief office of another's; they have reciprocal agreements. Don't be embarrassed to use these or any other Family Services offices. These organizations exist because there's a need for them. Along these lines, know that depending on your household income, family size, and children's ages, you may be eligible for WIC, the Department of Agriculture's Women, Infants, and Children's program. WIC provides checks for healthy foods tailored to your family's needs and helps stretch a dollar. The commissary takes WIC coupons. Visit *www.fns.usda.gov/wic/howtoapply* for more information.

INSURANCE

Insurance is a promise of reimbursement in case of loss. There are different kinds; a prudent family buys what it needs and no more. If you don't know anything about insurance and you speak to a persuasive agent, it's easy to buy too much and the wrong type. This is far more common among military families than not having any insurance at all. Most people don't need flight, rental car, or dread disease coverage; collision coverage on a clunker; life insurance for children; life insurance if they don't have children; or credit card/mortgage (the kind that pays off debt if you die). Why? Well, when you buy airline tickets with a credit card you probably get automatic flight insurance through the card. Your auto insurance probably already covers rentals, and your coverage for dread disease is probably already covered via any health or disability insurance. Collision insurance is expensive and if a clunker gets wrecked, replacing it is almost always the best option. There's little point in insuring a non-breadwinning child, and mortgage and credit card debt can be better paid off via a good term life policy.

Life Insurance

Life insurance is protection against financial loss in case of the death of a breadwinner. Its purpose is to enable family members to continue their lifestyle after a breadwinner's death. Figure out how much this sum might be before purchasing a policy. If you're a young, dual-income couple without children and haven't accumulated much debt, your needs may be quite different from a one-income couple with children and a mortgage. This is an example of where a spending journal and written budget are useful. You can't plan for what you'll need if you don't know what you'll need. One way to estimate what you'll need is to multiply your annual income five to ten times, with the resulting number being the amount of coverage needed. You can also find a calculator for this purpose at *www.insurance.va.gov/sglisite/ calcuator/LifeIns101.htm*. The higher the amount of insurance, the higher the premium you'll pay.

Once you figure out how much insurance you need, you must decide what kind of policy to buy. There are two major types of life insurance: whole life (also called permanent or regular) and term.

Whole Life. This protects the beneficiary over his or her entire life, as long as the premiums are paid. When you purchase whole life, you're actually purchasing three separate items: insurance, a savings account, and the ability to borrow money. You build cash value over the life of the policy and eventually pay it off, meaning you still have the coverage but no longer pay for it. Whole life is the most expensive type of insurance.

Term. This protects the beneficiary for a defined period of time, such as ten or twenty years, and expires without any monetary value if the insured survives that time period. Term is the cheapest insurance available. A small monthly premium buys a lot more coverage than a higher whole-life premium. Since no cash value is built, you can't borrow against it. Term is pure insurance. It has no investment features.

Term is further broken down into level and decreasing. Level means that the insured amount remains the same throughout the time period. Decreasing means that the insured amount decreases as you age on the premise that the older you get, the less you need insurance. This is valid, since children grow up and mortgages get paid off. Premiums increase as you age. Many term policies are sold as annually renewable, meaning that the policy cannot be canceled.

A word about affiliation marketing is in order. Many businesses market their financial products, such as insurance or mutual funds, on affiliations, which is a commonality. Professions are an example of an affiliation. When buying, don't let the fact that the agent may be retired military or similarly associated, influence you. Just because this person has an affiliation to you does not mean he or she will act in your best interests. And don't believe any claims that an insurance policy or any other product is "command endorsed" or "command sponsored." Such endorsement would be illegal.

Servicemember's Group Life Insurance (SGLI)

SGLI is a low-cost group life insurance policy available to active duty, ready reservists, cadets and midshipmen of the four service academies, and the Reserve Officer Training Corps. It's available in $50,000 increments up to $400,000. Premiums cost $0.07 per $1,000. SGLI also has a disability extension that allows service-members who are totally disabled at their time of discharge to retain the SGLI coverage they had in service at no cost for up to two years.

Enrollment for the maximum amount is done automatically upon joining the military. Although you can request to opt out, it is the best deal around. There are no eligibility requirements or medical questionnaires to fill out if the insurance is accepted upon joining the military. Premiums cost the same regardless of age and are deducted automatically from the paycheck. It will pay out regardless of what other policies are held. Coverage may be converted to VGLI (Veterans Group Life Insurance) upon retirement. Coverage is the same, but rates are higher and based on age. Individual ready reserve soldiers qualify for Veterans Group Life Insurance (VGLI). Call 800-419-1473 for more information on VGLI or direct questions to the base Finance office.

Make sure that the correct beneficiaries are listed. For instance, many single servicemembers list their parents and don't think to change this when they get married; ex-wives may be beneficiaries, too, if records are not updated.

Family Servicemembers' Group Life Insurance (FSGLI)

This is a policy for spouses and dependent children of members insured under the SGLI program. FSGLI provides up to $100,000 of coverage for spouses, in increments of $10,000. The amount cannot exceed the amount of SGLI the servicemember has. It also offers $10,000 for dependent children at no charge. Enrollment is done automatically upon joining the military, although, like SGLI, you can opt out. Such a policy, however, is useful for stay-at-home moms, since money would be needed for child care and other services that would have to be bought.

War and Aviation Clauses

On any policy you buy, beware of war or aviation clauses. A war clause exempts the insurance company from paying if the insured is killed in war; an aviation clause exempts it if the insured is killed in a plane crash in which he was a crewmember. These clauses are contained in many private policies, including some offered by companies that solicit military personnel. Considering the job, such clauses appear to negate any other desirable factors the policy might have. Before purchasing any insurance, read the policy carefully, note all exemptions, and look for clauses. And cost compare! Prices for life insurance vary drastically.

Auto Insurance

In today's litigious society, one is well advised to buy as much auto insurance coverage as can be afforded. The minimum amount required by each state's laws might not be enough if you're involved in a serious accident. The sum needed for auto liability is often higher than the sum needed for life insurance. Know if your insurance will still cover you when you move overseas or to another stateside location. Insuring your car overseas is much more expensive than it is in the States. Also find out if your policy covers you when driving rentals or someone else's car. Overseas insurers often don't cover that. Finally, when driving a rental car, make sure the model you're driving is covered under your regular auto or credit card policy, as some exclude certain vehicles.

You may lower your insurance premiums by taking the highest possible deductible (the amount you, not the insurer, pays in case of accident). For example, if you have a choice between paying the first $100 or $200 of car repairs, opting to pay the first $200 may be a better choice, as the price for that $100 deductible policy may be greater than the difference in deductibles.

Renter's Insurance

Landlords have insurance on the property they rent, but it doesn't extend to their tenants' personal possessions. A renter's, also called a tenant's policy, protects your personal property from fire, hurricanes, smoke, vandalism, and theft. Policies vary, but they generally cover everything you own whether it's stored at your house, a friend's house, in a storage shed, or another temporary location. (Possessions damaged during government moves are typically excluded.) Renter's insurance also covers you for unintentional bodily injury or property damage to others. Some even pay for legal bills in such cases and medical coverage for nonresidents. A popular company with military families for renter's and other types of insurance is *www.afi.org*.

The Military Personnel and Civilian Employees' Claim Act (PCA)

This is not an insurance policy; rather, it is a payment statute that compensates for personal property that is lost, damaged, or destroyed incident to service. This includes household goods damaged while transferring to an official duty station, while in an authorized storage place, in a government-provided residence, or in an overseas off-base rental. Other places to which the act applies are government offices, unit supply rooms, barracks, and warehouses. Loss or damage to personal property while in the performance of official duties, due to acts of war, riots directed against Americans overseas, or abandonment due to evacuation are included, and you may also be compensated if your automobile is damaged during a move, or by an unusual occurrence like a hailstorm while it's on base. You may even have a claim if property is stolen from it while it's parked on military property, in front of your overseas authorized quarters, or while it's being used for temporary or other military duty. However, any damage that is deemed the result, even partially, from your own negligence isn't included, nor are losses to any land or buildings you may own included.

Coverage is limited to an overall $40,000, with specific limits for individual categories. If you have a private insurer and loss or damage occurs, you must file with that insurer first, but in certain cases the government will pay for the policy's uninsured portion (the deductible).

INVESTING

It is unrealistic to think that the average wage earner can save enough to accumulate wealth; most do not have a large enough income to do that. Inflation and taxes take a large toll on simple savings accounts, money-market accounts, CDs, and savings bonds. So once you've built the financial foundation of a budget, savings, and insurance, you may want to consider investing in securities. Securities are financial instruments. They include certificates of deposit, stocks, mutual fund shares, bonds, and more. Know that investing does involve taking and tolerating risk. But this doesn't mean any risk; it means weighing options and taking action that is appropriate for your situation. For instance, the stock market has risks, but over the long term, history has proven that it provides good returns on wisely invested money. Just ask Warren Buffett, who made his fortune through prudent investing.

There are many books and websites on investing; some references are given at the end of this chapter. You may also visit with a no fee financial planner; visit The National Association of Personal Financial Advisors at *www.napfa.org* or the American Institute of Certified Public Accountants Web at *www.aicpa.org* to find one.

Popular investment securities include stocks and mutual funds. Unlike real estate or collectibles, they are liquid assets, meaning they can be quickly and easily sold at market price. Buy them through brokerage houses such as Charles Schwab or Ameritrade. Brokerages vary in how much they charge for executing trades (as buying stocks and mutual funds is called) and in how much help and what services they offer. Full-service brokerages offer a lot of help, in return for higher fees. Discount brokers offer little help, but have cut-rate fees. Some brokers have extensive online research centers for their customers that allow them to look up prices, histories, and other information for financial instruments they're interested in, and to screen for set criteria.

Stocks

Anyone can own a fractional share of a corporation by buying its stock. A stock is a share in a private company. The stock market is the giant market in which shares are bought and sold. There are several in the U.S., the largest being the New York Stock Exchange. By buying stock, you risk your money on the business's success. If it does succeed, you benefit by being able to sell your piece of it—your stock—at a higher price than you paid. Any business is risky because the future is uncertain, but some are riskier than others; people choose stocks based on the risk they're comfortable with. Generally, the riskier the stock, the greater its potential payoff is. In addition to appreciation, some stocks pay dividends, which are quarterly payments.

Mutual Funds

A mutual fund is a pool of money; as with a money-market fund, millions of dollars from millions of people are put together. But in this case, the fund manager buys stocks or other securities, such as corporate stocks, bonds, short-term money-market instruments, and CDs. Over 7,000 different kinds of mutual funds exist. There are funds that concentrate on gold stocks, oil stocks, junk bonds, Treasury debt, stocks of overseas companies, and socially responsible companies. Some are highly aggressive, meaning they have potentially high payoffs, but carry a larger risk of losing your principle (initial investment). Others are low-risk and have a lower potential payoff. Whatever your goals and needs in a fund are, you can find one that meets them. Remember that when you buy into a mutual fund, you are buying shares of the fund, not the actual financial instruments themselves.

Mutual-fund shares are bought in the hope that they'll increase in value, or for their dividends. They are professionally managed and thus good for people who want to invest but have neither the time nor the knowledge to buy individual stocks on their own.

All funds have a prospectus, which is a brochure that provides information about it. Read it and note the fees. Regardless of what securities they hold, all mutual funds are grouped into three fee types: no-load, low-load, and loaded funds (load means "fee"). No-loads don't charge a fee for buying into the fund. Low-loads charge a small fee, usually around 1 to 3 percent of the purchase price. Loaded funds usually charge 8 percent or more. This 8 percent does not guarantee better money management; in fact, over the years, most no-load and low-load funds have consistently outperformed most loaded ones. Some funds also have maintenance and "backend" (redemption) fees, which are charged when you sell your shares. Combined with a load, they can eat up any profits you might make from share appreciation and dividends. It's important to ask about loads and fees when you are solicited for mutual funds, because the types of funds salespeople offer are usually loaded and full of fees.

In the past few years, hybrid mutual funds called Exchange Traded Funds (ETFs) have hit the market. These are similar to mutual funds except they trade like stocks, so their value fluctuates every minute, instead of each day. There are many different ETFs to choose from, too.

TIPS FROM MONEY-SAVVY MILITARY FAMILIES

"Ask your insurer if you can get a discount by carrying all your policies—auto, life, homeowners—at that office."

"Spend your heyday creating wealth and value. What you do now will impact how you live in your old age. Assess your strengths and weaknesses, then nourish and capitalize on your strengths. Don't spend your heyday time watching TV six hours each day. Why watch others creating wealth and value for themselves?"

"You can fix almost anything with a glue gun and duct tape. One time, when I goofed up the sticky tape on my baby's diaper, instead of throwing the diaper away, I duct-taped it!"

"Keep a Rolodex, address book, or Blackberry containing frequently called business numbers. Enter your account numbers under the phone numbers to make calls to these places more effective."

"Ask about return policies before you buy. Merchants are not legally obligated to take back nondefective merchandise. They do so only to maintain goodwill."

"Ask the commissary and grocery stores what's the best day and time to find 'reduced for quick sale' items. Some stores set out a whole bin of such stuff in the early morning."

"Reflect upon, and analyze your financial decisions. You're going to make mistakes. Everyone does. Learn from them—not everyone does that."

"Visit www.coupons.com or www.coupons.mycoupons.com to download free grocery coupons. When shopping online, do a Google search for that store and "coupon code" to see if there are any codes you can take advantage of."

"Buy large-size clothing at thrift shops and yard sales to use as fabric to sew kids' clothes. Nice buttons and zippers on otherwise ugly clothes can also be cheaply obtained this way. Stock up on fabric and notions during fabric store sales. Since chain fabric stores are chaotic during advertised sales and sell out quickly, visit before the sale date, write down the pattern numbers you want, then go in and get them on the sale date. Or take the ad to Walmart, the exchange, or any other place that matches prices."

"Ask for a military discount. Some theme parks, hotels, car rental agencies, and restaurants offer them. When in Orlando, buy discount Disney, Universal Studios, and Sea World tickets at the Army Shades of Green Hotel."

"To help us save for a vacation, I bought a piggy bank that had to be broken to retrieve the money. This kept us from raiding the bank. When we finally did break it, we found over $300 in small bills and change. This money came mostly from nonpaycheck sources: grocery rebate checks, pop can deposits, consignment sales, reimbursements for paid medical bills. It was money we otherwise wouldn't have saved."

"If a bank or organization turns you down for a loan, it means its confidence in your ability to repay is low. When that happens, don't look for alternate loan sources—reconsider the purchase."

"Carry interlibrary loan cards in your purse, and when browsing in bookstores, jot down the title, ISBN number, author, and publisher of books that interest you. Or go to www.amazon.com, find the book, and cut and paste the information into your library's online request system."

"Buy baskets at yard sales and fill them with free samples to give as gifts. Request free samples at www.thefreesite.com. Try to give gifts that don't cost anything, such as free babysitting."

"If you own a home, perhaps you can get extra income from it by renting out a room, finished basement, or half of a garage for storage."

"Find nice plus-size clothing by putting up a card at a Weight Watchers office bulletin board."

"Search thrift stores on Monday mornings, since many people clean over the weekend and the good stuff goes fast."

"Don't search for satisfaction in your life at the mall, don't try to keep up with TV characters. Wait until the first wave of product hype has passed. People who waited a couple of weeks to buy iPhones paid a lot less than the ones who bought the first week, and they probably paid cash instead of using credit."

"The Tupperware ice pop set is a money-saver. Fill it with fruit cocktail, grape juice, orange juice, chocolate milk, Jell-O, lemonade, pudding, or yogurt to make your own frozen treats."

"Buy toys, cards, and gift wrap when they're on sale and stash them away for children's birthday parties. Buy Christmas gift wrap at 50 percent off the day after Christmas. Make your own cards using free clip art on websites."

"Buy kids' books at yard sales where they're cheap and plentiful."

"Ask if you can do a "pass-through" when buying your next car. On a car trade-in, you don't pay sales tax on the whole price, just on the difference between it and your old car's trade-in price. If you have a private buyer for your car, many dealerships will permit you to sell your car to them. They will then immediately sell it for that price to your private buyer. Technically this is a trade-in to the dealer, so you get that trade-in sales tax break when you purchase another car from the dealer."

"Don't pay to receive your tax refund 'early.' What you're really doing is buying a loan. If you've done without the money all year, why pay to get it a few weeks earlier? And get free tax preparation help from the base legal office."

"Minimize eating out by cooking in quantity and freezing small portions. Keep easy-to-prepare dinners, like good frozen pizzas, on hand for when you're too tired to cook."

"Find nice, cheap frames at yard sales. Throw away the art or embroidery it contains, and put your own art in it."

"When packing kids' lunches, skip the prepackaged snack-size packs. It's much cheaper to buy a large bag of that snack and repackage it yourself into sandwich-size zipper bags."

"Keep an envelope in your car with junk-mail coupons and discounts on movie rentals, dry cleaning, fast food, photo printing, and other services you use regularly or impulsively."

"Buy things before you need them, not when you need them. If you know you'll need tires in six months, start watching sales. When you wait until the last minute, price becomes a secondary consideration. The more costly the item, the further in advance you should plan to buy it."

"Ask your phone company which calling plan is best for your calling patterns. They never tell you; it's up to you to find out. They often don't even advertise their best plans, and there are many different ones.

"*Check out the newspaper classifieds, www.freecycle.com, and www.craigslist.com for ads for used exercise equipment, furniture, and other expensive items. Swap books for the price of postage on www.paperbackswap.com. Swap CDs on www.swapacd.com and DVDs at www.swapadvd.com.*"

"*Saving money isn't all about scoring bargains. Your attitude toward money matters more. Personal finance isn't about getting rich quick, but rather a disciplined execution of lifetime plans.*"

"*Figure out how to make things last longer instead of buying them when you don't have the money. Juggle money to stay out of debt rather than juggle it to buy new things. Anyone can make charges to a credit card. It takes no creativity for that.*"

"*Brainstorm ideas for pocket money. Tutor math or Spanish; put your name on tutor lists at the local schools and community colleges. Ask about substitute teaching; you don't always have to be a certified teacher. Sit for children, plants, pets, and houses. Charge to polish boots and iron uniforms for servicemembers who hate doing it. Arrange your schedule to accommodate dual-income families who want to come home to a clean home and a ready-made dinner. Offer sewing services or give sewing lessons. Teach music lessons, scrapbooking, faux finish painting, wallpaper hanging, or cake decorating. Teach dancing to children. Run errands for the homebound. Sell things for others on auction sites. Don't underestimate what you can do; a skill you consider mundane may be valuable to someone else.*"

MONEY CONSIDERATIONS FOR RESERVISTS

- Reserve families may claim a child-care tax credit if someone must be paid to babysit while the reservist drills. To qualify, the children must be under fifteen years old or disabled, and the spouse must be working or attending school full-time.
- Reservists may stay for free in government lodging while drilling. Off-base lodging is not reimbursed, but such expenses associated with drills may be tax-deductible.
- If you have a round-trip ticket for annual training and plan to use just the return portion of it, contact the airline with your plans. If you don't use the front-end part of a round-trip ticket, the airline considers you a "no-show" and will cancel your return reservation.
- Mileage to get to training exercises is not reimbursed unless the orders specifically state so. In that case, you are reimbursed per mile. If you are on group travel orders and elect to travel by yourself for personal convenience, you will not be reimbursed for mileage.
- Reservists are entitled to advance pay if ordered to active duty for at least 140 days. This interest-free loan must be repaid monthly before the active-duty tour ends.

BASE THRIFT SHOP

Thrift shops located on bases are resale shops that sell on consignment, meaning you retain ownership of the item until it sells, and receive most of the sale price. Investigate it for low-cost necessities. Bookcases, sofa beds, vacuum cleaners, irons, plants, and baby items are just a sample of what you might find. The thrift shop is a hit-or-miss place; sometimes you'll find junk, and sometimes it's golden. If you go once and are not impressed, try again another day. Someone about to make a permanent-change-of-station move might have brought in a load that contains just what you're looking for. Overseas, the thrift shop is the first place to check for transformers and 220V appliances from people who moved back to the States.

Low-price, useful items sell quickly. The thrift shop accepts items on consignment only and keeps between 10 and 25 percent of the selling price. This compares favorably with private consignment shops, which generally keep 40 to 60 percent. You must reclaim any unsold items after the specified time on your contract, or they become the property of the thrift shop. Clothes with rips, stains, broken zippers, or frayed collars are not accepted, and toys and appliances must be in working order. Because of space constraints, there's a limit to how many items you may consign at one time, but these limits are expanded if you're making a permanent-change-of-station move. Bring them a copy of your PCS orders, and a stamped, self-addressed envelope so the shop can forward the proceeds.

SCHOLARSHIP MONEY FOR CHILDREN

One of the largest expenses many families have is financing college for their children. Some financing avenues for spouses were discussed in chapter 4, and servicemembers can learn about their many options from the base education office. There are organizations that have scholarships specifically for military children. Here are a few. Additionally, look at the Tricare Supplemental Insurance policy list in the appendix to research which other organizations have scholarships; some of the military-affiliated ones offer scholarships for children of members.

> *Military Relief Societies* discussed earlier in this chapter have finance and scholarship programs for military children. Visit their websites at *www.aerhq.org*, *www.afas.org/*, *www.cgmahq.org/*, and *www.nmcrs.org/*.

> *Defense Commissary Agency (DeCa)* has a scholarship program for college-bound military children. Qualified children of U.S. military ID cardholders—active duty, retirees, reserve, and survivors of deceased servicemembers—may apply for a $1,500 scholarship, funded by vendors who provide goods to commissaries worldwide. Applications are available at your local commissary or at *www.militaryscholar.org*.

> The *Air Force Sergeants Association (AFSA)* and *Airmen Memorial Foundation (AMF)* have a joint scholarship program that assists eligible, dependent children of the Total Air Force with undergraduate studies. Visit *www.afsahq.org//AM/Template.cfm?Section=Home*.

The *American Legion* has a scholarship program for children of military parents killed on active duty. Visit *www.legion.org*.

The *Chief Warrant and Warrant Officer's Association* has scholarships for members' children (*www.cwoauscg.org/benefits.htm*).

IT'S UP TO YOU

Service families work hard for their money, and servicemembers take great risks for it. Therefore, we are obliged to spend and invest in the best ways possible. Others may assert that they know the "special needs of military money," but there really is no such thing. Aside from the unique risks and sacrifices service families make to earn it, this money is no different from the money that anyone else earns, and it needs to work for us the same way that the money of lawyers, accountants, and business owners work for them. So research all purchases, and consider how they affect your goals. No one cares as much about your financial well-being as you do.

FURTHER READING

Books

Belknap, Margaret, and Michael Marty. *Armed Forces Guide to Personal Financial Planning*, 6th edition. Mechanicsburg, PA: Stackpole Books, 2007.

Canfield, Jack. *The Success Principles: How to Get from Where You Are to Where You Want to Be*. New York: Collins, 2006.

Chatzky, Jean. *You Don't Have to Be Rich: Comfort, Happiness and Financial Security on Your Own Terms*. New York: Penguin, 2003.

Kiyosaki, Robert. *Rich Dad, Poor Dad: What the Rich Teach Their Kids about Money—That the Poor and Middle Class Do Not!* New York: Warner Books, 1998.

Lowe, Janet. *Warren Buffett Speaks: Wit and Wisdom from the World's Greatest Investor*. Hoboken, NJ: Wiley, 2007.

Mundis, Jerrold. *How to Get Out of Debt, Stay Out of Debt, and Live Prosperously*. New York: Bantam Books, 2003.

Stanley, Thomas J., and William D. Danko. *The Millionaire Next Door: The Surprising Secrets of America's Wealthy*. New York: Pocket Books, 2000.

Stein, Ben, and Phil DeMuth. *Yes, You Can Still Retire Comfortably! The Baby-Boom Retirement Crisis and How to Beat It*. Carlsbad, CA: New Beginnings Press, 2005.

Trump, Donald, and Robert Kiyosaki. *Why We Want You to Be Rich: Two Men, One Message*. Jackson, WY: Rich Press, 2006.

Walsh, Peter. *It's All Too Much: An Easy Plan for Living a Richer Life with Less Stuff*. New York: Free Press, 2007.

Internet Resources

www.ssa.gov. Social Security online. Contains information on planning your retirement, calculators, and more.

allrecipes.com. Lots of food ideas here.

www.orbitz.com, www.kayak.com, www.cheaptickets.com, www.priceline.com, www.hotwire.com, www.travelocity.com, www.webflyer.com, www.farecast.com/, www.travelzoo.com. Good sites for discount airline tickets, hotel rooms, rental cars, and other bargains.

www.GSAauctions.gov. Auction site run by the U.S. General Services Administration. Bid on cars and government surplus items.

www.google.com/products. Online shopping tool.

www.epinions.com. User reviews of millions of products and services.

www.aaii.com. American Association of Individual Investors. Contains lots of investment information.

www.idtheftcenter.org. Learn ways to prevent identity theft and deal with it when it occurs.

www.nfcc.org. National Foundation for Credit Counseling. Provides education and counseling services.

www.about.com, www.wisegeek.com. Lots of information and answers to common questions at these sites.

www.militarysaves.org. This website was created by the DoD for the military community. Contains information about debt reduction, money management, scams, banned financial advisors, and more.

www.Soldierfoundation.org. This foundation was created to assist servicemembers on extended duty and their families. The website has lots of information on education, family life, employment, and personal finance.

www.flylady.com. Popular site on organizing a household.

www.knowyourstuff.org. Download free home-inventory software here.

www.militarymoney.com. Financial website geared to military personnel.

www.kbb.com. Kelly Blue Book. Check the value of your car.

www.irs.gov/newsroom/article/0,,id=118104,00.html. Information on the Military Family Tax Relief Act of 2003.

www.indexcreditcards.com. Comprehensive list of credit card offers.

currentcodes.com, www.hotcouponworld.com/forums/index.php. Promotional discount codes and coupons.

www.insurance.va.gov/sglisite/SGLI/SGLI.htm. Information on SGLI and VGLI.

www.paypal.com. Popular payment system for online transactions.

6

Making a Home

Home is where you're sent! Military families live, love, and laugh in Washington D.C.; Anchorage, Alaska; Leavenworth, Kansas; and all over the world. This chapter discusses how to make a house a home wherever you are.

HOUSING OPTIONS

Living in government quarters, renting an apartment, or buying property are the options most relevant to military families. Visit the Housing office upon your arrival to a new base, even if you don't plan to live in quarters. It will have a list of landlords who have established good relations with military tenants. This stop will also clear you to live off base. Make your decision about where to live carefully, as the military will pay only for moves from duty station to duty station, not for moves in between.

BASE HOUSING

Base housing, also called quarters, is open to servicemembers who are living with their family members, and who have accompanied orders for that duty sta-

An Army family poses for a studio portrait circa 1910. Photo courtesy the Frontier Army Museum, Ft. Leavenworth, KS

135

tion. It is owned by the DoD or leased from private owners, who rent entirely to military families. (Such housing may even have other tenants from a DoD-approved list if the owner cannot fill the rentals with military families. In this case, you might find military retirees and civilian employees as your neighbors.) Most housing is on base, but some is not. Rent charged is the tenant's housing allowance and paid by allotment. Type and condition of housing varies with location. It may be a house with a yard. It may have a basement and storage shed. Some quarters are multistory apartments, condos, townhomes, duplexes, fourplexes, or eightplexes. Floor plans, appliances, window sizes, closet space, and construction type vary. Officer and enlisted families live in separate areas, and there are separate areas for junior and senior members. You may look at the outside of housing before deciding if you want it, but the inside isn't available for viewing. More information, and photos of some housing areas, can be found at *https://onestop.army.mil*, *www.housing.navy.mil/onestop*, and *www.afcrossroads.com*.

Junior enlisted housing at Pope Air Force Base, North Carolina. These are 1,500 square foot duplexes. Photo courtesy of the Department of Defense.

Many Housing offices allow you to apply for quarters before you move. You mail in an application and a copy of the PCS orders. Know that demand for housing is usually higher than supply, in which case you'll be put on a wait list. You can be on this list for a year or longer. Your place on the list is set by the date the application was received, your estimated time of arrival, the number of bedrooms required (this is based on family size and age of children), and servicemember rank (senior and junior personnel are put on different wait lists). The housing office can help arrange temporary lodging, if needed.

Quarters are not assigned on income or personal need. People in key jobs are usually required to live on base. Recruiters and others on independent duty can live in the quarters of sister services. In some instances, if quarters are available, you may be required to live in them or forfeit your housing allowance.

New recruits may be eligible for base housing once they finish basic training. They will attend school after that training, and receipt of accompanied orders will depend on how long the school is. If the school is short, housing eligibility will not occur until orders are received for the first duty station, assuming that duty station is an accompanied one.

Considerations for Living in Base Housing

Yardwork. Mowing, raking, weeding, and sidewalk shoveling may be handled by installation maintenance, but sometimes it will be your responsibility. If the latter, you will be held to strict standards for what the exterior should look like, and be ticketed or even asked to leave if that standard is not met.

Pets. You're limited to two pets per household (excluding fish, birds, and small, caged animals).

Quarters Must Be Occupied. If the servicemember is deployed and the family leaves to live elsewhere for several months, the quarters may be forfeited.

Rent and Utilities. You are not charged rent or utilities except for the phone and cable TV. When things break, the base engineers fix them at no charge. But quarters are not free; a servicemember pays for them by forfeiting his housing allowance. Higher-ranking families pay more for the same set of quarters than lower-ranking families because they give up a greater allowance; if they're childless, they'll probably even have smaller quarters. Some bases send out "mock bills" showing average costs, and may charge occupants for overages.

Furnishings. Most quarters are unfurnished. Washers and dryers usually are not provided, although hookups may be. Many quarters have a communal laundry area or conveniently located laundromat. Overseas, older quarters have 220V outlets, but newer ones will have 110V outlets. You will be charged for any damage to housing-provided furniture and appliances.

Proximity. Quarters are close to work, base facilities, and to other families.

Condition. You will be asked to return a signed inventory sheet soon after moving in. Check the condition of everything carefully before returning that sheet. Look at the draperies, carpet, doors, inside cabinets, and note every countertop chip, screen door tear, furniture scratch, window crack, carpet rip, and wall dent. When you clear (vacate) quarters, you'll be held responsible for everything on that list and its condition, whether it was actually present or not, and be charged for missing items or damage that wasn't noted at move-in. Clearing quarters involves cleaning them to strict standards, discussed in chapter 7.

Schools. DDESS (discussed in chapter 2) operates sixty-four schools on sixteen installations, with a total population of about 24,000 students. You typically have to live on base for your children to attend one.

Some comments from quarters occupants:

"I like how close we are to everything! Especially with gas prices what they are now. My husband comes home for lunch everyday and sometimes for an hour after PT. We are only minutes from the gym, PX, and commissary."

"I feel safer here. I don't worry about the kids leaving their bikes out or the water bottles on the front porch. There are also plenty of other kids in the neighborhood that they can play with and they have their choice of five different playgrounds in the immediate area."

"I like being surrounded by people who know what I'm going through, especially during a deployment. We don't know each other that well, but we are comfortable knocking on each other's doors if we need help."

"Call in a work order for anything that's broken before you move out, so you're not asked to pay for it."

OFF-BASE RENTAL

Rental apartments or houses are common options when quarters are unavailable. (Or even if they are, some people feel they can purchase a nicer environment for the money off base). Off-base housing, called "living on the economy" enables you to mix with the local population and better experience different localities. Overseas, it gives an authentic flavor of what life in another country is like, something not obtainable in the "little America" islands of government housing.

Choosing a Rental Location

Some wives send their husbands out alone to scout places and sign a lease. Since you may be unhappy with what he finds, try to accompany him to give input. Read the Yellow Pages for free rental locator services, or visit *www.rentals.com* or *www.apartment.com*. These are businesses that maintain free, searchable databases of local rentals and receive commissions from landlords when they place someone.

Considerations in Rental Living

Location. Is your rental near base, or near the facilities that you use? Are you near grocery stores, churches, fitness centers, malls? If you don't have a car, are you near a bus stop? What is the neighborhood like? Does it appear well kept and safe? Who lives nearby? Visit it at different times of the day to assess noise, neighbors, and traffic.

Schools. School district boundaries influence the residence decisions of most families with school-age children. You may find that you're asked to complete a lengthy questionnaire before enrolling your children. This is so the town may receive impact aid, which is federal money given to school districts whose tax bases cannot absorb the economic impact of military children.

Condition. Is the property well kept? Is there lots of natural light inside? Is it freshly painted and clean? Or are there leaky pipes, smelly drains and garbage disposals, mildewed surfaces, exposed wiring, torn screens, stained carpet, and old appliances? These are indications of poor upkeep. Is there a microwave, refrigerator, fireplace, balcony? Do all appliances work? Does the place have cable TV, high-speed Internet, and washer/dryer hookups? Storage areas? Smoke detectors? Dead-bolt locks? Is there adequate soundproofing between units? As with quarters, carefully record the contents and condition of the rental on an inventory sheet to protect yourself at clearing time. If the landlord doesn't have an inventory sheet, obtain one at the base housing office. Ask for any broken or missing items to be repaired or replaced before signing the lease. Note all items that are worn, damaged, or missing, and have the form signed by both you and the landlord.

Yard and Amenities. Who is responsible for yard work? Are the playground, swimming pool, party room, and other amenities nice? Is there outdoor lighting and convenient parking?

The Lease

A lease is usually required for a rental. It is a legal document, a contract agreement between you and the landlord. A comprehensive lease describes the following:

- the number of people who will live there and who they are
- the minimum amount of time you will live there
- rent charged, when it is due, and fees for late payments
- what utilities you'll pay
- pet restrictions, deposits, and charges
- cleaning upon vacating charges
- the upkeep for which you're responsible
- what constitutes damage and what is regular wear and tear
- the times when the landlord may enter and show the property
- security deposit

Read the lease carefully. If you don't understand it, ask someone at the base legal office to review and explain it. Negotiate points with which you have a problem. In a slow market rent, lease time, and incentives (e.g., one month's free rent), are flexible, and make sure any written changes in the lease are initialed by both you and the landlord. You may be able to negotiate more favorable lease terms if you offer to stay there longer than the lease requires. Some landlords will provide paint or other supplies to make small changes.

Most leases require a security deposit, and some require the first and last months' rent. Advance pay can be useful for this. Ordinary wear-and-tear charges may be deducted from the last month's rent. Alternatives to full rent payment might include tenants providing yard or handiwork. Some military spouses have served as resident managers in return for free rent. Use foresight when signing a lease; if you plan to expand your family, don't sign a long-term lease on a one-bedroom apartment. Know that most leases do not permit subletting, or allowing people the landlord hasn't contracted with, to live in your housing instead of you.

Consider purchasing renter's insurance, discussed in chapter 5. What would it cost to replace your furniture, electronics, clothing—the contents of all your cabinets, closets, and drawers? Most people could not afford to replace all these at once. An uninsured burglary or fire can have a large negative impact on your finances. For those living overseas, if your car is burglarized or damaged while on government property, or if your housing office–approved rental is burglarized, you may be able to file a claim against the government under the Military Personnel and Civilian Employees' Claims Act (PCA), also discussed in chapter 5.

If you really prefer to live in quarters but the wait is long, look for a month-to-month lease on a furnished apartment, and arrange with the transportation office to keep your household goods in storage. Servicemembers who make mid-month moves continue to receive their BHA or OHA for up to thirty days after they move into quarters to help offset the effects of breaking a lease.

The Military Clause

Any lease you sign should include this provision. It's a condition that releases you from the lease obligation in case of permanent-change-of-station orders, deployment, or if the servicemember is killed or missing in action. A typical one looks like this:

Military Clause Addendum

IN THE EVENT the Tenant is or hereafter becomes, a member of the United States Armed Forces on extended active duty and hereafter the Tenant receives permanent change of station orders to depart from the area where the Premises are located, or is relieved from active duty, retires or separates from the military, or is ordered into military housing, or is deployed for more than 90 days, then in any of these events, the Tenant may terminate this lease upon giving thirty (30) days written notice to the Landlord. The Tenant shall also provide to the Landlord a copy of the official orders or a letter signed by the tenant's commanding officer, reflecting the change which warrants termination under this clause. The Tenant will pay prorated rent for any days (he/she) occupies the dwelling past the first day of the month.

The damage/security deposit will be promptly returned to the tenant, provided there are no damages to the premises.

TENANT DATE

CO-TENANT DATE

LANDLORD/AGENT DATE

The clause has limitations. For instance, it doesn't apply to renters who wish to move simply to go on base or buy a home. It may not apply if the PCS move is less than fifty miles or for less than ninety-day temporary duty orders. Some states don't require a clause for landlords who offer only four-, six-, eight-, or twelve-unit dwellings. Some leases have had clauses that covered the military member, but not anyone living with him. If you are unclear of the wording in your lease, take it to the base legal office. Also know that the clause doesn't release you from properly cleaning the premises, and requires a thirty-day written notice.

MORTGAGE LOANS

Buying a house is beyond the scope of this book; if you're considering such a purchase, read some of the many books available on the subject. What we'll discuss here are financing options open to servicemembers.

Unless you have the money to pay cash, you'll need to finance your house with a mortgage loan. This is a lien on a property or house that secures the loan and is paid in installments over a set period of time. The mortgage secures your promise that you'll repay the money borrowed to buy your home. Banks, mortgage companies, credit unions, savings and loans, even insurance companies all offer mortgage loans. Comparison-shop by visiting a mortgage broker in your area. She or he will have information on loans offered by companies all over the country. Consult the yellow pages or search the Internet for online mortgage brokers. Interest rates, down payment required, and fees will vary.

Your credit history will be checked. The computers tell all; a bad history cannot be hidden. If you have unpaid debts or are overextended on current ones, obtaining a mortgage loan at a favorable rate will be difficult. Subprime mortgage lenders—lenders who cater to people with spotty credit histories—might accommodate you at a higher cost. But even those lenders have gotten much tougher now, due to rampant defaults from borrowers who bought homes they realistically couldn't afford.

It will be helpful if your financial records are organized, because detailed documentation is required, especially for first-time buyers. You'll be asked to supply Leave and Earnings Statements, bank and brokerage statements, references from landlords and/or utility companies on your bill-paying history, and proof of past employment. You'll also need your VA Certificate of Eligibility if you're using a VA-guaranteed loan.

There are many types of mortgage loans—Department of Veterans Affairs (VA), Federal Housing Authority (FHA), owner-financed, adjustable rate, balloon, and more—but all are obtained the same way: by going to a lender and applying. We'll discuss VA, FHA, conventional loans, and adjustable rate mortgages (ARM), as they are the most practical for most military families.

Department of Veterans Affairs Loans
The VA loan is a product of the Serviceman's Readjustment Act of 1946, designed to help servicemembers settle back into civilian life. Active-duty personnel, veterans, and reservists with six years of service or ninety days of active-duty service during wartime are eligible. IRR service does not count.

The word *loan* is actually a misnomer. The VA guarantees 80 percent of the loan. The money comes from a bank or other lender, and if the borrower defaults, the lender can collect the amount guaranteed from the VA. Since this greatly lowers its risk, a lender will lend to people it might otherwise turn down.

A VA loan can be used to buy a house, townhouse, condominium, co-op, mobile home (with or without a lot). It can be used for a farm if the property contains a residence and the owner lives in that residence. Commercial property may not be bought; however, a multi-tenant property of up to four separate units may be bought if the veteran occupies one of the units. As long as the purchase price doesn't exceed the home's appraised value, the VA doesn't require a down payment. The VA also doesn't require principal and mortgage insurance (PMI), a type of insurance which protects the lender in the event the borrower defaults on the loan. All other loan types require PMI when the borrower's down payment is less than 20 percent of the purchase price. Its premium is included in the monthly mortgage payment.

Generally, banks won't loan more than $417,000 on a VA loan ($625,000 in Hawaii, Alaska, Guam, and the U.S. Virgin Islands), unless the buyer makes up the difference with out-of-pocket funds. Those funds cannot come from a separate loan. Otherwise, the whole purchase price, including closing costs, can be financed. You may choose from among fifteen-year, thirty-year, or adjustable-rate loans.

VA loans are assumable, meaning they may be passed on to a subsequent buyer of that home, if the VA approves that buyer's credit. This is a selling point if your loan is at a lower interest rate than what the buyer can get. If you do let someone assume your VA loan, make sure you and the buyer sign papers releasing you from the VA obligation, as failure to do this will make you ultimately responsible for the loan until it's paid off. Know that your eligibility for a future VA loan guarantee will be lessened or even revoked until the person who assumed your loan pays it off, unless he eventually replaces your VA eligibility with his own VA eligibility. You may get as many VA loans as you want up to the total amount the VA will guarantee for your financial situation.

VA loans charge a funding fee that is required by law. A first-time buyer will pay 2 percent of the loan amount for a "no-money-down" loan, and a second-time buyer's fee is just above 3 percent. The fee's purpose is to reduce taxpayer burden by asking the servicemember or veteran to contribute to the cost of his VA mortgage. The higher fee for second-time borrowers presumes that there is equity in the home, or the borrower has had time to save. The funding fee is also charged on VA refinance loans.

FHA Loans

The Federal Housing Authority loan program began in 1934 to give people of limited income a chance to buy homes. Again, the word *loan* is a misnomer. The FHA guarantees most of the loan, but the money comes from the lender. A 3 percent down payment is needed, and borrowers must purchase insurance against default. The buyer must also fund closing costs. (The Coast Guard Mutual Aid Association and the Air Force Aid Society make loans to their members to cover closing costs.) The maximum mortgage amount that the FHA will guarantee varies greatly by area, due to the disparity in local property values.

The FHA sets a ceiling on interest that the lender may charge, and the rate is usually lower than that of a conventional loan. Like the VA, the FHA doesn't set a maximum purchase price, but the lender usually does. The Coast Guard will pay the mortgage insurance premiums for its members who purchase homes with FHA loans.

Conventional Loans

People who are not eligible for, or don't want, the VA or FHA loan may apply for a conventional loan. This is any mortgage loan other than VA or FHA. A conventional loan may be needed if the purchase price exceeds what the VA or FHA will guarantee. A down payment is usually required, although many banks accept a down payment as low as 1 to 3 percent of the loan amount. Private mortgage insurance (PMI) is required until 20 percent equity (see glossary) in the property is reached, at which point you can apply to have those premiums removed. Conventional loans may be more advantageous to the buyer who can afford a 20 percent down payment, since there is no funding fee like what the VA charges, and interest rates are often lower. They may also be more advantageous if you plan to keep the house for many years, since you won't have to worry about interest rate changes.

All loan types may be set up to be paid off in ten, fifteen, or thirty years. In certain high-cost parts of the country, some banks even set up forty-year loans. A fifteen-year mortgage will have relatively high payments, but save you a great deal of interest over the life of the loan. Longer term loans have cheaper monthly payments.

Adjustable Rate Loan (ARM)

The ARM is a mortgage loan that changes when interest rates change. Your monthly payments will increase or decrease at intervals determined by the lender. The change in monthly payment amount, however, is usually subject to a cap. The advantage of an adjustable rate is that the interest rate is below market for the first few years before it increases. If you plan to move in a few years, this is a feature worth taking advantage of. If you plan to retire in the house, it may not be, since you may find it difficult to meet the monthly payment if the loan resets to an unanticipated high rate.

Other Loans

Many states, cities, and counties operate special loan programs for specific markets: first-time homebuyers, low-income families, people with bad credit, immigrants, people who want to borrow without disclosing their income, and homeowners who want to buy second homes or investment properties. Ask a realtor or banker what programs are available in your area.

BEING A GOOD NEIGHBOR

Once you're in your home, you will probably find yourself surrounded with neighbors. Some people form lifelong friendships with them. Others find getting along a major problem. Although there are many reasons for arguments, most can be blamed on inflexibility and lack of communication.

No two families live alike. Some families sleep late on weekends, others don't; some have children, others don't; and everyone has different ideas about cleanliness, loud music, and parenting styles. It's important to acknowledge that in any multitenant situation.

Lack of communication can escalate the pettiest problem into an unnecessary incident. If another resident is doing something that bothers you, tell her. Knock on her door, be friendly, explain the problem and why it's affecting you. Calm, rational assertions often bring calm, rational solutions. Pounding on the ceiling, shouting out the window, and running to the building supervisor create animosity. Sometimes the person is not even aware that what she's doing is annoying you, and if you never speak up, she'll never know. If the problem can't be worked out between the two of you, use your housing area chain of command. A family member who is a chronic problem or a danger to others in the community can cause the whole family to lose housing privileges.

Some common courtesies when living in a multitenant building are:
- Be aware that sounds echo inside stairwell-type buildings. The sound of slamming doors and clomping up and down stairs is magnified.
- Be careful with your language when outside. Many families don't appreciate having their children listen to cursing.

- Do not play music so loud that it can be heard outside your front door. When it reaches that level, it vibrates the floors and walls of other units.
- If you live on an upper floor, do not roller-blade, bounce basketballs, or do other activities that create noise on the ceiling of the family below.
- Be aware that the construction in many multifamily dwellings isn't the highest quality and that voices carry through walls and ductwork. Don't argue in the bathroom or near open doors, windows, or air vents.
- Do not honk your horn when arriving to pick someone up. Call them on your cell phone, or ring their doorbell.
- Many civilians have unrealistic ideas about your privileges, such as what you can buy at the exchange and PX. Don't brag about your military benefits. There's no point, and it doesn't make for good neighbor relations.

Finally, make friends with your neighbors. While everyone wants to avoid drama queens and troublemakers, if the neighbor downstairs stops by for a chat, invite her in. Housework will always be there, but good friends are hard to find. Being friendly with your neighbors will make them more tolerant of things you do that bother them. When you move into a building, take advantage of your newcomer's prerogative and introduce yourself. Do the same thing when someone else moves in. Many people are too shy to introduce themselves but appreciate it when someone else does.

MAKING A HOUSE A HOME

Just because you are transient doesn't mean you have to live in surroundings you don't like. There are lots of books and websites on the subjects of budget and apartment decorating. Sites to start at include *www.diynetwork.com, www.marthastewart.com, www.hgtv.com,* and *www.rentaldecorating.com.* Meanwhile, here are some ideas for creating a space to enjoy.

- Pick a scheme of your favorite three or four colors and patterns, and build on it. This will pull your rooms together and enable you to interchange furniture, window treatments, and rugs from move to move.
- Buy colorful area rugs. Select ones of heavy wool to withstand a lot of traffic. Turn them occasionally so they'll wear evenly.
- Search thrift shops, garage sales, online auctions, flea markets, antique stores, and salvage stores for offbeat items at bargain prices.
- Unfinished furniture is inexpensive, and shops that sell it often hold free classes on staining and antiquing it.
- Faux-finish painting gives an expensive, custom look to a wall. Paint can be applied with sponges and rags for marbled effects. Paint stores and building supply stores often hold free classes in these techniques. Buy a large piece of gypsum board on which to experiment.

- In the kitchen, contact paper is a nice cover-up for ugly cabinets (remove the hardware before applying) and window ledges.
- Nonadhesive shelf liner is easier to use than the adhesive-backed type. Tape it down. You won't have to scrub shelves when you leave, which makes it easier to clear quarters.
- Mix and match old wooden chairs around a kitchen table, paint with bright colors, and spray lacquer for gloss.
- Don't skimp on your bed. A cheap mattress full of lumps and sags is not a bargain. Buy the best box spring and mattress you can afford. You can always buy the head- and footboards later.
- Put up nice window treatments. Bright blinds, valences, and curtains dress up a window and brighten a room that must remain "rental white." If you sew, make your own draperies and leave large hems for future adjustments, or puddle the extra fabric on the floor for a luxuriant look. For a valance, wrap material around a curtain rod, or quilting and fabric around a board. The advantage of the board-type valance is that if the windows are longer at the next place, you can hang the curtain rod lower and it will still be hidden.
- Unpack your boxes. Nothing says "temporary" like unpacked boxes piled to the ceiling. If they're packed for the whole tour, maybe you don't need the contents anymore.
- Freshen up tired rooms with new lampshades and throw pillows. Steam-clean your carpet and upholstery. That alone can make a big difference.
- Space in quarters kitchens is never generous, but to maximize it, store spices on a wall-mounted rack, use hanging baskets for fruits and veggies, hang pegboards on cabinet doors, hang mugs from racks, and use wall-mounted shelves for small kitchen tools. Keep cereal and spaghetti in pretty plastic containers on your countertops.
- Hang up your art and photographs. Group photos in a collage.
- Plastic shower curtains are made with all sorts of motifs. A jungle or underwater scene livens up a small bath.
- Use baskets to hold magazines, cosmetics, mail, and baby toys. Place one near the door to hold sunglasses and keys. Big baskets placed under sideboards and coffee tables utilize "underneath" space and hide a lot of stuff.
- Decorate a child's room with a theme from a favorite movie. Ask your movie store or the movie section in a local grocery store to save the posters for you when they are taken down. Travel agencies and airlines can be another source for free posters.

- Sofa beds can serve as your bed when you are first married and as a guest bed later.
- Lidded Rubbermaid tubs make good storage containers. Keep Christmas ornaments in them, military trinkets, occasionally used kitchen gadgets, papers, and baseball cards.

Whether you're living in a new apartment, old quarters, or your own house, you can create a home you enjoy and are proud to show off.

HAPPY FAMILIES

Getting into and fixing up a home is just part of what makes a family happy. Here are comments from military families about what they do inside those homes to make them happy and maintain harmony.

"*At each place we rent, I plant a shrub, small tree or flowering perennial as a reminder that my family was there.*"

"*We buy Christmas ornaments at each place we live and vacation.*"

"*I'm a stay-at-home, homeschooling mom with two small boys. I don't drive, so we're home most of the time. We're lucky to live in a nice neighborhood with a large park, a library, and a rain-forest conservatory within walking distance. Some other things we do regularly for fun are color with sidewalk chalk and blow bubbles outside; gather nature items (leaves, acorns, pine cones) to make simple crafts; go for walks to look for specific items (let's count all the dogs, cats, squirrels we see); color and draw; listen to music, dance, and march; play active games like Simon Says, Hide and Seek, Hokey Pokey, Follow the Leader; play pretend games with stuffed animals; cook and bake together; work with Play-Doh and clay; and play games on the computer.*"

"*As the Army encourages my husband to be all he can be, I strive to make my family all it can be.*"

The ornaments on this retired military couple's Christmas tree are a visual celebration of all the places they've lived and vacationed.

"I'm a big believer that positive thoughts bring you positive things and negative thoughts bring negative things. Whatever you're looking for, bad or good, you'll get it."

"Make time for yourself. Don't feel guilty about pursuing your own interests and needing 'alone' time. If momma ain't happy, no one is."

"We make dinner a celebration of being together. I let my family know I love them and enjoy being with them."

"Respond to others' welcoming efforts. If someone sends a plate of brownies, return the plate personally with your thanks."

"Take lessons with your kids. I've taken horseback riding, knitting, and 'Mommy and Me' classes with mine."

"I plant flowers or vegetables around my quarters, because I enjoy looking at their colors each time I drive up."

"Participate in a leisure-time activity with the whole family. The ten most popular activities among Americans, in ranked order, are gardening, swimming, bicycling, fishing, bowling, camping, weight training, jogging or running, golf, and hiking and backpacking."

"Physical fitness is important to soldiers, so I make it important to me, too. I try to keep myself looking like the woman he married. We have a gym membership and work out together. Put some equipment that you're likely to use in your home. A treadmill, ski machine, or exercise bike can be placed in front of the TV; an aerobic step can be stored in a closet when not in use. Buy exercise DVDs, or record morning exercise shows. Do sit-ups during a show's commercial break, take the stairs instead of the elevator. I take "power walks" each week with a neighbor. Agile bodies make for agile minds; a body that is sedentary is often accompanied by a mind that can't focus."

"Live in the present, enjoy what is happening now. Learn from the past and leave it in the past."

"When my husband had recruiting duty, I used to pack a picnic lunch and take it to him. I'd pack finger foods like cut-up fruit, cheese, crackers, carrots, green peppers, sweet pickles, muffins, and assorted nuts. We'd eat together several times a week. On days we wouldn't be eating together, I'd put a note in his lunch bag."

"On Valentine's Day I write 'I Love You!' in red lipstick on the mirror while he's in the shower. Sometimes I'll write it in red chalk on the sidewalk or with red food coloring in the snow. I've also made heart-shaped cookies, pancakes, sandwiches, and hamburgers."

"I made a coupon book for my husband with coupons for things like one day of no nagging, a backrub, and doing one of his chores around the house. This has averted many a fight, because when tempers were getting high, he'd present one to me!"

"If you're arguing a lot with people, read a book on communication skills. Be aware of what you're communicating via body language, tone of voice, and facial expres-

sions, and know that people can't read your mind. Criticizing, name-calling, and fault-finding are destructive. Hold family meetings where you listen to each other, not just talk. Acknowledge other opinions and grievances. When you lecture, it's not about you, but what people will take away with them."

"Gardening is fun for the whole family, and it beautifies your home. Even if your garden is on an apartment balcony or a set of concrete steps, you can grow things. Set containers out, pour in some potting soil, and grow anything you can grow in a regular garden. Fill them with tomato plants, pepper plants, and bright flowers, and enjoy the fruits of your labor as a family."

"Fun summer activities for our family are bubble baths in a wading pool and painting the sidewalk with house-painting brushes and colored water. Sometimes we pitch a tent in the backyard at night and tell ghost stories. At warehouse clubs, I buy big rolls of butcher paper. It's cheap and great for coloring and painting."

"Join Mothers of Preschoolers (MOPS); it's a great organization. Visit www.mops.com to find a chapter near you."

"I have a framed cross-stitch in my kitchen that says, 'Be not so busy making a living that you forget to live your life.'"

"Happiness for me was easier once I acknowledged and accepted that my husband's job is not nine to five and he isn't always able to call to let me know when he'll be late. He's away so much anyhow that every time I get irritated at him for doing or saying something silly, I ask myself, do I want to waste ten minutes fussing about this, or do I want to give him ten more minutes of kisses? I'm learning to fuss only about what I can change and deal with what I can't. It's not just his career, it's mine, too."

"When you or someone in your family makes a mistake, learn from it and move on. Don't waste your time worrying about it unless there's something you can do about it. Grudges are heavy baggage."

"Frequently tell your children any of the following: I'm so lucky to have you! You're a great helper! I like it when you try so hard! Let's talk about it. I'm sorry. You're very special to me. Thanks for being patient with me. You're a great kid! I love you."

"Explore your city. I learned my way around Oklahoma City with two kids in car seats. I am WOMAN. I can ask for directions."

"Celebrate each other's successes."

"Our far-away parents help our daughter feel closer to them by taping themselves reading books to her and sending us the audiocassettes. I also keep a framed photo collage of all her relatives in her room."

MAKING THE MOST OF IT

Some more comments from military families enjoying their duty stations:

"Annapolis was a great tour. I have fond memories of boat rides down the Chesapeake Bay and of eating tasty crab cakes and oysters."

"The high altitude and low humidity at Cannon AFB, New Mexico, make for great skiing at Angelfire, and you can play golf year round. The base has trailers for rent at Lake Conchas, for a nice weekend getaway."

"I didn't know anything about Caribbean history and culture until we moved to St. Thomas. I've enjoyed taking ferries to the different islands, seeing the hairstyles and hearing the accents."

"We're at Ft. Leonard Wood in Missouri. We love going to the Ozarks in the summer. There are lots of lakes, ponds, streams, and reservoirs filled with bass, trout, crappie, and catfish. The scenery is lush, and there are even caves and a water park."

"We live in Key West. There's lots to do there. There's a beach at the Navy's Truman Annex, and it's far less crowded than the public beaches. You can rent kayaks, snorkel sets, BBQ grills and fishing gear at the Navy Marina. It's weird and funny how wild chickens roam free here, down streets, courtyards, even into open-air restaurants. Apparently this is a 175-year-old historical feature."

"Don't spend a tour on the East Coast without taking a ferry to Nantucket. So much history and beauty on one island, and unlike Martha's Vineyard, all the beaches are public."

"I raised my kids in the Army with the belief that it was one big cultural learning experience. The most wonderful thing about it was the ability to live and work with people of so many ethnic backgrounds. My kids get surprised when confronted with the prejudices of people who have never worked in a multicultural setting."

"When we were at Ft. Monmouth, New Jersey, we drove to New York City to view Ground Zero. Standing on a platform there, looking at the wreckage, made it easier to explain to my kids the reasons behind deployments and the military's mission."

"While stationed at Ft. Huachaca, we took mini-vacations to see Arizona. Among them were a guided Jeep ride through the Sonoma Desert, where a retired National Park Service ranger showed us barrel cacti and 1,000-year-old Indian drawings on rocks, and how to distinguish them from modern-day graffiti. He told us lore of the Saguaro cactus and showed us packrat and tarantula nests. Another time we took a helicopter ride over the Grand Canyon."

"We're in Seattle, and on weekends we take a ferry ride to start a bicycling trip on the San Juan Islands. We bike past farmland, gigantic fir trees, and fields full of wildflowers, and sometimes we can even see whales out in the ocean and eagles and heron flying around."

"What fun to be stationed at Nellis Air Force Base! We love Las Vegas! We've seen world-class shows like the Blue Man Group and Celine Dion. It's fun to walk up and down the strip, looking at all the bizarre hotels."

"Hawaii is a great tour for the water-sport lover. It's all here: surfing, wind sailing, scuba diving, snorkeling, fishing, and sailing. I also recommend a tourist submarine ride through Waikiki's coral reef. The kids will love seeing all the colorful fish."

"Fort Bliss, Texas, offers the opportunity to take frequent trips to Mexico. Once you get past the border towns, it truly is another country, with its own customs and culture. You get the benefits of a foreign tour without moving to a foreign country."

"When stationed in Alaska, we took Gray Line's Grand Denali Explorer tour, and we also traveled through Denali National Park. We rafted on the Nenana River and went on wilderness safaris. People from all over the world spend a fortune to do these things that were right in our backyard. A frequent treat was the sight of people stopping their cars to let ducks and their ducklings cross the road."

FURTHER READING

Books

Hightower, Kathie, and Holly Scherer. *Help! I'm a Military Spouse—I Get a Life Too!: How to Craft a Life for You as You Move with the Military*, 2nd edition (Paperback). Dulles, VA: Potomac Books Inc., 2007.

Hopkins, Tom. *The Official Guide to Success.* New York: Warner Books, 1984.

Tyson, Eric, and Ray Brown. *Home Buying for Dummies*, 3rd edition. New York: Wiley, 2006.

Losier, Michael J. *Law of Attraction: The Science of Attracting More of What You Want and Less of What You Don't.* New York: Wellness Central, 2007.

Tannen, Deborah. *You Just Don't Understand: Women and Men in Conversation.* New York: Harper Paperbacks, 2001.

Internet Resources

www.citysearch.com. Information on the attractions of over eighty cities nationwide.

www.city-data.com. Statistical data on many cities.

7

Moving

It's permanent-change-of-station time—time to pack up and move to the next place!

Moving can be viewed as one of military life's greatest advantages. What opportunities to see the world! What luxury to expose your children to things their civilian playmates might only read about! In the span of nine years, you can enjoy cultural differences between Connecticut, Missouri, and Washington state. You can visit the San Diego Zoo on one tour and Opryland on the next. Camp in Gatlinburg, visit Disney World, be awed by the Albuquerque balloon festival—it might be in your backyard.

Moving is never easy, but it need not be an ordeal. It can be an adventure, especially if combined with a vacation. But unless you're a newly married couple with nothing to move except yourselves and a philodendron, you must actively plan and participate in your move. Smooth moves don't happen by themselves.

THE PURPOSE OF MOVES

Of course, you may be wondering why military members move so often. There are two reasons:

CONUS *vs.* OCONUS

Two terms you'll hear a lot are CONUS, meaning Continental U.S., and OCONUS, meaning Outside Continental U.S. Hawaii and Alaska are considered OCONUS stations, and overseas COLA (see chapter 5) is paid for those assigned to them.

1. Military success—readiness—depends on having the right people in the right places. Each year that a servicemember is in the military, he acquires new skills and may need a new job that fits those skills, a job that often is not at the base on which he is currently stationed. Moves almost always mean a better job, or at least a different one.

What's ahead? Moving brings new adventures.

2. The U.S. maintains bases all over the world. Some are in great places; others are not. But since all need to be maintained regardless of the lifestyle they offer, a system of rotation is observed.

DO YOU HAVE ANY SAY IN LOCATION?

After boot camp, only the Army guarantees a first duty station in the enlistment contract, and that is only for certain, hard-to-fill jobs. Additionally, the guarantee is only good for twelve months. After that, the person can be moved anywhere. The Guard and reserves also guarantee the duty station because they are recruiting to fill specific positions in their units.

But in the rest of the services (and the Army, if there is no guaranteed first duty), the first duty station selection is made either in basic training or technical school. Preferences are considered (servicemembers fill out the "dream sheet," a job and assignments worksheet), but there must be a need for his skills where he wants to go. Assignment to some Navy jobs considers A-school class standing; those who finished higher are more likely to be assigned where they want to go.

After the first duty assignment, those in their first enlistment who are assigned to a CONUS location must serve twelve months there before being eligible to move overseas, and twenty-four months before being allowed to move to another CONUS location. Career enlisted members assigned to a CONUS location must serve twenty-four months before moving overseas and thirty-six months before moving to another CONUS location.

In reality, though, CONUS-to-CONUS moves are getting less common due to costs. If you're at a CONUS base and want to move, volunteering for an overseas tour (or sea duty for Navy) is the most practical way to make it happen.

The amount of time spent on an overseas tour depends on where it is. Most of Europe and Japan are considered "standard" overseas tours, and servicemembers who bring their families are assigned there for three years. Another type of overseas assignment is "remote." This is an area that lacks family supports, and family members may not move there at government expense. A remote tour length is twelve months. Those returning from a remote tour usually get assignment preference over those returning from a standard tour.

When the servicemember is on a twelve-month remote tour, he can move his family anywhere they want in CONUS to live while he's away at government expense. When he returns, the government will pay again to move them from where they're living to his new location. But know that once he gets an approved follow-up assignment, he must agree to not relocate his family anywhere besides that follow-up location.

Some families—for example, one with a family member in the EFMP program—receive special consideration. There are also compassionate reassignments, given for hardship situations. Such a situation must be temporary (under a year), though; otherwise the military will consider a compassionate discharge instead.

THE RELOCATION OFFICE

Start your logistics planning early. Much of it cannot be done at the last minute. Each service has a Relocation Readiness office, whose purpose is to assist new and departing community members. You'll find moving packets, pamphlets on military bases worldwide, newcomer orientations, individual relocation counseling and classes, and sponsorship training (discussed in chapter 10). In the family services office there's a household goods loan closet from which you can borrow pots and pans, dishes, flatware, cribs, car seats, irons, sleeping mats, and perhaps furniture when arriving and leaving. Find branch-specific information at *www.myarmylifetoo.com* (Army), *afmove. hq.af.mil/default.asp* (Air Force), *www. nffsp.org* (Navy), and *www.usmc-mccs. org/rap/index.cfm* (MarineCorps).

It's estimated that up to 25 percent of Americans move every year. Retirees, corporate transferees, job-hoppers, young college graduates, and the recently unemployed actively seek new homes. Consequently, there are many online and print articles on the subject, especially in the late spring. Googling "military relocation" will return lots of relevant hits.

SEE YOUR TRANSPORTATION COUNSELOR

After the PCS orders arrive, make an appointment with the installation Joint Personal Property Shipping office. This is a DoD installation that oversees the shipping, receipt, and storage of personal property for all military branches. At this appointment you'll get information on shipping your household goods, cars, and pets, your moving entitlements, and a date will be set for the movers to arrive. Often only the servicemember goes to this appointment, but it's a good idea for you to go, too, to ask the questions your husband may forget. Such as: Are hanging wardrobe boxes authorized to keep your clothes from becoming a wrinkled mess? Can a special crate be built for your grandfather clock, marble tabletop, or antique piece? No two moves are alike, and the rules change. You'll be advised whether a do-it-yourself move is good for your situation, and what kind of storage is available. Go to this meeting with a written list of questions.

If you'll be handling the move by yourself, the transportation office will require a power of attorney (discussed in chapter 9). When you visit the office to set up a date, know when your husband must arrive at the new duty station, the type of shipments you'll have (do you have items stored in another state?) and their approximate weights, and any large or unusual items. Bring twelve copies of the PCS orders. After arrangements have been made, try not to change them. Changing moving dates, especially during the busy summer months, can mean a lengthy delay in getting your move rescheduled, and requires a letter from the unit commander.

MOVING PAYS, ALLOWANCES, ADVANCES, AND LEAVE

Moves often present families with unexpected expenses. Restaurant meals are consumed, duplicates of packed-away items may be bought. If the orders require reporting shortly before children's school lets out, some families send the servicemember first, a move that requires maintaining two dwellings. A family is only permitted to occupy one set of quarters; a new set cannot be assigned until the last one is cleared. At overseas stations, car registration may be expensive. While you can't predict all expenses, try to anticipate and budget for them. Here we'll discuss the pays, allowances, advances, and leave designed to help defray moving expenses.

Allowances

Dislocation Allowance. To help defray otherwise unreimbursable moving expenses, you are automatically issued a dislocation allowance based on pay grade and number of family members. It does not have to be paid back. Dislocation allowances are not given to servicemembers transferring to nearby duty stations, nor are they paid to those separating or retiring.

Temporary Lodging Entitlement. This payment helps defray up to ten days' living expenses on CONUS moves, when a family occupies temporary lodging. It pays up to $180 per day. If you're moving overseas from the states, up to five days TLE at the old duty station can be reimbursed. If you're moving stateside from an overseas location, up to ten days TLE at the new duty station can be reimbursed after arrival. TLE is not paid for lodging during the actual travel days between duty stations; a "per diem" is used for that. TLE is also neither paid on the first or last PCS when entering or leaving active duty, nor on Permissive Orders.

Temporary Lodging Allowance (TLA). Up to sixty days of temporary living expenses on overseas moves can be obtained from this allowance. The amount given depends on rank and family size. Up to ten days can be paid prior to departure. Servicemembers who start their tour unaccompanied but are later accompanied by their families may collect TLA if housing is not immediately available. TLA is not granted for new family members who are added after the effective date of the orders overseas, however. TLA must be applied for, and it doesn't have to be paid back. It is also available immediately before moving back to the States.

Per Diem. This is a flat rate of $91 per day for food and lodging for authorized travel (350 miles per day is the amount used when calculating how many days of travel should be taken) when the family moves using their personal car. If you combine your travel with a vacation, you are not allotted more mileage or per diem moneys. If you travel commercially (plane, train, bus), you'll receive a set per diem rate for the new duty station, or the rate for the delay point if you stop overnight. Per diem for family members is figured at three-quarters of the servicemember's rate for each person twelve years or older, and one-half of the servicemember's rate for each family member younger than twelve years.

Monetary Allowance in Lieu of Transportation (MALT). If you're driving to your new home, you will be reimbursed based on a commercial fare for the trip. MALT rates also are based on how many passengers are in the car. Reimbursement for two vehicles is generally authorized; in certain circumstances more can be. You may receive 80 percent in advance of the move, and it applies both to CONUS and overseas.

If family members travel within the U.S. by means other than their private car, the servicemember can be reimbursed for this travel up to what it would have cost the military to purchase a ticket. Know that if you buy your own commercial airline ticket for an overseas location, you will only be reimbursed for U.S. airlines, assuming they fly to that area. Tickets on foreign airlines are only reimbursed if no U.S. carrier flies to that location.

Move-In Housing Allowance(MIHA). This allowance is for overseas moves only, since you will find that the phrase "unfurnished apartment" takes on new meaning. Along with the furniture, you often must provide your own light fixtures, sinks, and cabinets! So a one-time move-in allowance may be autho-

rized to help pay the costs of these types of items. It can also apply to modifications for security. You must commit to a rental before applying. MIHA rates
change with currency fluctuations.

Miscellaneous Reimbursables. Items that may be eligible for reimbursement
include: postage, mileage for the distance driven from the old duty station to
the airport, cab fare, rental car, excess baggage, tolls, visa payments, ferry fees
from Alaska, and mandatory pet quarantine fees up to $550 for an overseas
move. Remember that reimbursements are not dollar for dollar, but up to a
maximum amount. Keep an envelope handy for saving all receipts, as you
must verify each expense to be reimbursed for it.

Advances

You can apply for advances for ten days before signing out of the unit. These are paid
by direct deposit, so don't close out your account before receiving them. The types of
advances you may apply for include the following:

Advance Pay. Servicemembers can apply for these interest-free loans of up to
three months' base pay to help with moving expenses. They can be given at
the old station, at the new one, or partially at both. Advance pay is not
automatic; if a servicemember wants it, he must apply at the base finance
office, with a written justification describing what it will be used for. The
money is usually advanced a day after applying; sometimes it's given in a few
hours. Even if three months' pay is requested, the finance office sometimes
approves only one. As a side note, advance pay can be applied for in cases
of hardship, even if no move is involved.

Advance Basic Allowance for Housing (BAH). Servicemembers may also apply
for this allowance, but it requires approval from the unit commander and
a copy of your lease (you must have already committed to a rental).
Advance BAH is neither given earlier than three days before the rent payment must be made, nor more than thirty days after. It is not available to
homeowners.

Advance Overseas Housing Allowance (OHA). For overseas moves, you may apply
for up to twelve months' advance BAH and overseas housing allowance
(OHA).

Consumables Allowance. Those assigned to some overseas stations may be authorized up to 1,250 pounds annually for consumable goods. These are products
that you consume (use up), such as canned soup, packaged cookies, cooking/
baking ingredients, and nonedible consumables such as toiletries and paper
products. The allowance doesn't include frozen or perishable foods. Automobile parts and supplies are not considered consumables. These items are
packed and weighed separately, from your weight allowance and the inventory should identify them as "authorized consumables."

Paying Back Advances

Allotments to repay advances are taken out of the paycheck for one year (two years in case of hardship) until the amount borrowed is paid back. The servicemember will continue to get his full allowances while paying back his advances. Don't spend advance money frivolously. Although this may sound obvious, many families get into financial trouble this way. Your finances may have some catching up to do in the months after you move, and that additional allotment isn't going to help. Use advance moneys for moving expenses only, and use them judiciously.

If you're financially sound and already have enough money to carry you comfortably through the move, a prudent use of advance pay is to pay off any debts that charge high interest rates. Since advance pay is interest-free, you're replacing an interest-bearing loan with an interest-free loan. Another idea is to put the advance pay in a savings account. That way you will earn interest on money that didn't cost you anything to borrow.

Moving Pay and Allowance Tax Considerations

TLA, TLE, dislocation, and move-in allowances are nontaxable. As for unreimbursed expenses, only direct moving costs, such as transporting family, pets, and household goods to the next duty station, are deductible, and only if they don't exceed the government allowance. Indirect expenses, such as house-hunting trips, meals during the move, closing costs, and spouse job-hunting trips, are no longer deductible.

Leave

Permissive TDY or TAD. Servicemembers can take up to ten days of noncharge-able leave for house-hunting trips prior to PCS moves, and also for house-hunting. TDY means "temporary duty," and TAD means "temporary additional duty." The servicemember must report to the on-post housing office prior to seeking off-post housing for the TDY to be approved. No extra money is provided for this, so most families take this leave ten days after clearing the last duty station.

Other Leaves. Other leaves for which you may apply include:

- Proceed time: a leave of absence of up to seven days at both the old and new duty stations to process in and out.
- Delay en route: leave for unforeseen delays. This must be approved by the new unit commander.
- Leave en route: personal travel time. This must be approved by the old unit commander. Proceed time for servicemembers on PCS orders to or from an unaccompanied tour overseas. Up to four days may be authorized to help family members move. This is typically done in conjunction with moving household goods or a car. Proceed time is not authorized for a servicemember's first or last PCS. It also is not available for moves between nearby stations or ships with the same home port or when orders require reporting within four days.

Throughout the entire moving process, monitor the LES to make sure your entitlements are correctly credited. Accidental over- and underpayments are sometimes made during moves. Save overpayments; if you don't report them, the finance office will eventually find out and withhold them in one lump sum from the military paycheck.

MOVING YOUR HOUSEHOLD GOODS

The most common method of moving is to allow the government to hire a commercial carrier to pack and move your property for you. Another method is to move your goods yourself. Either way, your moving entitlement has limits and parameters to observe, which we will now discuss.

Weight Allowance

You're given a weight allowance—a maximum weight that may be moved and/or stored at government expense—based on rank, family size, and whether the move is continental or overseas. The accompanying charts give general guidelines, but your transportation counselor will give you specifics for your situation.

Table of Joint Federal Travel Regulations Weight Allowances

GRADE	In Pounds		
	PCS WITHOUT DEPENDENTS	PCS WEIGHT DEPENDENTS	TEMPORARY ALLOWANCE
0-10	18,000	18,000	2,000
0-9	18,000	18,000	1,500
0-8	18,000	18,000	1,000
0-7	18,000	18,000	1,000
0-6	18,000	18,000	800
0-5	16,000	17,500	800
0-4/W-4	14,000	17,000	800
0-3/W-3	13,000	14,500	600
0-2/W-2	12,500	13,500	600
0-1/W-1	10,000	12,000	600
E-9	12,000	14,500	600
E-8	11,000	13,500	500
E-7	10,500	12,500	400
E-6	8,000	11,000	400
E-5	7,000	9,000	400
E-4	7,000	8,000	400
E-3	5,000	8,000	400
E-2	5,000	8,000	400
E-1	5,000	8,000	400

For a continental move, you may ship your entire allowance. But for an overseas move, if the PCS orders state that government furnishings will be provided, you are limited to 2,500 pounds, or 25 percent of your household goods allowance, plus nonavailable items. If washers and dryers are provided, you may be limited to 75 percent. The government will store what you leave behind free of charge in nontemporary storage (discussed later in this chapter), up to your full allowance.

One way to estimate your possessions' weight is to assume 1,000 pounds per room (excluding storage and bathrooms). Then add the estimated weight of any large items and appliances stored in the garage and basement. Another method is to add up the number of items on the movers' inventory sheets and multiply by forty. If you've moved at government expense before, use your previous paperwork as a baseline, then add items acquired afterward.

Keeping within your allowance is your responsibility, not the transportation office's or the mover's. The mover will give you a weight estimate, but it's not official and can't be used to refute excess weight charges. Actual charges are based on the weight tickets submitted by the moving company. If you exceed your allowance, you'll be billed later. It may be a whole year later, but it will come, and the entire amount will be withdrawn in one lump sum from the military paycheck.

Visit the website for your new base before moving. It may have information on items not to bring, saving you the trouble of packing and moving things you may not need or won't be able to use. For instance, if you're moving overseas, your land-line phones won't work. Small appliances, unless they're dual-voltage, won't work since they are 110V (the U.S. standard) and 220V is the standard overseas. Socket types are also different, and these even vary from country to country. You can buy plug adapters, step-down converters, and transformers to make your appliances work, but this may cost more than simply buying locally sold appliances. Apartments and government housing in most countries are not as spacious as what we're used to, so your furniture may not fit. In Japan, charcoal grills are not allowed on balconies, and there is no room for large propane grills. Space heaters may not be allowed. Most military housing overseas is equipped with communal washers and dryers, so you wouldn't need to bring those. Know that any outdoor items you bring, such as rakes and lawn-mowers, must be clean and free of soil and pest infestation to meet customs requirements. Chapter 8 has more information on transformers and using computers and small appliances overseas.

Call or e-mail the housing office at the new duty station to ask about the availability of quarters, apartments, quartermaster furniture, 110V outlets (if overseas), whether the family services office loans furniture for the duration of a tour, and so on. Ask the new Relocation office to send you a "welcome aboard" packet of information, if your sponsor (discussed in chapter 10) hasn't done so.

Non-Temporary Storage

Non-Temporary Storage (NTS), also called extended or permanent storage, is long-term household goods storage used for people who are:

- going overseas and can't take all of their property with them;
- being sent to a temporary duty station without a subsequent permanent duty station established yet; or
- leaving military service and have not yet decided where their home will be.

Nontemporary storage is also commonly used to store personal property pending shipment overseas when there is a shortage of housing for family members. Once that restriction is lifted, the household goods may be shipped to the new duty station.

You may have the government handle the storage of your property, in which case it will be inaccessible to you for the duration of the storage. You can also arrange storage with a service of your choosing, and the government will pay you as much as it would have paid its own storage contractor. You can even arrange to have it shipped elsewhere, such as to a relative's house, as long as the distance to that address is less than the distance from where you are now to the new duty station. Storage is provided in whatever approved commercial or government storage facility is nearest to the place where the household goods are located when PCS orders are issued.

The time length for storage allowed on overseas moves is the length of the overseas tour plus ninety days. Those ninety days allow you to obtain housing at the new location before calling for delivery. Storage beyond the entitlement time is at the customer's expense.

If a change in your status would affect your entitlement to NTS, such as consecutive overseas tours or extensions, you are responsible for notifying the transportation office that maintains your NTS account and for providing documentation showing your new return date. When you return, your storage items are sent to your new duty station.

Types of Baggage

Possessions that aren't stored are categorized as "unaccompanied," "household goods," and "professional books, paper, and equipment." To the fullest extent possible, physically separate items destined for these three categories. Otherwise, you'll get possessions put in storage that you wanted to take with you, and vice versa. If separating isn't possible, tag items with large paper labels detailing the category. Remove any stickers left from previous moves.

Unaccompanied Baggage. Also called "hold," unaccompanied baggage is a small shipment of things sent to the new duty station early so that you can set up basic housekeeping when you arrive. The following are useful items to include in it:

- food staples and condiment packets
- china, cups, glasses, mugs, silverware
- pots, pans, skillets, utensils, small appliances
- TVs, computers, stereos, MP3 docks

- pillows, bedding
- shower curtains, bath rugs, towels, washcloths, toilet paper
- light bulbs, lamps
- clocks
- coffee pots, coffee, tea bags
- large and small plastic bags
- paper, pens, and pencils
- contact paper
- clothes (If you're moving overseas, send lots of clothes, because the time it takes for your household goods to arrive is much longer than for continental moves. If the seasons are changing, send what's appropriate, and pack a raincoat and umbrella for each person. Some servicemembers mail uniforms to the new address in case their household goods are delayed.)
- clothes hangers, iron, ironing board
- tools, child's car seats
- computer accessories
- small TVs, DVD players

Household Goods. Furniture and all other personal possessions are your household goods. They may also include spare parts for your car, motorcycle, or even a boat less than fourteen feet long, with no boat trailer. (Families that ship larger items typically pay excess weight charges.) Boats more than fourteen feet long, or those with a trailer, can be shipped by a one-time-only rate method. You are responsible for all special service costs such as lift-on or lift-off, or handling charges. You may also ship golf carts, motorcycles, mopeds, jet skis, hang gliders, snowmobiles (and their trailers), and single-occupant ultra-light recreational or sport vehicles under 155 pounds if unpowered or under 254 pounds if powered.

If you want to send more than your unaccompanied baggage allowance permits, mail the items to yourself at your husband's new unit address. Third-class mail is less expensive than paying the movers. Even if you don't exceed your allowance, you still might want to do this, because mail arrives quicker than unaccompanied baggage, and it reduces the number of things to carry. Save your postal receipts for tax purposes.

Items you can't ship or store include outboard motors, propane tanks, perishable foods, live plants, pets, alcohol, cigarettes, live ammunition, explosives, aerosols, flammable products, acids, cordwood, or property for resale or commercial use.

Professional Books, Papers, and Equipment (PBPE). Servicemembers have a separate allowance for items that are required to perform official duties. The transportation counselor must be given an estimated weight, which is the official declaration of intent to ship. When properly listed on the inventory, these items are not counted as part of your weight allowance. They must be removed from the rest of your property so they may be packed and weighed separately. Before signing the movers' inventory, make sure PBPE items are labeled as such, not as "books" or "miscellaneous." Otherwise, they *will* count against your household goods weight allowance. PBPE does not include office furniture (e.g., bookcases, desks, file cabinets) or sports equipment. Typical PBPE items include:

> Before leaving each area, I take photos of my favorite places and friends to display at the new place. I also buy usable items, like dish towels and coffee mugs, to serve as happy reminders. Every time we vacate a home, I close the door slowly on all the happy times we had there.

- reference books, papers, and material
- instruments, tools, and equipment needed by technicians, mechanics, and other professionals
- specialized clothing such as diving suits, flying suits, band uniforms, and other nonstandard uniform or clothing items
- communication equipment used for the Military Affiliated Radio System (MARS)
- privately owned or issued field clothing or equipment, official awards, and other memorabilia given by a uniformed service, professional society or organization, or a U.S. or foreign government

PREPARING FOR THE MOVE

Keep a notebook with lists of things you'll need to do. Start disposing of unwanted items.

Sample Items for Your List

- Make copies of the PCS orders and keep them in your handbag. You'll often be asked for them while making arrangements.
- Close your local bank accounts if that's your plan. Give the bank at least five days' notice. Take to the bank any remaining checks, deposit and withdrawal slips, and ATM cards. Take your check register, too, so that the bank can determine which checks are still outstanding. If you know what

> If you buy U.S. Savings Bonds by allotment, your bonds will be mailed to your old address while you are in transit, and the post office will not forward them. Instead, they will return the bonds to the Defense Finance and Accounting Service (DFAS) center in Denver, Colorado. DFAS will release all of your bonds upon receipt of your new address. Change your bond address upon transferring in at your new base.

your new bank will be, you can open an account and have your money transferred, eliminating the need to carry a large cashier's check. Change your direct deposit and, if applicable, savings bond information, at myPay (discussed in chapter 5).

- Retrieve safety deposit box contents. Buy a lockable box in which to keep the contents on moving day and leave the box in your car trunk. Neither the movers nor the government is liable for watches, jewelry, cash, stocks, bonds, coin and stamp collections, antiques, bills, deeds, precious metals, or irreplaceable sentimental items. If the movers inadvertently pack them (or anything else you didn't intend to pack), you will be responsible for paying them to find and unpack them.

- Get change-of-address cards from the post office and send them to creditors, magazines to which you subscribe, and other businesses with whom you interact. Leave one with the post office so that your mail can be forwarded. Bulk mail is not forwarded, so pack catalogs that you like.

- Clean any rugs, draperies, and slipcovers you're keeping, and have the movers pack them in the cleaner's wrappers. It's a morale booster to have them fresh and ready when you move into your new place.

- Arrange for the transfer of your family's medical and school records. If you use a military treatment facility, they will give you the records for you to hand-carry to the next station. If you use a civilian provider, they transfer the records directly to your new provider, and will charge $15 per family member for photocopying costs. If your child has special needs, you should have your most current IEP, recent educational evaluation, school recommendations, and copies of any therapy services obtained through Tricare or the school. It is best to hand-carry rather than ship them, even in the hold baggage. New schools will ask to see all children's inoculation records before admitting them.

- Have utilities disconnected the day after you leave. You'll want to leave your phone, lights, and running water connected while the movers are there.

- Cancel your newspaper and any other home-delivery items.

- Disconnect your gas and electrical appliances and any window air-conditioning units you might own. Drain gas from the lawnmower. If you move your appliances, drain all water from appliance hoses, thoroughly wash the inside of your refrigerator and freezer, leave their doors open, and give them at least two days to dry out. Place several charcoal briquettes or a sock full of new coffee grounds or baking soda inside while in transit to prevent mold and mildew from forming. If plumbing, carpentry, or electrical work is needed to disconnect appliances, you must arrange and pay for that. Disconnect all electronics—stereos, TVs, DVD players, and computers.

- Remove pictures, mirrors, curtains, rods, lights, utensil racks, and other hardware from the walls. Stick tags on the items that belong to the apartment so that the movers won't remove them.
- Remove items from crawl spaces, the attic, and the roof. Movers are not required to go into areas that aren't accessible by a stairway (ladders don't count), aren't well lit, don't have a finished floor, or don't allow them to stand erect.
- Dismantle outdoor play equipment and sheds. Clean them, along with any other outdoor equipment and tools, making sure they are free of bug infestation. If you're moving overseas, a foreign customs office will be very strict about this.
- Get a health certificate for your pet, because you might have to put it in a kennel temporarily, and kennels require such certificates. If you know your new address, get it printed on a tag for your pet's collar. You never know what will happen at a rest stop! (See "Shipping Your Pet" later in this chapter.)
- Make advance reservations at hotels along the way and at your destination. Staying at military guest houses and lodges will save money, and your PCS orders entitle you to priority use. You can stay on any base, no matter what service you're in. Make reservations as soon as you can, because military guest houses fill up fast. Temporary lodging is open to all reservists (including gray area) with an ID card, on a space-available basis. Reservists are not required to be on orders or in training to utilize these lodgings. Know that most military guest houses do not accept pets, and they won't give a non-availability statement for pet owners. This statement is often needed to receive reimbursement for local hotel expenses before moving into a permanent residence. Another good option is an extended-stay hotel. These range from budget to luxury, have kitchenettes, and are larger than ordinary hotel rooms.
- Decide what you're keeping and get rid of the rest. Moving junk is a waste of your time and the government's money. It will also cost you if you exceed your allowance.
- Fill prescriptions; pick up developed film and dry cleaning. Retrieve loaned items, and return library books and other borrowed things.
- Give your landlord notice as required by your lease.
- Plan meals from what's in your freezer and pantry.
- Check expiration dates of major credit cards you plan to use en route. Check your family's ID card expiration dates.
- Assemble paperwork of any insurance policies you have on your property, a written and photographic inventory, with serial, make, and model numbers, and any appraisals. Don't keep appraisals in the same box as the valuables.

DISPOSING OF UNWANTED ITEMS

Moving offers a nice opportunity to declutter your life. Start this process about four months before you move. Go through every room, closet, and drawer. Ask your kids to contribute items they don't want; telling them that they can keep any monetary proceeds is a good motivator. Be ruthless when evaluating an item. Is it broken? Obsolete? Stained, unworn for years? Get rid of it. Know that storing dishwashers, washers, dryers, refrigerators, and freezers for several years is not a good idea. Freezers contain Freon, which goes dead after sitting idle and the others may rust. Sell or donate them.

You can sell items by placing ads in the newspaper classifieds or at one of the many online sites like *www.craigslist.com*. You can also auction them on *www.ebay.com*, hold a garage sale, or take them to the base thrift shop, a consignment store, or a used book shop. Be realistic about your prices; if people wanted to pay a lot, they wouldn't be looking in these places.

If you want to donate, Airman's Attic, Goodwill, the Salvation Army, and the family services lending closets and food locker might like your items. Or perhaps they're suitable for a shelter or library. Give neighbors your houseplants. Day-care centers and preschools might appreciate magazines and office/craft supplies you no longer need. Some charities will pick up large items in good repair. Get receipts for tax purposes. Please only donate items in good repair; nobody wants junk, and it costs charity manpower and money to sort and dispose of it. Junk would include, but is not limited to, stained and pilly clothes, items that don't work or are missing pieces, expired foodstuffs, shoes missing their mates, and twenty-year-old textbooks. Charities get a lot more of this stuff than you'd think.

PREPARE FOR MOVING DAY

Someone must be on premises when the movers arrive. If not, you will be charged for attempted pick-up or delivery. Once they are there, the movers work fast. Making sure that they're packing what you want and how you want requires your undivided attention, so it is helpful to hire a sitter for small children and pets. You must also be ready, as time is money for the movers. Keeping them waiting while you make decisions about things that should have been done already could cause problems.

Know what will go in your unaccompanied baggage, what will go in your household goods, and what you'll carry with you. Put the last items in a closet and tape up a "Keep Out" sign. Everything not in that closet will get packed. The movers will not verify whether you need particular items; they will simply pack everything they see. Essentials such as medicine, diaper bags, glasses, and contact lenses will be packed if you haven't set them aside. Heavy stacks of magazines and newspapers on which you didn't plan to waste your weight allowance will get packed too, if they're lying around. Anything that can be disassembled will be, so tell the movers in advance if you don't want a certain item taken apart.

Ideas for the "Keep Out" closet include:

- plastic bin with clean rags inside that fits under a car seat and can be used as a trash can while on the road
- plastic bucket and cleaning supplies for final once-overs and for the new place
- locked box containing your jewelry and other valuables
- briefcase or accordion file with papers you may need while on the road and when you first arrive, such as: monthly bills, creditor addresses, envelopes and stamps, a photographic inventory of possessions, all papers movers give you, port call papers, address books, realtor information, maps, and PCS orders. (You might put important papers from your files here, such as passports; immunization records; official birth, marriage, divorce, adoption, or death certificates; wills; powers of attorney; naturalization papers; property deeds; savings bonds; Social Security cards; car titles and shipping/storage papers; medical and school records; employment records and references; and pet records.)
- soft-sided case with makeup, soap, blow-dryer, Kleenex, contact lenses, extra glasses, sunglasses, ocular prescriptions, and over-the-counter and prescription medicines. (Keep prescription medicines in their original containers instead of generic reminder-type cases, especially if you're going overseas. A copy of the prescription itself may prove handy.)
- pet needs
- baby needs
- a backpack for each child, filled with nonmessy snacks, books, crayons, drawing paper, puzzles, magnetic board games, cassette player with headphones, cassette tapes.
- change for tolls and vending machines
- thermos and foam cups
- plastic bags, garbage bags, twist ties, plastic plates, quart bottles, plastic utensils, assorted condiments
- bag of food, napkins, paper utensils, cooler with soft drinks and bottled water, plastic ice substitutes
- paper napkins, packets of moist towelettes, washcloths
- pillows
- coats, sweaters, and jackets, even in the summer, for cool nights
- clothes and suitcases—jelly-roll entire outfits of kids' clothing to make on-the-road dressing easier
- big envelope for receipts pertaining to your move to save for tax purposes
- pet kennel
- telescoping clothes pole to set up in the backseat from which to hang plants or clothes
- flashlight, fresh batteries

In your hold baggage, fill luggage and duffle bags with clothing, sheets, towels, and other goods you want access to right away. This is easier than unpacking multiple boxes to find them. You also might want to get a large Rubbermaid tote for each family member to fill with the things they'll want right away in the new home.

Damage can be averted by paying attention to what's going on. Not that you should tell the movers how to pack, but if you see them handling things roughly or incorrectly, politely assert yourself. They're doing a job for you, not a favor. However, do not argue with them about anything; call the transportation office, which has the authority to dialogue with them.

Don't pack anything yourself; such items will be labeled "packed by owner," and if they are broken, you won't be reimbursed. If you're concerned about a special item, you may want to pack and move it yourself. Ask the movers to verify and note which appliances work so that if they get broken, you can back up your claim.

Make sure boxes are labeled with the name of the room or closet from which their contents came. This will make things easier when moving into your new place. Don't let toys get mixed with towels and forks, and then labeled "miscellaneous." Rugs should be rolled, mirrors and pictures individually wrapped, furniture disassembled, and mattresses put in individual cartons. Plastic bubble sheets and brown wrapping paper should be used. During disassembly, small, loose parts should be attached to the item they belong to with tape or placed in Ziploc bags, and then taped to the item. Keep a parts box open and fill it with miscellaneous cables, parts, and handles that are removed. Small parts have a way of getting easily lost and not found for years.

Packing and lifting furniture is hard work. Have ice water, soft drinks, and sandwiches on hand, or order a pizza. The movers will appreciate it, and it will show in the care your possessions get. It's also a good idea to have premade food for your family to eat, along with disposable plates and utensils.

Have lots of copies of the PCS orders on hand, and instruct the movers to put a copy in each box before it's taped up. That way, if a box goes astray, it'll be easier to locate you. Some families even put a sticker name and contact information tag on the outside of the boxes, in case they end up in someone else's delivery.

All your boxes and furniture will be put into large wooden crates. Ask that this be done in front of you, not at the warehouse. By watching your things get crated,

Try not to get too upset over damaged items; it's impossible to make a move without something getting broken.

you can ensure that boxes of dishes don't get balanced on sofa arms and sharp edges don't butt into bureaus. After the crates are nailed shut, ensure that a sealant is applied to all joints and doors to make them watertight.

Carefully check the inventory sheets before you sign them. Everything packed should be listed. If it's not, it can't be claimed. Expensive items should be specifically identified: "Lladró porcelain figurine," not "statue"; "Waterford crystal goblet," not "glass." Make, model, and serial number of electronics should be listed. Make sure computer equipment is specifically described: an iMac and accessories shouldn't be summed up as "computer." The same goes for your TV; a Sony fifty-inch plasma should be described as such.

If you disagree with the way an item's condition is described, note that on the comments part of the form. At this point, your interests and the mover's are not the same. Make sure that you understand all symbols used to describe damages. When you sign your name on the form, you are agreeing to all the mover's descriptions.

Clearing Quarters

Quarters have to be left in the same shape in which they were found. Excessive nail holes and other such damage must be fixed. Any changes made, such as interior painting or fence installation, must be returned to the original condition, unless the next occupant accepts it.

A deep cleaning is also required. The standards are strict, which prompts many families to hire a service to do it for them (but you are ultimately responsible for its work). Some bases hire cleaners at no charge to the occupants, but most require the occupants to do it. Other bases have an approved list of cleaners and act as a go-between. You pay the fee directly to the office and leave; clearing then becomes the cleaner's problem. If you hire a private party (find one in the classifieds under "house-cleaning"), make sure that your contract specifies for the cleaner to be there during the inspection. That way, if something doesn't pass muster, it can be redone.

Cost varies based on the condition of your quarters and whether yard work needs to be done, but $25 per hour is a common wage. A contract usually calls for you not to leave large items or an unusual amount of garbage and empty boxes for the cleaner to remove.

GETTING THERE

The following are suggestions from veterans of many moves.

"*Wrap plants in a plastic garbage bag with a few holes punched in it for air.*"

"*Get off the interstate once in a while and drive through some small towns. Make stops at tourist places, scenic vistas, and other highlights. That will make the trip seem like a vacation. Check a road map for indicators of whether or not the back road is an interesting one, though, as many aren't.*"

"*Try to plan your trips so you're not going through busy cities at rush hour.*"

"*On our drive from North Dakota to Alaska we knew driving the Alcan would be an adventure. Our middle daughter kept a daily journal and our oldest took photos. After settling in at Elmendorf, we put together a book of our journey. Digital*" photos were inserted into the text, copies were made, and on the last page was the dedication: 'No matter where in the world we go, we always know where home is.' We gave this to our families and my mom and in-laws still enjoy it."

"Stay at motels that have pools. Everyone will want to work off some energy after being cooped up in the car all day, and pools are a good place to do it."

"Have a good breakfast each day on the road. It makes sitting in the car easier."

"Carefully pack suitcases that will travel with you. Carrying around unnecessary items makes your suitcases heavier, and you waste time arranging and rearranging, folding and refolding their contents. Zip-closure bags are handy to hold bottles and tubes that might leak, to pack a wet washcloth in, or to store restaurant leftovers. Don't pack big supplies of things you can buy anywhere, such as detergent."

"Consider a satellite radio subscription. The traffic and weather reports alone may make it worth the cost to you. Regional radios are almost nothing but ads."

"When flying, ask at the airport if there's a USO lounge to relax in."

"Supplement your cell phone with a phone card. Your cell phone may not work well in an area in which you'll need to make a land-line call."

"Have all needed car and insurance documentation in the glove box."

"You can avoid a steady diet of fast food and the junk food sugar rush that tires you out by creatively stocking a cooler. Visit an ethnic foods store and a bakery shop for interesting treats. Buy chewy Italian or French loaves, bagels and containers of cream cheese. Fill Rubbermaid containers with exotic cheeses, pepperoni, tuna salad, summer sausage, grapes, melon chunks, kiwi fruit, oatmeal cookies, chocolate chips, snap peas, homemade trail mix, dried fruit, granola bars, and peanuts. Keep bottled water in the cooler."

"Buy Walmart gift cards for gas. Walmarts are everywhere and many have gas stations. When you use a gift card, the price per gallon is less than the advertised price."

"Keep the car clean. It's easy to let fast food wrappers and other trash pile up, and sitting with it gets tedious. Keep a hand-held vacuum cleaner in the trunk for regularly picking up crumbs and pet hair. You might keep sheets draped over leather seats to keep them from getting hot in the summer, and to help keep them clean."

"Join AAA or another roadside rescue service. You never know when you'll need it, and their 800 number will immediately hook you up with approved local tow services and mechanics."

MOVING IN

You've arrived! Call the transportation office with your contact information, even if you're living in a temporary quarters. You can arrange a direct delivery of your household goods when they come in, or place the shipment in temporary storage for up to ninety days while you look for a home.

Here are some tips for moving day.

- Accept your property as soon as possible after it arrives. Intermediate storage heightens the risk of loss or damage. It will also cost you money if it exceeds the amount of time for which the government will pay.
- Try to find a babysitter for small children. Moving in is just as hectic as moving out.
- When your household goods are delivered, the movers are only required to place each item once. You might sketch a floor plan showing locations of the furniture; if you're waiting to get into quarters, get a floor plan from the housing office. Some people designate a color for each room in the new home, with matching colored stickers on the boxes and on the door to each room.
- Disassembled items should be reassembled.
- Ask the movers to bring the boxes in through one door only, and check each box off as it's brought in. Don't sign the inventory until every box is accounted for. (You don't have to account for box contents, just the box.) Otherwise, filing a claim will be difficult.
- The movers are paid to unpack your stuff. If you wish them to do so, tell them. They will not organize your house, however. Carefully check each empty box before they cart it off; many a small item has gotten hidden in the wrapping paper and thrown out.
- Hang signs that correspond to the box labels on the door of each room, so that boxes can be put in their appropriate places.
- Finally, the movers will give you a form DD 1840 to sign, on which you should note any visibly damaged or missing items.

Filing a Claim

If items arrive damaged, you can file for their reasonable repair or full replacement cost. You can do this without your husband if you have power of attorney. Claims are processed through the personal property office responsible for the area where the goods were delivered. Air Force personnel may file for full replacement value directly with the moving company.

Bring the DD 1840 to the claims office within seventy days of the date your property was delivered. This form is the official notification that you are going to make a claim. You don't have to file the actual claim within seventy days; you have two years to do that. If you fail to file the official notification within seventy days, the government won't be able to collect any money from the moving company and will offset your claim by the amount it could have recouped. Personnel there will sign and date it and give you a copy. Keep this copy as proof that you did everything you were supposed to. At this time, pick up a claim packet. It contains all the forms you need.

Your claim needs to be accompanied by written estimates of everything that costs more than $100 to fix or replace. For items that have to be replaced, submit either copies of catalog pages of similar items or a signed note from a department store verifying the price. Sometimes the claims office will send an inspector to see your damaged goods. The mover has the right to inspect any damage reported to it and may ask a local repair firm for an estimate. Keep all broken items until the claim is settled, and then some. You might be asked to turn in any salvageable items for which you are paid replacement costs. Full replacement value of damaged items is given, not depreciated ones.

The claims system is not a substitute for insurance if you have substantial property. Total claims are limited to $40,000, regardless of the possessions' worth, and there are maximum amounts for specific categories, such as jewelry, crystal, and cameras.

PERSONALLY PROCURED TRANSPORTATION (PPT)

If you prefer to maintain complete control over your possessions, the PPT allows you to move your household goods yourself or hire your own commercial mover. You can also combine a PPT with a government move, up to your weight entitlement. If you move yourself, the government will reimburse you 95 percent of what it would pay a commercial carrier. Know that the source of your rental equipment must be bona-fide vendors such as U-Haul or Ryder. If you hire your own carrier, it will pay 100 percent of what it would pay a commercial carrier. If your move costs less than that, you pocket the difference. The average profit made by servicemembers who choose to move themselves is $600. If the move ends up costing more, you'll pay the difference. Know that you'll be issued a W-2 form to declare the profits as income on your taxes. Keep your receipts for everything—oil and gas for the rental truck, tolls, and any boxes and packing materials you buy, and the cost of the certified weight tickets—as these expenses will be subtracted before taxes are deducted from your payment. PPT reimbursement is for moving expenses only, entirely separate from personal travel, pay, and allowances. You can apply for an advance operating allowance.

Obtain PPT authorization from the transportation office, at which time you'll need to provide as accurate as possible an estimate of your weight. Then pack, load, and move your own possessions. Reserve a truck as soon as you know you'll need one. Prime moving season is May through September, and you'll be competing for rentals with college students and job-hopping civilians. Compare prices at www.123movers.com.

Obtain two weight tickets from a state-certified weigh station, one showing the weight of your truck or trailer empty and one showing it full. Your transportation office will have addresses of local weigh stations. The exact amount of money the government pays is tied to this weight. You must have both these tickets; if you fail to procure them, or you lose them, you'll be reimbursed nothing. You'll have the same weight allowance that you would if you were moved commercially. Calculate measurement tons with this formula: length × width × height ÷ 40.

Insure your possessions, as the military claims office will not pay for any loss or damages that occur during a PPT. Consider buying commercial insurance coverage, either through the moving company or through an insurance company. You may be held personally responsible if your insurance isn't enough to satisfy any third-party damage or claims resulting from an accident. If using a commercial carrier, ensure it provides insurance on your goods.

If you need temporary storage when you arrive at your destination, the government will reimburse you based on its cost to store a similar amount of weight. Claims for loss or damage to your household goods while in storage are not payable by the military claims office, so continue to insure your goods while they're in storage.

Packing Tips for PPT Moves

A PPT move isn't a bargain if everything gets broken. Ask the rental company for brochures and advice on packing boxes and loading the truck. Also consider that while you may have friends at your current duty station to help load your truck, will anyone be available at the other end? If not, a partial PPT move may be possible.

- Pack electronics and other fragile items in the area over the truck cab.
- Load heavy appliances toward the front, next to the cab (e.g., the refrigerator on the right and the washer and dryer on the left).
- Place desks and dressers facing the truck walls to keep the drawers from opening.

If you do your own move, find sturdy, manageable boxes, label them well, and don't pack them too heavy to comfortably lift.

- Use the tie-downs on the truck's inside walls to secure mattresses and tables.
- Stack boxes of similar size and weight together.
- Put lightweight, irregularly shaped items on top.
- Fill a box with moving essentials: a tape measure, strapping tape, marker pens, scissors, screwdrivers, wrenches, hammers, rope, soft soap, and paper towels. Load it last so that it can be unloaded first.
- Don't pack any of the boxes too heavy. Fill them solid with packing peanuts or balled-up paper so that they don't crush.
- An apron with big pockets is useful for wearing markers, tape, and other small items.
- Pack glass-framed art separately and pack them standing. Don't lay them flat.

Some tips from people who have done PPTs:

"Instead of renting an expensive city dumpster for serious decluttering, we rented a U-Haul. We filled it with bags of trash and unwanted furniture, then drove it to the dump."

"Scrounge for boxes anywhere you can find them. Small and manageable is the key. Grocery and liquor stores are good sources, as are bookstores and warehouse clubs. Collect copier and printer paper boxes from offices. Drive through military housing areas; many times you'll see lots of great boxes filled with packing paper from other people's PCS moves piled on a driveway. Good boxes bought from moving companies can be resold when you're done with them; place an ad for the whole lot; they'll fetch between $30 and $50."

"Buy rolls of unprinted newspaper on the roll from warehouse clubs or perhaps from the newspaper itself. They make good packing material. Don't use printed newspaper; it's dirty and the ink rubs off on your possessions."

"I've successfully wrapped dishes and breakables in my towels and dishcloths, and even my clothes. You can also cushion glass plates by putting paper plates in between them."

"Our move was a short distance. For clothes, we took drawers out of dressers, carried the dressers to the truck, and then replaced the drawers."

"While we were planning the move, I laid out my kitchen on a floor plan, choosing convenient locations for dishes, silverware, pots and pans, to make unpacking easier. I took out my plan and began unpacking shortly after the movers left. We had been living in a furnished condo and it gave me insight into what I did and didn't need. I ended up getting rid of much of the plasticware I had brought as most was just useless stuff to dig through."

MOVING YOUR MOBILE HOME

If you want to move the homestead, you can do that, too. Transportation of a mobile home is authorized in lieu of household goods within CONUS, within Alaska, and between CONUS and Alaska. When moved by commercial transporter, reimbursement includes carrier charges, road fares and tolls, permits, and charges for the pilot car. If you tow it yourself, you will be reimbursed for actual costs. Self-propelled mobile homes are reimbursed at 36.5 cents per mile up to your household goods weight entitlement.

The government will pay as much to move a mobile home as it would pay to move your maximum weight allowance. You must pay anything over that. It's rare for anyone to break even when shipping a mobile home. What the government pays usually doesn't cover even half the cost. Transportation personnel have seen bills in the thousands presented to the servicemember.

Setting up a mobile home in the new location may involve expenses such as earthquake bracing required by some state laws. Furthermore, mobile homes are made for the requirements of the state where they're manufactured; ones built for the South may not be warm enough for the North. Lots may not be readily available, and your home must meet standards in appearance and construction. Selling your mobile home and buying another after relocating is almost always wisest. Know that mobile homes don't appreciate like site-built homes; they depreciate like cars.

What a mobile home can hold while stationary and what it can hold while being pulled down the interstate are two different things. People moving overloaded trailers have had them break down en route. For this reason, a carrier may decline to move a mobile home after deciding that it's overloaded, but you would then have to pay an attempted-pickup charge.

SHIPPING YOUR VEHICLE

POV shipment within the U.S. is typically authorized only when the owner is medically unable to drive, when there is a home-port change, or if there isn't enough time to drive. A vehicle can be stored when the servicemember has overseas orders in which shipping isn't authorized or is sent TDY on a contingency operation for more than thirty days.

One vehicle may be shipped for many overseas assignments (and be shipped back at the end of the tour). Restrictions may apply. For example, for assignments to Korea, military members must be "command sponsored" (allowed to be accompanied by family members), or pay grade E-7 or above, to ship a vehicle. Servicemembers may also be authorized shipment for a replacement POV during any four-year period while assigned overseas. If you have a lease over twelve months on your vehicle, written permission from the leasing company is required. If your vehicle exceeds twenty measurement tons in size, you'll have to pay for the excess. A motorcycle or moped may be shipped as long as another vehicle isn't shipped under the same set of orders.

The vehicle needs to be delivered to the port before you go overseas. If a spouse delivers the vehicle to the loading port, a power of attorney is required. You can apply for mileage reimbursement to the authorized port for shipment, as well as from picking it up at the authorized receiving port. If you're going to an area with minimal service facilities, consider shipping some spare parts (e.g., tires, fan belts, windshield wipers, hoses), also. If the place you're going only sells leaded gas, you'll need to have your car's catalytic converter removed before shipping. Keep the paperwork. You'll need to put it back on before your stateside return and show proof of this before the U.S. authorities will let you drive it away. While you are allowed to ship some property in it, such as jumper cables, tools, and a car seat, this is not advisable due to the high incidence of theft. Ship these things with your unaccompanied baggage. Any TVs or other electronics in the car need to be factory installed and bolted down, or removed.

With few exceptions, you can't ship back at government expense a foreign-built vehicle that was bought overseas. You can pay to ship a vehicle yourself, space available, on the Military Sealift Command. Naturally, it must meet all U.S. safety and emission standards before you can drive it away. Converting a foreign-specification car to meet U.S. standards is expensive, so before you buy one with this in mind check prices.

While en route, the status of your vehicle can be found at *www. whereismypov.com*. A list of vehicle processing centers is in the appendix. When picking up your car, wash it before signing the inventory sheet. Most ports have car washes on the premises. Dirt accumulated on the way over can obscure new nicks and scratches. Be careful about hiring other people to pick up your car for you; they don't know your car as well as you do and won't be as meticulous about noting new scratches. Once the inventory sheet is signed and the car driven away, scratches not noted will be difficult to claim.

SHIPPING YOUR PET

You can ship Fluffy three ways: on the Air Mobility Command (AMC), on a commercial carrier, or through a pet-shipping service. Shipping a pet requires months-in-advance planning. Since pets don't travel at DoD expense, cost is involved.

Discuss your pet at your moving appointment, and reserve space for it at the same time; do not just show up at the AMC with a pet. Airlines require a health certificate issued within ten days of departure. That is not enough time, however, to treat some ailments that prevent certification. For instance, if rabies shots are required, they must be given between thirty days and one year before departure. You may also need to obtain bilingual health certificates.

AMC is the least expensive carrier. Shipment is for a permanent move only, and service ends at the port of entry, so you must make arrangements for any continuing flights. Your pet must stay with you until boarding time. Only dogs and cats can be shipped, two per family. Animals must be at least six weeks old and weaned, and the pet and its carrier must weigh less than 99 pounds. It costs $85 for a pet weighing up to 70 pounds and twice that for a pet weighing between 71 and 99 pounds. If you need a waiver because of the number, type, and weight of your pets, fax a request to 618-229-7876 or to *petwaivers@scott.af.mil*.

Ask your veterinarian about foreign countries' quarantine requirements, since you must pay most associated expenses (e.g., lab tests and food). Quarantining on military facilities, if available, is cheaper. Some countries require microchipping. When your tour is over, you'll have to comply with the quarantine requirements in the States (for instance, Hawaii has a 120-day quarantine). AMC will not ship pets to England, Korea, or Japan due to their lengthy quarantine requirements. Some countries restrict what they consider dangerous dogs, such as pit bulls. Carry a leash to walk your pet before and after the flight. Don't put the leash inside the carrier or attach it to the outside. Clip your pet's nails to prevent them from hooking the carrier. Carry your pet's rabies certificate during travel and attach a copy to the carrier, along with a copy of the orders. If your pet bites someone while traveling, you must provide proof of current vaccinations (a rabies tag isn't enough) or your pet will be impounded. In some places, if proof of current vaccination cannot be provided, the animal may be destroyed in order to be tested.

If you use a commercial airline, research their often-changing rules. Most airlines won't board pets as cargo during the summer because of a risk of injury to the pet in the hot cargo hold. If the pet is very small, the airline might allow you to stash it in an approved container under your seat, for an extra charge. A pet-shipping service offers shipping plus extras, such as home pickup, boarding at airport kennels, and delivery at the cargo terminal. This option is the most expensive.

If you're traveling by car, a health certificate is legally required to take your pet across state lines. Though this law is rarely enforced, your pet could be impounded without one.

NONCONCURRENT TRAVEL

If the overseas area you're going to has a severe shortage of housing both on base and off, concurrent travel orders for you and your husband will not be issued. Your husband will still have to report to his new assignment, but you will not be authorized to travel with him. You will be issued travel authorization when the housing situation improves.

If you marry *after* he has moved, inquire about a paid move to join him, which may be possible if he didn't use up all his moving entitlement. You will have to be command-sponsored for this to happen.

HOMEOWNER'S ASSISTANCE PROGRAM (HAP)

Two items military homeowners will be interested in knowing about are the Homeowner's Assistance Program and the tax relief law for military homeowners.

Homeowner's Assistance Program (HAP). Base closings have a negative effect on home prices. If you are moving from a base that has announced a closure, you might qualify for the HAP. It assists military people from all services, DoD civilians, and homeowners employed near the base if they owned and occupied their homes when the closure was publicly announced. (Occupancy can be waived if the owners were stationed overseas at the time.) Homes must be one- or two-family dwellings. Most mobile homes do not qualify.

HAP works like this: If you are unable to sell your house, the government will buy it for 75 percent of the prior market value or the balance of the existing mortgage, whichever is greater. Even if you do find a private buyer, HAP can reimburse you for part of your financial loss. The government will make up the difference between the sale price and up to 95 percent of the house's value before the base closure announcement. HAP is not designed to make you money or even let you break even; it just softens the financial blow.

Military Exemption for Home Sale Capital Gains Tax. The Internal Revenue Service (IRS) allows anyone who profitably sells a home they owned for at least five years to exclude up to $250,000 of that profit from their taxable income if they owned and lived in the home as their principal residence for at least two years (those two years don't have to be consecutive).

Since many servicemembers retain ownership of their homes while away on duty and eventually sell them without returning to live in them, they may meet the criteria for an exemption to the two-year rule. If they are on qualified extended duty, defined as the duty station being at least fifty miles from the residence sold, they may suspend this five-year test period for up to ten years of such duty time. This provision may be used for only one property at a time and may exclude gain on only one home sale in any two-year period.

> A servicemember's legal residence doesn't change just because he moves to another state. The Servicemember's Civil Relief Act (see chapter 9) allows him to live in one state but claim another as his legal residence.

MAKE IT HOME

Get acquainted with your new neighborhood and base. Go with your husband to the newcomers' briefing; it is a good source of information about available services and facilities. Spouses are welcome. Find out where the town library, parks, gyms, and other leisure spots are. Actively seek friendships. Go to your unit wives' coffee or Family Readiness Group. If you're an extrovert, take advantage of the newcomer's prerogative and introduce yourself to your neighbors. If you're an introvert, hang around outside washing the car, sitting on the porch, or playing with your pet to give someone more outgoing a chance to introduce herself. There's no better way to start a new tour than by making new friends.

FURTHER READING

Books

Cline, Lydia Sloan. *Architectural Drafting for Interior Designers.* New York: Cengage-Delmar, 2007. Contains instructions on sketching floor plans.

Internet Resources

www.mapquest.com, www.mapsonus.com, www.mapblast.com. Get driving directions and maps.

www.weather.com. Get local forecasts.

www.petswelcome.com. Website listing places that welcome pets while on the road.

www.defenselink.mil/specials/itsyourmove. Comprehensive information on military moves.

www.yardsalequeen.com/yardsale.htm, www.mahalo.com/How_to_Hold_a_Successful_Yard_Sale. Sites with useful information about holding a yard sale.

jppso-sat.randolph.af.mil/ecaf/faq4.htm. Frequently asked excess cost questions about weight allowances.

www.militarystudent.dod.mil. Information on education transitions for military children.

www.biz-stay.com. Has information about extended-stay hotels.

www.defenselink.mil/mtom. Site that helps military kids and teens make new connections when they move.

www.militaryhomefront.dod.mil. Military Homefront is a DoD website with lots of quality-of-life information, including tools for planning a move.

www.sas.usace.army.mil/hapinv. Information on homeowner's assistance programs.

www.jiwire.com. Find wireless access for your laptop or handheld device at this hotspots site.

www.homefair.com. Compare what the same salary buys in different cities.

www.kidon.com/media-link/us_military.php. Links to base newspapers and other military-related newspapers.

https://www.navy-lodge.com. List of military lodges worldwide.

www.sddc.army.mil/sddc/Content/Pub/8808/dbcn8808.pdf. Pamphlet on shipping your vehicle.

8

Living Overseas

So your husband has orders to a foreign country, and you're going with him—lucky you! You're being given the opportunity of a lifetime. You can see world landmarks, meet citizens of other countries, experience new cultures, and learn different viewpoints. In short, you will be able to see what makes a foreign country "foreign." Think of this tour as your overseas vacation. People pay big bucks for this!

Q: Why are servicemembers stationed overseas?
A: Because America's defense rests not only on its home bases but on its overseas installations as well. Overseas bases are needed to support the personnel that keep sea routes open by which goods critical to our economy (e.g., petroleum, chromium, steel, rubber, ball bearings, sugar, coffee, DVD players, bicycles, toys, and cars) travel. These stations are also needed to support personnel sent to areas where they might be needed in case of hostilities.

MULTICULTURALISM
In the United States, much is said about the need to appreciate diversity and multiculturalism. This appreciation will serve you especially well overseas. Things don't always appear the same to people from different cultural backgrounds. For instance, in the Orient, avoiding loss of face is important; people don't want to offend if they can't answer a question, so their behavior is what we might perceive as evasive. In the Middle East, conservative dress is required and physical contact between the genders is discouraged. In Australia, rowdiness and physical contact are common. In many countries, wearing shoes in some religious temples is sacrilegious, as is displaying religious symbols as art. It is improper to show up at a European's home for dinner empty handed, but red roses or white asters are inappropriate.

Gestures, greetings, appropriate eye contact, working style, listening style, and interpersonal relations differ everywhere. But culture isn't inborn; it's learned. If you're open to host-citizen behavior and willing to ask questions and exchange information, you'll pick up what's accepted and what's not. As soon as you learn which country you're going to, learn something about it. Browse the message boards at sites like *www.fodors.com*, *www.frommers.com*, *www.tripadvisor.com*, and *www.igougo.com*, where enthusiastic travelers swap tips and report experiences. Read up on the country's customs; be mindful of your dress and where you point your camera (taking photos of strangers is rude anywhere). And remember that it takes more than one person to accurately represent how an entire culture thinks, feels, and behaves.

LEARN THE LANGUAGE

Make a goal to become conversational in the language of the country to which you're moving. Think of all you do throughout the day: You ask for directions, read gas pumps, question clerks, read bills, count money. Unless you plan to lead a very limited and restricted life, you'll want to do the same overseas. Knowing the language will also make your time in that country more fun. You'll get better buys because shops where English is spoken charge more for the service. You may make host-citizen friends more easily. If you can't carve out the time to take structured classes, try an online course at a community college, or investigate some of the free or inexpensive courses at *www.word2word.com/course.html*. Advertise for a tutor. Borrow CDs from your library or buy a set and play them in your car while commuting. Practice instead of watching TV. Make learning the language a family project.

Once in country, accompany your husband to any language and orientation classes he's required to attend. Perhaps sign up for classes offered through the education center, where the instructors are host citizens who will also share their knowledge of the area.

PREPARING TO GO

You have a lot of stuff to do! In addition to all that's involved in a stateside move (see chapter 7), there are additional considerations when moving overseas.

Should You Ship Your Car?

Considerations for shipping your car overseas include:

- The streets in many countries are narrower than what we're used to, making a big vehicle hard to maneuver and park.
- Your car is a foreign import to the country to which you ship it. Even if it was made in that country, it was made to American standards and specifications and is still a foreign import. Getting parts and repair work done can take months.
- Insurance is more costly overseas and many stateside insurers do not cover you abroad (USAA does). If your insurer won't cover you, ask your sponsor

in advance for names of companies that insure Americans. You will need proof of insurance to register and insure your car, and have it pass a vehicle inspection.

- Some countries restrict vehicle characteristics such as type, color, and optional equipment. CB radios and radar detectors are often illegal.
- The car must be in top condition. The government has strict rules on the condition of a vehicle before it's shipped, but the host country's rules can be even stricter. Tire treads a millimeter too thin, rust on the exhaust, a hairline crack in the windshield, even an unadjusted light can cause your vehicle to sit at the host-country port until you can afford to correct it. The engine, windshield wipers, brakes, horn, battery, and lights must work. The exhaust system must be sound and body fenders free of breaks or tears. Rust protection is needed if you're going to humid areas such as Panama or the Pacific. Your car will also have to meet the host country's emission control standards.
- After-market items, such as tinted windows, undercarriage lights, loud exhausts, and "spinners" are illegal in Europe. So if you've "pimped your ride," you may have to spend more removing it all.

It may be more practical to sell your car and buy one from an overseas military family that is moving back home.

STORING YOUR VEHICLE
This option is available for those with PCS orders to an area where vehicles cannot be shipped, or if extensive modifications to their car are needed to conform to the host country's standards. Only one self-propelled, wheeled motor vehicle may be stored—no trailers, boats, or snowmobiles. No property may be stored inside the vehicle except for car-related items (e.g., jacks or tire chains). The vehicle will be covered and stored indoors, and started once a month, the air-conditioner and heater cycled, and fuel stabilizer added as needed. It will be moved occasionally to prevent flat spots on tires. You might ask your insurer if you can save money by dropping all coverage except for comprehensive loss. The storage facility maintains some insurance on it.

Driver's License
In some countries, your U.S. driver's license will suffice; in others, you need a local or military license. To get this, simply present your valid U.S. license, pass a test on international symbols, and pay a small fee.

Firearms
Gun ownership is easy in the U.S., but this isn't the case in most countries. Stringent gun-control laws are common with accompanying fines and jail terms if you break them, and they apply whether you live on or off base. Make sure that you're permit-

ted to possess firearms. Even in countries where private guns are permitted, hunting licenses, permits, and guides (often required) are costly. Many overseas bases have sports clubs where firearms can be rented. If you do take your own firearm, register it.

Obtaining a Passport

If you accompany, or even just visit, your sponsor overseas, you'll need a passport. This is an internationally recognized travel document that verifies the bearer's identity and nationality. A valid U.S. passport is required to enter and leave most foreign countries. It is not the same as a passport card, which is a document that facilitates entry at U.S. land and sea ports of entry from Canada, Mexico, the Caribbean, and Bermuda, and cannot be used for air travel. Only the U.S. Department of State has the authority to grant, issue or verify United States passports.

Apply for a standard tourist passport at over 9,000 locations, including many U.S. post offices. Visit *iafdb.travel.state.gov* to search for the closest location to you by zip code. Overseas, apply at a U.S. embassy, consulate, or the base legal office You can also apply online at *https://pptform.state.gov*. The fee is $100 for adults and $85 for children under sixteen. There's a $10 to $15 charge for the required two × two–inch photos, which you can have taken at the post office or at many Kinko's, Walgreen's, or other photo shops. Bring the following when you apply for a passport:

- an original or certified copy of your birth certificate or a Certificate of Naturalization or a previous U.S. passport (If you don't have a birth certificate, contact the Office of Vital Statistics in the state where you were born for a copy.)
- an original or certified copy of your children's birth certificates
- a passport application
- two recent, identical, two × two–inch photographs
- proof of identity (a valid driver's license or other valid photo ID)
- the application fee

The country you're moving or traveling to may also require you to have a visa (permission to enter) in your passport. The same office that takes your passport applications can tell you if you'll need a visa and how to apply.

Both parents must sign the forms for a child under fourteen to receive a passport and visa. If you are geographically separated, whoever applies for the passport needs a notarized statement from the absent parent. If your child is born overseas, get a passport for him or her as soon as possible, since you won't be able to remove the child from the country without it, a problem if you must leave for an emergency. If your passport picture shows you and your child together, neither you nor he will be able to leave independently.

Family members can get a no-fee passport at the base passport office if they are PCSing overseas. Since the sponsor's military ID permits him entry into the country he's ordered to, he has to buy his own if he wants one (advisable, since he'll need one to vacation in other countries). The no-fee passport looks identical to the tourist passport except for a line in the back stating that the holder is military affiliated. If you plan to do a lot of traveling, you may not want this. In addition to the documents listed, bring a copy of the travel orders. Some military assignments entitle the sponsor and his family to official or diplomatic passports. Call the passport office before going because some bases process passport applications only on certain days and times.

Don't leave this until the last minute, as both no-fee and tourist passports generally take six weeks to issue, although you can pay $60 extra per passport for expedited service.

Passports are important identity documents and, as such, valuable to identity thieves. Guard yours. Don't routinely carry it on your person, making it vulnerable to pickpockets. Make a copy of it and carry it if you feel the information on it may be needed.

MANAGING YOUR FINANCES OVERSEAS

Which banks, credit cards, and cash instruments will meet your needs in the most cost-effective way? You'll need to research fees, charges, and access to services.

Bank Accounts. Canceling your stateside bank account isn't necessary, but most families find it useful to open an account with the bank that has contracted to serve the military overseas. However, if you make trips stateside while stationed overseas, be aware that overseas customers of a bank may not be able to cash checks at stateside branches of that same bank.

Credit Cards. MasterCard and Visa are widely accepted overseas, but some places accept one and not the other. American Express is less accepted, and Discover almost not at all. Inform the issuing bank about your move; otherwise, the company's fraud detection software may shut your card down on your first attempt to use it overseas. Also, know that 800 numbers only work in the U.S. and Canada, so ask for an alternative customer service number. When you use the card, the purchase amount will be converted from the local currency into dollars at whatever exchange rate the bank uses on the day the bank receives the charge, not the day the purchase was made. Most banks charge a 1 percent fee for foreign usage plus a 2 percent fee for currency conversion. Capitol One (*www.capitalone.com*) is a popular card with overseas travelers because it doesn't charge either of those fees.

Debit Cards. As discussed in chapter 5, these are used as credit cards. When traveling, some people prefer prepaid debit cards instead of regular debit cards because they're not connected to a checking account, making them less vulnerable in case of loss or theft. You can buy a prepaid debit card with the amount of money you think you might need while traveling, and use it in

ATM machines. But know that prepaid debit cards have purchase fees, reloading fees, international transaction fees, and cancellation fees. An advantage is that there is no cash advance fee.

Travelers Checks. These are preprinted, fixed-amount checks that are bought at a bank, typically for 1 percent of the face value. They're available in different currencies. You must sign it when using it for a purchase, and it's basically a same-as-cash transaction. Since they can be replaced if lost or stolen, many people consider them safer than cash. However, being that credit cards are so widely accepted, traveler's checks aren't as popular as they used to be, and, in fact, some places don't accept them, particularly if the issuer is small and not widely known. Some banks sell what are called "travelers check cards" which are used like credit cards.

Automatic Teller Machines (ATMs). If your ATM card is linked to the PLUS or Cirrus networks, you can use it to obtain local currency in over 210 countries. Each network has over a million ATMs. Know that many ATMs, especially in Europe, don't accept personal identification numbers (PINs) longer than four digits. If your PIN is longer, change it before you go, and use numbers, not letters, since many overseas ATMs only have numbers on the keypad. Most ATMs abroad will only let you access the primary account on your ATM card. Some major U.S. banks partner with overseas banks, which may save you from paying ATM fees to your hometown bank.

If you plan to use your ATM or debit card in an overseas ATM, make sure the card contains a Visa, MasterCard, Cirrus, or Plus logo, because those cards are used internationally. If you use a Cirrus or Plus card without a Visa or MasterCard logo you might avoid Visa and MasterCard fees for foreign use and currency conversions. Many banks charge higher fees for international ATM withdrawals, and you may also be charged a fee by the foreign ATM's owner. Otherwise, charges are the same as with credit cards.

Cash. Obtain some local currency before you go, as you may need it immediately upon arrival. Otherwise, you may find that expensive currency exchange booths and ATMs are your only options, and even they either may be closed or have long lines. You can obtain foreign currency from your hometown bank. Some savvy travelers offer to buy excess currency at a more favorable rate from recently returned travelers.

Exchange currency and travelers checks at major financial institutions when you can. Avoid changing money at airports, train stations, hotels, and kiosks. Between the low exchange rate and high fees, you can lose 10 percent of the original amount. Also try to avoid the ubiquitous cash-to-cash machines. These machines work similar to ATMs, but instead of inserting a card, you insert money, and it returns a different currency. While convenient, they have poor exchange rates and charge a fee for their use. Likewise, avoid transactions where the merchandise is quoted in dollars and the merchant converts to local currency. While this seems tourist-friendly, such transactions have inflated exchange rates.

Hidden travel wallets (worn around the neck), ankle holsters, money belts and socks with zippered pouches are prudent ways to carry cash and passports. Fanny packs are not. Loop the strap around yourself a few times to discourage pickpockets and other types who routinely survey foreigners for possibilities. Don't retrieve the contents from hidden packs in public, as that defeats their purpose.

TELEPHONES

Phone service overseas can initially be confusing. Prefixes, rings, and busy signals are different, country codes have to be dialed, and the bills may be hard to read. Ask your sponsor (discussed in chapter 10) to help you out with this. Meanwhile, here's some general information about phone service overseas.

Landline phones. Phone service is nationalized in many countries, and you will need to apply for it. You may pay an initial setup fee plus monthly charges. Internet access usually costs extra. Calling charges may vary with time of day. If you don't specifically ask for an itemized monthly bill when you apply, the default may be a simple, nonitemized bill that is impossible to check for accuracy. Know that local calls made from a home land-line phone are generally not free; you're charged for each one. So if you make calls from someone else's home phone, it's polite to offer reimbursement. Generally, long-distance calls on land-lines are more expensive when they originate overseas than stateside.

Phone Cards. Buy an international phone card. While some cards can be used both stateside and overseas, most calling cards are not designed for overseas use. You can buy competitively priced prepaid cards and calling cards from the exchange and AT&T (*www.usa.att.com/military/index.jsp*).

Voice over Internet Protocol (VoIP). Also called IP Telephony, this is the transmission of voice traffic over computers. It is popular because of its cost advantages over traditional telephone networks; on overseas calls, the monetary savings is huge. VoIP calls can be placed across the Internet for no additional charge other than the flat monthly fee you already pay for Internet service; there is no per-minute fee for long distance. Some services offer an optional small monthly fee that will enable you to make unlimited calls to land-line and cell-phone users.

Skype and Net2Phone are two VoIP services. Download their software at *www.skype.com* and *www.net2phone.com*. Equipment needed is either a standard telephone with a VoIP adapter, a computer with speakers and a headset, or a VoIP telephone. This equipment can be bought at places like Radio Shack or Best Buy.

Cell Phones. Most U.S. cell phones will not work overseas due to different transmission frequencies. If your phone is a "tri-band" it will, but it must be unlocked, meaning it can work with any service provider. However, if you use your U.S. service provider, you'll incur large roaming charges. Fortunately, cell-phone coverage is excellent overseas, and in many places is better than in the U.S. It is best to just purchase a GSM (Global System for Mobile communications) world cell phone overseas. These are unlocked, and you can buy a service contract in the country you're in. These contracts are typically for two years duration and require payment by direct withdrawal from an account. However, you might find that buying a local prepaid SIM card is a cheaper and easier route. A SIM card is a small chip that contains your cell phone number and any additional services subscribed to, like voicemail. A prepaid SIM card for each country you visit will give you a local phone number and local calling rates (typically twenty-five cents per minute). Incoming calls are free regardless where they originate. You can replenish your SIM card by purchasing an airtime voucher in the local currency. Airtime vouchers are available at newsstands and convenience stores. They're scratch cards with a pin code that you key into your phone for immediate credit.

Generally, cell-phone rates are higher than land-line rates. Calling from a cell phone to a land phone or from a land phone to a cell phone is more expensive than calling from a cell to a cell or a land phone to another land-line.

HEALTH CARE

Tricare, a managed health and dental plan, was discussed in chapter 2. It exists outside the U.S. in the form of Tricare Prime Overseas (TPO), Tricare Standard Overseas (TSO), and Tricare Global Remote Overseas (TGRO). These plans cover routine, urgent, and specialty care. Active-duty servicemembers and their eligible, command-sponsored family members who reside with them overseas are eligible.

Tricare Prime Overseas. Characteristics of this option are:

- no enrollment fees (although enrollment is required)
- fewer out-of-pocket costs than Tricare Standard Overseas
- enhanced coverage for vision and clinical preventive services
- a primary care manager (PCM), from which most care is received
- referral from the PCM to specialists when necessary
- usually no claims to file
- transfers from one overseas area to another or back to the United States
- point-of-service option may be available for receiving care without needing a referral from the PCM (which, of course, usually results in higher out-of-pocket costs)
- is not available at all overseas locations

Tricare Global Remote Overseas. TRGO is an option where TPO isn't. Tricare partners with International SOS to find the best local providers and facilities and develop a network of licensed, qualified physicians for quality care. Only physicians who are licensed and who have graduated from an accredited medical school are included in the core network. A list of TGRO providers is at *www.internationalsos.com/private/tricare*. It's updated daily.

Characteristics of TGRO are:

- no enrollment fees (although enrollment is required)
- fewer out-of-pocket costs than Tricare Standard Overseas
- you receive most care from your primary care manager (PCM)
- your PCM or TGRO call center refers you to specialists when necessary and will tell you when you need to go to another city, country, or the U.S. for quality care
- generally no claims to file

Tricare Standard Overseas. This is a fee-for-service option. Retirees and their families are also eligible for this option, as are noncommand sponsored family members and survivors who live overseas. Characteristics of TSO are:

- higher out-of-pocket costs than Tricare Prime Overseas
- ability to choose from any qualified host nation provider
- referrals are not required, but some care may require prior authorization
- services must be paid for upfront when received
- you may have to submit claims for reimbursement
- there is no assigned primary care manager
- no enrollment is required
- care may be received in a military treatment facility on a space-available basis

Employment Overseas

Finding a job overseas can be difficult. Federal jobs are limited, and in remote areas they are practically nonexistent; they are limited by law and by agreement with the host nation. You will compete with a group that has equal or greater priority for these federal jobs: citizens of the host country. And if you don't speak the language, the federal government is about the only employer available to you.

Employment procedures overseas must meet legal, regulatory, and mission requirements and must uphold host-government agreements. The government has only the jobs required to accomplish its mission, and there are far more applicants than jobs. Congress places limits on the number of DoD civilians allowed overseas; it's virtually a no-growth market. For what jobs there are, qualified host citizens have as much right to them as you do, as spelled out in the Status of Forces Agreement (SOFA) discussed later in this chapter. Furthermore, local nationals bring stability and knowledge of the language to the job. For many jobs, such characteristics are essential. That isn't to say it can't be done, though.

Federal and NAF Jobs. Some job slots are reserved for military spouses. Review the websites and information in chapter 4 for instructions on applying. Those interested in being a DoDDS teacher should e-mail *Recruitment@ hq.dodea.edu* or call 703-588-3983.

Independent Contracting Companies. These are large companies that contract with the DoD to provide specific services. While most are looking for high-tech telecommunications and computer specialists, there are other opportunities. Contract employment is available via direct hire for set time periods, such as twelve months. Each contractor advertises for and hires its own employees; there is no central administrative office. Some contractors post listings on the job board at the family services office.

Adult Education Program. You may work directly or indirectly for the base education center. Schools and colleges under contract with the DoD offer courses almost everywhere Americans are stationed and routinely recruit people to teach a wide variety of subjects. A master's degree isn't necessarily needed; depending on the subject, you may be qualified with a two-year associate's degree, a vocational-technical degree, or a bachelor's degree. Teaching online classes is another possibility. You can do this for any college in the world, from any place in the world.

Private-Sector Jobs. If you have a working knowledge of the language, it will boost your chances for finding a job on the local economy. Gift shops that cater to tourists seek English-speaking employees; sometimes knowing the native language isn't even needed, since few native-language speakers are their customers. However, getting a work permit is difficult for nonresidents and also introduces tax issues. Discuss with the base legal office before accepting a private-sector position.

Other Suggestions. If you have a professional or occupational license, ask your professional organization before moving about certification and/or licensing procedures abroad. Many professional organizations have overseas branches that will permit you to participate in networking opportunities, conferences, and continuing education. At *www.state.gov/m/dghr/flo/c21671.htm* you'll find a listing of websites the Department of State's Family Liaison Office assembled to help with both stateside and overseas job searches. Finally, countries where many American multinational companies operate usually have an American Chamber of Commerce (there are currently 105 in 91 countries). There you'll find a list of American companies, some of which might be hiring.

MEDIA

The Armed Forces Radio and Television Service is a military program that provides radio and television to overseas commands. It broadcasts television and radio channels in 177 countries and aboard Navy ships at sea. The TV channels entertain overseas families with varied English-language programming that is available via direct cable connection for quarters residents and with a decoder available for those living outside quarters. These decoders may be issued, but they often have to be purchased or rented. Because programs are provided at a low fraction of what stateside networks pay, Armed Forces Network (AFN) is dependent on what distributors make available. News, sports, movies, talk shows, sitcoms, and children's shows are common, and with some fiddling, you may get TiVO functionality. Visit *myafn.dodmedia.osd.mil* for more information.

Stars and Stripes is an English-language newspaper, published seven days a week for military and civilian DoD families overseas. It's an NAF activity and contains a mix of international, U.S., and local news. It also includes AFRTS program schedules. There are different editions for different parts of the world. Visit it online at *www.stripes.com*.

USING U.S. STANDARD APPLIANCES AND COMPUTERS OVERSEAS

The standard electric current in the U.S. for small appliances is 110 volts (V). Overseas, the standard is 220V. The "hertz" (Hz), or cycles per second, that the current runs is also different. The U.S. standard is a 60Hz current, but overseas, it's 50Hz. If you plug a 110V appliance into a 220V circuit, you will ruin it.

A transformer is a device that enables you to operate some 110V appliances on 220V circuits. However, since the transformer only changes the voltage, not the Hertz, appliances with motors—such as clocks, fans, refrigerators, and computers—will run significantly slower. This will cause the appliance to heat up more, shortening its life span. If you still decide to use a transformer, choose one that is rated 20 percent above the appliance's maximum wattage. The chart below shows you transformer sizes needed for typical appliances.

Transformer Size	Appliances the Transformer Can Handle
75 W	Small, low-wattage appliances such as radios, tape recorders, and some TVs
300 W	Large radios, stereos, electric blankets, hand mixers, small fans, most TVs
500 W	Upright mixers, blenders, some stereo equipment
750 W	Projectors, sewing machines, broom-type vacuums
1000 W	Small space heaters, coffee makers, vacuums
1600 W	Most appliances that contain heating elements such as toasters, electric frying pans, irons, hair dryers, and stovetop grills

Small appliances without speed controls can be successfully used with a transformer. If the appliance is one that is moved, such as a vacuum cleaner, the transformer will have to be moved with it. Since small appliances are generally not used for a continuously long time, the issue of motor burnout is minimal. When the transformer isn't in use, unplug it, as it consumes electricity when plugged in, which will wear it out faster.

Most computers built after 1995, including laptops, have a built-in power supply located in the back with a switch that you can flip to convert for use on a 220V system. Hertz isn't an issue. Peripherals, such as the monitor, printer, speakers, and scanner, may work, depending on how they're built. Many newer monitors will operate on both 110V and 220V, but older ones will not. Read their printed specifications or ask the manufacturer. Peripherals often work off a separate power pack that can be replaced relatively cheaply with a 220V equivalent.

STATUS OF FORCES AGREEMENT (SOFA)

SOFAs are contracts between the U.S. government and the governments of the countries in which we have bases. The United States signs one with each host country. Directly or indirectly, they affect you. Each SOFA varies, but the subjects covered are the same. They spell out such things as how many civilian jobs on base must be reserved for host citizens; what kind of commissary items must be procured from the host country; who has authority over problems between host and U.S. citizens; how large a school or hospital may be; how much housing may be built; which host-country taxes and fees we're exempt from; cottage industry and commercial solicitation rules; broadcasting of the Armed Forces Radio and Television Station; and who may shop at the commissary and exchange.

Commissary and exchange shopping is regulated because many of these countries' economies are dependent on tourism, and every dollar you spend in an American military facility is a dollar lost to their own businesses. The host governments realize that since we're here by the hundreds of thousands and are not tourists, we need our own supply centers, so they allow us to build them. But our facilities do exist at their courtesy, and taxes are waived as a matter of diplomacy. If a lot of tourists who happen to be military use them, that's money lost to them. So host governments may—and many do—decide which Americans may use the facilities and which may not. Even if the SOFA does allow military tourists to shop at base facilities, the commander may disallow it, as items are often limited, and his primary responsibility is the people stationed there.

The U.S. law requires SOFAs, not Department of Defense policies. Showing how our presence benefits the local economy is one of the ways we persuade countries to keep us there. Bases have been saved from being shut down simply because our hosts were reminded how many host citizens would lose their jobs.

ABSENTEE VOTING

For voting purposes, your legal state of residence can be the state you've claimed as your home state since being in the military. To claim a new legal residence, you must have simultaneous physical presence and intent to reside at the location as your primary residence. Military families have the choice of changing their legal residence every time they move or retaining the same legal residence.

Registration requirements vary from state to state. Many allow the voter to register and request an absentee ballot by submitting a single Federal Post Card Application (FPCA). Other states require two separate FPCA forms—one to register and one to request an absentee ballot. Some states allow you to register to vote, request your ballot, and cast it by fax. (Note: Not all states that fax blank ballots will accept them back by fax.) Those sending voting materials by fax must go through the Federal Voting Assistance Program in Washington, D.C., 703-693-5527. Request your ballot at least forty-five days before the election. States generally mail ballots thirty to forty-five days before the election. Visit *www.fvap.gov* for details.

If you're politically active and wish to remain so overseas, you might want to contact Democrats Abroad at *www.democrats-abroad.org* or Republicans Abroad at *www.republicansabroad.org*.

TAXES

Whether you are stateside or overseas, the rules for filing income tax are the same. Your income, filing status, and age determine whether you need to file an income tax return. American citizens working abroad for foreign employers don't have to pay taxes on their first $80,000 they earn, but this doesn't apply to servicemembers or federal/NAF employees. Taxes are due April 15 for those who file on the calendar year system.

You can file your taxes electronically (a fee is charged) or mail them. If you mail them, the date "filed" is the postmark. You can get an extension, but if you pay tax due after the regular due date you'll be charged interest from that date until the day it's paid.

You may be eligible for a two-month extension to file your tax return if, on the due date:

- you are living outside of the United States and Puerto Rico and your main place of business is outside the United States and Puerto Rico, or
- you are on active military service outside the United States and Puerto Rico. If you served in a combat zone or qualified hazardous duty area, you may be eligible for an even longer extension of time to file.

To get an extension, attach a statement to your return explaining which qualifying situation applies to you, or file Form 4868, available at *www.irs.gov/pub/irs-pdf/f4868.pdf*, electronically. You will need to estimate your tax liability. If filing jointly, either you or your husband can qualify for the automatic extension. If you and your husband file separate returns, the extension applies only to the one who qualifies for it.

SHOPPING

Much of the fun of living overseas is shopping in new and exotic stores. When you shop in European stores, you are exempt from paying the value-added tax (VAT). This benefit applies strictly to active-duty families, DoD civilian employees, contractors in Europe on a military contract, and people in Europe on temporary duty. Go to your base VAT office to fill out a form, which must be presented to the store personnel before purchasing the item. It cannot be done afterward. Stores are not obligated to participate in the VAT program, and some don't, due to the paperwork. But many do, and it is a nice savings on expensive items.

If you prefer shopping in stores you're familiar with, the Internet and a credit or debit card will allow you to do that. You will have a military post office box number, called an APO (Air Post Office) or FPO (Fleet Post Office), and it has a U.S. address. Don't add in the country you're in, as that may result in misdirected mail. With an APO or FPO address, you can send and receive mail at the same cost as if you were actually living in the U.S. Keep in mind, some businesses will not ship to these boxes; a solution to that is *www.shipitapo.com*, a company that forwards catalog merchandise for a small fee.

Before placing any merchandise order, ask the base post office or U.S. embassy what restrictions exist on what may be received by mail. For instance, it's common for a country's Customs service to disallow certain fruits, vegetables, or plants due to health or pest infestation concerns.

GASOLINE

While living overseas, you will purchase gas with coupons from the exchange. These coupons enable you to pay about half the price posted on the pump. (The filling station owners are reimbursed the difference when they turn in the coupons.) These coupons can only be used at specific gas chains, such as BP and Esso, so plan your fill-ups accordingly. There are separate coupons based on octane level and by country, and they are not interchangeable. For an extra fee you can buy coupons that are good in multiple countries. If you don't use the full amount of a coupon, you don't get the difference refunded. Coupons must be presented at the time of gas purchase. You are allowed 400 liters per month and must present a registration document each time you fill up at an AAFES gas station. If you rent a house where you have to buy fuel oil, arrangements for tax-free purchase can be made through the exchange. Those purchases are separate from your gasoline ration.

ENJOY THE PLACE!

Don't hang around the apartment waiting for your husband to come home. Download a city map from MapQuest, Google Maps, or Yahoo Maps, maybe buy a portable GPS device, write your address on a slip of paper, and drive, walk, or get on a bus. You'll find buses all over; many countries have more advanced public transportation than the United States. If you get lost, just show someone that slip of paper with your address. Hand signals are universal. Or hail a cab. Successfully making your way around a new place is a self-esteem and confidence booster. Don't be daunted by the cultural differences. Part of the learning experience is discovering why they're different. Here are some tips and comments from people enjoying their overseas tours.

> *"Expensive trips aren't needed to enjoy yourself. Ordinary things make a tour fun, too. Even with the low dollar, it's not so bad. You just have to realize that currency fluctuations are a way of life and budget for them. I always figure my bills at less than what the dollar is trading for, to leave myself a cushion. We don't own a car, so public transportation and cabs are as much a part of our budget as food. It's not always convenient, but it beats car and insurance payments. Seek out fun things to do that cost little or nothing. You only live once, this ain't no dress rehearsal."*

> *"When stationed in Japan, we took a trip to Australia. We chose it for its blue skies, no smog, and elbow room for a couple of weeks! Bondi Beach was the highlight. Shaped like a horseshoe, it's miles of white sand, clear surf and sunshine, framed with large rocks and Mediterranean-style houses. We took a cruise down Sydney Harbour, visited the Royal Botanic Gardens (fab views of the city skyline), and took pictures of the famous Opera House. We loved the Taronga Zoo with its koala bears, kangaroos, dingoes, and wallabies, and the Aquarium with its sharks and enormous stingrays. There are sidewalk cafés everywhere. Order pizza, kebabs and sandwiches, or kangaroo steaks or vegemite for the more adventurous!"*

> *"During a tour in Europe, go to Keukenhof, the world-famous flower garden outside Lisse. Over ninety growers exhibit seven million bulbs. You can spend all day walking paths that take you by gardens, flower beds, fountains, sculptures and a lake. There's even a nineteenth-century windmill you can climb to take some great, panoramic photos."*

> *"Blend in. Try not to wear clothes that identify your nationality or scream 'tourist.' Observe what the locals wear. In most countries, people don't wear athletic shoes, shorts, and baseball caps as street wear; rather, they dress business casual. Leave the bling at home; all it does is attract those who target tourists for theft. Of course, as soon as you talk, the locals will know that you're not one of them, but being pleasant and polite goes a long way. Be aware of pickpocket ruses like women coming up to you with children or people spilling condiments on you."*

> *"When we were in Korea, we'd go to the ocean market on Saturdays. The mama-sans and their children sell fresh fish, mussels, lobsters, clams, shrimp, and prawns. In dozens of tiny stalls you'll find soaps, mink blankets, or a restaurant where the man cooks your food right in front of you in a wok. Drives in the country allow you to admire light, airy oriental-style homes with tipped roofs, surrounded by vegetable and flower gardens. They're certainly different from those rows of aluminum-sided houses we left in Ohio! Once we went to where the kings*

are buried. The ancient Koreans buried their kings by laying them on the ground and pouring dirt over them. There are mounds of buried kings and a display under glass that allows you to see the mummified body of one, with his gold and jewels. Their temples are incredible—intricate confections with solid gold interiors."

"On three-day weekends we tie our bikes to the car, load up some field gear, and drive to the Black Forest. We put our baby in a bike seat, strap a helmet on him, and cycle the paths to Switzerland. He's a 'go-baby,' always rolling on our bikes, in a stroller, or on my back. Everyone loves a baby, and he gets a lot of attention. In fact, he's our icebreaker! We've met Germans, Swiss, Austrians, and Italians cycling with their own babies. Other weekends we ride around town, exploring new neighborhoods and discovering parks and monuments. One monument listed all the men from that area who had been killed in World War I, and the dates and places. The first hundred or so were killed in France, but the last few were killed in nearby Kloppenheim and Wiesbaden. It illustrated very graphically how the Germans were in France for a long time but toward the end were reduced to just defending their own territory."

"We attended CeBit, a huge technology trade show in Hannover's Exhibition Center. There were 6,200 exhibitors from seventy countries showing the latest and greatest in business, home, and mobile technology. Since I'm a gadget geek, this sort of thing is better than Epcot for me!"

"In Italy, a tank of gas or a few dollars' worth of bus tickets will take you on a decent day trip anywhere. We take local buses and sightsee. We've been on a gondola in Venice, and we've seen the Sistine Chapel and the Colosseum. Going to the Vatican City and attending services at St. Peter's was an emotional experience for me. My son has developed an interest in Roman history as a result of this tour."

"We live on the economy. Once we had a Texas barbecue and invited our Spanish neighbors. We served American food: hamburgers, fried chicken, chips, kosher pickles, and Häagen-Dazs ice cream. Two months later they were still telling us how much they had enjoyed it. They've also invited us to their homes. I can't imagine living in a place for three years and not making civilian friends, whether stateside or overseas. I've been taking night classes in Spanish. Americans who don't enjoy it here say, 'Well, you like it because you speak Spanish!' I didn't speak any more than they did when I got here. Our tour is up in four more months. I wish I could thank all the Spaniards who have made it so memorable. Hasta la vista."

"The Greek Islands are paradise. Olive trees, hot sun washing over stucco buildings. Simple. And the fact that we don't get American TV is a blessing. My kids used to be glued to it, now they read more. I laugh at the letters in the Stars and Stripes from people in Germany complaining about the programming on AFRTS. One lady said she couldn't find anything interesting on during the day. Personally, I had that problem in the States."

"We're homeschoolers in Turkey. The wild currency fluctuations here are a fact of life and make a great opportunity to teach my kids about macroeconomics."

"I took a University of Maryland art course that was held in Florence! What better place to study Renaissance architecture, painting, and sculpture."

"Here in Germany, my husband and I go to Kontakt club meetings. The club organizes activities: evenings at the local swimming pool or a restaurant, a day at the circus, a tour of a car factory, trips to amusement parks and flea markets. Last Fourth of July we had a medieval weekend. We slept in a castle and roasted a boar and ate it with our hands while listening to madrigal music."

"I love to cook. I spice up the offerings at the commissary with ingredients from the German food markets. I've discovered a lot of interesting things on their shelves and have made some very nice dishes. I'll miss spätzel, Italian eis, and those little cartons of strawberry milk when we go back."

"Okinawa is awfully expensive, but that's OK because we don't buy things. We travel. From here we can take hops all over the Orient. We've hopped to Bangkok, Hong Kong, and the Philippines. It's the best remedy for island fever. We also check in to Okuma, the military R&R resort at the north end of the island, once in a while for mini-vacations."

"I took an Officer Wives Club tour to Russia. I loved seeing St. Basil's Cathedral in real life after seeing it in so many magazine pictures. We took a bus ride through a forest. There was a heavy mist all around the silver birch trees; it was like a scene from a Baba Yaga fairy tale."

"These Bavarian villages at Christmastime are like something out of a Grimm fairy tale: cross-timbered, pointed-roof buildings topped with snow and strung with lights. I love walking through the Christkindlmarkt, smelling the hot, spicy wine and the lebküchen and eating those sticks of cherries and chocolates and the big, soft, hot pretzels. Glittery ornaments and gold angels hang from the booths, and decorated horses and carriages ride through the town."

"England is a great overseas tour; you get all the benefits of a foreign tour and don't have to learn a new language! London is only sixty miles away. We've toured the Tower and saw the crown jewels. We've been to the beaches at Brighton, too. I studied Stonehenge in school; it was fun seeing it in real life. We'll get to Scotland and Ireland before it's time to go."

"I couldn't find a job when living in Belgium so I completed an MBA online instead."

"While living in Japan, a bunch of wives embarked on a fitness program. When we felt ready, we climbed Mt. Fuji together. I mailed my family a postcard from the top."

"My parents came over here for three weeks. My husband and I got time off from work, and we took some organized bus tours to Holland, France, and Italy. My parents couldn't afford trips to Europe when I was growing up, but our being stationed here made it possible."

"If you like people-watching, sit yourself down in a café on the French Riviera."

"I've bought lots of oriental rugs here in Saudi Arabia. They're much cheaper than in the U.S. We plan to build a home when we return and I look forward to decorating my house with them."

"Instead of carrying around a whole guidebook, copy the sections you'll need. Use page-size printouts of maps so you won't have to stand in the middle of sidewalks unfolding large papers."

"Since moving to Frankfurt, we've gotten into refurbishing affordable and usable antiques. We scour flea markets, particularly for old baskets, the kind with the quilted tops that are used to store potatoes and onions. We restore them and do a brisk business selling them at the wives' club bazaars. It's been a good family project that even our teenagers enjoy. My son sews the quilted tops, and my daughter runs our booth."

"When we first got to La Maddelena, I isolated myself and wasn't happy. Then I got brave enough to walk out the front door, make friends, and take my chances. Some of my fondest memories are of sitting on the terrace with my landlady in the early morning with an Italian-English dictionary, sipping coffee, and teaching each other how to say things."

"When a host citizen says that he doesn't speak English, don't get annoyed because you know that he was required to study it in school. How many Americans do you know who studied French or Spanish and still can't speak it?"

"Don't compare peaches and pears. If you dwell on all the wonderful things you left in the old country, you'll miss all the wonderful things the new one has to offer."

"I love market day in Bassano del Grappa! The narrow streets and squares are filled with merchants selling veggies, fruits, clothes, cloth, cheese, and flowers from stalls. Old men sit at café tables gossiping, and children run around their mamas."

"Do whatever you can to enjoy your overseas tour so that you won't be saying, 'I wish I had done . . .' when you return."

"Guam is fun if you like snorkeling, diving, or just wandering in the boondocks. But my favorite aspect of Guam was hopping to Korea to shop!"

"Check the thrift shop for plug adapters, step-down converters, and transformers before you buy them new."

"If you take driving trips, research any toll roads first. They cost a lot more than toll roads in the U.S. In some countries, a toll road can cost as much as $70 each way. Also, carry a roll of toilet paper with you because not all restrooms have it (many dispense it via vending machines). Carry coins, too, since many public restrooms charge for admission!"

Sometimes you can judge a book by its cover! A store in Italy.

"I keep an online, password-protected account with jpg scans of my wallet contents, my passport, and a text list of account numbers and emergency numbers for my credit cards. If my room gets burgled while I'm out, this will help me. If you access such information from an Internet café, know that keyloggers are often installed on their computers. Clear the browser cache when you're done, and change your password. Consider a graphical password system where you click images on a page instead of typing, or use a flash drive."

"I buy an ornament for the Christmas tree in each city where we vacation. I also seek to incorporate host-country holiday traditions into my own. It's not always possible to buy everything you're used to buying for holidays. For instance, in some places you won't be able to buy a real Christmas tree. So buy a native tree or shrub to decorate. Or make a tree out of wire and papier-mâché. If you can't find pureed pumpkin and turkey, consider apricot jam and roast duck."

IF YOU CHOOSE NOT TO GO

Although many people enjoy this chance of a lifetime, others aren't interested. You may have family obligations or a job you don't wish to leave. Or you know that overseas living just isn't for you. In this case, your husband might look into getting a humanitarian transfer or temporary deferment, which is given if you can prove hardship. Or he can go alone, in which case you'll be moved at government expense to the location of your choice and he'll serve a shorter "without dependents" tour. Know that after this happens, if you change your mind and decide to join him later, you will have to pay your own way, as the government will only move you once per travel order. He will also have to apply for command sponsorship, and getting it is not guaranteed. Without command sponsorship your husband won't get any increased allowances, you won't have use of the base facilities (only medical care is guaranteed), and you can't live in quarters. If you are currently living in quarters, you won't be able to stay there if he's on a long OCONUS tour (or on any CONUS one). You may be able to stay if he is on a short OCONUS tour, but you will need permission from the base commander. You'll also need a power of attorney to conduct any business on his behalf.

MAKE THE MOST OF IT

Pursue your hobbies. Seek clubs where you'll find others who share your interests. The woman who paints will discover new vistas; the sewer, new patterns; the cook, new recipes. Ask your language teacher if she knows of sports or hobby clubs, or ask at stores where the wares are sold. Investigate swimming pools, gyms, and other recreational facilities. The host citizens are interested in these places, too, and they're good places to meet them. Ask the public affairs office if there's a club that brings Americans and host citizens together, like Germany's famous *Kontakt* clubs.

Don't use a lack of money or low currency exchange rates as an excuse to spend three years cocooned in your quarters. The host citizenry is living on the same economy you are, and no matter how little you think your household income is, most of them have even less. And they don't have the benefit of the military support systems you do.

Talk to people who have just come back from where you're going for ideas on what you should and shouldn't take in the way of household goods, furniture, appliances, and clothing. Enjoy your tour—lucky you! Make the most of this chance of a lifetime.

FURTHER READING

Books
Keats, John. *See Europe the Next Time You Go There*. Boston: Little, Brown, 1968.
Savage, Barbara. *Miles from Nowhere*. Seattle: The Mountaineers, 1984.

Internet Resources
www.asknumbers.com. Online conversions for distances, cooking, clothing, and more.
www.iys.fi. International Youth Service website. Obtain pen pals for children.
www.tricare.mil/mybenefit/index.jsp. Information on TPO, TSO, and TGRO.
travel.state.gov/passport/passport_1738.html. Information on obtaining a passport.
www.usa.att.com/military/index.jsp. Information on phone service abroad.
www.journeywoman.com. Travel site for women.

www.independenttraveler.com, www.tripadvisor.com. Sites with good travel tips.

www.mastercard.com/us/personal/en/cardholderservices/atmlocations/index.html. Master-Card Global ATM locator.

visa.via.infonow.net/locator/global/jsp/SearchPage.jsp. Visa Global ATM locator.

www.earthcalendar.net/index.php. A daybook of holidays and celebrations around the world.

www.countrycallingcodes.com. Country calling codes.

www.uschamber.com/international/directory/default. Directory of overseas American Chambers of Commerce.

afrts.dodmedia.osd.mil. AFRTS website. Find answers to frequently asked questions and more.

www.usa.gov/Topics/Americans_Abroad.shtml. Government website with information for Americans living abroad.

www.sddc.army.mil/sddc/Content/Pub/8810/DBCN8810.pdf. Pamphlet on storing your vehicle.

9

Separations

Oone of the aspects that makes military service a unique job is separations, which is time away from the family. Temporary duty assignments, unaccompanied tours, and deployments are essential parts of military training and work. "No overtime" means pay, not hours, as regular working days can be twelve or thirteen hours long. The nation's defense does not operate on a forty-hour workweek with guaranteed weekends, anniversaries, and holidays at home.

TYPES OF SEPARATIONS

Most separations are due to field exercises, unaccompanied tours, temporary duty assignments, and deployments. Other separations are due to flight time and alerts. They are all part of the operational experience of classroom military training. Although the specific job a servicemember holds influences over how often he's away, sooner or later everyone goes. With today's smaller military and the Iraq and Afghanistan situations, each person now deploys longer and more frequently than in

A woman waves goodbye to her husband as the USS Russell deploys from Hawaii to support the global war on terrorism. Photo courtesy U.S. Navy

the past. Time away can be a week, a month, even eighteen months. There is also the possibility of sudden deployment, in which case you may not even be told that your husband has left the area or where he has gone, until that information is safe to release, and may not be told when he's coming back until a few hours before he arrives.

During separations, it may seem that the military is coming before the family. It is. It has to. It won't work any other way. A servicemember wouldn't be doing his job if he were giving anyone or anything else first priority. Take pride in your husband's commitment to our country. Such commitment by anyone to anything is rare these days. You can complain or show him some love . . . either way, he has to go.

Field Exercises

A field exercise combines multiple tasks in a simulated war atmosphere. The commanding officer determines how much money he has for the exercise and what facilities are available. Then he draws on experience to determine how much time the tasks should take. He must be sure that his people know what they're doing and are ready to do it. If things do not go properly, they must be redone. This might involve staying away extra days or coming home for the weekend just to go out again on Monday. Training facilities are often limited, and many units must share them. While the people in your husband's unit are waiting their turn, they might find themselves with a free evening. To you this might seem like needless time away from the family, but it's a part of training.

Just as you would not be able to easily contact your husband if there really was a war, so it must be with many field problems. Consider this your own basic training. You must be self-reliant enough to care for the children, pay the bills, and handle whatever comes up to keep things running smoothly at home.

Sometimes units invite spouses out for a "field day" so they can get a taste of an operational experience. Army and Marine Corps wives get to wear the "steel pots" on their own heads and run an obstacle course. Navy wives can sail on a family cruise. If you're interested in this firsthand look at military life, bring it up at the next family support group meeting. One day spent on a submarine or among camouflage tents may give you a new appreciation for your husband's job.

Deployment

A "deployment" is what servicemembers currently in Iraq and Afghanistan are serving. They are assigned to their home tour location, but they are deployed, not assigned, to Iran or Afghanistan. When their mission is complete, they will return to the same base and unit they came from. Most deployments last for six months or less, although some may be for as long as eighteen months.

Unaccompanied Tours

There are areas around the globe that, because of their strategic locations or special facilities, need to be maintained. While some have family support facilities such as schools, exchanges, and hospitals, others don't. Or they're not safe for families. But since all servicemembers must share the responsibility of maintaining them, unaccompanied tours, which are tours without the family, are part of service life. They're shorter than accompanied tours precisely because they are unaccompanied. In these cases, the service will pay to move you back to your family, job, or school.

Sometimes a servicemember is sent to an area where adequate support facilities exist, but authorization for his family to accompany him is still denied. This occurs because the number of families that are allowed to be command-sponsored is limited by law and budgetary constraints. It costs a lot to command-sponsor a family, and the money may just not be there. Before deciding to accompany your husband on a unaccompanied tour, know what you're getting into. The lack of official support will make a big difference in your standard of living.

Temporary Duty Assignments (TDY)/Temporary Additional Duty (TAD)

These short-term, out-of-town assignments typically last between two weeks and six months. Allowances are paid to help compensate for expenses (see chapter 5), but since these are unaccompanied orders, families are not moved.

SHOULD YOU JOIN HIM?

Some wives join their husbands on unaccompanied tours or TDY/TAD orders. Some also temporarily move to a different town (e.g., to be with their parents). Before making either of these decisions, consider these points.

- If you are in quarters and vacate them for three or more months, you are subject to forfeiting them. You may also lose some allowances.
- You may be interfering with an assignment that requires a lot of study time and concentration. The point of such orders is not for vacation.
- The orders may be for multiple locations, not just one. If you are stationed overseas, you may be able to fly Space-A, but otherwise, your transportation is not paid for.
- What are the housing options? If he's on an unaccompanied tour, it may be unaccompanied because of difficulty obtaining quality housing. Your husband also may be required to live on base.
- If you aren't command-sponsored, you may not have access to a military treatment facility for routine medical care. Ask your Tricare office what facilities are available where you will be going and if you are entitled to use them. The same goes for commissary and exchange shopping; SOFA agreements (see chapter 8) may prevent you from using them.

- If you have children, what will the impact on their education be? Overseas, admittance to a DoDDS school would be on a space-available basis, and your child could be displaced any time to accommodate a space-required student. There might not even be a DoDDS or other American-accredited school there.
- You may miss the support of other military wives who understand your situation. Some wives say that while their civilian friends are sympathetic, they get tired of hearing, "I don't know how you do it." Other military wives will also know the importance of OPSEC, and understand why you are reluctant to discuss anything that might compromise it.

THE FAMILY CARE PLAN

Family care plans are required for all single soldiers and dual-military couples. These are formal documents kept on file with commanding officers that describe contingency plans for the care of servicemembers' families during deployment and field duties. Your family deserves one, too, even if you are a civilian. It's part of personal readiness. For instance, if you became incapacitated while your husband was deployed, who would care for your children? Are you authorized to deal with businesses on your husband's behalf? Do you know how money, car maintenance, and repairs are handled? Emergencies don't leave time for planning; this must be done in advance. Having your own personal readiness program can ease family-related stress and enable your husband to concentrate better at his job. Here's what a comprehensive family care plan involves.

Your Files

You should have a file system set up as discussed in chapter 5. Review its contents to bring them up-to-date. Add the following items if they're not there already.

Legal Authorizations. A power of attorney (POA) is a legal document necessary to take action on another's behalf. There are two types: durable (also called general) and special (also called limited). In theory, a durable POA issued to you by your husband allows you to conduct all business in his behalf. This includes cashing his paycheck, shipping household goods, signing damage claim forms, moving into and clearing quarters, opening a STAR card account at the exchange, and buying or selling a home or car registered in both your names. A special POA enables you to do one or two specific tasks. For example, a real estate POA would enable you to sell a car or rent an apartment in his name or both of yours. A medical POA would enable a caregiver to seek treatment for your minor child. If a POA doesn't have a specified time limit, it's in force until you revoke it or die. A POA can be obtained at your base legal office.

That said, know that POAs aren't universally accepted. Due to rampant instances of fraud and POAs' liability, some businesses prefer to deal with the principal or with all the principals in a transaction, not a representative. Some families have discovered that certain banks (even right on base), car dealerships, and real estate agencies will not accept POAs. General POAs are not accepted for a child's passport anymore, either. One possible solution is to list specific contingencies on the durable POA, such as real estate transaction authorization. Another is to obtain multiple, specific POAs for whatever situations you think are likely to surface. These can be filled out in advance even if details, such as address, are not yet available. Powers of attorney for those missing in action are automatically extended.

Guardian for Your Children. Appoint a guardian, someone who will care for your minor children if you died or became incapacitated while your husband was deployed. Actually, this is a good thing to do as a matter of course, in the event you both died or became incapacitated. If the guardian lives far away or might be temporarily unavailable, appoint a closer, temporary guardian as well.

Forms. Prepare paperwork that gives the guardian access to the base and to the PX, commissary, and hospital to care for your children, and to pick them up from school.

Financial Affairs. Arrange for money to be transferred to your children's guardian, perhaps via a bank account that the guardian has access to.

Hard-Copy Address Book. Include the names, addresses, and telephone numbers of everyone involved in your family care plan (emergency contacts, guardians). Also keep the names, phone numbers, and addresses of every business with whom you associate. Write your account number on the same card as the phone and address. It's prudent to have a hard copy of this information (such as in a Rolodex) along with any electronic means you use to store it.

Wills. A will is a legal document that describes how you want your property divided after you die and who is to be your child's legal guardian. Having a will ensures that the survivors receive what you intended to give them with a minimum of hassle. Although each state has laws for the division of property, if a person dies "intestate" (without a will), more paperwork is involved, it takes longer to resolve affairs, and the division of your estate may not be what you wanted it to be. Don't laugh at the word "estate" when thinking of your possessions. Remember, it contains insurance policy payoffs, and SGLI alone is $400,000. In intestate deaths, property is distributed in accordance to state law. Keep your will current; marriages, divorces, births of children, and changes in legal residence are reasons to revise your will. You also need to appoint an executor to administer and settle your estate. Along these lines, both of you should know what each other would prefer in case of serious injury (e.g., life-saving measures to take). A living will is a good document to have. See your base legal office to make or revise a will.

Your Husband's Military File. Out-of-date personnel records have caused problems for "geographical bachelorettes." These records are kept at the base personnel or administrative office and describe the servicemember's marital status, number of family members, emergency contact data, past and present assignments, special skills and training, civilian and military education, awards, disciplinary measures taken, photographs, security clearances, and efficiency reports. It's the servicemember's responsibility to keep this file up-to-date, not the office's. Only primary and secondary next of kin are notified in case of death. Outdated records have resulted in ex-wives and other outdated contact people being notified—and awarded benefits—instead of the current family. Is there an address where you'll temporarily move during a deployment?

Transportation Arrangements. How will the children get to their guardians if they're overseas?

Special Instructions. This includes anything not covered elsewhere, such as information about medications.

Military ID Cards. Check their dates to ensure they don't expire during the deployment.

OTHER READINESS CONCERNS

Besides a family care plan, these items should be attended to:

Car Maintenance Information. Keep papers showing the date of the last oil change, receipts for repair work, and phone numbers of trusted repair shops. Where and when do you send loan and insurance payments? Are the registration and base ID stickers current? Do you have a proof-of-insurance statement in the glove box? Do the tires need to be replaced? Do you have an emergency medical kit, jumper cables? Do you know basic maintenance requirements and the car's maintenance schedule?

Home Maintenance Information. What are the filter sizes for the furnace and air conditioner? What are the light bulb types and wattages for your different fixtures? Where is the circuit breaker box? Which switches control which outlets? Get your home in good repair; check and fix the furnace, hot water heater, smoke detector, refrigerator, range, washer, dryer, TV, and other appliances if necessary. But since Murphy's Law dictates that things break the day after the ship sails and the battalion marches off, keep phone numbers of handymen, repair shops, lawn services, and the gas, electric, and water companies in your address book.

A Plan for Your Money. Most separations involve allowances that are given and others (e.g., BAS) that are taken away. Will you have a net gain or loss? What additional expenses will you incur (e.g., travel, phone bills, babysitting)? Are any current disputes and problems being handled? They're harder to resolve when the principal person involved is away. If your husband has an allotment that needs to be stopped while he's deployed, do the paperwork before he leaves. If he'll be leaving a car behind that won't be driven, consider saving money by canceling all insurance on it except comprehensive. Make sure life insurance payments are up-to-date; policies in arrears (payments that are behind) don't pay off.

Arrange for split pay; that is, most of the paycheck will be deposited in the home account for the family's use, and spending money will be sent to the service-member. Emergency aid officials will tell you that something often goes wrong with the "Just send me a check each month" system. Separate accounts are also an option. Consider filling out a preauthorization form for a loan at the emergency aid office; without it, aid may not be given to the family.

Extra Keys. Keep extra car and house keys in the house. Leave a set with someone, or put them in a plastic container and bury them in the backyard in case you lock yourself out.

Supplies. Keep one week's food supply in the house in case of illness, bad weather, lack of money, transportation problems, or drop-in visitors who need to share your company. Have emergency light sources such as flashlights or battery-powered lanterns, plus extra batteries and bulbs. Have a first-aid kit stocked with bandages, pain relievers, and any prescriptions. Keep one gallon of water per person handy. Don't let your gas tank go under one-quarter.

PREDEPLOYMENT BRIEFING

Before a deployment you will be asked to attend a briefing. It's in your best interest to go, as you'll receive, and be asked to give, a lot of information. The service needs to know where you'll be if they have to notify you in case of casualty. You'll be asked whom you'd like to be with when notified, and for phone numbers and addresses of family members. You'll need to ensure that the correct beneficiaries of insurance policies and the death gratuity are named. A representative from every organization on post or nearby will explain their services.

Operational Security (OPSEC)

At the deployment briefing you will be reminded about OPSEC, short for "operational security." This refers to protecting information you know about your husband and his unit, an updated version of "loose lips sink ships." Random bits of information may not seem useful by themselves, but when pieced together with other bits by skilled puzzle-assemblers, they become very useful. Military and family members need to practice OPSEC in their dealings with each other and with the public at large. Be careful what you post on Internet boards (the Internet is a treasure trove of information) and say in conversation. Don't nag servicemembers to discuss things that they shouldn't discuss with you.

OPSEC information includes servicemembers' exact location overseas, troop movements (especially dates and times), weapons systems, training programs and photos, as many photos from abroad can easily violate OPSEC. If your husband is in a special operations unit, the OPSEC guidelines can be even stricter. He may not be able to say if he's even deployed at all, much less where. A predeployment briefing will provide guidelines. Remember that just because information is on the news doesn't mean you can or should talk about it. By doing this, you're actually verifying the news information.

Here are examples of good and poor ways to discuss this sort of information.

Good: "My husband is deployed in support of Iraqi Freedom."

Poor: "My husband is in Alpha Unit, stationed at [Name of] Camp in Basra."

Poor: "My husband's unit is returning from deployment and flying into [Name of] Airport at 8 P.M. this Friday."

Poor: "Please pray for my husband! He called today and told me his Marine unit is going out on a dangerous mission tonight. They will be gone for three days and I'm worried."

PERSONAL SECURITY

Along with OPSEC, practice PERSEC, or "personal security." Here are some tips for that.

- Many crimes arise from opportunity. Criminals look for an easy mark. Survey your home for weaknesses; ask your police station for suggestions. A burglar's worst enemies are time, visibility, and noise.
- Don't tell phone solicitors or other unknown callers that your husband's away. Tell them you'll relay a message. Hang up on anyone who wants more information. You don't owe them anything, including politeness.
- Don't change the answering machine message to one that greets him or indicates that he's away. And don't hang a yellow ribbon on your tree. It advertises that the man of the house is gone.
- Don't share unit phone trees with anyone outside the unit.
- Keep shrubs trimmed low, and install bright exterior lights.
- Buy dead bolts for exterior doors and locks for the storm and screen windows and doors. Keep your door locked and the garage door down even when you're home.
- Don't wear obviously expensive items in public. Try to shop with a companion; police statistics show that the chance of being targeted for crime drops 90 percent when three people are together versus alone. Don't overburden

yourself with packages; place them in the trunk of your car before acquiring new ones. Some retailers provide escorts to the car at night. Have your keys in hand when walking to your car, park where the lighting is good, keep your car locked, and place valuables out of view.

- Get call-block to spare yourself the nuisance of anonymous numbers (which are usually from solicitors). At *www.whocalled.us* you can look up phone numbers that show up as "anonymous" on Caller ID.
- Buy timers for your TV and lights. A house lit at all times announces that it's empty, just as a dark house does.
- Verify the ID of repairmen before admitting them, and don't admit anyone you haven't made arrangements with in advance.
- If you keep a weapon in the house, take classes in using it, and practice occasionally.
- Be prudent with what you post on the Internet (as well as say in public). It is easy to track down people's phone numbers and addresses, as discussed in the ID theft portion in chapter 5. Don't post deployment tickers, especially ones that show the number of days until servicemembers return. Blank out name tape, rank, and unit affiliation in photos.

SERVICEMEN'S CIVIL RELIEF ACT (SCRA)

The nature of military service may compromise a servicemember's ability to fulfill certain financial obligations and to assert some legal rights. Congress enacted protections during the Civil War, and that legislation has evolved into what is called the Servicemen's Civil Relief Act (SCRA). Its protections may be of particular interest to Guardsmen and Reservists called to active duty for more than thirty consecutive days. National Guard members called to state duty are covered if the duty is a federal emergency and the activation is longer than thirty days. Protections begin on the first day of active duty, including basic training. Some protections extend for a limited time beyond active duty discharge. Some protections even extend to family members. The major points of the SCRA are:

Termination of Leases. A residential, professional, business, or agricultural lease may be broken when servicemembers go on active duty, if they entered into the lease before going on active duty. A thirty-day notice is required. Car leases can also be terminated if the lease was signed before going on active duty if that active duty is at least 180 continuous days. Servicemembers who make permanent-change-of-station moves or who deploy for at least 180 days may also terminate a car lease. The lessor may not charge an early lease termination fee, but any taxes, summonses, title and registration fees, and charges for excess wear, use, and mileage are still valid.

Evictions from Rental Housing. Service families may not be evicted from their homes if the monthly rent is less than $2,400.

Installment Contracts. If a contract was signed prior to active duty and at least one payment was made before that time, the creditor cannot repossess the property while the member is on active duty. Nor can the creditor terminate the contract for breach without a court order.

6 Percent Interest Rate. If a servicemember's military obligation has affected his ability to pay financial obligations such as credit cards, loans, and mortgages, the servicemember can have his interest rate capped at 6 percent for the duration of his military obligation.

Private Practitioners. Physicians, lawyers, and other professionals who have purchased malpractice insurance to cover their private practices are able to stop paying premiums while on active duty and reinstate the insurance without penalty. While the insurance is suspended, court actions for damages are also suspended.

Court Proceedings. If a servicemember is a defendant in a civil court proceeding, the court may grant a ninety-day delay in the proceedings. If a default judgment is entered in a civil action against a servicemember during the period of military service (or within sixty days after it), the court must reopen the judgment if the servicemember requests it.

Star Card. If you have a balance on an Exchange Star card, the Exchange Credit Program offers two options to servicemembers who are deployed to hostile-fire/imminent-danger areas for more than ninety days: You can choose either a 6 percent interest rate with no monthly payments and use of the account during the deployment period, or a 0 percent rate with no monthly payments, but no additional charges can be made during this time. The command must fax a letter to the exchange for this to take effect. USAA may also lower credit card interest payments and pay for three months' service with home security company ADT during a deployment. It, too, must receive deployment orders to do this.

Know that if any creditor does not believe that the military service affects the ability to pay, they may go to court about it.

The Uniformed Services Employment and Re-Employment Rights Act (USERER)

Employers under this law are prohibited from discriminating or retaliating against any employee or applicant because of his military service. Employers are required to permit reservists unpaid, nonvacation time off to perform active training and other military duties. The law also gives a reservist reemployment rights to his former position (or one of similar status, seniority, and pay) if the reservist must leave his job temporarily for military duties. These reemployment rights apply whether the reservist's service is voluntary or mandatory and during war or peace.

It is unlawful for a reservist to be denied a promotion or other advantage of employment because of military duties. When the reservist returns, the law mandates that he return to the same seniority, status, and pay rate that he would have reached without interruption. If the reservist was a probationary employee, or in a training program, he is entitled to reinstatement in the probation period or training program.

To exercise these rights, a reservist must meet certain criteria.

- He must have had an "other than temporary" civilian job (but not necessarily a permanent one). The job may be part time or probationary. Temporary workers and independent contractors are not protected.
- He must have left the civilian job to go on active duty.
- He must have been released from active duty under honorable circumstances.
- He must apply for reemployment within thirty-one days after release from active duty, or within ninety days if on active duty for at least ninety-one days. Reservists who are injured or disabled while on active duty have one year to apply for reinstatement in order to cover a period of hospitalization. If the reservist can no longer perform his old job because of a service-related injury, he may request reemployment in the nearest comparable job that he is able to perform.

The same law that protects reservists gives these rights to employers:

- *The right to know the employee's military training schedule as far in advance as possible*. The annual drill schedule published by reserve centers fills this requirement. Some problems can be avoided by giving an employer the annual drill schedule and active-duty training and annual training dates as soon as you know them. It is also good practice to return to work the first working day after completing the training or after a reasonable time of rest. Since it is sometimes impossible for a reservist to say exactly when he will return, an employer may not demand it. Try to give an approximate date.
- *The right to receive proof of a reservist's military duty*. This could be an unclassified set of orders or an official letter from the commanding officer.
- *The right to deny pay or special work rescheduling for periods of military duty*. Employers are not required to assist reservists in making up pay or work lost because of military obligations.

MILITARY RESERVIST ECONOMIC INJURY DISASTER LOAN PROGRAM (MREIDL)

The purpose of the Military Reservist Economic Injury Disaster Loan program (MREIDL) is to provide loans of up to $1,500,000 over up to a thirty-year period to eligible small businesses so they can meet their ordinary and necessary operating expenses when an essential reservist employee is called to active duty. These loans are intended to only provide the amount of working capital needed to pay its necessary obligations until the essential employee is released from active duty. They are not intended to cover lost income or lost profits. Nor can MREIDL funds be used to take the place of regular commercial debt, to refinance long-term debt, or to expand the business. An application can be made on the day the essential employee is ordered to active duty and ends ninety days after he is discharged.

Because these loans are taxpayer subsidized, Congress requires that applicants who are financially able to meet their business expenses while deployed are not eligible for them. Loans over $5,000 require collateral, typically a first or second mortgage on the business property. Personal guarantees by the business principals are also required. And since this assistance is in the form of loans, the borrower must be creditworthy. The maximum interest rate for this program is 4 percent. Call 800-659-2955 or e-mail *disastercustomerservice@sba.gov* for details.

OTHER RESERVIST CONCERNS
Reservists activated for more than thirty days are eligible for Tricare. They and their families are eligible for medical care up to ninety days before a deployment. After the deployment, they are eligible for one year of Tricare Standard coverage for each ninety days of active duty service. They pay 28 percent of the cost for care and must agree to stay in the Selected Reserve.

Additionally, the Consolidated Omnibus Budget Reconciliation Act (COBRA) generally allows them to continue their employment-based group health plan for up to twenty-four months. If their military service is for thirty days or less, they can continue coverage at the same cost as before that short service. If the service is longer, they may be required to pay as much as 102 percent of the full premium for coverage.

If a reservist's family member wants to continue with a current doctor or hospital, COBRA continuation coverage can be elected for just that person. If the family was already on COBRA when he was called for active duty, COBRA coverage can be kept even after enrolling in Tricare. If a reservist had health coverage under his employer's group health plan and let it lapse due to belonging to Tricare, he should be able to reenter it with no waiting period. The exception to this is for an illness or injury incurred in, or aggravated during, performance of service in the uniformed services, which is covered by the military health plan.

The military service is not considered a break regarding eligibility to participate in an employer's retirement plan, vesting, or benefit accrual. That said, there is no requirement for your employer to make contributions to your 401(k) plan while you are on active duty. Once you return from military duty and are reemployed, your employer must make the employer contributions that would have been made if you had been employed during the period of military duty.

For more information, call the Department of Labor at 866-444-3272 or visit *askebsa.dol.gov*.

RESOLVING PROBLEMS

When you have a question, it's important to get your answer from the source. Don't rely on your neighbor who had "the same problem last year." Details get lost in translation, and policies change. When you ask anyone but the proper authority how to solve a problem, you run the risk of getting an incorrect answer, or an answer colored by that person's experience or perceptions.

When asserting yourself to solve a problem, dress professionally before visiting the office. People who are "dressed for success" are responded to better than people who look casual or unimportant. The civilian power suit isn't called that for nothing.

Of course, while many of the people who staff phones and desks are sharp and helpful, others aren't. Don't assume that just because people work in a particular office they know (or care) what they're doing. If you're not satisfied with an answer—it doesn't sound right, it isn't clear, it isn't complete—push for more. The person working there is doing a job, not a favor. Speak to the manager. If it still doesn't sound right, speak to that person's manager. Enlist the aid of the unit's first sergeant, chief petty officer, unit commander, chaplain, or ombudsman. Write a letter to the inspector general, the base commander, your congressman. There are a lot of links in the chain of command. Just be sure that you use the chain without skipping any links. If you do, your problem will take longer to resolve, because it will be passed back down to the person it should have been given to in the first place. Be assertive, polite, and firm. And if none of that works—well, be a witch! They'll take care of you just to get you out of there.

When you call or visit an office, have all necessary documentation. Know your account number and your husband's Social Security number. Take an LES printout, your receipt, your power of attorney, a copy of your husband's orders and your Tricare explanation of benefits. Calling in advance to ask what's needed often avoids a wasted trip. And be succinct; customer service representatives get ten-page complaint letters in which the writer doesn't identify herself or her sponsor, leave a phone number, or coherently explain the problem. The more documentation you bring, the less time it will take to research the problem and resolve it.

When writing a complaint letter, you have the best chance of getting your issue resolved if your letter is coherent and well written. Here are some tips:

- Type it in dark print. Handwritten letters are difficult and time-consuming to read. Don't type in all capital letters.
- Keep it short and to the point. If it's longer than one single-spaced typed page, it's probably too long.
- Don't use abbreviations or acronyms.
- Keep it factual. Don't include your opinions, speculations, perceptions, or other irrelevancies. Stick to the subject.

- Proofread for spelling, grammar, and punctuation.
- Include your signature, name, and contact information.

Whether you write a letter, call, or visit in person, here is a list of base agencies and the topics they handle:

Finance and Accounting Office. Basic pay, allowances, allotments, U.S. savings bonds, federal income tax, life insurance and health benefits deductions, leave balances.

Housing Office. Assignment of family quarters, certificates of nonavailability of quarters, clearing of quarters, complaints about housing, furniture, local economy housing referrals.

Military Police. Criminal complaints, customs clearance, disturbances, driver's licenses, firearm registration, installation passes, pet registration, traffic tickets, vehicle registration.

Legal Office. Income tax law, leases and rental contracts, notarizing of legal documents, legal problems.

Red Cross. Notification of next of kin, emergency communication to family, emergency financial aid, counseling.

Family Services. Babysitters, child care, household lending items, counseling.

Inspector General. Community dissatisfaction, host-nation problems, military-oriented complaints, unsatisfied complaints. You can complain anonymously.

Chaplain's Office. Marital counseling, personal counseling, religious retreats and services. You don't have to be of the chaplain's faith or be religious to use this resource.

Transportation Office. Unaccompanied baggage, household goods, shipment of privately owned vehicles on orders, temporary storage of household goods.

Facilities Engineers. Quarters repairs.

First Sergeant or Chief Petty Officer. Good sources of information, and able to help solve problems.

Ombudsman/Key Volunteer (for Navy, Coast Guard, and Marine Corps). General and command-related concerns.

CARE PACKAGES

Servicemembers away from their loved ones live for letters and care packages! They're the number-one morale booster. Even people who don't like to write still love to get letters. In remote areas, food, candy, and sundries become de facto currency.

Packing and Mailing

You have your choice of carriers: the U.S. Postal Service (USPS), DHL, Federal Express, and United Parcel Service. Each has rules about what they won't ship; for instance, the USPS prohibits sending aerosols, due to the danger of exploding in transit. It's generally cheaper to send one large box than multiple small ones.

The USPS offers choices of Express (not available in all locations), Priority, First Class, Parcel Post, Media Mail, and Space Available Mail. Flat-rate priority boxes are popular for care packages since they cost one amount to mail domestically no matter what the weight. Know that when mailing something priority, it only travels fast to a U.S. destination. Once it leaves the country, it becomes part of military mail, where it may or may not be handled faster. Parcel post is a cheap, weight-based rate. Media mail is an even cheaper rate but is strictly for books and magazines. Space available mail goes to overseas bases only and is the cheapest, but delivery time is unpredictable.

Most of the Middle East has been designated a free zone, meaning servicemembers stationed there can send their own personal correspondence mail free. The postal service has a special flat-rate box for these addresses that is bigger and cheaper than the domestically mailed ones, with "America Supports You" printed on it.

The Postal Service provides free priority packing materials (boxes, envelopes, tape, address labels, customs forms). They'll mail these materials to you, and they'll even pick packages up from your home. Call 800-610-8734 and request "Care Kit 4" or visit *www.usps.com* for more information.

Ask the post office what is prohibited in the region you're sending to. Some areas forbid pork products, alcohol, tobacco, nude/seminude and pornographic pictures, or multiples of religious material. A customs form must be filled out for overseas packages, listing contents. While you are instructed to fill out the forms as accurately as possible, many people fill them out vaguely, especially if expensive or sketchy items are inside, and write a low amount for the value to discourage theft. Know that spot checks are made; your package can be opened at any time and contraband items confiscated.

Write the address exactly how it was given to you. Put the servicemember's first and last name only, no rank or unit. Do not decorate the outside of the box; it must be plain. Boxes printed with the names of alcohol or hazardous materials (e.g. bleach or cleaning fluids) will not be delivered. If you put something on the address that you're not supposed to, like a unit identifier, it may also not be delivered. Such mail typically goes in a dead-letter file or is returned to you. Some units may have additional restrictions, such as for size and weight. The maximum length a package in any category can be is forty-eight inches.

Pack things well. Boxes can take up to four weeks to arrive, and they undergo a lot of handling. Use the smallest box possible and fill it with air pillows, Styrofoam peanuts, or bubble wrap to keep the contents from shifting. Small boxes weighing ten pounds or less are recommended. Check the shipper's website for mailing dates to ensure arrival at a specific time.

Include a contents list inside the box so the recipient can see if anything is missing (or the mail service, if the box breaks in transit). Some wives put stickers on the tape to let the recipient know if it was opened, but due to the plain packaging requirements, these should be packaging stickers.

Mail-by dates vary by the delivery location and method of delivery. Here are approximate dates for mailing to APO and FPO boxes. These dates will differ slightly each year.

Military Mail Addressed To	Express Mail® Military Service (EMMS)[1]	First-Class Mail® Letters/ Cards	Priority Mail®	Parcel Airlift Mail (PAL)[2]	Space Available Mail (SAM)[3]	Parcel Post®
APO/FPO AE ZIPs 090–092	Dec 18	Dec 11	Dec 11	Dec 4	Nov 27	Nov 13
APO/FPO AE ZIP 093	N/A	Dec 4	Dec 4	Dec 1	Nov 27	Nov 13
APO/FPO AE ZIPs 094–098	Dec 18	Dec 11	Dec 11	Dec 4	Nov 27	Nov 13
APO/FPO AA ZIP 340	Dec 18	Dec 11	Dec 11	Dec 4	Nov 27	Nov 13
APO/FPO AP ZIPs 962–966	Dec 18	Dec 11	Dec 11	Dec 4	Nov 27	Nov 13

[1]EMMS: Express Mail Military Service is available to selected military post offices. Check with your local post office to determine if this service is available to your APO/FPO address.

[2]PAL: Parcel Airlift Mail (PAL) is a service that provides air transportation for parcels on a space-available basis. It is available for parcel post items not exceeding 30 pounds in weight or 60 inches in length and girth combined. The applicable PAL fee must be paid in addition to the regular surface rate of postage for each addressed piece sent by PAL service.

[3]SAM: Space Available Mail, or SAM, parcels are paid at the parcel post rate of postage, with maximum weight and size limits of 15 pounds and 60 inches in length and girth combined. SAM parcels are first transported domestically by surface and then to overseas destinations by air on a space-available basis.

Contents

Now that you know how to address and ship your package, here are ideas for what to put in it.

Food Items. Nuts, beef jerky, pretzels, Slim Jims, crackers, Rice Krispy treats, tuna packaged in fresh pouches, gum, Pop Tarts, boxed doughnuts, applesauce, dried fruit, sunflower seeds, Chex mix, Cracker Jacks, Pop Rocks, noodle soup cartons, oatmeal packs, sports drinks, drink mixes, cocoa, tea, coffee, cartons of nonrefrigerated milk and cookies for dunking, power bars, restaurant-sized condiment packets (barbecue, soy and taco sauce, mustard, ketchup, mayo, relish, salt, pepper, ranch dressing, creamer, sugar, cheese in a can).

Pack popped corn in baggies and use to fill spaces. Not only will it protect your items, it will be an edible treat! Pack a slice of bread in the sealed bag with homemade goodies. It will absorb moisture. And ship homemade goods the fastest way possible so that they'll arrive fresh, and pack them well. One time my husband called, upset because the cake I sent him arrived as tiny crumbs!

Food should be sturdily packaged; chips in cans and cookies in tins are more likely to arrive intact than bagged items. Single serving sizes work best for the small shipping boxes recommended. Put liquid and powdered items in a Ziploc bag to protect the rest of the contents from leakage. Avoid chocolate or anything with a low melting point. Don't forget to include plastic utensils, paper plates and napkins, and foam cups.

Entertainment. DVDs, CDs, and portable players with headphones, MP3 players, handheld games, PS2 games, batteries (all sizes), puzzles, word search and manga books, novels, magazines, newspapers, books on tape, silly putty, water guns (include enough for him and friends), Silly String, door basketball hoop and Nerf ball, small rubber ball, keychain and jigsaw puzzles, Rubik's Cube, dominoes, yo-yo, playing cards, Frisbee, hacky sacks, magic tricks, and travel-sized checkers and chess games. Make recordings of his favorite shows or sports games.

Medicine/Hygiene. Baby powder and wipes, deodorant, lip balm, Kleenex, lotion, hand sanitizer, toothpaste/brush, mouthwash, dental floss, Q-tips, eyedrops, sunscreen, aloe vera, Band-aids, aspirin, Icy-Hot, Neosporin cream, A&D

Don't pack soaps and deodorants in the same box with food, since the soap smell will permeate the food even when wrapped separately.

ointment, cold medicine, Gold Bond powder, Tums, soft toilet paper, gel boot inserts, cough drops, and bug repellent. Browse travel-size bins and dollar stores for useful little things that are easily carried.

Other Useful Items. Pens, writing paper, stamps, envelopes, blank birthday and event cards, filled-out address book, international phone cards (prepaid cards will give you more control over your budget), sunglasses, disposable camera, fan/water bottle, and coloring books and crayons to give to local children.

218 • TODAY'S MILITARY WIFE

Special Occasion Packages

Birthday. Put a party in a box! Send cake in a jar, candles, party blowers, confetti, and a file of you singing "Happy Birthday" copied onto a CD. Make message balloons by blowing up a balloon, writing a message on it with marker, and then deflating it. Include a card with his age in that number of lipstick kisses. Or leave it one kiss short and tell him he'll get that one upon return.

Anniversary. Send a CD of favorite songs, a scented candle, a list of favorite dating memories, and a card with a description of how you will celebrate your anniversary when he's home. Trace your handprints so you can "hold hands." Send brochures of the places you want to vacation to when he returns.

New Year's. Party blowers, confetti, a plastic champagne glass with a paper toast inside. Include some for his friends. Send a calendar with Post-it notes on each month that have a happy message. Buy a mouse pad that holds pictures (you can find these at Kinko's), and send it along with twelve photos that he can switch out each month.

Valentine's Day. Send a package of red, with candy hearts and licorice. Burn a CD with special songs; make a small photo album and a book of coupons for his return. Spray a pillowcase with your perfume (enclose it in a Ziploc bag so the scent doesn't dissipate in transit).

St. Patrick's Day. Send a package of green, with paper shamrocks, green candy, drink mix, a "Kiss Me, I'm Irish" button or shirt, and some good-luck charms.

Easter. Fill a basket with jellybeans, hard candy, and marshmallow Peeps. Put shiny coins and hand-written messages from your family inside plastic eggs.

Halloween. Fill your package with themed candy, maybe even some costume pieces, a foam pumpkin to carve, and DVDs of scary movies, if he has means to play them. Make treat bags for the people in his unit.

Thanksgiving. Record your dinner and his chair at the table. Send him the movie to watch while he eats his own dinner, along with a small decoration. Perhaps send along a meal of canned turkey, canned cranberry sauce, instant mashed potato cups, hard breadsticks, jarred gravy, Hostess apple pies, and a small can of corn. Or send a self-heating dinner, such as the ones sold at *www.heatermeals.com.*

Christmas. Send a miniature tree, battery-operated lights (include batteries), a stuffed stocking, and Christmas CDs and movies. Record your church service. Send some ornaments to hang in his room or on the ship's tree. Make bread-dough ornament rings and put family pictures inside. If he's coming home soon, take a picture of his present and send it wrapped.

Make boxes around themes: "Jamaica," where you might send jerk sauce, Caribbean coffee, and music; "Tea Time" with a plastic, push-button jug filled with tea bags and sugar packets; "Mexico" with chips, a jar of cheese, and jalapeños; "Poker Party" with poker chips, cards, pepperoni pieces, nonalcoholic beer, and a lucky rabbit's foot; "Movie Night" with DVDs, flavored popcorn (microwave or popped in a bag), movie candy, and a movie poster; "Break Time" with a photo cut into jigsaw pieces to assemble, humor books, comedy tapes, a home movie of your friends and family clowning around; a mug or pillowcase with a photo of yourself scanned on it, a mirror-writing letter; "Taste of Home" with a running tape of background noise (cars going by, dogs barking, kids playing), graded school papers, some home-baked goods.

MANAGING STRESS AND ANGER

Separations bring on stress or tension. Some are more stressful than others. But any separation is stressful when you're not used to being by yourself or are experiencing problems. How you manage your stress can affect your relationship.

Life is largely a process of adapting to the positive and negative changes around us. Whether it's moving, waiting out a traffic jam, saying good-bye, or coping with the demands of single parenthood, a means to adapt is necessary. How happy and healthy we are depends in large part on how successful this adaptation is. Different things are stressful to different people, but stress is something that we ourselves create, and it depends on how we interpret situations and relate to the world. Many people think that others and situations around us are responsible for our stresses. But no one can make us feel sad, angry, jealous, foolish, incompetent, or stressed except ourselves.

We can't avoid stress; such a thing isn't even desirable. Positive stresses are beneficial. However, negative stresses can be debilitating. They can make you unhappy and physically sick. Ulcers, high blood pressure, strokes, and even allergies are linked to stress. Clearly, knowing how to manage stress successfully is an important life skill.

One of the biggest stressors is the feeling that you lack control over what is happening to you. If you feel that you lack control, why? What, exactly, is stressing you out? Children, money, job, environment, poor relationships, bad health? Can you isolate your stresses and deal with them constructively? Seek counseling if your methods of dealing with them aren't working.

Proven Stress Reducers

You can't control the amount of stress a separation will give you, but you *can* control how you respond to it. People who cope with stress best have these things in common: optimism, a sense of being in control of their lives, a reliable network of friends or family, the ability to be flexible, the ability to take care of themselves, and a sense of spirituality. In addition, studies have shown that people who incorporate the following steps deal with stress well.

- Get up fifteen minutes earlier in the morning, and leave before you have to. Unanticipated delays will then be less stressful.
- Practice preventive maintenance on cars and appliances.

- Restrict the amount of caffeine, alcohol, tobacco, and junk food in your diet. Eat healthy.
- Don't procrastinate. If you have an unpleasant task to do, do it early to get it over with. That way, you won't worry about it all day.
- Don't tolerate something that doesn't work right. Fix it or buy a new one.
- Avoid unproductive, negative, "high-maintenance" people. If you find yourself thinking angrily about them a lot, they're high maintenance.
- Prioritize what's important and what's not. Relax your standards about what's not (e.g., housecleaning). Maintain a routine.
- Regularly set aside "me" time for yourself. Hire a sitter and do something you enjoy. Indulge regularly in a hobby: cross-stitching, gardening, scrapbooking, singing in a choir, making crafts. The Air Force Aid Society runs a "Give Parents a Break" program, which provides several hours of free babysitting at regularly scheduled times to families of deployed servicemembers. A referral from the family services office, Family Advocacy, or the child-care center is needed.
- "Anticipatory grief" is very real. Try "inoculating" yourself against a dreaded event. Just as a vaccine can protect you from an illness, if you expose yourself to one or more of the dreaded aspects of an unpleasant experience, you can sometimes mitigate your fears. Differentiate between a worry and a concern. A worry is something you can't do anything about, and it's unproductive; it accomplishes nothing. Turn it into a concern. Ask yourself what's the worst thing that could happen and what you'd do if it did. Then make plans for that incident and stop worrying. Or try setting aside a specific amount of time to worry, and then move on. Recognize the things over which you have no control.
- Borrow library books on visualization, meditation, and relaxation techniques.
- Exercise. It is a terrific stress buster. Thirty minutes on an exercise bike, a brisk swim, or an aerobic walk around the neighborhood can make your problems seem more manageable. Find room in your home for a small treadmill, exercise bike, or mini-trampoline. Perhaps set it in front of the TV.
- Get lots of sleep. Perhaps ask for a sleep aid; some people swear by Ambien.
- Vent to a friend or on an online message board as an anonymous screen name. (Remember, that no one is truly anonymous though; you can be traced via the post's IP address.)
- Count your blessings. For everything that's wrong in your life, there are a dozen things that are right. Remember the adage about the man who was upset over no shoes until he met a man who had no feet.
- Slow down and take five deep breaths when you find yourself starting to spin with concerns. Exhale slowly.

- Meditate, pray and read books that feed your spiritual side.
- If you're still stressed, ask why your plan isn't working and look for concrete ways to change your routine and situation.

Anger Management Techniques

Like stress, bottled-up anger can create real and serious health problems. Venting anger can have disastrous effects on you and those around you. Studies on anger show that people who brood have the highest blood pressure, people who blow up have the second highest, and people who take steps to resolve their anger have the lowest. Strategies for resolving anger include:

- Make a list of the things you're angry about. This might help clarify the problem so that you can take steps to solve it.
- Instead of brooding or blowing up when someone says something rude or cuts you off in traffic, tell yourself the person is either having a bad day or is just a jerk not worth your time. Will it really matter a week from now, anyway?
- Try not to say anything in anger when you're hot, hungry, tired, or have a headache. Have something to eat, get some sleep, or take a shower or aspirin first.
- Recognize that people don't have to act like we think they should and that things will not always go the way we want them to.
- Discuss problems constructively. Focus on solving them instead of venting anger.
- Don't give people you dislike "real estate" in your head. It elevates their importance—why bother?

TIPS FROM THE PROS

Take advantage of the time your husband is away to get those chronically postponed chores done, take those classes, do that craft project, and participate in the

> Ask at the family services office for deployment coloring books for children.

things you've been wanting to do. Here's what some veterans of separations have to say about keeping it together.

"*Keep your freezer and pantry full. Buy easy-to-make food. Eat well and healthy, but you don't have to copy a TV chef to do it.*"

"*I bought my husband a Blackberry so he could download e-mails quickly during his limited shipboard computer time, then read and respond at his leisure.*"

"*If there's something you had planned to do together, such as play tennis or see a movie, do it yourself regardless of your husband's unit schedule. Unexpected interruptions like alerts may ruin his plans, but they don't have to ruin yours. Don't cancel, sulk, and make your husband feel bad for disappointing you. I'd rather see a few movies without him than never go to them at all.*"

"Take a cue from the older wives. Most have been through deployments, wars, schools, etc., and have grown stronger for it. In four years you might look back and be amazed at how much you've changed. Of course, you might go day to day doing the exact same things you are now, and never change. Some people get older and wiser; some just get older. We have a limited time on earth and the countdown begins the day we're born. Use each day wisely."

"Tuck homemade cookies, sandwiches, a small thermos of hot coffee, and love notes into his field gear before he goes. Discovering them will be a pleasant surprise."

"My husband was in Iraq for a year. My faith in God sustained me; I knew God would never give me anything I couldn't handle."

"Learn new recipes to surprise him with when he returns."

"Choose another day to celebrate. If he has to be away or must work on a holiday, pick a day when everyone's home to have your dinner or party or to open gifts. Celebrate Thanksgiving on a Saturday, or when he gets home."

"Buy some holiday decorations that will last until the family is reunited, like a living Christmas tree in a pot. Relive holiday excitement when he's home again by looking at photos or watching videos of the family opening presents."

"Spend the holiday helping the down-and-out and doing random acts of kindness. It will keep you busy and give you a new perspective about feeling sorry for yourself."

"Keep in touch! With e-mail, instant messaging, telephony, cell phones, and web-cams there's no reason not to. Deployed dads can even send e-mail to their kids at their DoD school. Set a time and date for each communication as much as you're able. (Be realistic; his schedule is more unpredictable than yours.) When you do talk, keep it healthy. Don't rehash old arguments or bad news that he can't do anything about. You never know exactly when you'll be able to talk again. Think about how you'd feel if you never saw him again. Don't forget that they have limited computer time and their e-mails are subject to interception and monitoring. It may be the reason he's not as forthcoming or affectionate as you might like him to be."

"To my surprise, I didn't find the six months Tom spent on his unaccompanied tour so bad. I don't have kids, and free of the need to accommodate another adult, I actually rearranged a lot of things to suit myself. I had time to do things I couldn't do when he was home. Sure, there were drawbacks to being alone, but I also discovered advantages."

"I used to do count-downs until I realized that I was putting my life on hold for them, and there were just too many: count-downs until graduation from Basic; to the first PCS; until he deployed; until he returned. Instead of living my life, I was counting it down. Life is a journey, not a destination."

"Get your craft projects done. Take classes in sponge and tole painting. Every true Navy wife cross-stitches! When Tim was away for six months, I made an entire queen-sized quilt. We broke it in when he got back!"

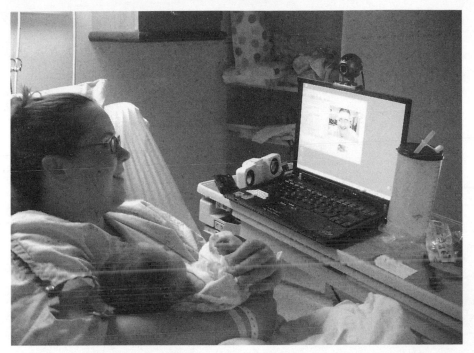

An Air Force wife at Ellsworth Air Force Base in South Dakota talks to her husband in Southwest Asia via Web cam after their son is born. Photo courtesy U.S. Air Force

"I got a job when my husband was deployed, with the intent of saving the money to take him on a nice vacation or shopping spree (his choice) when he returned."

"Before Mike goes, I think of all the things I want to do that I don't, or wouldn't, do when he's here, like eating with the kids on the floor in front of the TV instead of at the table, and doing jigsaw puzzles afterward. Or pitching a tent in the backyard and sleeping in it. Doing different, special things that we don't do when he's here helps the children adjust better to his absence instead of viewing separations as something to dread. And we really do have fun. I feel special bonding with my children during these times."

"I scan pages of our kids' schoolwork and e-mail them to him."

"There are benefits to training exercises. For two weeks there's no green laundry, and I can watch something on TV besides sports. The kids and I enjoy more macaroni and cheese, turkey franks, soup, and PB&Js when he's gone, which means I save money on food."

"Separations are good in that you get a break from each other. When you realize how many little things he does around the house—coaxing a bad TV or DVD to work, changing light bulbs in high places, starting the grill—you appreciate him all the more when he gets back. I don't get mad over silly nothings like not putting the cap back on the toothpaste, because we don't have enough time together as is to waste it like that. Furthermore, if you successfully make it through a long separation, it makes anything that follows easy."

"I maintain Pete as the house authority figure even when he's away. If the children are pressing me for something and I'm not sure what to do, if the decision doesn't have to be made immediately, I'll say, 'Wait until Dad calls. We'll see what he says.' If the decision has to be made right away, I'll make it and say, 'I think Dad would agree with this.'"

"Strong marriages have little problem surviving a separation. It's the shaky ones that are pushed over the edge. Get your marriage in the best possible shape. Talk out nagging concerns, and don't trivialize or dismiss what the other is worried about. If either of you is worried about something, that's enough to make it a valid, legitimate concern. There's no such thing as 'small stuff' where marriage problems are concerned; all become 'big stuff' when unaddressed."

"Keep your routine, preserve your home and sense of normalcy. A separation needs to be viewed as a time to miss your husband, not a time of complete disruption."

"Join a gym, take Pilates, spinning, aerobics, or yoga classes. Lose weight. Get your hair colored, get a makeover, buy contact lenses. Surprise him with a sharp-looking wife when he returns. Visit www.weightwatchers.com or www.freeweightloss.com for inspiration."

"Being a military spouse involves sharing and mutual support. So participate in FRG meetings. When my husband was in Operation Enduring, I didn't hear from him for weeks on end. I wasn't even sure exactly where he was. I befriended other Special Forces wives in the unit, and that helped. No one else—not your family, not your civilian friends, not even military wives whose husbands aren't deployed—will truly understand what you're going through. Plus it's nice to have a group of anybody to meet, greet, and eat with one night a month.

"Don't get worked up over gossip and stuff that comes down on the 'unofficial' phone tree. As an ombudsman, I assure you that much of what you hear is BS. Some gossipers appear persuasive and knowledgeable, but I assure you that the commanding officer doesn't call them with information personally. As spouses, we all have the responsibility of controlling gossip and nasty rumors. Have faith in the official information systems: the ombudsman, the key volunteers, the family support groups."

"I keep the speakers on my computer turned way up so I can hear instant message beeps throughout the house."

"Do what you can to help other wives get through whatever it is they're going through. Offer 'been there, done that' advice. Don't play the 'who's got it worse' game. Don't say things like, 'You're lucky your husband only deploys for short times,' or 'Be happy your deployment is almost over,' or 'Be happy he's not in a real war zone.' Separations from our loved ones are separations, whether they're for peacetime disaster assistance or for war."

"I enrolled in online classes when Jan was deployed for a year. They're great opportunities to pursue a degree from a university 100 miles away while holding down the home front. A friend of mine got a degree as a medical transcriptionist in that time."

"Pamper yourself at a day spa. A hot oil or hot stone massage and a facial will melt stress away. Get an aromatherapy treatment. It's expensive, but like that old commercial said, you're worth it!"

"Reservist wives, don't let the fact that your husband isn't on active duty lull you into a false sense of security that you don't need your affairs in order. Reservists can be called up anytime; the September 11 attacks showed that. And you need to be prepared to live on a military income if that happens."

"Keep your husband informed of your activities during a separation. Being surprised with a major purchase upon return or with huge bills that you've run up can cause problems."

"My husband has a three-week training course after Thanksgiving. I'm already thinking about all the Christmas crafts I'll make."

One time when my husband went away, I opened a savings account for his birthday present. Was he surprised! Now every time he goes away I scrimp and add to it. I enjoy showing him a bigger balance when he gets back. It's our 'reward.' Sometimes quite a bit of money can be made during a TDY, which I consider a separation benefit."

"Keep a notebook for writing down all the things you want to tell him, so that when he calls, your mind won't go blank. I have friends who keep an online blog for this. The benefit there is their husband can check it anytime—of course, this may not be a benefit!"

"I tend to not mention problems in letters or phone calls until I have a solution. I don't bother him with small stuff. And if nobody's dead or hospitalized, it's small stuff!"

"Keep your letters, e-mails, and phone calls upbeat. When he's away, it's easy to blow things out of proportion. Things that wouldn't ordinarily bother us suddenly get honored with three pages. If you write a letter while you're depressed, don't mail it right away. Read it again after a good night's sleep and reevaluate it. Separations are just as hard on them, and when they're flying or in other dangerous situations, they're much harder. Don't add to the difficulty; don't distract him with trivia."

"Don't feel like you have to defend to anyone why he's deployed. That is Congress's job. Just support and be proud of your soldier."

"When I know he's in his quarters, I send him a pizza."

"Every day he's away I do one thing to improve myself, such as flip through a dictionary to learn a new word, flip through a history book to learn an important date, or study a map to see what countries border Qatar. Once I started a self-education program where I chose a subject a month and read everything the library had on it."

"During a six-month deployment, my husband's ship docked in Charleston for a week. I flew out with my AAA tour book (those books are terrific!), and we had a mini-vacation."

"I hate separations, but I would no sooner ask my husband to give up a career he loves (and that he had before we met) than I would give up my own career as a mother. My mission is to support him, and he's worth it! Face it, in a marriage someone is going to have to sacrifice something."

"Before my husband leaves, I write some cards to him. I pack them in his gear with the envelopes labeled 'Save This for a Bad Day,' 'Save This for When You Need a Laugh,' and so forth."

"I start my 'deployment routine' a few weeks before he leaves. It helps me make a mental transition. For instance, John does routine things such as lowering the shades and checking the locks before we go to bed. Before he leaves for a long separation, I start doing them."

"When you've handled something especially challenging, reward yourself with something you've been wanting to buy. Put it on layaway if you can't afford it right away; don't charge it."

"When I accepted my husband's proposal thirteen years ago, I gave him a hand-carved 'yes.' It hangs in the kitchen to remind me that I agreed to separations and other challenges of this way of life."

"I thought nothing was worse than separations. When my husband got recruiting duty I learned I was wrong."

"As soon as my husband leaves for a long deployment, I take most of his clothes out of the closet to let mine spread out a little. Then I throw all his toiletries into a Rubbermaid container and stash it out of the way so I have the whole bathroom to myself. I do keep a picture of him on my dresser."

"We can be apart and be miserable or be apart and make it work—I choose the latter. But it is a choice; it doesn't just happen."

"Someone once asked me why be married if you can't be together. Well, to me, togetherness is a state of mind. No matter where Mike is, I know he's my husband and loves me. What he does, he does for us. He does it so we will have a good future. These sacrifices are not one sided, we both make them, and we do so for each other. I would rather have him as my husband part-time than anyone else full-time."

"I'm too proud of being a soldier's wife to feel sorry for myself. And how can I feel sorry for myself? I'm the one able to see our daughter start walking, barbecue a steak whenever I want, sit on the furniture he's still paying for. He's out in 120-degree heat, wearing full field gear."

"When my husband is gone, I hit the road and travel, visiting my old high school friends and family. I have a home-based business, so I have lots of flexibility. There are other pluses—I let the house get trashed and stop shaving my legs! Also, separations make for great 'Sorry I was gone' guilt gifts! I love that gold from Saudi Arabia!"

"I listened to some Anthony Robbins 'personal power' tapes once, and something in particular struck me. He said that if you were overweight, you could ask yourself, 'Why am I so fat?' but a better question is, 'What can I do to lose weight?' An even better one is, 'What can I do to lose weight and enjoy the process?' That got me thinking about things I could do to be more active and enjoy this separation more."

Tips from the Pros on Dealing with Loneliness

"I talk to his picture and hold his dog tags. I keep a picture of him in his blues in my car. I save some of the texts he sends me and re-read them."

"When our husbands were gone over Valentine's Day, we wives got dressed up and went to an upscale restaurant. Other times we've gotten together, baked brownies, and watched rented movies. It beats staying home alone."

"I let an item remain just the way he left it during a deployment. If he leaves his running shoes under the desk or a shirt draped over a living room chair, I'll let it stay there as a way to feel close to him."

"Drugs, booze, and junk food don't cure loneliness. When you're feeling down, work on a hobby. Don't make that hobby partying with other men, though, even if they're just friends. I've seen divorces occur over long deployments because of that. Your husband deserves a partner he can count on. Who wants to put up with the demands of two men, anyway?"

"I look at his picture, kiss my wedding ring, and hold our son (he's his clone). If it gets really bad I scrub the house from top to bottom or bake a lot of good stuff."

"I sometimes leave the TV on all night to sound like someone's home with me. I offer to work lots of overtime at my job. I also go to the gym and work out right before bed so I'll be tired."

"I smell his clothes that I never washed. Sometimes I sleep with his shirt on. I look at pictures or I write in my journal assuming that someday, whether I'm here or not, he'll read it and see what I was thinking and feeling."

"I spray his cologne on me or around the room. I leave his pillowcase on the bed and snuggle up to it. I also carry a picture of him on my keychain. I also have a medal of St. George, the Patron Saint of the Military on it. The inscription on the back reads: 'Keep us safe, day and night. Give us courage, strength and might.' It's sort of like a prayer for me."

"I listen to some of our favorite slow songs, drive his car, and I wear one of his T-shirts or other clothes."

"During Juan's last deployment, I got very active with our family support group. I published its monthly newsletter and added innovations such as a coloring page for kids, a penny-pinching hints column, and inspirational poems."

"Before he left for Korea, I made a video of our whole extended family. He didn't know I did this until I took him to the airport. Before he got on the plane, I handed it to him. When he gets lonely, he watches it."

"I write letters and assemble care packages with his photo in front of me. At the end of an hour of doing that I often feel as if I've spent some special time with him."

"It's not the days that drag by, because during the day he's not home anyway. It's the nights. So I invite the other women whose husbands are away and their kids over for dinner. We go to movies, come back, gab all night. The kids fall asleep on the floor."

"When I'm feeling blue, I write my husband a long love letter. I remind him of the first time we met, how we fell in love, our wedding day, and the wonderful memories I have of our courtship and married time together. It feels good to put my most precious thoughts down on paper and share them with him. Sometimes he is inspired to do the same, and the separation reaffirms our love."

"The sooner you learn to get along on your own, the better, because the higher up the ladder your husband goes, the more he'll be working. My husband's a first sergeant and works late all the time, often picking up the slack for subordinates who have to go home to attend to their families' problems. I always thought it was the first sergeants and company commanders who got out of going to the field and went home early every day. Instead they're the ones who work the most!"

CHILDREN'S ISSUES

Children's anxiety about separations and what they see in the news about world situations can affect their family, school, and social lives. Strategies to ease their anxieties include:

- Explain where their dad is going. Look at maps and books; learn a bit about the place. Making the unknown a bit more known may make it less scary.
- Assure them that their dad is as well trained and equipped as possible. Perhaps view some of the many impressive images at *www.defenselink.mil* (click on "photos").
- Assign responsibilities. This can range from caring for the family pet, to cooking dinner, to mowing the lawn.
- Answer their questions. Not answering them won't make them go away. Just do it in an age-appropriate manner.
- Keep a calm exterior. There is a correlation between wives' and children's behavior during absences. If the parent is obviously stressed and nervous all the time, the kids are likely to be the same way. Assure them that you're there for them and won't go anywhere.
- Have your husband record bedtime stories on videotape or cassette before he goes, or as an ongoing project while deployed. Perhaps have him buy gifts or write notes to present to them when they're having a bad day.
- Do a visual countdown. Put a number of Hershey's Kisses in a jar equal to the anticipated separation days and take one out each day for a kiss from dad. Make a paper link chain and remove one link each day, or stick playing cards

to poster board and remove one each day. Add a few days to the countdown in case of delays.

- Minimize watching news on TV. Much of it is negative; it's not even good for you to constantly watch it.
- Save answering machine messages and play them back when everyone wants to hear dad's voice.
- Let the school know he's deployed so they will be more sympathetic and alert about behavior changes. Along those lines, don't deny when there is a problem.
- Don't expect a child to become the man or woman of the house in a parent's absence.
- Don't bad-mouth the military, the schools, or the base. You may not like certain aspects, but it is more constructive to help children see the positive factors and seek solutions.

EMERGENCIES

In the event of a death, serious illness, or injury, a servicemember can be called back to the family. But before you initiate this, be sure that the situation is grave. Calling your husband out of the field, out of school, or back from deployment for anything but the most serious of problems is a distraction to his training, an irritant to his superiors, and a burden to his coworkers. It cheats him of what might someday be critical knowledge and reflects poorly on you and your ability to cope. Do try to deal with it yourself first, as there is little he can do from where he is, and telling him about problems he can't solve is frustrating and distracting on his end.

Depending on where he is, calling him can be as simple as calling the unit and having your message relayed. Other times you might have to contact the Red Cross, which will verify the emergency and send a message. If you're unsure what to do, contact your ombudsman or the wife of your husband's supervisor or commanding officer. She's been a part of service life longer than you and will know what to do.

HOMECOMINGS

Is there anything better than hearing the key caller on the phone, telling you to hurry to base because the plane has landed? However, if the separation has been a long one, the reunion can be hard. People sometimes change during long separations. Perhaps you've assumed responsibilities your husband may want back, but which you may not be willing to relinquish. You may be unsure of his reactions to your decisions about the children and money or your newfound enjoyment in nights out with friends. He may be wondering if the kids will recognize him, if his parenting skills are up to par, and how things went overall while he was away. Even the children may have concerns, such as wondering if any rules will change and how long he'll be home this time. New interests may have been cultivated, bringing new problems, and old problems are still there.

You may have had this glorious fantasy of what he will look like, and when he steps off the plane, ship, or five-ton truck, he's tired, dirty, unshaven, has lost or gained weight, and just wants to go home and sleep. Or it may be the opposite. One woman recalled a homecoming when she was in the hospital recovering from a difficult childbirth and her husband walked in tanned, smiling, and wearing a new leather jacket. Even though for the past seven months she'd looked forward to their reunion, she fixated on that jacket and became furious.

Communicate. Listen, notice body language, and don't trivialize concerns. If something is important to him, it should be important to you, too (and vice versa). If he wants time alone, that should be respected, just as your space should be.

Some women make reservations in a luxury hotel for a night to reconnect with their husbands before dealing with anything else. Others feel a need to reestablish the family and get the servicemember reacquainted with young children before whisking him away on an adults-only vacation. Do what works best for your family. Some thoughts from wives who have been there:

"Don't schedule a lot of activities or chores right away. Your husband probably won't want a list of demands made on him."

"I love watching my children run at breakneck speed across the tarmac to their daddy and jump in his arm as he climbs out of his jet. I love seeing the look of joy and happiness on his face as he sets eyes on the loves of his life for the first time in months."

"Money is often a major issue during our homecomings. I offer to show Aaron the checkbook and bank statements before he asks, and we discuss how I spent our money."

"Don't play an 'I had it harder than you' game when he returns. Both of you had stresses."

"Don't make inflexible plans for the homecoming day; it leaves less room for disappointment if the schedule changes."

"The time after a separation can be as hard as the time during, for different reasons. If you've become self-sufficient, learn to work as a team again. Don't continue trying to fix all issues on your own. Let him know the processes in the house."

"My husband's in a field that takes him from his family often. So I look at our homecomings as a gift—a gift given each time he comes home."

"Treat each other courteously. Jamie doesn't come home and throw his field gear all over; he puts it away. Then he takes the kids to the park while I cook dinner. I don't ask him to help with the housework afterward."

"The day Leon comes home I have his space in the family room just as he left it: the ottoman in front of his chair, the remote handy, and his magazines in the basket next to the chair."

"My in-laws always want to be there when he returns. I love them, but don't want to share the moment. If you have the same situation, I suggest keeping the return date a secret or adding a week to it."

"Tricare covers marriage counseling. We starting going when we felt we were losing touch with each other after his last deployment. It really helped. The counselor helped us make time for each other and remember why we fell in love."

"Have a nice dinner ready when he gets home, but don't be surprised if he just goes to sleep instead of eating. Don't have any activities planned for the day he comes home or the day after."

"I love planning our reunions. I make hotel reservations and buy new lingerie and refer to the books 1001 Ways to Be Romantic *and* 1001 Ways to Be More Romantic *for ideas."*

"Make a separation something to grow through, not something to go through. The rewards of being able to shop, buy a house, sell a car, discipline the children, move, resolve problems, and cope on your own are the wonderful feelings of independence, assurance, self-esteem, and self-confidence, and they're known only to those who have done it. It makes the separation worth it."

FURTHER READING

Books

Davidson Tom and Lorna Gentry. *The Complete Idiot's Guide to Home Security.* New York: Alpha Books, 2001.

Leyden-Rubenstein, Lori. *The Stress Management Handbook.* New York: McGraw-Hill, 1999.

Internet Resources

www.verybestbaking.com/promotions/programs/troops.aspx. Nestle's tips and recipes for sending baked goods abroad.

www.operationhomefront.org/Help/help_volunteer_delivery.shtml. Information on free doula care for expectant wives of deployed or injured servicemembers.

www.usps.com. Postal service website. Allows you to calculate the postage costs of packages, including additional services such as insurance or return receipt.

www.nmfa.org/site/PageServer?pagename=camp_locations. Free summer camp for children of deployed parents.

www.booksforbrats.net/hero/ecards/library.php. E-cards for kids to send to deployed relatives.

www.sesameworkshop.org/tlc. Bilingual educational outreach kits for children from Sesame Street.

www.insurance.va.gov/Sglisite/SGLI/deployFAQ.htm. FAQ page for deployed and mobilized Reservists.

www.cellphonesforsoldiers.com. Donate your old cell phone here. They're recycled to provide phone talk time for deployed servicemembers.

www.guardfamily.org. National Guard families online.

https://www.jagcnet.army.mil. Find a comprehensive deployment checklist here.

www.usuhs.mil/psy/CTChildrenCopeDuringDeployment.pdf. Tips on helping children of deployed servicemembers.

www.guardianangelsforsoldierspet.org. Pet foster care for deployed servicemembers.

10

Sponsoring a Family

The military offers a way to make friends immediately upon arrival at each new duty station: the Sponsorship Program. It was created to help servicemembers comfortably settle into their new location, thus get up to speed on the new job as soon as possible. The program extends to the whole family, as there are youth sponsorship programs for preteen and teen children, too.

HOW THE PROGRAM WORKS
When the gaining unit learns of an incoming person, they'll send an official welcoming letter, and then assign a sponsor, which is basically an outreach person from that unit. The sponsor is typically of equal or higher in rank, the same sex, military career field, or occupational series as the incoming person. He will also be the same marital status, in hopes that you, the family member, will assist the new family member while your spouse assists the new servicemember. The sponsor is typically not being replaced by the incoming person or scheduled for a PCS move soon.

IMPORTANCE OF SPONSORING
Being a sponsor is an important responsibility. Sponsors represent the unit and are a newcomer's first contact with it. These first impressions can be longlasting. Just as being well treated makes a newcomer and his family feel like an important and integral part of the unit, a poor reception can create negative feelings that spread to the whole family. For the program to work properly, both the sponsor and the sponsored have obligations to fulfill.

THE SPONSOR'S RESPONSIBILITIES
Upon receiving a sponsorship assignment, a servicemember should send an e-mail or letter and welcome packet to the newcomer immediately. It doesn't matter if the newcomer isn't due for another ten months; the sooner communication starts, the

better. Welcome packets are available at the family services office, and sample letters might be available at the unit. Typical letters contain information on the housing situation, availability of quartermaster furniture, length of time for car shipment if overseas, duty uniform and patches worn, anticipated temporary duties, mission of the unit, and so on. One soldier ended his letter with the friendly advice, "Our physical training runs take us up hills, down valleys, and it's HOT here in the summer! We run at least two miles, so I advise you to keep in shape!" Such efforts give a form letter a nice personal touch.

A gesture that is sure to be appreciated is for you to e-mail or enclose a letter to the new spouse. Here is a letter that a wife wrote to the wife of an airman her husband sponsored.

Dear Emma,

I hear you'll be joining us at Kirtland! W00t! I hope you'll like it here! Albuquerque is a large city surrounded by beautiful mountains. The cost of living isn't too bad, there are nice shops—if you're into silver and turquoise, this is the place!—and things to do. Ski buffs have Sandia Peak. Santa Fe is an hour's drive, lovely historic buildings there. The desert sun really heats things up in the summer, so I hope you have lots of light clothes.

Do you have children? Kids here attend the Albuquerque public school system, and I can give you a heads up on some good private ones, too.

Do you plan to live on post or in town? Let me know. We live in quarters, so I'm not too familiar with what's on the economy, but I'm told that rents are reasonable.

Looking forward to hearing from you. Maybe we can do lunch in Old Town, a historic area here.

Sincerely,

Beth

Nothing elaborate, that took research, or more than twenty minutes to write. Just a short description of what Beth found enjoyable. But this simple effort sure made Emma's day!

Notice how upbeat Beth was. If you have negative opinions about the place, they're best kept to yourself. There's no need to add to the apprehensions the newcomers are sure to have, and your worst tour may turn out to be their best ever.

When you sponsor someone, it helps to review relocation videos, information packets, and brochures about your own duty station from the family services office. Refreshing your memory about what your town offers will give you ideas to pass along to newcomers. Offer practical advice, such as where the nice neighborhoods, good places to buy furniture, favorite hair salons, and other places you like.

The first letter should be addressed to the newcomer's home. If you don't get a response within a month, send another, this time to the unit. People with orders are people on the move. They visit relatives, take vacations, attend schools, and tie up all the loose ends a move creates. If the newcomer isn't there anymore, the unit will forward your letter. If you still don't receive an answer, your husband should let his commander know; he can then phone the newcomer's unit to investigate. You've both done your jobs.

When you receive a letter with the family's exact date of arrival, acknowledge it. It makes people nervous when they get no response to important information like that. A phone call at this point is a nice touch.

WHEN THEY ARRIVE

What would you have liked someone to have done for you? There are no rules, common sense and courtesy govern. Think about what your sponsor could have done to make life easier when you were moving in. Here are some suggestions:

- When the family arrives, serve them dinner, either at your house or in their hotel room. They've had a long drive and probably feel too tired to go to the commissary and too scruffy to go to a restaurant. A hot meal is a nice gesture, as they've probably had their fill of cold cuts and fast food.
- While the new servicemember gets in-processed and introduced to his chain of command, the spouse often sits neglected in the hotel room. Give her a call. Better yet, show her around base. Show her where the PX, commissary, hospital, library, and child-care center are. Take her into town and point out your favorite shops, flea markets, historical sites, picnic, and recreation spots.
- In the event the family is able to move into quarters immediately, take her to the commissary while the guys are at work.
- If the family has special needs, find out what accommodating programs are available or gather some phone numbers to give them.
- Drive with her to the next coffee or FRG meeting.

- Let her know that she can call you with questions.
- If you want to do a really super job, do something for the children. If your own children are similar ages, ask them to write letters.

OVERSEAS

There's a special need to be helpful when you're sponsoring a family overseas. The adjustments can be overwhelming. A few more considerations will help ease the frustrations a new arrival might encounter her first week.

- Write suggestions of what to bring and what not to in the way of clothing and household goods.
- Assume the family has a lot of luggage, since vacationing and visiting prior to overseas moves is common. Pick them up in the largest car available to you.
- Have some extra money in the local currency available that they can buy from you if they want. The banks might be closed, and they might need to purchase food or other essentials on the local economy. Explain the currency system.
- Explain how the phone system works. It's frustrating not to be able to place calls due to lack of knowledge of the local signals, recordings, and prefixes.

This is all a lot of work. But as difficult as it may be for you to accomplish these tasks, imagine what it would be like for the newcomer's wife with no help at all. The efforts involved take only a few hours of your life, and they won't go unappreciated. You'll have helped the military in its mission of giving a warm welcome to newcomers, and you will have laid groundwork for a new friendship.

If you can't help the new spouse, see whether your husband or someone else can. If you're having car problems, arrange with someone else in the unit to pitch in. If you had planned to go on leave during the time they'll be arriving, make arrangements to have someone else sponsor them. Have a backup plan.

FOR THE SPONSORED

When you, the incoming family, receive your welcome packet, thank your sponsors for their communication, and ask any questions you might have. Let your sponsor know how many children and pets you have and what your special needs are. It's essential that you keep your sponsor and his chain of command aware of any changes to your plans, such as orders to a different unit, an earlier date of arrival, or attendance at a school first. All it takes is an e-mail. If the sponsor hears of such plans, he needs to keep you informed. Don't count on the units to do it for you. Granted, both units should have up-to-date information about your present and future whereabouts and be in constant communication with each other, but sometimes wires get crossed. The problem of arriving and having no sponsor is rarely the fault of an uncaring unit; it's often just the result of the unit's being unaware of the latest plans. This is why early and constant communication between newcomer and sponsor is critical. If you haven't heard anything from your sponsor, feel free to contact the unit and ask for another.

SPONSORSHIP SUCCESS STORIES

Here are some comments from people who have had good sponsoring experiences.

"We've always been lucky to get a warm welcome when moving into housing, and I pass that on. I give people we sponsor and new neighbors a notebook of helpful hints. I list my favorite places to get my hair cut and eat out, veterinarians, where to get the best produce and meats, and babysitter numbers. I also give the new family some freezer meals that get them through the first three days. At one place we lived, we implemented a system in which an updated notebook with this information was passed from one newbie to the next."

"I was worried what Altus Air Base would be like. After four years at Wichita, we'd put down roots. I wasn't sure I could ever like another place as much. Getting a letter from our sponsor's wife made me feel better, that there was someone who cared, who would welcome us."

"The couple we sponsored stayed in a hotel for three weeks before they found an apartment. I bought two bags of groceries for them when they arrived and lent them a small refrigerator to use in the hotel."

"Our sponsor's wife baked chocolate chip cookies and presented them to us at the airport, tied up in a red ribbon."

"We took the family we sponsored around town and invited them for dinner, and I bought her a welcome gift. We're good friends now; we exchange babysitting hours, and she even made me a dress for a Christmas formal. I often hear people say that commanders should enforce the Sponsorship Program. In my opinion, commanders shouldn't be expected to enforce a program that simply asks people to be nice to each other."

"When we moved to Mystic, our sponsor gave us a cutting from one of her plants. That was two moves ago, and I still have it; it's big and bushy and looks lovely on my windowsill. Every time I see it, it brings back good memories."

"The family we sponsored had a big dog, and none of the hotels would accept it, so we kept it for them until they got quarters. It was fun having a dog for a few weeks."

"Our sponsor knew that I was looking for work as a paralegal, so he asked around town for me. He got some contacts that landed a few interviews."

"Our sponsors treated us so well that when they PCSed, we returned the favor and sponsored them! We drove them around their last week here (they were going overseas and had sold their car) so they could out-process and do other errands."

Clearly, the Sponsorship Program can benefit both the sponsors and the sponsored family. It takes some effort, but has its rewards.

11

Getting Out

Most departing military personnel leave after completing their first educational or enlistment obligation, which typically lasts three to five years. Others leave after a longer time, and some leave after they are eligible for retirement pay. This chapter discusses transition issues and benefits available to those who leave voluntarily, involuntarily, and retire. Additional benefits for those wounded on active duty are discussed in chapter 12.

Plan your new view.

DISCHARGE VS. SEPARATION

Let's clarify two words: *discharge* and *separation*. They aren't synonymous. "Discharge" means that all legal ties a person has to the military are cut. Discharged soldiers cannot be recalled to active duty. "Separation" is a general term which *includes* discharge but also includes release from active duty, transfer to the inactive reserves (IRR), and other changes in active or reserve status.

Once joining the military, getting discharged before the contractual obligation time is up is difficult. Those in the Delayed Enlistment Program (See chapter 1) may request to leave, and it is a long-standing DoD policy to permit it. But for everyone else, once the oath is taken, the contract signed, and training money invested, a compelling case to leave must be made.

The military can, however, discharge people for failing to meet or maintain standards. This is called an "involuntary administrative discharge." People can also be forced out for not meeting standards via what the Navy and Air Force call the "High Year of Tenure" (HYT) and what the Army calls the "Retention Control Point" (RCP). Both are known in all services as the "up or out" policy, meaning that if a servicemember does not make a certain rank within a certain amount of time, he is not allowed to reenlist. For example, if a solder does not reach the grade of E-4 by ten years, he won't be promoted, hence won't be allowed to remain in the military. This policy applies to officers, too. They must reach a certain pay grade based on their date of rank, meaning the day they entered the service.

CHARACTER OF SEPARATION PAPERS

A separation's character is described on the discharge/separation papers. Administrative discharges include honorable, general (under honorable conditions), under other-than-honorable conditions, or entry level separation. There are also bad conduct and dishonorable discharges, which are punitive, not administrative, and result from a court-martial.

An honorable discharge is granted when the standards of conduct and performance have been met. A general discharge is granted if the military service was good but there are some "warts" on record, such as several Article 15s (nonjudicial punishments); or bad performance evaluations. An other-than-honorable discharge is given for a pattern of bad behavior. An entry level separation is given if separation processing began within the first six months of active duty. It's considered neither honorable nor less-than-honorable because no military record was developed. Bad conduct and dishonorable discharges are punitive, not administrative. They are given by a court-martial (a military court) and are preceded by jail time.

Holders of honorable and general separations are entitled to veterans' benefits. An other-than-honorable may result in a loss of benefits. An entry level separation is not entitled to veterans' benefits, nor is a bad conduct or dishonorable discharge holder. The latter two do not receive payment for transportation home, accrued leave, or any veterans' benefits.

SERVICE COMMITMENT

Everyone who joins the military incurs an eight-year service commitment at minimum. It is a contractual obligation. Whether the active-duty contract was for two, four, or six years is irrelevant. The total military commitment is eight years. Whatever amount of that time not spent on active duty must be served in the active or inactive reserves. This makes servicemembers eligible for a mobilization call-up until their contractual time frame has elapsed.

Reservists who served at least one day in any U.S. altercation are eligible to join the American Legion. This organization serves U.S. veterans, their widows, and their survivors. It offers scholarship funds, tuition assistance, and life insurance.

PREFERENCE FOR THE RESERVES

Eligible veterans have preference over other equally qualified applicants for reserve slots, as long as they apply for a reserve or guard position within one year of the separation date. This is a good way to preserve one's investment in the military and earn extra money, benefits, and eventually retired pay.

AMERICAN COUNCIL OF EDUCATION (ACE) CREDITS

When leaving the service, any education credits earned can be claimed. The American Council on Education (ACE) is an organization composed of over 1,800 accredited, degree-granting colleges, universities, and higher education–related associations. Military experience can be converted into ACE credits. To do this, servicemembers need to request a transcript from their branch. Unofficial personal copies will be given him, and official ones sent at no charge to schools he applies to.

Each military branch has its own system for converting military education, job experience, training, and educational testing into a transcript that colleges and employers can understand.

Army. The AARTS system automatically captures academic credits from military training and standardized tests. It is available to enlisted soldiers only. Officers report their training and experience on form DD 295 (Application for Evaluation of Learning).

Navy and Marines. The SMART system automatically captures training, experience, and standardized test scores.

Air Force. The Community College of the Air Force (CCAF) automatically captures training, experience, and standardized test scores.

Coast Guard. The Coast Guard Institute (CGI) requires each servicemember to submit documentation of all training (except correspondence course records), along with an enrollment form, to receive a transcript.

Veterans. Veterans are generally eligible to use their former service branches' transcript program. However, if, for whatever reason, they are not eligible, they need to fill out form DD 295 and provide their DD-214 Discharge Document to receive credit for their experience.

ACE credits are generally used to fulfill free-elective requirements. However, each college determines the number of credits it will accept and how they will be applied toward a degree. Know that some schools don't grant any credit for military experience. Shopping around for military-friendly schools may be necessary. Official transcripts from previous colleges and service branches should be sent for evaluation to the college applied to before any classes are taken. Many students waste time and money taking unnecessary classes because they signed up before their military and prior college transcripts were completely evaluated.

PREFERENCE FOR CIVIL SERVICE JOBS

All veterans with at least 180 days of service (a reservist can have less if time served was during a war) have a five-point preference for federal jobs and ten points if they are disabled. (Seventy points total are typically needed to qualify for a federal job.) They're also eligible for a Veterans Readjustment Appointment, which is a special authority by which federal agencies may, if they wish, appoint an eligible veteran without nonveteran competition. They have postal service preference, can take the postal exam at times other than when it's officially offered, and, upon passing it, are immediately put on the hiring list. Former active-duty personnel who don't qualify for retired pay may have their active-duty time count the same as their federal civilian job time for calculation of leave per pay period and protection from cutbacks.

TROOPS TO TEACHERS (TTT)

This program helps eligible personnel transition to careers as public school teachers in targeted schools. A network of state TTT offices counsels on certification requirements, state certification, and employment. Stipends of up to $5,000 may be available to help pay for teacher certification costs, and bonuses of $10,000 to teach in schools that primarily serve students from low-income families. Those who accept a stipend or bonus must agree to teach for three years. Visit *www.proudtoserveagain.com* or call 800-231-6242 for details.

SGLI CONVERSION

There are two options for Serviceman's Group Life Insurance:

1. Conversion to Veteran's Group Life Insurance (VGLI), which is a term policy.
2. Conversion to a whole life policy with a specific commercial provider. Proof of good health is not required. This option doesn't allow for term, variable life, or universal life, and supplementary policy benefits such as Accidental Death and Dismemberment or Waiver of Premium for Disability are not considered part of the conversion policy. Download a brochure of participating providers at *www.insurance.va.gov/sglisite/forms/forms.htm*.

To be eligible for VGLI, applicants must be at least one of the following:

- an SGLI-insured servicemember who is leaving active duty (or active duty for training that lasted at least thirty-one days)
- an SGLI-insured Ready Reservist who is being separated or released from drilling assignment
- a member of the Individual Ready Reserve (IRR) or the Inactive National Guard
- a member of the Public Health Service (PHS) or Inactive Reserve Corps (IRC)
- a member who had part-time SGLI and who, while performing duty (or traveling directly to or from duty), suffered an injury or disability that makes him uninsurable at standard premium rates

Applicants have one year plus 120 days from their date of discharge to convert SGLI to VGLI. However, proof of good health will be needed if the application is done over 120 days.

TERMINAL LEAVE

This type of leave is granted after the last day of work until all accrued leave time is used up. Full pay and allowances are received.

UNEMPLOYMENT BENEFITS

These benefits vary by state; depending on where you live after separation, the servicemember may be able to apply for unemployment benefits. Contact your state unemployment insurance office for more information; visit *www.servicelocator.org/OWSLinks.asp* to find the closest one to you. You can file in person or online.

CONTINUED HEALTH CARE BENEFITS PROGRAM (CHCBP)

This is a premium-based health-care program run by Humana Military Health Care Services, Inc., that bridges military health-care benefits and a civilian health plan. It offers health coverage for eighteen to thirty-six months after Tricare eligibility ends, and its benefits, providers, and rules are comparable to Tricare Standard's. Eligible beneficiaries can purchase it within sixty days of becoming ineligible for Tricare or TAMP (discussed later in this chapter) coverage. Premiums cost $933 per quarter for one person and $1,996 per quarter for families.

Eligible beneficiaries are:

- Former active-duty servicemembers released from active duty (excluding those leaving under adverse conditions) and their eligible family members. They have eighteen months of coverage.
- Unremarried former spouses who were eligible for Tricare on the day before the date of the final decree of divorce, dissolution, or annulment. They typically have thirty-six months of coverage.
- Children who cease to meet the requirements to be eligible family members and were eligible for Tricare on the day before ceasing to meet those requirements. They have thirty-six months of coverage.
- Certain unmarried children by adoption or legal custody. They have thirty-six months of coverage.

For more information about CHCBP, visit *www.humana-military.com/chcbp/main.htm* or call 800-444-5445.

TRANSITION ASSISTANCE PROGRAM (TAP)

The DoD Transition Assistance Program is a joint effort between the Departments of Defense, Labor, Transportation, and Veterans Affairs. The program helps servicemembers who are within 180 days of separation or retirement transition to the civilian world. It is also open to spouses. The TAP has three-day workshops on job hunting, resume preparation and interviewing tips, career decision making, current labor market conditions, veterans' benefits, and evaluations for civilian employability. Help is given after you fill out DD Form 2568, which summarizes military education, training, and job experience in recognizable terms to civilian employers, and DD Form 295, which is the application for the Evaluation of Military Learning Experiences. Participants are told about the Defense Outplacement Referral System (DORS) and the Public and Community Service (PACS) registries, which are national networks that connect separating servicemembers and their spouses with public-, private-, and community-sector employers. Leave time is not charged for attending these workshops.

TAP services are provided on major military installations by the Transition Assistance Office, located in ACAP Centers on Army bases, the Family Support Service Center on Navy and Marine Corp bases, the Airmen and Family Readiness Flight Centers on Air Force bases; and through the Work-Life offices for the Coast Guard. Visit *www.militaryinstallations.dod.mil/ismart/MHF-MI* to find one closest to you.

A separation briefing is part of the transition program. It is mandatory for servicemembers and encouraged for spouses. Go to it! You have many steps to take and decisions to make, and some of the consequences are irrevocable. So it's in your best interest to attend. Many topics—such as the difference between DoD and VA compensation, what deductions might be made from the final paycheck, how to arrange a different method for any installment payments currently made via allotment, pros and cons of selling unused leave versus taking terminal leave—are covered in depth.

What your husband forgets, you might remember, and vice versa. If you are both fully informed, you can make the right decisions together.

Financial planning advice is given, too. This can never start too soon, as even a large nest egg can dissipate quickly with the expenses of job hunting, relocation, and possible extended unemployment.

Servicemembers traveling on permissive TDY orders to attend TAP workshops are authorized Space-A travel. They may be accompanied by their spouses between CONUS and OCONUS, and within and between OCONUS. However, family members are not authorized Space-A travel within CONUS to attend.

BENEFITS FOR INVOLUNTARILY SEPARATED
ACTIVE-DUTY FAMILIES

Those who are involuntarily separated receive benefits to help their transition, as long as the discharge or separation is not due to poor performance or bad conduct. They are not available to service families who are voluntarily leaving. However, those families may purchase extended transitional health-care coverage (CHCBP), discussed later in this chapter, for up to eighteen months. They may purchase it up to sixty days after the separation date, and coverage starts the day after separation.

If a family member is pregnant and Tricare eligibility ends during the pregnancy, Tricare does not cover any remaining maternity care unless the family qualifies for TAMP (discussed later in this chapter). She may, however, request space-available maternity care in a military treatment facility that provides obstetric care, and she may enroll in CHCBP.

ID Card

Service and family members are issued identification cards stamped with the dates when they may use transitional services and base facilities.

Involuntary Separation Pay

Also called severance pay, this is given to servicemembers with over six but less than twenty years of service, a good record, and an honorable discharge. Pay is 10 percent of their annual basic pay multiplied by the amount of years of service completed. It is fully taxable. Most who receive it do so due to a military draw-down or the up-or-out system. Servicemembers who are eligible for retirement pay or who are in their initial periods of active duty are ineligible. Those who ask to be separated from active duty, decline a new assignment, or are discharged for unsatisfactory performance are also ineligible. However, officers who have been passed over and request early separation prior to their mandatory separation date will not negate their entitlement to separation pay as long as they will have six years active duty upon separation.

Drilling guardsmen and reservists who are not on full-time active duty generally do not receive separation pay. They may be eligible if involuntarily separated from the service due to their unit's deactivation, and if they performed federal duty, not state. At minimum, they must have had at least six years on active duty, an honorable discharge, and be separated from the unit due to a reduction in force or if they are passed over for promotion. In some cases, permanent medical disability can qualify a reservist for benefits.

The Transitional Assistance Management Program (TAMP)

This program provides 180 days of transitional health-care benefits to service families beginning on the separation date. During TAMP, sponsors and family members may enroll in Tricare Prime, Tricare Prime Overseas, or use Tricare Standard and Extra or Tricare Standard Overseas.

To qualify, the sponsor must be one of the following:
- involuntarily separating from active duty under honorable conditions
- a reservist separating from more than thirty consecutive days in support of a contingency operation
- separating from active duty following involuntary retention ("stop-loss") in support of a contingency operation
- separating from active duty following a voluntary agreement to stay on active duty for less than one year to support a contingency operation

If a different coverage plan hasn't been found after the 180 days are up, the family may enroll in CHCBP within 60 days of TAMP eligibility ending.

NAF Employment Preference

Servicemembers and their family members are entitled to a one-time hiring preference for NAF positions UA-8/NF-3 and below, for which they are fully qualified. The positions must be competitively recruited ones.

Commissary, Exchange, and MWR Privileges

Servicemembers and their eligible family members have unlimited commissary and exchange use, as well as MWR facilities, for two years after their date of separation.

Continued Use of Military Family Housing

Service families may remain in military housing for up to 180 days after the separation date, space permitting, and with the base commander's permission. (Where there is a long wait for active-duty families to move into housing, this benefit is usually denied.) Rent equal to the servicemember's VHA and BAQ rates will be charged, although the base commander may waive in hardship cases.

Excess Leave or Permissive TDY

Excess leave (maximum thirty days) or permissive TDY (maximum thirty days if OCONUS, twenty days if CONUS) for job and house hunting may be authorized by the unit commander, solely at his discretion. Excess leave is anything beyond the thirty days that servicemembers get each year and must be repaid, either as time worked or as cash. If a servicemember owes the government for excess leave on his last day of active duty, it'll be deducted from his final paycheck. Only one of the two kinds of time off may be selected.

Transportation Entitlement

Eligible members are authorized travel allowances for up to one year after separation to a home of record or selection within CONUS. Only residents whose official home of record is Hawaii or Alaska can ship their property to those states. This benefit is good for up to one year after leaving active duty. The same weight limits apply as for any other move, and travel benefits are paid. Know that if the home of selection is farther from the servicemember's current location than his home of record is, he will have to pay the difference. Nontemporary storage for household goods, and their subsequent shipment to the home of selection, will be paid for up to one year after the date of separation. Those on separation or retirement orders who need additional time may request an extension; however, they will have to pay for storage costs.

> Make sure that the home of record in your file is correct. Some servicemembers have learned only upon separation or retirement that their home of record is different from where they assumed it to be.

DoDDs

Children enrolled or authorized to enroll in an overseas DoDD school, or who have completed their junior year on the servicemember's separation date, may stay at that school, at no charge to them. Their education must be completed within twelve months from the separation date.

Enrollment/Reenrollment in the Montgomery G.I. Bill (MGIB)

Servicemembers may enroll or reenroll in the MGIB, even if they initially turned it down.

RETIREMENT BENEFITS

One of the major benefits of military service is its generous retirement system. Most retirees are thirty-seven to forty-two years old, making them young enough to start a new career. This section discusses the current systems. As a side note, the government spends about $40 billion yearly on military retired pay. Due to this, DoD is studying retirement options that are similar to civilian retirement plans.

Retired ID Cards

Retired personnel retain their ID cards; the status is just switched to "retired." They have full access to all base facilities; commissary, exchange (except when overseas, where access is governed by SOFA agreements; see chapter 8), MWR, Space-A travel, and Tricare medical and dental coverage until they are eligible for Medicare. They have one year from the effective date to ship their goods to their home of selection. They can also utilize nontemporary storage for one year at government expense. Retirees may have to pay very high taxes when shipping their POV to their home of record overseas (e.g., Puerto Rico or the Philippines).

Active-Duty Retired/Retainer Pay

Active-duty retired pay is an immediate, lifetime, inflation-protected annuity to those who complete at least twenty years of active duty. It's a portion of the monthly base pay (allowances are not calculated). It differs from civilian pensions in two ways:

1. There is no "vesting"; that is, no money is set aside to keep if a service-member's employment is terminated. He either qualifies for retirement by serving twenty years or he doesn't. If he is discharged one day short of twenty years, he will qualify for some early retirement programs, but not for retired pay.
2. A retired military member can be recalled to active duty. Nondisability retirees under age sixty who have been retired less than five years are the ones most likely to be recalled if there is a need.

In the Army and Air Force, members with over twenty years of service are classified as retired, and receive retired pay. In the Navy and Marine Corps, an enlisted member with over thirty years, or a warrant or commissioned officer, is classified as retired. Enlisted Navy and Marine Corps personnel with less than thirty years are transferred to the Fleet Reserve or Fleet Marine Corps Reserve, and their pay is called "retainer pay." When a Navy or Marine Corps member completes thirty years, including time receiving retainer pay, his reserve status is changed to retired status, and his pay is called retired pay. However, despite being named differently, retired and retainer pay are treated the same. Retired and retainer pay is taxable, but not subject to FICA (Social Security) deductions, nor is it reduced when the recipient becomes entitled to Social Security payments.

There are three nondisability retirement systems. The date that the service-member *first* enlisted or joined active duty or the reserves determines which system applies to him. This date, known as DIEMS (Date of Initial Entry to Military Service) is fixed; leaving and then rejoining the military does not change it. Exceptions are academy and ROTC cadets and midshipmen and those enlisting under the delayed-entry program (DEP). These people are eligible for the retirement system that was in effect when they entered the reserves, academy, or DEP.

The three retirement systems are:

Final Pay. This applies to those who entered the service on or before September 8, 1980. Each year of service is worth 2.5 percent toward the retirement multiplier. Hence, 2.5% × 20 years = 50%, and 2.5% × 30 years = 75%. The longer an individual stays on active duty, the higher the multiplier and the higher the retirement pay. Annual cost-of-living adjustments are made.

High-3 Year Average. This system applies to members who entered on or between September 8, 1980, and August 1, 1986. It also applies to individuals who entered on or after August 1, 1986, who do not elect the CSB REDUX retirement system at their fifteenth year of service.

Each year of service is worth 2.5 percent toward the retirement multiplier. Hence, 2.5% × 20 years = 50%, and 2.5% × 30 years = 75%. The longer a servicemember stays on active duty, the higher the multiplier and the higher the retirement pay. This multiplier is applied against the average basic pay for the highest thirty-six months of the servicemember's career. This usually equals the average basic pay for the final three years of service. Know that commissioned officers and enlisted personnel with prior commissioned service must have at least ten years of commissioned service to retire at their commissioned rank. If they have less than ten years of commissioned service and voluntarily retire, only the highest thirty-six months of active duty enlisted base pay will count for retirement computation, and they will retire at their enlisted rank.

CSB/REDUX. This is the Military Reform Act of 1986. It applies to all servicemembers who joined on or after August 1, 1986. This group may choose between High-3 and REDUX. It must be chosen at a servicemember's fifteenth year. If it is chosen, a taxable Career Service Bonus (CSB) of $30,000 is given at that time. The servicemember must agree to finish out twenty years; if he leaves before then, a prorated part of the bonus must be given back.

The REDUX multiplier calculation and annual cost of living adjustments differ from the other systems. Each of the first twenty years of service is worth 2.0 percent toward the retirement multiplier. But each year after the twentieth is worth 3.5 percent. A thirty-year career is computed by 2.0 percent times the first twenty years, plus 3.5 percent for the next ten years beyond twenty. There is a catch-up increase at age sixty-two that brings it to the same amount paid under the High-3 system.

The combination of the bonus and retirement may make this advantageous for some people, as they will get retirement income plus discretionary cash. The bonus may be taken in a lump sum or in payments to reduce the tax bite. Prudent service families will invest this money, buy a house or a business, or pay off debt. However, the other options are ultimately higher paying.

This chart summarizes the differences the three retirement systems.

Retirement System	Basis	Multiplier	COLA	Readjustment	Bonus
Final Pay	Final basic pay	2.5% per year	CPI*	None	None
High-3	Average of highest 36 months of basic pay	2.5% per year	CPI	None	None
CSB/ REDUX	Average of highest 36 months of basic pay	2.0% per year for the first 20 years; 3.5% for each year beyond 20	CPI −1%	At age 62, (1) changes multiplier to 2.5% per year; (2) adjusts COLA to full CPI for past retired years	$30,000 at 15th year of service with commitment to complete 20-year career

*CPI: Consumer Price Index

Army and Air Force enlisted servicemembers who have been cited for extraordinary heroism receive an additional 10 percent of retired pay.

Unlike active-duty pay, retired/retainer pay cannot be garnished for commercial debts (e.g., credit cards and car loans). Military retirement pay can, however, be garnished for alimony, child support, and debts owed to the government, such as IRS tax levies, student loans, and STAR card debt. State courts may treat military retired pay as joint property between the member and the spouse during a divorce.

Visit *www.defenselink.mil/militarypay/retirement* for more information on the military retirement system.

Retired Pay for Selected Reservists
National Guard and reservists receive retired pay, also; it is a major incentive for most to stay in. To receive it, they must meet these minimum requirements:
- be at least sixty years old
- have performed the last six years of creditable service while a member of the Active Reserve
- not be entitled to retired or retainer pay
- have at least twenty creditable years of service

A creditable year is one in which at least fifty retirement points were earned through Reserve activities: unit training assemblies, attending service school, accredited correspondence courses, funeral duty, attending professional conventions that enhance military skills, and so forth. There are also "gratuitous" points for membership in the reserve component and participation in civil defense activities. If fifty points are not accumulated in a year, that year is not creditable (but the points for that year are still figured in the calculation of retired pay). An excess of points from one year cannot be carried over to make up for a deficiency in another year.

A maximum of 365 points may be accumulated in one year. However, when calculating retired pay, no more than 60 (for reserve years ending before September 23, 1996) or 75 (for reserve years ending after September 23, 1996) points per year are used.

If reservists are combining active and reserve service to equal twenty years, at least six of those years must be in the reserves. For example, someone with fifteen years of active duty who transferred to the reserves would need a combined total of twenty-one years to qualify for retirement. Both active and reserve personnel must have twenty years of service before reaching age sixty to be retirement-eligible. After age sixty, a person must leave, retirement-eligible or not. That is also the age at which retirement pay starts. You need to apply for it, as it's not mailed automatically.

To calculate the retired reservist's paycheck, first calculate the number of "equivalent years of service." That formula is:

Total number of Creditable Retirement Points ÷ 360 = retired paycheck.

Then, depending on the date a reservist initially entered military service, his monthly retired pay is calculated under the "Final Basic Pay" or "High-3" formula.

Final Basic Pay (for those with an entry date before September 8, 1980). Multiply the years of equivalent service by 2.5 percent. Multiply the result by the basic pay in effect on the date your retired pay starts. That is the monthly retired pay.

High-3 (for those with an entry date on or after September 8, 1980). Multiply the years of equivalent service by 2.5 percent. Multiply that result by the average of the highest thirty-six months of basic pay. The highest thirty-six months for a member who transfers to the Retired Reserve until age sixty are the thirty-six months before they turn sixty.

The Twenty-Year Letter
When a reservist has served enough years to collect retired pay, a letter titled, "Notification of Eligibility for Retired Pay at Age 60," known as the twenty-year letter, is mailed. At this point the reservist may opt for discharge or retired reserve status. Discharged soldiers cannot be recalled to active duty; retired reserve soldiers are subject

to an involuntary recall to active duty in the event of a full mobilization. Service-members who don't specifically request assignment to the Retired Reserve are discharged. Know that retired pay is calculated based on which option is chosen! Reservists who request a discharge from the Retired Reserve before sixty can only use the basic pay for the thirty-six months prior to their discharge; Reservists who opt for Retired Reserve status will have their basic pay for the thirty-six months prior to age sixty calculated. The latter will result in a much larger retired paycheck.

Between the time the twenty-year letter arrives and age sixty, a reservist is a "Gray Area" retiree. Gray Area retired guard and reserve members and their authorized family members retain their ID cards, which entitle them to the same base facilities benefits as retired active duty.

Sanctuary

Sanctuary is the period in a servicemember's career where enough creditable service to be within two years of retirement eligibility has been earned, hence he may not be easily involuntarily separated until that point is reached. It applies to active duty, reservists, officers, and enlisted personnel. To enter sanctuary for an active-duty retirement, eighteen years of active duty is required; reserve years do not count for sanctuary purposes. If his mandatory separation date is approaching or he has been twice passed over for promotion, the required date to leave will simply be pushed back.

Reservists also have sanctuary after eighteen years. If a reservist cannot find or maintain a spot in a reserve unit, he may be assigned to a Nonaffiliated Reserve Section and continue to earn points via education.

Sanctuary does not guarantee that a servicemember will be able to continue past retirement eligibility; for example, it can't be used as a basis for staying in until an "up or out" point is hit. Nor does it guarantee promotions, remove negative notes in the files, or exempt a servicemember from evaluations or fitness reports.

Survivor Benefit Program

Retired pay stops with the death of the servicemember. The Survivor Benefit Plan is an insurance plan designed to provide income for the wife and/or kids. Enrollment is automatic, and spousal written consent is required for it to be reduced or declined.

Upon death of the wife, coverage passes to the children. With no spouse and children, coverage can be chosen for a former spouse, dependent grandchildren, or an "insurable interest" (e.g., business partner or parent). Only one opportunity to enroll is given, and that is during retirement transition.

A monthly premium based on the benefit level is charged. The base amount can be any amount from full coverage to as little as $300 a month. Full coverage is a premium of 6.5 percent of full retired pay, in return for 55 percent of the retired pay. If lesser coverage is selected, then you will receive 55 percent of the selected base amount. Premiums stop when the survivor reaches age seventy and 360 payments into the program have been made. Premiums and annuity payments have annual cost-of-living adjustments.

Reservists can enroll once they receive the twenty-year letter. The plan works similarly for them, but they can choose from three options:

- No coverage, but with the option to enroll upon marrying or reaching age sixty
- Coverage elected, but survivor benefits don't start until the retiree would have been age sixty even if he were to die sooner
- Coverage elected, with survivor benefits beginning immediately upon the retiree's death

Retiree Medical Care

Retirees may keep their Tricare coverage, but deductibles, premiums, and other costs become higher. They are not eligible for active-duty-specific programs and benefits such as Tricare ECHO and hearing aids. Remember that Tricare is a second payer behind any civilian program the retiree might have, such as through a civilian employer.

Tricare for Life (TFL) is a program available to all Medicare-eligible Tricare beneficiaries, regardless of age, if they have Medicare Parts A and B (see glossary). If they have Part B, they are enrolled in TFL automatically. Medicare remains their primary insurance, but Tricare will be a secondary payer, minimizing out-of-pocket expenses. Tricare for Life benefits include covering Medicare's coinsurance and deductible.

Even though Medicare doesn't provide coverage outside the continental United States, retirees who live in foreign countries can use TFL because it becomes their primary source of health benefits. But they still must be enrolled in Medicare Part B. TFL provides the same level of coverage that retirees under sixty-five get, and the cost shares and deductibles are the same as for under-sixty-five retirees. Tricare Plus may be available for care at some military treatment facilities.

Retiree Dental Program

Tricare offers a separate dental program for military retirees and their family members. Premiums are based on where the retiree lives and the number of family members covered. Some costs are covered completely; others have a cost-share. Visit *www.ddpdelta.org* for details.

VA MEDICAL CARE

This treatment option is not open to all veterans. To receive medical care from the VA, one must be a veteran (over 180 days of military service); an honorable discharge; and either have a service-connected illness, injury, or disability, or fall into a certain range of poverty.

DIVORCE

If you are leaving the military due to divorce, here are some things to know.

Under the 1982 Uniformed Services Former Spouse Protection Act (USFSPA), retired pay is considered an asset, thus state courts may treat it as they want. There are no requirements for how long the marriage must have lasted for the ex-wife to receive it, nor are there formulas for how it should be divided. Base privileges are granted based on length of the marriage. For instance, one formula, called the 20/20/15 rule, allows commissary, exchange, and medical privileges if the marriage lasted for at least twenty years to a person who had twenty years of creditable service toward retirement, and there was fifteen years of overlap between the marriage length and years of service. If the divorcée remarries, she loses those privileges but some may be reinstated if that marriage ends. Unremarried former spouses may be eligible for medical care for one year from date of divorce, followed by the eligibility for CHCBP for eighteen to thirty-six months.

If you and your spouse are living apart but not legally separated, he is required to provide monetary support to you and any dependent children. If there are no court-ordered support documents, the military has guidelines that call for a portion of base pay and basic housing allowance. You might contact his command, the base legal office, or a private attorney to set up an allotment. However, these guidelines are not legally binding, so unless there is court-ordered support, the military does not have the ability to force him to provide it. For emergency assistance, you may contact the Red Cross or one of the relief services on base (see chapter 5).

If your spouse is deployed and you wish to initiate or continue with a divorce, the Soldiers and Sailors Civil Relief Act can delay any court proceedings. It can also make obtaining support more difficult. Base attorneys may advise you, but you will need to personally hire a civilian lawyer to initiate proceedings.

If you divorce while on an overseas tour, you may lose your ability to stay there or keep your job, as you no longer are sponsored.

PREPARING EMOTIONALLY

No matter the length of time, being a service family makes one feel part of a large, worldwide community. This often makes leaving it harder than leaving most jobs. Here are some comments from people who made the transition.

> "When Mike got passed over and had to leave, I never ragged about his not doing his job well enough. Nor did I allow myself to feel guilty over my contribution to the pass-over. It's unproductive. Accepting what's given, refusing to focus on what we couldn't change, and taking active control of the future were critical to our successful next chapter. You can't change the past, but you can influence the future."

> "When job hunting, we met regularly with two other families who were in the same situation. We gave each other job leads and met for potlucks every Saturday night to encourage each other and keep our spirits up. Knowing that there were others in this situation made us feel less alone."

"We knew that we would have to leave the military in fifteen months. We started making plans early. When we PCSed to another base, we deliberately didn't move into quarters, even though they were available; we wanted to adjust to living as civilians. Since we knew we'd buy a house wherever we ended up, we moved into a rental house. This enabled us to experience living in a house, learn about maintenance issues, qualities we liked and didn't like in a neighborhood, and so on, without having the accompanying financial responsibilities."

"Before the separation, my family became less involved with military groups and facilities and more with civilian ones. We started going to the local church instead of the post chapel and joined the YMCA for its gym. I stopped volunteering on post and started volunteering for an animal rights group."

"We researched different parts of the country for places to live. We considered not only the job market but also climate, cost of living, nearby recreational facilities, and educational opportunities. It was fun knowing that we were going where we wanted to go, not where we were ordered."

"I investigated the job market when we learned that Tim was leaving the Air Force. I hadn't worked in three years, and learning that there were employment options for myself made my worries about a drop in his income more manageable."

"I visited civilian supermarkets to ease 'sticker shock' and was pleased to learn that warehouse clubs and stores where you bag your own groceries had favorable prices."

"Leaving the Army turned out to be positive. It forced our family to sit down, clarify our goals, and decide what we wanted out of life. In the military we were always told what to do, which made us complacent. I suggest that you evaluate your interests, values, and abilities. It's critical in creating a life you'll be happy with."

"Take this opportunity to make a fresh start with your life, finances, career, even your appearance. Get vocational counseling, take tests to see what career fields match your interest. Get financial counseling. Acknowledge that the way you've done things up until now may not be the way you want to continue to do them."

"Start planning a year before moving, so you can evaluate things at your leisure, not in a rush because your lease is up or you have to leave quarters. Do you want to change your lifestyle from suburban to city? Would you like a bigger house, or maybe a condo? Do you want to be near family? How important is climate and lifestyle activities like beaches or golf? What are real estate costs where you want to live? Use this transition time to inventory your personal abilities, interests, needs, and values."

"Discuss your options with people whose judgment you trust. They may add insight about things you hadn't thought of."

"Use vacation time to take a trip to a town you're considering. Visit friends who live in places that appeal to you."

FURTHER READING

Books

Enelow, Wendy, and Louise Kursmark. *Expert Resumes for Military to Civilian Transitions*. St. Paul, MN: Jist Publishing, 2005.

Budahn, P. J. *Veteran's Guide to Benefits*, 4th edition. Mechanicsburg, PA: Stackpole Books, 2005.

Armstrong, Elizabeth. *America's 100 Best Places to Retire: The Only Guide You Need to Today's Top Retirement Towns*, 4th edition. Houston, TX: Vacation Publications, 2007.

Internet Resources

www.myhealth.va.gov. Gateway to veteran health benefits and services.

www.legion.org/homepage.php.

www.dfas.mil/money/retired. Retired and annuitant pay information, including advice on preparing for retirement.

www.transitionassistanceprogram.com/register.tpp. The official Transition Assistance Program website. It supplements the services offered by the Transition Assistance Offices and other groups.

www.dmdc.osd.mil/ot. Operation Transition website.

www.troa.org. The Retired Officers Association. Lobbies on behalf of, and provides services to, retired officers and warrant officers.

www.myhealth.va.gov. Website designed for veterans and their families. Users can store medical records, research the library of health and wellness information, and partner with health-care providers.

www.va.gov/vso. Find the Directory of Veterans Service Organizations here, which lists military service organizations, such as the Air Force Benefit Association, the Warrant Officer Association, and the Navy League. Such organizations operate online job boards for their members.

www.dol.gov/vets. Veterans Employment and Training Service.

tricare.osd.mil/chcbp/default.cfm. Information on the CHCBP program.

online.onetcenter.org/crosswalk. This site generates job titles and descriptions that are civilian equivalents of military jobs.

12

Survivors and
Wounded Warriors

This chapter discusses benefits and resources for the surviving spouses and children of active-duty servicemembers and for wounded warriors.

BENEFITS FOR SURVIVING SPOUSES AND CHILDREN

Spouses and children of servicemembers who die on active duty are eligible for a broad range of benefits and services from the Department of Defense (DoD), the Department of Veterans Affairs (VA), the Social Security Administration (SSA), and the Department of Labor (DoL).

Casualty Assistance

If an active-duty servicemember or a reservist on active duty dies, the family is assigned a person called the Casualty Assistance Officer (Army), Casualty Assistance Representative (Air Force), or Casualty Assistance Calls Officer (Navy, Marines, and Coast Guard). He notifies the family (or whoever is listed on the servicemember's emergency contact sheet), provides what information is available about the circumstances of the death, and helps with funeral and memorial arrangements and filing benefit claims. He is available as long as needed.

Death Gratuity

The DoD pays a one-time death gratuity of $100,000 (nontaxable). It is paid whether the death was combat related or not, and it applies to:
- servicemembers who died while on active duty
- servicemembers who died while performing authorized travel to or from active duty
- reservists who die while on inactive duty training
- in certain cases, to those who die within 120 days after discharge or release from active or inactive duty, if the death results from an injury or disease incurred or aggravated during duty or during travel to or from the duty

The entire amount goes to the primary next of kin unless the servicemember designated otherwise. Up to $50,000 can be designated in advance to someone else, even if the servicemember is married. For instance, it can go to someone who would care for minor children. Or a single servicemember could leave it to his fiancée instead of a parent or sibling. The other half is required by law to go to the spouse first, then children in equal shares (legitimate, adopted, stepchildren who were part of the household at the time of death, and extramarital, with certain conditions of proof), and then to parents or siblings.

Pay
All outstanding pay and allowances, including accrued leave, up to the maximum allowed by law are paid.

Serviceman's Group Life Insurance
SGLI (discussed in chapter 5) is paid. The payment can be made as a lump sum or in thirty-six installments, as previously designated by the servicemember.

Housing
Families currently in quarters may continue to remain there for up to one year, with permission of the base commander, or receive the appropriate housing allowance (BAH or OHA). If families are in a rental leased in the servicemember's name, a landlord cannot evict (or change locks or cut off utilities) without going through proper legal channels. Family members may be able to suspend legal proceedings under the Serviceman's Civil Relief Act. (Know that many of its protections do terminate upon the servicemember's death.)

ID Cards
Survivors retain their ID cards; however, the card is changed to "retired" status. They retain commissary, exchange, and MWR benefits, unless they are overseas, where such benefits are contingent on SOFA agreements (see chapter 8). Upon remarriage, survivors lose their ID card and accompanying base benefits.

Tricare
Two terms to know are "transitional survivor" and "survivor." These describe beneficiary status, which determines the payment rate and benefit level for medical and dental claims processing. Transitional survivor status means that active-duty family member payment rates are charged. Survivor status means that retiree payment rates are charged. Minor children and unmarried dependent children remain in transitional survivor status and are Tricare eligible for one of the following periods of time, whichever is longer:

- three years after the sponsor's death
- until age twenty-one
- until age twenty-three if full-time students or mentally/physically incapable of self-support (incapacitated) and if their sponsor provided more than 50 percent of their financial support at the time of death

They are eligible for Tricare Prime, Prime Remote for Active Duty Family Members, Overseas Prime, Global Remote, the Extended Care Health Option (ECHO), and hearing aids.

Spouses have transitional survivor status for three years after the active-duty sponsor's date of death. Afterwards, DEERS will automatically change their status to retiree, with its payment and benefit rate. Retired family members are not eligible for Tricare Prime Remote for active-duty family members, Overseas Prime, ECHO, and hearing aids. They remain eligible for Tricare Prime, Extra, and Standard at the retiree family member payment rate.

After the transitional survivor period ends, surviving spouses and incapacitated dependent children who become entitled to Medicare Part A must purchase Medicare Part B to remain Tricare eligible. To avoid the Medicare surcharge for late enrollment, surviving active-duty family members must purchase Medicare part B coverage when they first become eligible.

If a reservist is covered by Tricare on the day of his death, surviving family members may buy or continue coverage for an additional six months from the date of death. If member-and-family coverage is in effect at the time of death, DEERS will automatically convert coverage to survivor coverage. If member-only coverage is in effect at the time of death, the coverage will terminate, and survivors may purchase survivor coverage within sixty days. Survivors are responsible for paying monthly premiums. Visit *www.tricare.osd.mil/survivors/default.cfm* for details.

Widows and widowers remain eligible until they remarry, whether that remarriage ends in death or divorce. Children remain eligible until age twenty-one unless they meet the exceptions noted.

Social Security

Social Security is best known as a retirement program. However, it's also an income source for families with children. The Social Security Administration (SSA) provides survivor's benefits to:

- widows or widowers—full benefits at full retirement age (currently age sixty-five), or reduced benefits as early as age sixty
- disabled widows or widowers—as early as age fifty
- widows or widowers at any age if they take care of the deceased's child who is under age sixteen or disabled, and receiving Social Security benefits
- unmarried children under eighteen, or up to age nineteen if they are attending high school full-time (Under certain circumstances, benefits can be paid

to stepchildren, grandchildren, or adopted children; children at any age who were disabled before age twenty-two and remain disabled are eligible).

- dependent parents age sixty-two or older

Among young families, the most common recipients are unmarried children under age eighteen (or under nineteen and still in high school) and a widowed spouse caring for those children. Children of a former marriage and children born out of marriage are eligible, as is an ex-spouse caring for an eligible child. Survivor benefits are typically not paid to young widows without children.

You can receive Social Security survivor benefits and also work. However, depending on your age, your benefits could be reduced if you earn more than certain amounts. If you are divorced and your former spouse dies, you can even receive benefits as a widow if the marriage lasted ten years or longer and you are age sixty or older (or age fifty if you are disabled).

You typically cannot receive survivor benefits if you remarry before age sixty unless that marriage ends (be it by death, divorce, or annulment). If you remarry after age sixty (fifty if disabled), you can still collect benefits on your former spouse's record. When you reach age sixty-two, you may get retirement benefits on the record of your new spouse if they are higher. Your remarriage has no effect on any benefits paid to your children.

Benefit amounts are based on the deceased's average earnings. Higher earnings result in higher benefits. The following chart shows some benefit amounts.

APPROXIMATE ANNUAL
SOCIAL SECURITY SURVIVOR BENEFITS BY EARNINGS LEVEL
AND NUMBER OF ELIGIBLE FAMILY MEMBERS*

Annual earnings	One child survivor	Two eligible survivors	Three or more survivors
$18,000	$7,740	$15,490	$15,820
$24,000	$9,180	$18,370	$21,040
$30,000	$10,670	$21,330	$26,410
$45,000	$14,220	$28,450	$33,190
$60,000	$16,220	$32,450	$37,860
$90,000	$19,600	$39,200	$45,710

*Current amounts should be verified by issuing office.

At *www.ssa.gov/planners/calculators.htm*, you'll find calculators to help you figure your exact benefits. Or call 800-772-1213 (800-325-0778 for TTY) for more information.

VA Benefits

The VA also pays survivor benefits; unlike Social Security, it pays them to widowed spouses with or without children. Families of active-duty and of federally activated National Guard and reserve personnel are also eligible. These payments are called Dependency and Indemnity Compensation (DIC). A set amount is given for each widowed spouse, regardless of the deceased's pay grade, with incremental pay added for each child. Know that the Survivor Benefits Plan annuity (discussed in chapter 11) is reduced by any DIC amount received.

The following chart shows DIC amounts.

APPROXIMATE MONTHLY DEPENDENCY INDEMNITY COMPENSATION (DIC) PAYMENTS FOR FAMILIES OF SERVICEMEMBERS WHO DIED OF SERVICE-RELATED CAUSES*

Surviving Spouse and Children	
Type of Family Member	Payment
Spouse only	$1,033
Each child under age 18	257
Each student child age 18–23	218
Each disabled adult child	438

Eligible Children Only	
Number of Children	Total Payment (this is divided between children)
One	$438
Two	629
Three	819
Four	976
Five	1,133
Six	1,290

*Current amounts should be verified by issuing office.

The VA adds another $250 transitional assistance to the surviving spouse's monthly DIC if she has children under eighteen. It is paid for two years from the date that the DIC entitlement starts and stops when there is no child under age eighteen or there is no child on the surviving spouse's DIC for any reason. There is also a parents' DIC, based on income, which is a monthly benefit amount for the deceased's parents.

Families eligible for benefits from both SS and the VA receive all benefits in full. Both SS and VA benefits have annual cost of living increases.

Moving

One-time transportation of you, your children, and your household goods to anywhere in the continental United States is provided. Overseas survivors of servicemembers who die on active duty are entitled to two government-paid moves. One is an interim move, to allow them time to decide where they wish to settle permanently. On an interim move, the government will ship household goods but will not unpack them. The moving must take place within one year from the servicemember's death; an extension may be granted if applied for within that year. Temporary property storage is limited to ninety days from the date of death; nontemporary storage is limited to one year from that date.

Burial Benefits

Servicemembers may be buried with honors in any of the U.S.'s 125 national cemeteries, assuming there is space. The gravesite, opening and closing of the grave, perpetual care, a government headstone or marker, a burial flag, and a Presidential Memorial Certificate are provided at no cost to the family. Upon request, the VA will furnish a medallion that signifies the deceased's veteran status for attachment to an existing headstone or marker that was furnished at private expense. Cremated remains are buried or inurned in national cemeteries in the same manner and with

Honor guard at a military funeral.

the same honors as casketed remains. Know that there is no charge for the headstone or marker itself, but arrangements for its placement in a private cemetery and all setting fees are at private expense. Some veterans may be eligible for burial allowances for a nonmilitary burial. If a reservist dies while on inactive duty, his unit may furnish a ceremonial escort at his funeral.

Burial benefits for spouses and dependents include burial with the veteran, perpetual care, and an inscription included on the veteran's headstone, at no cost to the family. Eligible spouses and dependents may be buried even if they predecease the veteran. There are no burial benefits for spouses and dependents in private cemeteries.

The body or remains of servicemembers killed in a war theater are flown to Dover Air Base in Delaware, and then transported to the final resting place, at government expense. The government will also provide transportation to the burial site for members of the servicemember's immediate family. If family members prefer to make their own arrangements, they may be reimbursed up to the government rate. Certain family members may receive travel and per diem expenses to attend the funeral.

For more information on VA benefits, visit *www.va.gov*.

Job and Education Benefits

The Survivors' and Dependents' Educational Assistance Program (DEA) is a VA program for students who have never served in the military. It evolved from the 1956 War Orphans' Educational Assistance Act of 1956. DEA provides educational assistance to spouses and children of living veterans when the veterans meet one of these conditions:

- are permanently and totally disabled because of a service-connected disability
- have been listed for more than ninety days as missing in action
- were captured in line of duty
- are detained or interned in line of duty by a hostile force or foreign government

DEA provides educational assistance to surviving spouses and children of veterans when the veterans meet any of these conditions:

- died while on active duty
- died as the result of a disability arising from active duty
- died from any cause while rated permanently and totally disabled from service-connected disability

The program offers up to forty-five months of education benefits, currently $404/month, which may be used for degree and certificate programs, apprenticeship, and on-the-job training. Remedial, deficiency, and refresher courses may be approved under certain circumstances. Professional, educational, and vocational counseling is also provided upon request.

Spousal benefits end ten years from the date of eligibility or from the date of death of the veteran. Spouses of servicemembers who died on active duty have twenty years from the date of death. Remarriage ends the benefits.

Children must be between the ages of eighteen and twenty-six to receive school or job training benefits (in certain instances, they may be younger or older). They may be married and still receive these benefits.

Work-Study Employment
This type of employment is available to eligible survivors while they are studying or training under the DEA program.

Montgomery GI Bill
If your husband was contributing regularly to the Montgomery GI Bill and died before using it, built-up funds are returned to the designated life insurance beneficiary or surviving spouse.

> A widow may sign her husband's' retirement benefits over to her children to avoid the steep "military widow's tax."

Home Loan Guaranty
The surviving spouse of a veteran who died in service or as the result of a service-connected disability may be eligible for a guaranteed loan from a private lender. The loan may be used to buy, build, or improve a home (including a manufactured home) or lot or to refinance the existing mortgages on the surviving spouse's. This benefit has no time limit.

State Benefits
Many states have passed laws providing certain rights, benefits, and privileges to the surviving spouse and children of deceased servicemembers. They may include free college tuition, property tax savings, employment opportunities, and low-interest home loans to survivors. Contact local government officials, the nearest VA office, and local veterans' organizations such as the American Legion, Veterans of Foreign Wars, and Disabled American Veterans for details.

OBTAINING VETERANS' RECORDS
Copies of evaluations, medical records, and other official documents are stored at the National Personnel Records Center, 9700 Page Blvd., St. Louis, MO 63132. It is a central repository of military and civilian personnel records, and one of the National Archives and Records Administration's largest operations. The NPRC provides services to government agencies, military veterans, former federal civil service employees, family members, next-of-kin, and authorized third-party requestors (e.g., doctors, lawyers, genealogy researchers, and historians).

Copies of most military and medical records on file are made upon request. Veterans and the next-of-kin of deceased veterans have the same rights to full access to the record. "Next-of-kin" refers to the unremarried widow or widower, son or daughter, father or mother, or brother or sister of the deceased veteran. Standard Form 180 must be filled out, with an original cursive signature. All requests must be done in writing; telephone and Internet requests are not accepted. Download the request form at *www.archives.gov/research/order/standard-form-180.pdf*.

DISABILITY BENEFITS FOR WOUNDED WARRIORS

Access to medical care, restorative services, rehabilitation services, tuition, other educational assistance and training, and disability payments are available to help injured veterans pursue a new line of work. The main programs are discussed here.

Disabled Transition Assistance Program (DTAP)

DTAP is the portion of the Transition Assistance Program (see chapter 11) that assists servicemembers released due to disability issues. It assists and intervenes on behalf of those who may be eligible for the VA's Vocational Rehabilitation and Employment Program (VREP; a service that provides vocational rehabilitation services to veterans with military-related disabilities), and helps them file an application for vocational rehabilitation benefits. You will learn about VREP, be given educational and vocational counseling, and discuss barriers to successful employment and other potential difficulties.

VA representatives have individual sessions for servicemembers who are unable to attend the classes due to being hospitalized, convalescing, or receiving outpatient treatment for a disability. For more information, visit *www.dol.gov/vets/aboutvets/contacts/main.htm* for details.

DoD Disability Retired Pay

If a servicemember is found to be physically unfit for further military service, he will be removed. Those with less than twenty years of active duty may be either separated or retired. If the military rates their disability at 20 percent impairment or lower, they will typically be discharged with severance pay (see chapter 11) unless the condition existed prior to service and was not permanently aggravated by service. They may also be eligible for monthly disability compensation from the Veterans Administration, discussed later in this chapter.

If their condition is rated at or above 30 percent, and other conditions are met, they are typically disability retired. This retirement may be temporary or permanent. If temporary, the status should be resolved within five years. The difference between temporary and permanent disability is the stability of the medical condition. When deemed temporary, the servicemember is reevaluated every eighteen months. At the five-year point, if not sooner, he is removed from the temporary list and either found fit, retired permanently, or discharged with severance pay. Disability compensation and retirement pay are not taxed.

Social Security Disability Payments

Social Security disability payments are only made to those who have a work record. A person needs to have worked in at least half of the last ten years or, for younger workers, half of the elapsed time since age twenty-one, with a minimum of six calendar quarters. It also has a very strict requirement for disability: "inability to engage in substantial gainful activity because of a physical or mental impairment(s) that is expected to last at least 12 months or result in death." The disability can be of any cause. Benefits begin five months after the onset of the impairment that precludes work. Social Security benefits vary with past earnings level; see the chart below.

APPROXIMATE SOCIAL SECURITY ANNUAL DISABILITY BENEFITS BY EARNINGS LEVEL AND PRESENCE OF DEPENDENTS*

Annual Earnings	Disabled Worker	Disabled Worker plus Dependents
$18,000	$10,330	$15,300
$24,000	12,270	18,370
$30,000	14,170	21,250
$45,000	18,970	28,450
$60,000	21,630	32,450
$90,000	26,139	39,200

*Current amounts should be verified by issuing office.

Social Security benefits are paid in full regardless of what DoD or VA benefits are paid.

VA Disability Compensation

The VA Veterans' Compensation pays monthly, nontaxable benefits for disabilities resulting from injury or disease incurred or aggravated by active military duty, whether in wartime or peacetime. Unlike Social Security, it pays for partial as well as total disabilities. It's a separate program from DoD retirement pay and uses different standards to determine service-connected disability. VA disability ratings range from 10 percent to 100 percent disability.

Veterans' payments are not based on rank or pay grade. Rather, the disability severity is rated on a scale from 10 percent to 100 percent impairment. Additional increments are added for each dependent, which can include a spouse, children, and in some cases, parents. When a 30 percent rating is reached, additional allowances are given for dependents.

Amounts are shown in the chart below.

APPROXIMATE MONTHLY VETERANS' COMPENSATION FOR SERVICE-RELATED DISABILITIES*

Disability Rating (percent)	Veteran Alone	Veteran with Spouse and One Child
10	$115	$115
20	225	225
30	348	420
40	501	597
50	712	832
60	901	1,045
70	1,135	1,303
80	1,319	1,511
90	1,483	1,699
100	2,471	2,711

*Exact amounts should be verified by issuing office.

Veterans eligible for Social Security disability and Veterans' Compensation receive both payments in full. However, military retirement pay is forfeited on a dollar-to-dollar basis to receive VA disability compensation. The gross amount of the VA compensation is deducted from the retired pay.

VA compensation offers these additional benefits:

- VA approved disability gives priority admittance to VA hospitals for medical treatment for the disability.
- VA compensation is nontaxable.
- VA outpatient facilities are available for treatment of the disability.
- Even a rating by VA of 0 percent (although of no monetary benefit) documents your physical condition as service connected.
- VA disability percentage (and compensation) can be increased based on a request and approval of reevaluation.
- Up to $10,000 of National Service Life Insurance may be purchased without a physical exam.

Visit *www.ssa.gov/woundedwarriors* and *www.vba.va.gov/bln/21/* for more information.

Additional VA Compensation

Under a recently enacted law, certain severely disabled military with a VA-reported disability are entitled to special compensation. Monthly, it is:

- 70 percent to 80 percent disabled = $100.00
- 90 percent disabled = $200.00
- 100 percent disabled = $300.00

To qualify you must:

- not be retired from the military for a disability
- be in a retired status receiving retired pay
- have twenty or more years of service for the purpose of computing retired pay; a reservist must have at least 7,200 points to qualify

The VA rating for disability of 70 percent or higher must be awarded within four years of retirement and must be that level for each month. If the rating falls below 70 percent any given month, then there is no special compensation for that month.

A servicemember undergoes rehabilitative treatment at the Navy Comprehensive Combat and Complex Casualty Care Center in San Diego. Photo courtesy of DoD.

Job Preference

All veterans have preference for Federal and NAF jobs, but disabled veterans have preference even over other veterans. Under the Veteran's Readjustment Appointments program (discussed in chapter 11), the minimum requirement for a minimum of 180 days of service is waived if the veteran was separated from active duty because of a service-connected disability. This preference also applies to reservists who served on active duty during a period of war or in a military operation for which a campaign or expeditionary medal is authorized.

Traumatic Servicemembers' Group Life Insurance (TSGLI)

Veterans may be able to file claims for TSGLI. Coverage applies to active-duty members, reservists, National Guard members, funeral honors duty, and one-day muster duty (the latter two are covered for no charge). Everyone who has SGLI also has TSGLI.

TSGLI coverage will pay a benefit of between $25,000 and $100,000, depending on the loss directly resulting from the traumatic injury.

If the member has lost . . .	. . . then the amount paid is:
sight in both eyes or hearing in both ears	$100,000
sight in one eye	$50,000
one hand at or above the wrist or one foot at or above the ankle	$50,000
thumb and index finger of same hand	$50,000

Also, SGLI has a disability extension that allows servicemembers who are totally disabled at time of discharge to retain the SGLI coverage they had in service at no cost for up to two years.

Homes

Certain seriously injured veterans and servicemembers may receive multiple grants for constructing or modifying their homes. Special adaptive housing grants of $10,000 or $50,000 may be obtained three times, so long as the total grants stay within specified limits outlined in the law. For more information about the adaptive housing grants available to veterans, visit *www.homeloans.va.gov/sah.htm* or contact a local VA regional office at 800-827-1000. They are also exempt from paying the funding fee on a VA loan (see chapter 6).

Veterans getting disability compensation for service-related medical issues, or who are getting compensation if not retirement pay, do not pay the funding fee on VA loans. Nor do surviving spouses of those who died in the service, or from service related disabilities.

The Family and Medical Leave Act (FMLA)

This permits a spouse, child, parent, or next-of-kin to take up to twenty-six work weeks of leave to care for a servicemember who is receiving medical treatment, therapy, or recuperation therapy, or is otherwise on the temporary disability retired list, for a serious injury or illness.

Traveling to Wounded Servicemembers

If the attending physician determines it is essential to a seriously injured patient's recovery, and this is verified by the hospital commander, three "primary next-of-kin" (spouse, children, parents, siblings) may be issued Invitational Travel Orders to visit him. Transportation and lodging is provided in two-week increments. Housing may be in a local hotel, military guesthouse, or a Fisher House.

Other Programs

Along with the government programs mentioned, there are private programs that help veterans and survivor families. Each has its own target, mission, and goal. Some work to ensure that families have food on the table, some provide getaways in vacation spots, some help with the job search, some help with the home. Active research and contact is needed on your part, as the military does not check with other agencies to see if a veteran is eligible for private programs. The Internet Resources at the end of this chapter list some websites that survivors and veterans might investigate as a starting point.

Many spouses speak of the need to proactively advocate for their wounded warriors and some obtain legal assistance to do so. It is suggested that you thoroughly review everything you're offered, make sure you understand it, do not make hasty decisions about what to accept, and don't downplay or underestimate the extent of injuries to expedite the process.

FURTHER READING

Books

Steen, Joanne M., and M. Regina Asaro. *Military Widow: A Survival Guide*. Annapolis, MD: U.S. Naval Institute Press, 2006.

Internet Resources

www.saluteheroes.org. Provides financial aid and career assistance.
www.cominghomeproject.net/cominghome. Provides workshops and retreats.
woundedwarriorproject.org. Provides career and benefits counseling.
www.operationfirstresponse.org. Provides clothing, toiletries, phone cards, and more.
www.taps.org/mission. Tragedy Assistance Program for Survivors.
www.americasupportsyou.mil. List of organizations that help.
www.fallenheroesfund.org. Provides financial support.
goldstarfamilysupport.org. Gold Star Wives of America, a group of 10,000 military widows that lobbies Congress and the Pentagon.
www.silverstarfamilies.org. Helps wounded servicemembers.
www.militaryspousesforchange.com. Advocacy group.
www.lastwishfoundation.org. Provides funds to help support and educate children of American servicemembers killed during Operation Iraqi Freedom.
www.homesforourtroops.org. Builds specially adapted homes for severely disabled soldiers and their families.
www.woundedwarriorhospitalfund.org. Provides time in resort areas for families of injured servicemembers.
www.heromiles.org. Joint effort by multiple airlines that accepts public donations of frequent flyer miles for servicemembers' use.
www.ssa.gov/reach.htm. How to contact Social Security in the U.S. and overseas.
www.vba.va.gov/survivors. VA Survivor Benefits Homepage.
www.va.gov/statedva.htm. Find a VA office in each state.

13

Wrapping It Up

Well, we've covered a lot of ground! Money and moving, customs and careers, separations and sponsors—it's a start. You pick up the ball from there. Military life is what you make it. The person who brings to it enthusiasm, joy in living, and a willingness to grow, change, and be flexible will find it a good life. Certainly there are trade-offs. Your attitude toward accepting those trade-offs will determine how well you adjust to them.

Attitude is everything. A positive attitude will give you the flexibility, humor, and patience that are needed to make military life fun no matter where you're stationed, what benefits you have access to, and what your husband's rank is.

What is a positive attitude? It's a state of mind that booms, "Now I'm going to get something done!" instead of "Today is a drag like every other day." It affects how you look, how you feel, what you do, and what you say. It determines your success in achieving your life goals. It's the most important characteristic you have.

Your willingness to help make your world a better place will indeed make it a better place. Work with people, not against them, to obtain what you want. Most installations have programs that solicit advice on how to make things work better. Suggestions are welcomed from all quarters, not just from military or civilian employees. You may even be rewarded financially for suggestions that save money.

Discover what's offered at your base. Learn the structure of what surrounds you and the reasons behind the rules that affect your life. There are a lot of people who feel that the military is their spouse's job, not theirs. They feel that they have nothing to do with it, that the military doesn't affect them. They must be asked: Do you shop at the commissary? Do you eat at the club? Are your baby's checkups performed by an Army doctor, a Navy nurse, an Air Force physician's assistant? Does your child attend a DoDDS school? Is your blouse from the exchange? Do you live in quarters? Did you obtain your federal job with an edge from the Military Spouse Employment Act? Do you survive separations? Did you quit a good job to move with your spouse—did you move with your spouse? Does your morale boosting benefit him, or does your negativity make him a chronic complainer? Is your spouse's paycheck the main source of income in your family? Do you still say you have nothing to do with the military?

The person who marries a servicemember but expects to have nothing to do with the system is mistaken. If your spouse is an E-1, in for the minimum two years, this might be true. Otherwise, the higher up the ladder he goes, the more things will be expected of him—and of you. Hardly anyone can give 100 percent, but 15 percent, 10 percent, even 2 percent will be observed and appreciated. Things aren't as rigid as they once were, but some guidelines remain. Learn what they are, what protocol exists, what is and isn't expected, what can and can't be done. Those who aren't willing to make such an effort should reevaluate whether military life is for them, because with each increase in rank, a lack of understanding and concern is sure to bring friction.

Follow current events. The combined strength of the 5 million active-duty servicemembers, reservists, retirees, and family members could be a powerful voting force indeed. You might wish to support organizations that lobby on the military's behalf, such as the National Military Family Association (*www.nmfa.org*).

VOLUNTEERS

A book on the military lifestyle wouldn't be complete without some words about the people responsible for making many quality-of-life programs work: volunteers. The willingness of people to give of themselves—not for money, but simply to help make the world a better place—provides those thousand points of light a former president once spoke of. Government alone does not and cannot do it all. Through volunteering you can make another person's life happier and more meaningful. You can make it a little more bearable or comfortable, maybe less desperate or hopeless. Charitable and social service agencies could not function without volunteers. Volunteers provide the extras for which there will never be enough paid staff.

Volunteers have helped the previously unemployable, such as former prison inmates and inner-city youth, get jobs by teaching skills, tutoring them for general equivalency diplomas, accompanying them to interviews, and boosting their self-confidence. Most political workers are volunteer grassroots campaigners who pass out information and offer rides to the polls. The USO and Red Cross depend on volunteers, operating with donated money. Churches, the Humane Society, soccer clubs, senior citizens' centers, Little League, the United Way, Big Brothers/Big Sisters, and Scout troops are just a few of the many important organizations that rely on volunteers. A person who gives even two hours a week makes herself part of the solution. You'll find volunteers teaching crafts to kids and comparison shopping to adults. You'll find them serving as directors of the Red Cross, as newspaper publishers, and as public-relations personnel.

Volunteering can help people who have lots of education but little experience. Many volunteers have successfully used their experience to land a paying job. The federal government is just one of many employers that give credit for volunteer experience.

Can you answer a telephone? Can you listen to problems? Can you type, translate, file, phone the homebound, take kids to a ball game? Can you fix toys, play games, take photographs? Then you can volunteer. Can you sew, knit, tutor, arrange flowers, sort clothes, shop for groceries, or operate a cash register? Then you can volunteer. Volunteer duties range from the routine to the professional. Some volunteer slots have job descriptions and accompanying qualification requirements. Programs exist to recruit, train, and supervise volunteers and to recognize good work. Volunteers are limited only by their imagination and that of the organization using them.

CLOSING THOUGHTS

Here are some more comments from military spouses:

"To help make your world a better place, start with your unit. Be part of a 'chain of concern,' or a 'wife-on-call' system, where you might take a young mother lacking transportation on a diaper run, an errand, or to a doctor's appointment. Offer to babysit. This shows that people in the community care, and it cuts down on calling servicemembers away from their jobs. If your wives' group has neither a chain of concern nor a wife-on-call system, start one. If it has one, participate in it. Befriend a foreign-born spouse whose lack of knowledge of the language may be inhibiting her social life."

"Your mind and your attitude are very strong. If you tell yourself things will be bad, that's what the universe will give you. If you look for the good, the good will find you. The universe doesn't care if you succeed or fail. Choose wisely."

"Your husband probably has single friends. Welcome them over. Set time and day limits if you feel they're there too much, but still, welcome them over. Both of you need friendships besides each other's."

"There's a story in a Chicken Soup for the Soul book that tells of a wife who wrecked the family car. When she tells her husband, he says there's no need to be upset. We can have a wrecked car and be angry about it or we can have a wrecked car and be happy about it—either way we have a wrecked car. Use this philosophy to guide your own unpleasant experiences."

"Check your attitude and recharge your ambitions. Have you become complacent, lost your creativity, feel as if you're plodding? Write down self-improvement goals. Have you put on weight? Make some fitness goals. Cull your wardrobe, get rid of old, faded, and tired-looking clothes, buy some new ones. Make an effort to find new social outlets and friends. Read an important book instead of watching TV. Make a long-term financial plan."

"My favorite saying is 'Give flowers to the living while they can enjoy them.' You don't have to literally give flowers, but rather acts of kindness. Like they say, pay it forward. Share happiness with strangers. If there's an organization that has helped you, such as the thrift shop or hospital, turn around and volunteer to help it. If you've been treated well by a sponsor, pass it on. If you've learned something helpful—some tip, hint, or way to make life easier—pass that on, too. Cast your bread upon the water. What goes around comes around."

"I try not to see good vs. bad. I see good vs. hard or good vs. different."

"Learn and grow. Ideally, you'll look back at a military career and be amazed at how much you've changed. Or you might go day-to-day and not change a thing. That's up to you, though."

"Be flexible in everything. Military life leaves no room for rigidity. Make the best of things, roll with the punches. Whenever we get 'rained on' by higher-ups or powers that be, my husband and I just remember a private joke between us: you can put steak sauce on a hot dog, but it's still just a weenie. This makes us laugh, and we move on."

> "Do not go where the path may lead, go instead where there is no path and leave a trail."
> —Ralph Waldo Emerson

"If the youth activities aren't all you would like them to be, offer to be a team mom or coach. Help DoDDS instructors do paperwork so that they can spend more time teaching your children. When you're invited to a planning session for a morale-boosting activity, go! If there's no Girl Scout troop around, start one. If you would like to see something done, there must be others who feel the same way."

"No marriage is easy, but a military marriage is especially challenging. Never assume anything—discuss everything with your partner. Both of you should act as individuals; both of you should participate in decisions. One shouldn't be completely dependent upon the other. Maintain other adult friends and contacts; at some time you are going to need them."

"Don't overlook the single servicemembers. Invite them over on holidays and other occasions for a home-cooked meal. They'll love it. Meat loaf in a family setting beats steak in the mess hall. Bake cookies at Christmas and send them to the barracks. At planning sessions for unit parties, include activities and gifts for them. Send holiday gifts to those who are deployed; this can be an FRG activity. Not all of them have friends and parents who send them things. On one WESPAC cruise, the spouses and significant others got together and sent the complete fixings for a Christmas party, down to monogrammed stuffed stockings."

"When you marry a soldier, you become part of the largest family in the country, for better or for worse."

"*Anyone can be a spouse, but it takes a special person to be a military spouse. I love the travel, having friends of all races and creeds, and how handsome my husband looks in his uniform. Live life to its fullest—it's too short to spend fretting over careless movers, unfamiliar surroundings, and deployments.*"

"*As a Marine wife of twenty-two years, I can say that you're in for the time of your life! It's a challenging life, but one that will make both you and your spouse better people. We've lived in fourteen homes and have visited some of the most interesting places on earth. How I envy you, just starting out. Hang on for a great ride!*"

"*Take ownership of your life. If things aren't going the way you want, don't blame others. Only you have the power to change things. Make a plan and stick with it.*"

"*Learn as much as you can, because one day you'll be providing the legacy of leadership and advice.*"

Military service isn't a job. It's a lifestyle. At retirement ceremonies, you will often observe the moving sight of spouses shedding tears, evidence of the ties they have formed after years of this lifestyle. A large number of the military's volunteers are retired servicemembers and spouses who desire to keep in touch with the military and its young, active-duty members. Can any civilian company boast of this?

If you have adventure in your soul, you will enjoy military life. The opportunities it affords to see the world, to meet different people, and to instill patriotism and pride are endless. As the Navy Lifelines crowd says, "Good luck and HAVE FUN!"

Appendix A

Army, Navy, and Air Force Leave and Earnings Statement

Fields 1 through 9 contain the identification portion of the LES.

1. NAME: The member's name in last, first, middle initial format.
2. SOC. SEC. NO.: The member's Social Security number.
3. GRADE: The member's current pay grade.
4. PAY DATE: The date the member entered active duty for pay purposes in YYMMDD format. This is synonymous with the Pay Entry Base Date (PEBD).
5. YRS SVC: In two digits, the actual years of creditable service.
6. ETS: The Expiration Term of Service in YYMMDD format. This is synonymous with the Expiration of Active Obligated Service (EAOS).
7. BRANCH: The branch of service: Navy, Army, Air Force.
8. ADSN/DSSN: The Disbursing Station Symbol Number used to identify each disbursing/finance office.
9. PERIOD COVERED: This is the period covered by the individual LES. Normally it will be for one calendar month. If this is a separation LES, the separation date will appear in this field.

Fields 10 through 24 contain the entitlements, deductions, allotments, their respective totals, a mathematical summary portion, date initially entered military service, and retirement plan.

10. ENTITLEMENTS: In columnar style the names of the entitlements and allowances being paid. Space is allocated for fifteen entitlements and/or allowances. If more than fifteen are present, the overflow will be printed in the remarks block. Any retroactive entitlements and/or allowances will be added to like entitlements and/or allowances.
11. DEDUCTIONS: The description of the deductions are listed in columnar style. This includes items such as taxes, SGLI, mid-month pay, and dependent dental plan. Space is allocated for fifteen deductions. If more than fifteen are present, the overflow will be printed in the remarks block. Any retroactive deductions will be added to like deductions.

12 ALLOTMENTS: In columnar style the type of the actual allotments being deducted. This includes discretionary and nondiscretionary allotments for savings and/or checking accounts, insurance, bonds, etc. Space is allocated for fifteen allotments. If a member has more than one of the same type of allotment, the only differentiation may be that of the dollar amount.

13 +AMT FWD: The amount of all unpaid pay and allowances due from the prior LES.

14 +TOT ENT: The figure from Field 20 that is the total of all entitlements and/or allowances listed.

15 −TOT DED: The figure from Field 21 that is the total of all deductions.

16 −TOT ALMT: The figure from Field 22 that is the total of all allotments.

17 =NET AMT: The dollar value of all unpaid pay and allowances, plus total entitlements and/or allowances, minus deductions and allotments due on the current LES.

18 −CR FWD: The dollar value of all unpaid pay and allowances due to reflect on the next LES as the +AMT FWD.

19 =EOM PAY: The actual amount of the payment to be paid to the member on end-of-month payday.

20–22 TOTAL: The total amounts for the entitlements and/or allowances, deductions, and allotments, respectively.

23 DIEMS: Date initially entered military service: This date is used *solely* to indicate which retirement plan a member is under.

24 RET PLAN: Type of retirement plan: Final Pay, High 3, REDUX, or CHOICE (CHOICE reflects members who have less than fifteen years service and have not elected to go with REDUX or stay with their current retirement plan).

Fields 25 through 32 contain leave information.

25 BF BAL: The brought-forward leave balance. Balance may be at the beginning of the fiscal year, or when active duty began, or the day after the member was paid Lump Sum Leave (LSL).

26 ERND: The cumulative amount of leave earned in the current fiscal year or current term of enlistment if the member reenlisted/extended since the beginning of the fiscal year. Normally increases by two and a half days each month.

27 USED: The cumulative amount of leave used in the current fiscal year or current term of enlistment if member reenlisted/extended since the beginning of the fiscal year.

28 CR BAL: The current leave balance as of the end of the period covered by the LES.

29 ETS BAL: The projected leave balance to the member's Expiration Term of Service (ETS).

30 LV LOST: The number of days of leave that have been lost.

31 LV PAID: The number of days of leave paid to date.

32 USE/LOSE: The projected number of days of leave that will be lost if not taken in the current fiscal year on a monthly basis. The number of days of leave in this block will decrease with any leave usage.

Fields 33 through 38 contain Federal Tax withholding information.

33 WAGE PERIOD: The amount of money earned this LES period that is subject to Federal Income Tax Withholding (FITW).

34 WAGE YTD: The money earned year-to-date that is subject to FITW.

35 M/S: The marital status used to compute the FITW.

36 EX: The number of exemptions used to compute the FITW.

37 ADD'L TAX: The member-specified additional dollar amount to be withheld in addition to the amount computed by the Marital Status and Exemptions.

38 TAX YTD: The cumulative total of FITW withheld throughout the calendar year.

Fields 39 through 43 contain Federal Insurance Contributions Act (FICA) information.

39 WAGE PERIOD: The amount of money earned this LES period that is subject to FICA.

40 SOC WAGE YTD: The wages earned year-to-date that are subject to FICA.

41 SOC TAX YTD: Cumulative total of FICA withheld throughout the calendar year.

42 MED WAGE YTD: The wages earned year-to-date that are subject to Medicare.

43 MED TAX YTD: Cumulative total of Medicare taxes paid year-to-date.

Fields 44 through 49 contain State Tax information.

44 ST: The two-digit postal abbreviation for the state the member elected.

45 WAGE PERIOD: The amount of money earned this LES period that is subject to State Income Tax Withholding (SITW).

46 WAGE YTD: The money earned year-to-date that is subject to SITW.

47 M/S. The marital status used to compute the SITW.

48 EX: The number of exemptions used to compute the SITW.

49 TAX YTD: The cumulative total of SITW withheld throughout the calendar year.

Fields 50 through 62 contain additional Pay Data.

50 BAQ TYPE: The type of Basic Allowance for Quarters being paid.

51 BAQ DEPN: A code that indicates the type of dependent. A—Spouse; C—Child; D—Parent; G—Grandfathered; I Member married to member/own right; K—Ward of the court; L—Parents in Law/own right; S—Student (age

21–22); T—Handicapped child over age twenty-one; W—Member married to member, child under twenty-one.

52 VHA ZIP: The zip code used in the computation of Variable Housing Allowance (VHA) if entitlement exists.

53 RENT AMT: The amount of rent paid for housing if applicable.

54 SHARE: The number of people with whom the member shares housing costs.

55 STAT: The VHA status: accompanied or unaccompanied.

56 JFTR: The Joint Federal Travel Regulation (JFTR) code based on the location of the member for Cost of Living Allowance (COLA) purposes.

57 DEPNS: The number of dependents the member has for VHA purposes.

58 2D JFTR: The JFTR code based on the location of the member's dependents for COLA purposes.

59 BAS TYPE: An alpha code that indicates the type of Basic Allowance for Subsistence (BAS) the member is receiving, if applicable. This field will be blank for officers.

- B–Separate Rations
- C–TDY/PCS/Proceed Time
- H–Rations-in-kind not available
- K–Rations under emergency conditions

60 CHARITY YTD: The cumulative amount of charitable contributions for the calendar year.

61 TPC: This field is not used by the active component of any branch of service.

62 PACIDN: The activity Unit Identification Code (UIC). This field is currently used by the Army only.

Fields 63 through 75 contain Thrift Savings Plan (TSP) information/data.

63 BASE PAY RATE: The percentage of base pay elected for TSP contributions.

64 BASE PAY CURRENT: Reserved for future use.

65 SPECIAL PAY RATE: The percentage of Specialty Pay elected for TSP contribution.

66 SPECIAL PAY CURRENT: Reserved for future use.

67 INCENTIVE PAY RATE: Percentage of Incentive Pay elected for TSP contribution.

68 INCENTIVE PAY CURRENT: Reserved for future use.

69 BONUS PAY RATE: The percentage of Bonus Pay elected toward TSP contribution.

70 BONUS PAY CURRENT: Reserved for future use.

71 Reserved for future use.

72 TSP YTD DEDUCTION (TSP Year-To-Date Deduction): Dollar amount of TSP contributions deducted for the year.

73 DEFERRED: Total dollar amount of TSP contributions that are deferred for tax purposes.

74 EXEMPT: Dollar amount of TSP contributions that are reported as tax exempt to the Internal Revenue Service (IRS).

75 Reserved for future use.

76 REMARKS: This area is used to provide you with general notices from varying levels of command, as well as the literal explanation of starts, stops, and changes to pay items in the entries within the "ENTITLEMENTS," "DEDUCTIONS," and "ALLOTMENTS" fields.

77 YTD ENTITLE: The cumulative total of all entitlements for the calendar year.

78 YTD DEDUCT: The cumulative total of all deductions for the calendar year.

DEFENSE FINANCE AND ACCOUNTING SERVICE MILITARY LEAVE AND EARNINGS STATEMENT									
ID	NAME(LAST,FIRS,MI) 1	SOC.SEC.NO 2	GRADE 3	PAY DATE 4	YRS.SVC 5	ETS 6	BRANCH 7	ADSN/DSSN 8	PERIOD COVERED 9

ENTITLEMENTS		DEDUCTIONS		ALLOTMENTS		SUMMARY	
TYPE	AMOUNT	TYPE	AMOUNT	TYPE	AMOUNT	- AMT FWD	13
A B C D E F G H I J K L M N O 10		11		12		- TOT ENT	14
						- TOT DED	15
						- TOT ALMT	16
						"NET ALMT	17
						- CR FWD	18
						"BOM PAY	19
TOTAL 20		21		22		DIEM 23	RET PLAN 24

LEAVE	BF BAL 25	ERND 26	USED 27	CR BAL 28	ETS BAL 29	LV LOST 30	LV PAID 31	USE/LOSE 32	FED TAXES 33	WAGE PERIOD	WAGE YTD 34	M/S 35	EX 36	ADD'L TAX 37	TAX YTD 38

FICA TAXES	WAGE PERIOD 39	SOC WAGE YTD 40	SOC TAX YTD 41	MED WAGE YTD 42	MED TAX YTD 43	STATE TAXES 44	ST	WAGE PERIOD 45	WAGE YTD 46	M/S 47	EX 48	TAX YTD 49

PAY DATA	BAQ TYPE 50	BAQ DEPN 51	VHA ZIP 52	RENT AMT 53	SHARE 54	STAT 55	JFTR 56	DEPNS 57	2D JFTR 58	BAS TYPE 59	CHARITY YTD 60	TPS 61	PACIDN 62

Thrift Saving Plan (TSP)	BASE PAY RATE 63	BASE PAY CURRENT 64	SPEC PAY RATE 65	SPEC PAY CURRENT 66	INC PAY RATE 67	INC PAY CURRENT 68	BONUS PAY RATE 69	BONUS PAY CURRENT 70
	CURRENTLY NOT USED 71		TSP YTD DEDUCTION 72		DEFERRED 73		EXEMPT 74	CURRENTLY NOT USED 75

REMARKS   YTD ENTITLE _____   YTD DEDUCT _____

76   77   78

WWW.DFAS.MIL

Appendix B

Reserve and National Guard Leave and Earnings Statement

(This statement looks the same as the LES for the Army, Navy, and Air Force, but some explanations are different.)

Fields 1 through 9 contain the identification portion of the LES.
1 NAME. The member's name in last, first, middle initial format.
2 SOC. SEC. NO. The member's Social Security number.
3 GRADE. The member's current pay grade.
4 PAY DATE. The date the member entered active duty for pay purposes in YYMMDD format. This is synonymous with the Pay Entry Base Date (PEBD).
5 YRS SVC. In two digits, the actual years of creditable service.
6 ETS. The Expiration Term of Service in YYMMDD format. This is synonymous with the Expiration of Active Obligated Service (EAOS).
7 BRANCH. This field reflects branch of service *or* program in which the service member is enrolled.
8 ADSN/DSSN. The Disbursing Station Symbol Number used to identify each disbursing/finance office.
9 PERIOD COVERED. This field will show the "Check Date" for Reserve or National Guard members.

Fields 10 through 22 contain the entitlements, deductions, allotments, their respective totals, a mathematical summary portion, and date initially entered military service.
10 ENTITLEMENTS. In columnar style, the names of the entitlements and allowances being paid. Space is allocated for fifteen entitlements and/or allowances. If more than fifteen are present, the overflow will be printed in the remarks block. Any retroactive entitlements and/or allowances will be added to like entitlements and/or allowances.
11 DEDUCTIONS. The description of the deductions is listed in columnar style. This includes items such as taxes, SGLI, and dependent dental plan.

Space is allocated for fifteen deductions. If more than fifteen are present, the overflow will be printed in the remarks block. Any retroactive deductions will be added to like deductions.

12 ALLOTMENTS. Reservist and National Guard do not have allotments.

13 AMT FWD. The amount of all unpaid pay and allowances due from the prior LES.

14 TOT ENT. The figure from Field 20 that is the total of all entitlements and/or allowances listed.

15 TOT DED. The figure from Field 21 that is the total of all deductions.

16 TOT ALMT. Reservist and National Guard do not have allotments.

17 NET AMT. The dollar value of all unpaid pay and allowances, plus total entitlements and/or allowances, minus deductions due on the current LES.

18 CR FWD. The dollar value of all unpaid pay and allowances due to reflect on the next LES as the +AMT FWD.

19 EOM PAY. The actual amount of the payment to be paid to the member on that specific payday.

Fields 20 through 22—TOTAL. The total amounts for the entitlements and/or allowances, and deductions, respectively.

Fields 23 and 24 are not used by Reserve and National Guard members.

Fields 25 through 32 contain leave information.

25 BF BAL. The brought-forward leave balance. Balance may be at the beginning of the fiscal year, or when active duty began, or the day after the member was paid Lump Sum Leave (LSL).

26 ERND. The cumulative amount of leave earned in the current fiscal year or current term of enlistment if the member reenlisted/extended since the beginning of the fiscal year. Normally increases by two and a half days each month.

27 USED. The cumulative amount of leave used in the current fiscal year or current term of enlistment if member reenlisted/extended since the beginning of the fiscal year.

28 CR BAL. The current leave balance as of the end of the period covered by the LES.

29 ETS BAL. The projected leave balance to the member's Expiration Term of Service (ETS).

30 LV LOST. The number of days of leave that have been lost.

31 LV PAID. The number of days of leave paid to date.

32 USE/LOSE. The projected number of days of leave that will be lost if not taken in the current fiscal year on a monthly basis. The number of days of leave in this block will decrease with any leave usage.

Fields 33 through 38 contain Federal Tax withholding information.

33 WAGE PERIOD. The amount of money earned this LES period that is subject to Federal Income Tax Withholding (FITW).

34 WAGE YTD. The money earned year-to-date that is subject to FITW.

35 M/S. The marital status used to compute the FITW.

36 EX. The number of exemptions used to compute the FITW.

37 ADD'L TAX. The member-specified additional dollar amount to be withheld in addition to the amount computed by the Marital Status and Exemptions.

38 TAX YTD. The cumulative total of FITW withheld throughout the calendar year.

Fields 39 through 43 contain Federal Insurance Contributions Act (FICA) information.

39 WAGE PERIOD. The amount of money earned this LES period that is subject to FICA.

40 SOC WAGE YTD. The wages earned year-to-date that are subject to FICA.

41 SOC TAX YTD. Cumulative total of FICA withheld throughout the calendar year.

42 MED WAGE YTD. The wages earned year-to-date that are subject to Medicare.

43 MED TAX YTD. Cumulative total of Medicare taxes paid year-to-date.

Fields 44 through 49 contain State Tax information.

44 ST. The two-digit postal abbreviation for the state the member elected.

45 WAGE PERIOD. The amount of money earned this LES period that is subject to State Income Tax Withholding (SITW).

46 WAGE YTD. The money earned year-to-date that is subject to SITW.

47 M/S. The marital status used to compute the SITW.

48 EX. The number of exemptions used to compute the SITW.

49 TAX YTD. The cumulative total of SITW withheld throughout the calendar year.

Fields 50 through 62 contain additional Pay Data.

50 BAQ TYPE. The member's type of Basic Allowance for Quarters status.
    • W/O DEP—Member without dependents.
    • W DEP—Member with dependents.
    • WDAGQT—Member with dependents assigned government quarters.

51 BAQ DEPN. Indicates the type of dependent.
    • Spouse
    • Child
    • Parent
    • Grandfathered

- Member married to member/own right
- Ward of the court
- Parents-in-law
- Own right
- Student (age twenty-one to twenty-two)
- Handicapped child over age twenty-one
- Member married to member, child under twenty-one
- No dependents
- N/A

52 VHA ZIP. The zip code used in the computation of Variable Housing Allowance (VHA) if entitlement exists.

53 RENT AMT. The amount of rent paid for housing if applicable.

54 SHARE. The number of people with whom the member shares housing costs.

55 STAT. The VHA status: accompanied or unaccompanied.

56 JFTR. The Joint Federal Travel Regulation (JFTR) code based on the location of the member for Cost of Living Allowance (COLA) purposes.

57 DEPNS. The number of dependents the member has for COLA purposes.

58 2D JFTR. The JFTR code based on the location of the member's dependents for COLA purposes.

59 BAS TYPE
- STAND—Separate Rations
- (blank)—Rations-in-kind not available
- OFFIC—Officer Rations

60 CHARITY YTD. The cumulative amount of charitable contributions for the calendar year.

61 TPC. This field is not used by the Active Component. Army Reserves and National Guard use this field to identify Training Program Codes.
- A—Normal pay status code for a regular service member on regular duty.
- C—Funeral honors duty.
- M—Annual training tours over thirty days.
- N—Death.
- O—Training for HPSP, ROTC, and Special ADT over thirty days.
- T—ADT over twenty-nine days (school).
- U—Undergraduate pilot training, in-grade pilot, navigator, and advance flying training officers.
- X—Stipend tour of HPIP participants or subsistence for ROTC participants.
- Z—Administrative and support training (exclusive of recruiting).

62 PACIDN. The activity Unit Identification Code (UIC).

Fields 63 through 75 contain Thrift Savings Plan (TSP) information/data.

63 BASE PAY RATE. The percentage of base pay elected for TSP contributions.

64 BASE PAY CURRENT. The amount of Base Pay withheld for TSP from current pay entitlement

65 SPECIAL PAY RATE. The percentage of Specialty Pay elected for TSP contribution.

66 SPECIAL PAY CURRENT. The amount of Special Pay withheld for TSP from current pay entitlement.

67 INCENTIVE PAY RATE. Percentage of Incentive Pay elected toward TSP contribution.

68 INCENTIVE PAY CURRENT. The amount of Incentive Pay withheld for TSP from current pay entitlement.

69 BONUS PAY RATE. The percentage of Bonus Pay elected toward TSP contribution.

70 BONUS PAY CURRENT. The amount of Bonus Pay withheld for TSP from current pay entitlement.

71 Reserved for future use.

72 TSP YTD DEDUCTION (TSP Year-To-Date Deduction): Dollar amount of TSP contributions deducted for the year.

73 DEFERRED: Dollar amount of pay elected to be deferred during the tax year.

74 EXEMPT: Dollar amount of TSP contributions that are reported as tax exempt to the Internal Revenue Service (IRS).

75 Reserved for future use.

76 REMARKS. Notices of starts, stops, and changes to a member's pay items, as well as general notices from varying levels of command may appear.

77 YTD ENTITLE. The cumulative total of all entitlements for the calendar year.

78 YTD DEDUCT. The cumulative total of all deductions for the calendar year.

Appendix C

Marine Corps Leave and Earnings Statement

SECTION A: IDENTIFICATION INFORMATION
Box 1—NAME. Last name, first name, and middle initial.

Box 2—SSN. Social Security number.

Box 3—RANK. Pay grade (Rank) for which basic pay is determined.

Box 4—SERV. Branch of service (e.g., "USMC" or "USMCR").

Box 5—PLT Code. The section which assigned.

Box 6—DATE PREP. Date Prepared. This is the date the LES was prepared by DFAS in Kansas City.

Box 7—PRD COVERED. Period covered. Used to specify the span of days covered by this leave and earnings statement.

Box 8—PEBD. Pay entry base date.

Box 9—YRS. Years of service for pay purposes.

Box 10—EAS. Expiration of active service.

Box 11—ECC. Expiration of current contract.

Box 12—MCC-DIST-RUC. Monitor command code, district, and Reporting Unit Code (MCC-RUC for USMC, DIST-RUC for USMCR).

SECTION B: FORECAST AMOUNTS
Box 13—DATE AND AMOUNT.
1. DATE. Date of mid-month payday.
2. AMOUNT. Forecast of amount due on mid-month payday of the upcoming month.

Box 14—DATE AND AMOUNT.
1. DATE. Date of end-of-month payday.
2. AMOUNT. Forecast of amount due on end-of-month payday of the upcoming month.

SECTION C: SPLIT PAY DATE

Box 15—START DATE. The date Split Pay started.

Box 16—AMOUNT. The amount of Split Pay elected.

Box 17—BALANCE. The balance of Split Pay not received.

Box 18—POE. Payment Option Election. The POE code is used to designate distribution of monthly pay.

SECTION D: DIRECT DEPOSIT/EFT ADDRESS

This section contains the name and address of the financial institution where payments are being deposited.

SECTION E: LEAVE INFORMATION

Box 19—LV BF. Leave brought forward. The number of days leave accrued at the end of the preceding period.

Box 20—EARNED. Number of days leave earned during the period covered. Normally this will be two and a half days.

Box 21—USED. Number of days leave charged since the previous LES was prepared.

Box 22—EXCESS. Number of days leave charged without entitlement to pay and allowance, in excess of leave that can be earned prior to ECC.

Box 23—BAL. Balance. The number of days of accrued leave due or advanced.

Box 24—MAX ACCRUAL. Total number of days that can accrue based upon the ECC date. Value is obtained by using the first day of the month following the period covered, up to and including the ECC date.

Box 25—LOST. Number of days in excess of sixty days dropped due to the change in the fiscal year.

Box 26—SOLD/AS OF. The cumulative amount of leave earned in the current fiscal year or current term of enlistment if the member reenlisted/extended since the beginning of the fiscal year. Normally increases by 2.5 days each month.

Box 27—CBT LV BAL. Reserved for future use.

SECTION F: AVIATION PAY INFORMATION

Boxes 28 through 32 pertain only to Officers in the aviation field.

SECTION G TAX INFORMATION

Box 33—STATE TAX.

1. STATE CODE. State tax code. An alphanumeric code is used to identify the state (or territorial possession) designated by the member as his or her legal residence.
2. EXEMPTIONS. State tax exemptions. Marital status and number of exemptions claimed for state tax purposes.
3. WAGES THIS PRD. Total state taxable income for the period covered.

4. WAGES YTD. State taxable income year-to-date. This is the amount of taxable income earning by the Marine from the date of entry into service or from January 1 of the current year through the last day of the period covered.
5. STATE TAX YTD. State taxes year-to-date. Total amount of state income tax withheld for the year.

Box 34—FEDERAL TAX.

1. EXEMPTIONS. Federal tax exemptions. Marital status and number of exemptions claimed for federal tax purposes.
2. WAGES THIS PRD. Total federal taxable income for the period covered.
3. WAGES YTD. Federal taxable income year-to-date. This is the amount of taxable income earned from the date of entry into service or from January 1 of the current year through the last day of the period covered.
4. FED TAX YTD. Federal taxes year-to-date. Total amount of federal income tax withheld for the year.

Box 35—FICA (SOCIAL SECURITY TAX)

1. SSEC WAGES THIS PRD. Social Security wages this period. Moneys earned during period covered that are subject to deduction under the Federal Insurance Contributions Act.
2. SSEC WAGES YTD. Social Security wages year-to-date. The amount of wages earned for the year that are subject to Social Security tax.
3. SSEC TAX YTD. Social Security tax year-to-date. The amount of Social Security tax withheld for the year. This includes withholding on the amount shown in Social Security wages this period.
4. MEDICARE WAGES THIS PRD. Medicare wages this period. Moneys earned during period covered that are subject to deduction under Old Age Survivors Disability Insurance.
5. MEDICARE WAGES YTD. Medicare wages year-to-date. The amount of wages earned for the year that are subject to Medicare tax.
6. MEDICARE TAX YTD. Medicare tax year-to-date. The amount of Medicare tax withheld for the year. This includes withholding on the amount shown in Medicare wages this period.

SECTION H: RIGHTS OF MARINES INDEBTED TO THE GOVERNMENT

SECTION I: ADDITIONAL BAH INFORMATION
Boxes 36 through 42 are no longer used. VHA and BAQ have been replaced with BAH, which will be shown in Section O.

SECTION J: CAREER SEA PAY
Box 43.

1. DATE. The date career sea duty ended.
2. TOTAL CAREER SEA SVC. The total number of years, months, and days served on sea duty.

SECTION K: EDUCATION DEDUCTION

Box 44—TYPE. The educational program enrolled.

Box 45—MONTHLY AMT. The monthly amount being deducted for the educational program.

Box 46—TOTAL. The total amount that has been deducted for the educational program; this amount includes the current month.

SECTION L: ADMINISTRATIVE INFORMATION

Box 47—PAY STATUS. This code identifies the particular pay status on the last day covered by the LES.

Box 48—PAY GROUP. A three-digit code that identifies if officer or enlisted.

Box 49—CRA DATE. Clothing Replacement Allowance date for active-duty enlisted.

Box 50—RESERVE ECC. Reserve Expiration of Current Contract.

Box 51—DSSN. Disbursing Station Symbol Number. A number used to identify the servicing disbursing/finance officer account.

SECTION M: RESERVE DRILL INFORMATION

Box 52—Reg. Total Regular Drills Performed This Period.

Box 53—Reg Fytd. Total Regular Drills Performed This Fiscal Year.

Box 54—Reg Annytd. Total Regular Drills Performed This Anniversary Year.

Box 55—Add. Total Additional Drills Performed This Period.

Box 56—Add Fytd. Total Additional Drills Performed This Fiscal Year.

Box 57—Add Annytd. Total Additional Drills Performed This Anniversary Year.

SECTION N: RESERVE RETIREMENT INFORMATION

Box 58—Bf Annytd. Ending Balance of Retirement Credit Points for Anniversary Year From Prior Month.

Box 59—Acdu This Prd. Total Days Active Duty This Period.

Box 60—Drill This Prd. Total Drills This Period.

Box 61—Other This Prd. Total All Other Credit Points Awarded This Period.

Box 62—Mbr This Prd. Total Membership Points Awarded This Period.

Box 63—End Bal Annytd. Total Retirement Credit Points after This Period for Anniversary Year-to-Date.

Box 64—Total Sat Yrs. Total Satisfactory Years Credited for Retirement Purpose.

Box 65—Total Ret Pts. Career Total Retirement Credit Points.

SECTION O: REMARKS

Section O of the LES gives an itemized listing of entitlements, deductions, and payments, and also explanatory remarks concerning specific LES data.

Entitlements. The Marine will receive entitlements based on the information mentioned in the above sections, their marital status, and dependents. The type and amount of the entitlement will be listed at the top of this section, along with a total.

If there have been changes to either the type or the amount of the entitlement, this will be noted in this section, along with a note saying whether the entitlement was being stopped or started. For example, if a Marine is promoted, there will be an annotation stopping the amount of base pay under his old rank and another annotation starting the base pay of his current rank. These entitlements can include:

- Basic Pay
- Pro/Sep Rations
- Clothing Replacement Allowance
- BAH
- Other types of special pay

Deductions. This portion in section O gives an itemized listing of what was deducted from your entitlements. Again, there will be an annotation for starting and stopping amounts as necessary, such as when you start, stop, or change an allotment. If a Marine takes advanced pay, such as when he PCSes, the amount of the monthly will be noted here. These deductions can include:

- Allotments
- Bonds
- Medicare
- Serviceman Group Life Insurance (SGLI)
- Other special deductions based on the individual or government needs
- FITW (Fed Tax)
- Dental
- Social Security
- Medicare
- SGLI/TSGLI/Spouse SGLI
- USN/MC Retirement Home
- Checkages

Payments. This portion represents the last month's regular payments, which occurred on the first and the fifteenth.

Explanatory Remarks. This includes information that is not found on other parts of the LES, as well as information messages.

MARINE CORPS TOTAL FORCE LEAVE AND EARNINGS STATEMENT

A ID INFO	1 NAME (LAST, FIRST, MI)		2 SSN ********	3 RANK LCPL	4 SERV USMCR	5 PLT CODE UTIL	6 DATE PREP 20070401	7 PRD COVERED 1-31 MAR	8 PEBO 20060503	9 YRS 00	10 EAS	11 ECC	12 MCC DIST RUC S4L O1 00540

B FORECAST AMOUNTS	13 DATE	AMOUNT	14 DATE	AMOUNT	C SPLIT PAY	15 START DATE	16 AMOUNT	17 BALANCE	18 POE	D DIRECT DEPOSIT/EFT/ADDRESS FIRST NATIONAL BANK PO BOX 92055 CAMP PENDELTON 920550000

E			LEAVE INFORMATION					F		AVIATION PAY INFORMATION			
19 LV BF	20 EARNED	21 USES	22 EXCESS	23 BAL	24 MAX ACCRUAL	25 LOST	26 SOLD AS OF	27 CBT LV BAL	28 ASED	29 D/FOP TOTAL	30 PRIOR D/FOP START	31 PRIOR D/FOP STOP	32 OPFLY GATE INFORMATION
	0.0						7.5 20060729			YRS MO			

C		TAX INFORMATION				H RIGHTS OF MARINES INDEBTED TO THE GOVERNMENT YOU HAVE THE RIGHT TO

33 STATE TAX		34 FEDERAL TAX		25 FICA (SOCIAL SECURITY TAX)		
STATE CODE EXEMPTIONS WAGES THIS PRD WAGES YTD STATE TAX YTD	CT $00 $255.70 $897.93 $.18	EXEMPTIONS WAGES THIS PRD WAGES YTD MED TAX YTD	$01 $255.70 $897.93 $47.97	SSEC WAGES THIS PRD SSEC WAGES YTD SSEC TAX YTD MEDICARE WAGES THIS PRD MEDICARE WAGES YTD MEDICARE TAX YTD	$255.70 $897.93 $55.67 $255.70 $897.93 $13.02	- INSPECT AND COPY RECORDS PERTAINING TO DEBT - QUESTION VALIDITY OF A DEBT AND SUBMIT REFUTING EVIDENCE - NEGOTIATE A REPAYMENT SCHEDULE - REQUEST A WAIVER OF DEBT MORE INFORMATION ABOUT YOUR RIGHTS CAN BE OBTAINED FROM YOUR COMMANDER OFFICER VIA YOUR CHAIN OF COMMAND

I		ADDITIONAL BAH INFORMATION					J	CAREER SEA PAY		K	EDUCATION DEDUCTION	L	ADMIN INFO
36	37 BAH ZIP	38	39	40	41	42	43 DATE	TOTAL CAREER SEA SVC YRS MO DA	44 TYPE	45 MONTHLY AMT	46 TOTAL	47 PAY STATUS 77000	

M	RESERVE DRILL INFORMATION		N		RESERVE RETIREMENT INFORMATION					48 PAY GROUP 231	49 CRA DATE
52 REG FYTD	53 REG ANNYTD	54 REG FYTD	55 ADD	56 ADD FYTD	57 ADD ANNYTD	58 BF ANNYTD	59 ACDU THIS PRD	60 DRILL THIS PRD	61 OTHER THIS PRD	62 MBR THIS PRD	63 END BAL ANNYTD	64 TOTAL SAT YRD	65 TOTAL RET PTS	
0	020	027		000	000	036	05	000	0	00	042	01	00145	50 RESERVE ECC 20130801	51 DSSN 6102

66 AFADBD 00000000	67 DEAF 00000000	68 TSP TAX DEFERRED $ .00	69 TSP TAX EXEMPT $ .00

O REMARKS

BROUGHT FORWARD   .00   200 702 28

ENTITLEMENTS	RUC	AMT	DATES
BAH W/O DEPN	00540	13.57	20070305 - 20070305
BAH PARTIAL	00540	1.04	20070301 - 20070304
BAS (MONTHLY)	00540	46.65	20070301 - 20070305
BAH PARTIAL	00540	1.30	20070301 - 20070305
BASIC PAY	00540	255.70	20070301 - 20070305
TOTAL		318.26	

DEDUCTIONS	RUC	AMT	DATES
SGLI FULL TIME 400,000	00540	28.00	
FED TAX		13.95	
SOCIAL SECURITY		15.85	
MEDICARE		3.71	
STATE TAX		.10	
BAH PARTIAL	00540	1.30	20070301 - 20070305
RES FILL TIME TSGLI	99999	1.00	20070301
TOTAL	-	63.91	

PAYMENTS	AMT	DATE	VOU/PRNO	DSSN
PMTS - REGULAR	254.32	20070319	00087	6102
TOTAL	254.35			

CARRIED FORWARD   .00
REMEMBER TO FILE   YOUR FEDERAL AND STATE TAX RETURN ON TIME.
OUR NATION IS AT WAR - OUR CORPS IS AT WAR - FIGHTING A
DETERMINED ENEMY BENT ON TERROR AND DOMINATION.   NOW, MORE THAN
EVER, YOUR MARINE CORPS NEEDS YOU. MANY OF YOU HAVE ALREADY
SACRIFICED A GREAT DEAL - AND HAVE ALREADY SERVED YOUR COUNTRY
IN A COURAGEOUS AND HONORABLE MANNER. AMERICA AND YOUR CORPS
THANK YOU

DFASKC 7220139 (REV 1-04)   www.dfas.mil   EFT INFO-DFAS-KC 1-800-594-8302

World Time

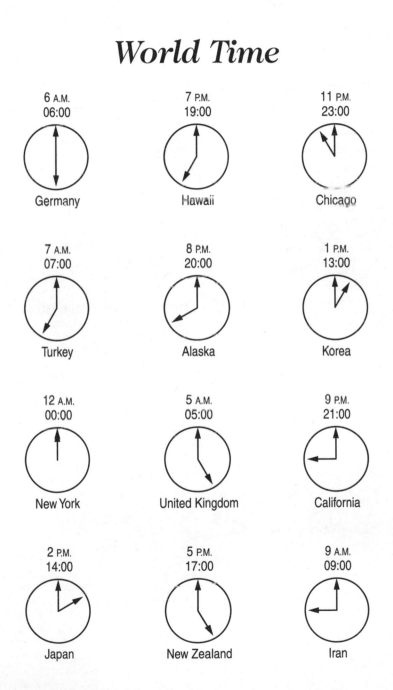

6 A.M. 06:00	7 P.M. 19:00	11 P.M. 23:00
Germany	Hawaii	Chicago

7 A.M. 07:00	8 P.M. 20:00	1 P.M. 13:00
Turkey	Alaska	Korea

12 A.M. 00:00	5 A.M. 05:00	9 P.M. 21:00
New York	United Kingdom	California

2 P.M. 14:00	5 P.M. 17:00	9 A.M. 09:00
Japan	New Zealand	Iran

Appendix E

Fisher House Locations

CALIFORNIA
Zachary & Elizabeth M. Fisher House
David Grant USAF Medical Center
100 Bodin Circle
Travis Air Force Base, California 94535
Manager: Charlene Hall
Tel: (707) 423-7550; Fax: (707) 423-7552
E-mail: charlene.hall@travis.af.mil
Affiliation: Air Force
Number of houses at this location: 1

Zachary & Elizabeth M. Fisher House
San Diego Naval Medical Center
34800 Bob Wilson Drive
Building 46
San Diego, California 92314-5000
Manager: Belle Esposito
Tel: (619) 532-9055; Fax: (619) 532-5216
E-mail: belle.esposito@med.navy.mil
Affiliation: Navy
Number of houses at this location: 1

Zachary & Elizabeth M. Fisher House
Palo Alto VA Health Care System
3801 Miranda Drive
Palo Alto, California 94304
Tel: (650) 493-5000, ext. 63967; Fax:
Affiliation: VA
Number of houses at this location: 1

COLORADO
Zachary & Elizabeth M. Fisher House
Denver VA Medical Center
1055 Clermont Street
Denver, Colorado 80220-3873
Manager: Jann Griffiths
Tel: (303) 364-4616; Fax: (303) 393-4679
E-mail: jann.griffiths@med.va.gov
Affiliation: VA
Number of houses at this location: 1

DISTRICT OF COLUMBIA
Fisher Houses I, II, & III
Walter Reed Army Medical Center
6900 Georgia Avenue, N.W.
Building 56
Washington, D.C. 20307-5001
Manager: Kate Deyermond
Tel: (202) 545-3218; Fax: (202) 545-3202
E-mail: kate.deyermond@us.army.mil
Affiliation: Army
Number of houses at this location: 3

FLORIDA
Zachary & Elizabeth M. Fisher House
Bay Pines VA Medical Center
10000 Bay Pines Boulevard
Bay Pines, Florida 33744
Manager: Richard Kippings
Tel: (727) 319-1350; Fax: (727) 319-1106
E-mail: richard.kippings2@va.gov
Affiliation: VA
Number of houses at this location: 1

Zachary & Elizabeth M. Fisher House
West Palm Beach VA Medical Center
7305 N. Military Trail
Route 136
West Palm Beach, Florida 33410
Manager: Theresa Ringel
Tel: (561) 442-5554; Fax: (561) 422-8793
E-mail: theresa.ringel@va.gov
Affiliation: VA
Number of houses at this location: 1

Zachary & Elizabeth M. Fisher House
James A. Haley VA Medical Center
13000 Bruce B. Downs Boulevard
Tampa, Florida 33612
Manager: Paula Welenc
Tel: (813) 910-3000; Fax: (813) 910-3088
E-mail: paula.welenc@va.gov
Affiliation: VA
Number of houses at this location: 1

GEORGIA

Zachary & Elizabeth M. Fisher House
Dwight David Eisenhower Army Medical
    Center
Fisher House Road
Building 280
Fort Gordon, Georgia 30905
Manager: Francisco Cruz
Tel: (706) 787-7100; Fax: (706) 787-5106
E-mail: francisco.cruz@amedd.army.mil
Affiliation: Army
Number of houses at this location: 1

HAWAII

Fisher Houses I & II
Tripler Army Medical Center
315 Krukowski Road
Honolulu, Hawaii 96819
Manager: Theresa Johnson
Tel: (808) 433-1291, ext. 28;
    Fax: (808) 433-3619
E-mail: theresa.johnson@amedd.army.mil
Affiliation: Army
Number of houses at this location: 2

KENTUCKY

Zachary & Elizabeth M. Fisher House
Blanchfield Army Community Hospital
652 Joel Drive
Fort Campbell, Kentucky 42223
Manager: Vivian Wilson
Tel: (270) 798-8330; Fax: (270) 798-8804
E-mail: vivian.wilson@amedd.army.mil
Affiliation: Army
Number of houses at this location: 1

MARYLAND

Zachary & Elizabeth M. Fisher House
Malcolm Grow Medical Center
1076 West Perimeter Road
Andrews Air Force Base, Maryland 20762
Manager: Janet Grampp
Tel: (301) 981-1243; Fax: (301) 981-7629
E-mail: janet.grampp@andrews.af.mil
Affiliation: Air Force
Number of houses at this location: 1

Fisher Houses I & II
National Naval Medical Center
24 Stokes Road
Bethesda, Maryland 20814-5002
Manager: Becky Wood
Tel: (301) 295-5078; Fax: (301) 295-5632
E-mail: bwood@mwrbethesda.com
Affiliation: Navy
Number of houses at this location: 2

MINNESOTA

Zachary & Elizabeth M. Fisher House
Minneapolis VA Medical Center
One Veterans Drive
Minneapolis, Minnesota 55417
Manager: Maggie Swenson
Tel: (612) 467-2157; Fax: (612) 970-5864
E-mail: margaret.swenson@med.va.gov
Affiliation: VA
Number of houses at this location: 1

MISSISSIPPI
Zachary & Elizabeth M. Fisher House
Keesler Medical Center
509 Fisher Street
Keesler Air Force Base, Mississippi
  39534-2599
Manager: Larry Vetter
Tel: (228) 377-8264; Fax: (228) 377-7691
E-mail: larry.vetter@keesler.af.mil
Affiliation: Air Force
Number of houses at this location: 1

NEW YORK
Zachary & Elizabeth M. Fisher House
Stratton VA Medical Center
113 Holland Avenue
Albany, New York 12208
Manager: Jerry Jensen
Tel: (518) 626-6919; Fax: (518) 626-5452
E-mail: fisherny@aol.com
Affiliation: VA
Number of houses at this location: 1

NORTH CAROLINA
Zachary & Elizabeth M. Fisher House
Womack Army Medical Center
12 Bassett Street
Fort Bragg, North Carolina 28307-5000
Manager: Paula Gallero
Tel: (910) 432-1486; Fax: (910) 432-3825
E-mail: fhwamc@aol.com
Affiliation: Army
Number of houses at this location: 1

OHIO
Zachary & Elizabeth M. Fisher House
Cincinnati VA Medical Center
3200 Vine Street
Cincinnati, Ohio 45220
Manager: Karrie Hagan
Tel: (513) 475-6571; Fax: (513) 487-6661
E-mail: karrie.hagan@med.va.gov
Affiliation: VA
Number of houses at this location: 1

Fisher Houses I & II
Wright-Patterson Medical Center
415 Schlatter Drive
Wright-Patterson Air Force Base, Ohio
  45433
Manager: Karen Healea
Tel: (937) 257-0855; Fax: (937) 656-2150
E-mail: karen.healea@wpafb.af.mil
Affiliation: Air Force
Number of houses at this location: 2

TEXAS
Fisher Houses I & II
Brooke Army Medical Center
3623 George C. Beach Drive
Fort Sam Houston, Texas 78234
Manager: Inge Godfrey
Tel: (210) 916-6000, ext. 1;
  Fax: (210) 916-6488
E-mail: fhbamc@aol.com
Affiliation: Army
Number of houses at this location: 4

Zachary & Elizabeth M. Fisher House
Darnall Army Community Hospital
36000 Darnall Loop
Fort Hood, Texas 76544
Manager: Isaac Howard
Tel: (254) 286-7927; Fax: (254) 286-7929
E-mail: issac.howard@amedd.army.mil
Affiliation: Army
Number of houses at this location: 1

Zachary & Elizabeth M. Fisher House
Michael E. DeBakey VA Medical Center
2002 Holcombe Boulevard
Houston, Texas 77030
Manager: Frank Kelley
Tel: (713) 794-8095; Fax: (713) 794-7971
E-mail: frank.kelley@va.gov
Affiliation: VA
Number of houses at this location: 1

Fisher Houses I, II, & III
Wilford Hall Medical Center
1445 Foster Avenue
Lackland Air Force Base, Texas 78236
Manager: Paula Lewis
Tel: (210) 671-6037; Fax: (210) 292-3031
E-mail: plewis-fisherhouse@satx.rr.com
Affiliation: Air Force
Number of houses at this location: 3

Zachary & Elizabeth M. Fisher House
Wiliam Beaumont Army Medical Center
5005 North Piedras Street
El Paso, Texas 79920-5001
Manager: Harry Hicks
Tel: (915) 569-1860; Fax: (915) 569-1862
E-mail: fhwbamc@aol.com
Affiliation: Army
Number of houses at this location: 1

VIRGINIA
Zachary & Elizabeth M. Fisher House
Portsmouth Naval Medical Center
853 Fisher Drive
Building 287
Portsmouth, Virginia 23708
Manager: Loretta Loveless
Tel: (757) 953-6889; Fax: (757) 953-7174
E-mail: fishrhouse@msn.com
Affiliation: Navy
Number of houses at this location: 1

WASHINGTON
Zachary & Elizabeth M. Fisher House
Madigan Army Medical Center
9999 Wilson Avenue
Fort Lewis, Washington 98433
Manager: Jodi Land
Tel: (253) 964-9283; Fax: (253) 968-3619
E-mail: jodi.land@nw.amedd.army.mil
Affiliation: Army
Number of houses at this location: 1

EUROPE
Fisher Houses I & II
Landstuhl Regional Medical Center
CMR 402, Box 669
APO, AE 09180
Manager: Kathy Gregory
Tel: (011) 49-6371 6183311;
    Fax: (011) 49-6371-866679
E-mail: mary.gregory@lnd.amedd.army.mil
Affiliation: Army
Number of houses at this location: 2

Appendix F

Metric Conversion Charts

Overseas, you'll find things measured in meters, liters, and grams, and temperatures quoted on the Celsius scale. Here are some conversions.

TEMPERATURE

To convert Fahrenheit temperatures into Celsius:
1. Subtract 32 from the Fahrenheit number.
2. Divide the answer by 9.
3. Multiply by 5.

To convert Celsius temperatures into Fahrenheit:
1. Multiply the Celsius temperature by 9.
2. Divide the answer by 5.
3. Add 32.

Common Temperatures

5° F = –15° C	61° F = 16° C
10° F = –12° C	66° F = 19° C
16° F = –9° C	70° F = 21° C
24° F = –6° C	75° F = 24° C
25° F = –4° C	81° F = 27° C
30° F = –1° C	86° F = 30° C
32° F = –0° C	90° F = 32° C
36° F = 2° C	95° F = 35° C
41° F = 5° C	99° F = 37° C
5° F = –15° C	100° F = 38° C
46° F = 8° C	106° F = 41° C
50° F = 10° C	111° F = 44° C

Oven Temperatures

Fahrenheit	Celsius	Description
300	150	Slow
325	160	Moderately slow
350	175	Moderate
375	190	Moderately hot
400	205	Hot
425	220	Very hot
450	230	Very hot
475	245	Extremely hot

WEIGHT

To convert Ounces to Grams, multiply by 28.35
To convert Grams to Ounces, multiply by 0.035
To convert Pounds to Kilograms, multiply by 0.45
To convert Kilograms to Pounds, multiply by 2.21

Common Weights

½ oz.	=	15 g
1 oz.	=	30 g
1 lb.	=	455 g
1 lb., ½ oz.	=	500 g
2 lbs., 3 oz.	=	1 kg

Cooking Equivalents

U.S. Measure	British Measure	U.S. Fluid Ounces	Metric
Teaspoon	Teaspoon		5 ml
Tablespoon	½ oz.	½ oz.	15 ml
¼ cup	2 oz.	2 oz.	59 ml
⅓ cup	Coffee cup	2⅔ oz.	79 ml
½ cup	⅕ pint	4 oz.	118 ml
1 cup	Breakfast cup	8 oz.	237 ml
1 pint	About ⅘ pint	16 oz.	473 ml
1 quart	33⅓ oz.	32 oz.	946 ml
½ gallon	66⅔ oz.	64 oz.	1.89 l
1 gallon	133 oz.	128 oz.	3.78 l

CAN SIZES

Can Size	Equivalent Weights
No. 300	14–16 oz.
No. 303	16–17 oz.
No. 2	20 oz.
No. 2½	29 oz.
No. 3	46 oz.

VOLUME

When You Know	Multiply By	To Get
teaspoons (tsp.)	5	milliliters
tablespoons (tbsp)	15	milliliters
fluid ounces (fl oz)	30	milliliters
ounces (oz)	28	grams
cups (c)	0.24	liters (l)
pints US	0.47	liters (l)
pints Imperial	.568	liters (l)
quarts US	0.95	liters (l)
quarts Imperial	1.137	liters (l)
gallons US (gal)	3.8	liters (l)
milliliters	0.034	fluid ounce (fl oz)
liters	2.1	pints US
liters	1.76	pints Imperial
liters	1.06	quarts US
liters	0.88	quarts Imperial
liters	0.26	gallons US
liters	0.22	gallons Imperial
gallons Imperial (gal)	4.546	fluid ounce (fl oz)
pounds	0.45	kilograms (kg)
cubic feet (ft.^{3})	0.03	cubic meters (m^3)
cubic yards (yd.^{3})	0.76	cubic meters (m^3)
grams	0.035	ounces

LENGTH

When You Know	Multiply By	To Get
inches (in)	25	millimeters (mm)
feet (ft)	30	centimeters (cm)
yards (yd)	0.9	meters (m)
miles (mi)	1.6	kilometers (km)
millimeters (mm)	0.04	inches (in)
centimeters (cm)	0.393	inches (in)
meters (m)	1.1	yards (yd)
meters (m)	3.3	feet (ft)
kilometers (km)	0.6	miles (mi)

AREA

When You Know	Multiply By	To Get
square inches (in.^{2})	6.5	square centimeters (cm^2)
square feet (ft.^{2})	0.09	square meters (m^2)
square yards (yd.^{2})	0.8	square meters (m^2)
square miles (mi.^{2})	2.6	square kilometers (km^2)
acres	0.4	hectares (ha)

INTERNET RESOURCES

http://www.worldwidemetric.com/metcal.htm. Metric conversion calculator.

Appendix G

Military Time

Military time utilizes the twenty-four-hour clock. This is done because each of the twenty-four hours in a day is identified with a unique two-digit number. A.M. and P.M. time is less clear, hence not used.

During operations, servicemembers need to coordinate with people in other time zones. The location of Greenwich, England, is used as a common reference, and it's called Greenwich Mean Time (GMT). U.S. military personnel refer to this time zone as "Zulu Time" and attach a "Z" suffix. For example, a message might say, "The ship will arrive at 1300Z." This means 1:00 P.M. in Greenwich, England. They call it "Zulu Time" because the world is divided into 24 time zones, with an alphabet letter assigned to each time zone for easy reference. The time zone letter for Greenwich, England is "Z." The military phonetic alphabet for the letter "Z" is "Zulu."

Local time is employed for daily use. "Report for PT at 0600" means be ready to run at 6:00 A.M. ("Zero dark thirty" is a joke referring to Physical Training time.) Daylight Savings Time is observed if the state or country uses it.

Following are A.M./P.M. standard times and their corresponding military times. Note that 1300 through 2300 are converted to standard time by subtracting 2, and then either dropping the first digit or changing it from a 2 to a 1. Both time systems treat minutes the same. For instance, 5:15 P.M. is 1715; 11:30 P.M. is 2330.

Time	Military	Time	Military
Midnight	0:00	Noon	12:00
1 A.M.	1:00	1:00 P.M.	13:00
2 A.M.	2:00	2:00 P.M.	14:00
3 A.M.	3:00	3:00 P.M.	15:00
4 A.M.	4:00	4:00 P.M.	16:00
5 A.M.	5:00	5:00 P.M.	17:00
6 A.M.	6:00	6:00 P.M.	18:00
7 A.M.	7:00	7:00 P.M.	19:00
8 A.M.	8:00	8:00 P.M.	20:00
9 A.M.	9:00	9:00 P.M.	21:00
10 A.M.	10:00	10:00 P.M.	22:00
11 A.M.	11:00	11:00 P.M.	23:00

The Phonetic Alphabet

The phonetic alphabet is an internationally adopted list of words used to identify letters in radio- or phone-transmitted messages. It was introduced in 1913, and its current version was adopted in 1957. The phonetic alphabet's purpose is to make messages easier to understand by substituting words from a recognized list for letters. For example, the word "Navy" is "November Alfa Victor Yankee" when spelled in the phonetic alphabet. This helps to solve the problem of messages being unclear due to some letters sounding alike (e.g., "m" and "n") or to poor reception.

Letter	Word	Letter	Word
A	Alfa	N	November
B	Bravo	O	Oscar
C	Charlie	P	Papa
D	Delta	Q	Quebec
E	Echo	R	Romeo
F	Foxtrot	S	Sierra
G	Golf	T	Tango
H	Hotel	U	Uniform
I	India	V	Victor
J	Juliet	W	Whiskey
K	Kilo	X	X-ray
L	Lima	Y	Yankee
M	Mike	Z	Zulu

Appendix I

Space-A Locations and Contacts

Location	Phone Number	Fax	Flight Info Recording
Altus AFB OK	DSN: 866-6428 Commercial: (580) 481-6428		DSN: 866-5333 Commercial: (580) 481-5333
Andersen AFB, Guam	DSN: 315-366-5135 or 5165/Commercial: (671) 366-5165/5135	DSN: 315-366-3984 Commercial: (671) 366-3984	DSN: 315-366-2095 Commercial: (671) 366-2095
Andrews AFB MD	DSN: 858-1854 Commercial: (301) 981-1854	DSN: 858-4241 Commercial: (301) 981-4241	DSN: 858-5851 or 3527 Commercial: (301) 981-5851 or 3527
(NAS) Atlanta GA	DSN: 625-6359 Commercial: (678) 655-6359		
Aviano AB, Italy	DSN: 314-632-7680/7520 Commercial: 39-434-66-7680	DSN: 314-632-7782 Commercial: 39-434-66-7782	
Baltimore-Washington IAP MD	DSN: 243-6900/Commercial: (410) 918-6900 (1-877-429-4262)	DSN: 243-6932 Commercial: (410) 918-6932	DSN: 243-6900 Commercial: 410-918-6900
(NAS) Brunswick ME	DSN: 476-2682 Commercial: (207) 921-2682		DSN: 476-2689 Commercial: (207) 921-2689
Ben Gurion IAP, Israel	Commercial only: (972) 3-935-4333	Commercial: (972) 3-935-8697	
Cairo East AB, Egypt (See Note)	DSN: 725-1456 ext. 3212 Commercial: 20-2-797-3212	Commercial: 20-2-797-1290	
Charleston AFB SC	DSN: 673-3083/3048 Commercial: (843) 963-3083/3048	DSN: 673-3060 Commercial: (843) 963-3060	DSN: 673-3082 Commercial: (843) 963-3082
(NAS) Corpus Christi TX	DSN: 861-2505 Commercial: (361) 961-2505		DSN: 861-3385 Commercial: (361) 961-3385
Davis-Monthan AFB AZ	DSN: 228-2322 Commercial: (520) 228-2322	DSN: 228-7229 Commercial: (520) 228-7229	DSN: 228-2322 Commercial: (520) 228-2322

Location	Phone Number	Fax	Flight Info Recording
Diego Garcia	DSN: 315-370-2745/2795 Commercial: 246-370-2745/2795	DSN: 315-370-2787 Commercial: 246-370-2787	
Dobbins ARB GA	DSN: 625-4903 Commercial: (678) 655-4903	DSN: 625-6155 Commercial: (678) 655-6155	
Dover AFB DE	DSN: 445-4088 Commercial: (302) 677-4088	DSN: 445-2953 Commercial: (302) 677-2953	DSN: 445-2854 Commercial: (302) 677-2854
Eielson AFB AK	DSN: 317-377-1854 Commercial: (907) 377-1854	DSN: 317-377-2287 Commercial: (907) 377-2287	DSN: 317-377-1623 Commercial: (907) 377-1623
Elmendorf AFB AK	DSN: 317-552-8588/4616 Commercial: (907) 552-8588/4616	DSN: 317-552-3996 Commercial: (907) 552-3996	DSN: 317-552-8588 Commercial: (907) 552-8588
Fairchild AFB WA	DSN: 657-3406 Commercial: (509) 247-5435	DSN: 657-3399 Commercial: (509) 247-3399	DSN: 657-3406 Commercial: (509) 247-3406
F. E. Warren WY	1-800-832-1959 (Option 7)		
Forbes Field ANG, KS	DSN: 720-4210 Commercial: (785) 861-4210	DSN: 720-4555 Commercial: (785) 861-4555	DSN: 720-4210 Commercial: (785) 861-4210
(JRB) Fort Worth TX	DSN: 739-5677 Commercial: (817) 782-5677		DSN: 739-6289 Commercial: (817) 782-6289
Grand Forks AFB ND	DSN: 362-7105 Commercial: (701) 747-7105	DSN: 362-3448 Commercial: (701) 747-3448	DSN: 362-7105 Commercial: (701) 747-7105
NAS Guantanamo Bay, Cuba	DSN: 660-6408/6397 Commercial: 011-53-99-6408/6397	DSN: 660-6170 Commercial: 011-53-99-6170	
Hickam AFB HI	DSN: 449-1515 Commercial: (808) 449-1515	DSN: 448-1503 Commercial: (808) 448-1503	DSN: 449-1515 Commercial: (808) 449-1515
Hill AFB UT	DSN: 777-3089/2887 Commercial: (801) 777-3089/2887	DSN: 775-2677 Commercial: (801) 775-2677	DSN: 777-1854 Commercial: (801) 777-1854
Holloman AFB NM	DSN: 572-3150 Commercial: (505) 572-3150		
Homestead ARB FL	DSN: 791-7518 Commercial: (305) 224-7518		
Incirlik AB, Turkey	DSN: 314-676-6424/6425 Commercial: 90-322-216-6424 or 6425	DSN: 314-676-3420 Commercial: 90-322-216-3420	
MCAS Iwakuni Japan	DSN: 315-253-5509 Commercial: 81-6117-53-5509	DSN: 315-253-3301 Commercial: 81-6117-53-33	DSN: 315-253-1854 Commercial: 81-6117-53-1854

Location	Phone Number	Fax	Flight Info Recording
Jackson IAP MS (Thompson Field)	DSN: 828-8761 Commercial: 601-936-8761	DSN: 828-8698 Commercial: 601-936-8698	DSN: 828-8761 Commercial: 601-936-8761
(NAS) Jacksonville FL	DSN: 942-3825 Commercial: (904) 542-3956/3825	DSN: 942-3257 Commercial: (904) 542-3257	DSN: 942-3956 Commercial: (904) 542-3956
Kadena AB, Japan	DSN: 315-634-2159 Commercial: 011-81-6117-34-2159	DSN: 315-634-4221 Commercial: 011-81-6117-34-4221	
Keesler AFB MS	DSN: 597-2120/2123 Commercial: (228) 377-2120/2123	DSN: 597-2488 Commercial: (228) 377-2488	DSN: 597-4538 Commercial: (228) 377-4538
Keflavik, Iceland	DSN: 450-6139 Commercial: 354-228-6139	Commercial: 354-228-4649	
Kelly Annex, Lackland AFB TX	DSN: 945-8715 Commercial: (210) 925-8715	DSN: 945-2732 Commercial: (210) 925-2732	DSN: 945-8714 Commercial: (210) 925-8714
Kirtland AFB NM	DSN: 246-7000 Commercial: (505) 846-7000		DSN: 246-6184 Commercial: (505) 846-6184
Kunsan AB, Korea	DSN: 315-782-4666/ 5403 Commercial: 82-63-470-4666/5403	DSN: 315-782-7550 Commercial: 82-63-470-7550	
Lajes AB, Azores	DSN: 535-3227/Commercial: 351-295-57-3227	351-295-57-5110	
Langley AFB VA	DSN: 574-3531 Commercial: (757) 764-3531	DSN: 574-3722 Commercial: (757) 764-3722	DSN: 574-5807 Commercial: (757) 764-5807
Little Rock AFB AR	DSN: 731-3342 Commercial: (501) 987-3342	DSN: 731-6726 Commercial: (501) 987-6726	DSN: 731-3684 Commercial: (501) 987-3684
(NAS) Lemoore CA	DSN: 949-1680 Commercial: (559) 998-1680		
MacDill AFB FL	DSN: 968-2440/2485 Commercial: 813-828-2440/2485	DSN: 968-7844 Commercial: (813) 828-7844	DSN: 968-2310 Commercial: (813) 828-2310
McChord AFB WA	DSN: 382-7259 Commercial: (253) 982-7259	DSN: 382-6815 Commercial: (253) 982-6815	DSN: 382-7268 Commercial: (253) 982-7268
McConnell AFB KS	DSN: 743-4810 Commercial: 316-759-4810	DSN: 743-1032 Commercial: (316) 759-1032	DSN: 743-5404 Commercial: (316) 759-5404
McGuire AFB NJ	DSN: 650-5023/2864/2749 Commercial: (609) 754-5023 or 2864	DSN: 650-4621 Commercial: (609) 754-4621	800-569-8284, then dial 754-9950
March ARB CA	DSN: 447-2397 Commercial: (951) 655-2397		DSN: 447-2913 Commercial: (951) 655-2913

Location	Phone Number	Fax	Flight Info Recording
Maxwell AFB AL	DSN: 493-7372 Commercial: (334) 953-7372	DSN: 493-6114 Commercial: (334) 953-6114	DSN: 493-6760 Commercial: (334) 953-6760
RAF Mildenhall, United Kingdom	DSN: 238-2248/ 2526 Commercial: 44-1638-54-2248 or 2526	DSN: 238-2250 Commercial: 44-1638-54-2250	
(NAS) Miramar CA	DSN: 267-4283 Commercial: (858) 577-4283		
Misawa AB, Japan	DSN: 315-226-2370/2371 Commercial: 011-81-3117-66-2370/2371	DSN: 315-226-4455 Commercial: 011-81-3117-66-4455	DSN: 315-226-2852 Commercial: 011-81-3117-66-2852 (after 7 P.M. local time)
Naples, Italy (Capodichino Airport)	DSN: 314-626 5247/5283 Commercial: 39-081-568-5247/5283	DSN: 314-626-5259/5499 Commercial: 39-081-568-5259/5499	
Nellis AFB NV	DSN: 682-2562 Commercial: (702) 652-2562	DSN: 682-2561 Commercial: (702) 652-2561	
Naval Station Norfolk VA	DSN: 564-4148 Commercial: (757) 444-4148	DSN: 565-7501 Commercial: (757) 445-7501	DSN: 564-4118 Commercial: (757) 444-4118
(NAS) North Island CA	DSN: 735-9567 Commercial: (619) 545-9567	DSN: 735-9532 Commercial: (619) 545-9532	DSN: 735-8273/8278 Commercial: (619) 545-8273/8278
Offutt AFB NE	DSN: 271-8510 Commercial: (402) 294-8510		DSN: 271-7111 Commercial: (402) 294-7111
Osan AB, Korea	DSN: 784-1854 Commercial: 011- 82-31-661-1854	DSN: 784-4897 Commercial: 011-82-31-661-4897	DSN: 784-1854 Commercial: 011-82-31-661-1854
Patrick AFB FL	DSN: 854-5631 Commercial: (321) 494-5631	(321) 494-7991	
Pease ANGB NH	DSN: 852-3323 Commercial: (603) 430-3323	DSN: 852-3335 Commercial: (603) 430-3335	
(NAS) Pensacola FL	DSN: 922-3311 Commercial: (850) 452-3311		DSN: 922-3311 Commercial: (850) 452-3311
Peterson AFB CO	DSN: 834-4521 Commercial: (719) 556-4521	DSN: 834-4979 Commercial: (719) 556-4979	DSN: 834-4707 Commercial: (719) 556-4707
(NAS) Point Mugu CA	DSN: 351-7731/7026 Commercial: (805) 989-7731/7206	DSN: 351-8540 Commercial: (805) 989-8540	
Pope AFB NC	DSN: 424-6527/6528 Commercial: (910) 394-6527/6528	DSN: 424-6526 Commercial: (910) 394-6526	DSN: 424-6525 Commercial: (910) 394-6525
Ramstein AB, Germany	DSN: 479-4440/4299 Commercial: 011-49-6371-47-4440-4299	DSN: 480-2364 Commercial: 011-49-6371-47-2364	

Location	Phone Number	Fax	Flight Info Recording
Randolph AFB TX	DSN: 487-3725 Commercial: (210) 652-3725	DSN: 487-5718 Commercial: (210) 652-5718	DSN: 487-1854 Commercial: (210) 652-1854
Robins AFB GA	DSN: 468-3166 Commercial: (478) 926-3166	DSN: 468-5835 Commercial: (478) 926-5835	DSN: 468-4446 Commercial: (478) 926-4446
(NAS) Rota, Spain	DSN: 727-2411/ 2171 Commercial: 34-956-822411 or 34-956-822171	DSN: 727-1734 Commercial: 34-956-821734	
Scott AFB IL	DSN: 576-2014/3017 Commercial: (618) 256-2014/3017	DSN: 576-1946 Commercial: (618) 256-1946	DSN: 576-1854 Commercial: (618) 256-1854
Sigonella Airport, Sicily	DSN: 314-624-5576 Commercial: 39-95-86-5576	39-95-86-6729	
Souda Bay, Crete	DSN: 314-266-1275/ 1383 Commercial: 30-2-821-02-1275/1383	DSN: 314-266-1525 Commercial: 30-2-821-02-1525	DSN: 314-266-1387 Commercial: 30-2-821-02-1387
Spangdahlem AB, Germany	DSN: 314-452-8866/8867 Commercial: 49-6565-61-8866/8867	DSN: 314-452-8665 Commercial: 49-6565-61-8665	DSN: 314-452-8860 Commercial: 49-6565-61-8860
Stewart ANG NY	DSN: 636-2226 Commercial: (914) 563-2226	DSN: 636-2228 Commercial: (914) 563-2228	
Tinker AFB OK	DSN: 339-4339 Commercial: (405) 739-4339	DSN: 339-3826 Commercial: (405) 739-3826	DSN: 339-4360 Commercial: (405) 739-4360
Travis AFB CA	DSN: 837-5770 Commercial: (707) 424-5770	DSN: 837-2048 Commercial: (707) 424-2048	DSN: 837-1854/5770 Commercial: (707) 424-1854/5770
Westover ARB MA	DSN: 589-3453/2622 Commercial: (413) 557-3453/2622	DSN: 589-3147 Commercial: (413) 557-3147	DSN: 589-2589 Commercial: (413) 557-2589
Willow Grove JRB, PA	DSN: 991-6217 Commercial: (215) 443-6217		DSN: 991-6216 Commercial: (215) 443-6216 or (1-866-608-2976)
Wright-Patterson AFB OH	DSN: 787-7741 Commercial: (937) 257-7741/8549	DSN: 986-1580 Commercial: (937) 656-1580	DSN: 787-6235 Commercial: (937) 257-6235
Yokota AB, Japan	DSN: 315-225-5661/ 5662 Commercial: 81-3117-55-5661	DSN: 315-225-9768 Commercial: 81-3117-55-9768	DSN: 315-225-7111 Commercial: 81-3117-55-7111

Note: To arrive at Cairo East, individuals must have a sponsor stationed in Egypt to escort them off base. To depart Cairo East, individuals must request a base access letter from the Office of Military Cooperation at the U.S. Embassy at least five days prior to intended departure.

Appendix J

Tricare Supplemental Insurance

Many military associations and private companies offer supplemental insurance policies. A supplemental policy pays after Tricare pays its portion of the bill. It reimburses the holder for what Tricare didn't pay.

Each supplemental insurance plan has its own rules for eligibility, preexisting conditions, cost-shares, deductibles, and what it covers (e.g., pregnancy, well-baby care, long-term disability care). You need to understand what, exactly, your Tricare plan pays; for instance, people who subscribe to Standard and Extra will have more out-of-pocket expenses than people who subscribe to Tricare Prime. Prime subscribers may find that a supplemental policy costs more than the benefits it provides.

Policies are offered by most military associations and by some private companies.

Before committing to a policy ask:

1. What services are covered?
2. Does the supplement pay for services not covered by Tricare?
3. How much does the premium cost? Are there deductibles and cost-shares?
4. Do active-duty, retired, and family members pay different premium rates?
5. Will the premiums increase?
6. Is there an annual or yearly maximum limit on benefits?
7. Is there a preexisting condition clause? If so, how long is the waiting period?
8. Does the supplement cover Tricare enrollment fees and copayments?
9. Will the policy convert to a Medicare supplement?
10. Does the policy cover inpatient, outpatient, long-term, and overseas care?
11. How do I file a claim? What is the time limit?
12. Does the plan have higher rates for smokers and the overweight?
13. Does the plan cover college students who live in a different part of the country?

Here are some organizations that offer supplemental policies.

Air Force Association: *www.afa.org*

Air Force Sergeants Association: *www.afsahq.org*

The American Legion: *www.legion.org*

American Military Retirees Association: *www.amra1973.org*
Armed Forces Benefit Association: *www.afba.com*
Armed Services Mutual Benefit Association: *www.asmba.com*
Army Aviation Association of America: *www.quad-a.org*
Association of the U.S. Army: *www.ausa.org*
Chief Warrant and Warrant Officers Association: *www.cwoauscg.org*
Fleet Reserve Association: *www.fra.org*
Marine Corps Association: *www.mca-marines.org*
Marine Corps League: *www.mcleague.org*
Military Benefit Association: *www.militarybenefit.org*
The Military Officers Association of America: *www.moaa.org*
Military Order of the Purple Heart: *www.purpleheart.org*
National Association for Uniformed Services: *www.naus.org*
National Defense Transportation Association: *www.ndtahq.com*
Naval Enlisted Reserve Association: *www.nera.org*
Naval Reserve Association: *www.navy-reserve.org*
Navy League of the United States: *www.navyleague.org*
Pentagon Federal Financial Services: *www.pentagonfcu.orgpfiscpfisc.htm*
Reserve Officers Association: *www.roa.org*
Retired Association for Uniformed Services: *www.raushome.com*
The Retired Enlisted Association: *www.trea.org*
Society for Military Widows: *www.militarywidows.org*
The Uniformed Services Benefit Association: *www.usba.com*
USAA Life Insurance Co.: *www.usaa.com*
U.S. Army Warrant Officers Association: *www.penfed.orgusawoaindex.html*
U.S. Coast Guard Chief Petty Officers Association: *www.uscgcpoa.org*
U.S. Naval Institute: *www.usni.org*

Appendix K

Vehicle Processing Centers (VPC)—CONUS and OCONUS

Ask your local transportation office which VPC to ship your car from.

CONUS
Operating Hours for POV processing: 8:00 A.M.–4:00 P.M. Monday–Friday. Closed on federal holidays. Hours of operation are strictly enforced. VPCs are not open on weekends or holidays, so plan your trip accordingly.

Atlanta, GA VPC
2579 Campbell Boulevard
Ellenwood, GA 30294
Tel: 404-363-4449/3753
Fax: 404-363-1858
Toll Free: 800-965-9155

Baltimore, MD VPC
2501 Broening Highway
Baltimore, MD 21224
Tel: 410-631-5751
Fax: 410-631-5756
Toll Free: 800-631-5751

Charleston, SC VPC
1510 Meeting Street Road
Charleston, SC 29405
Tel: 843-805-6667
Fax: 843-805-6671
Toll Free: 800-747-9223

Dallas, TX VPC
500 North Stemmons Freeway
Lake Dallas, TX 75065
Tel: 940-497-1036
Fax: 940-497-1076
Toll Free: 866-438-2046

Los Angeles, CA VPC
23803 South Wilmington Avenue
Carson, CA 90745
Tel: 310-549-8277
Fax: 310-549-7438
Toll Free: 800-887-3344

NY/NJ Metro VPC
260 Meadow Road
Edison, NJ 08817
Tel: 732-339-0591
Fax: 732-339-0595
Toll Free: 877-269-3702

New Orleans, LA VPC
5481 Crowder Boulevard
New Orleans, LA 70127
Tel: 504-246-2102/0770
Fax: 504-246-2111
Toll Free: 800-721-9632

Orlando, FL VPC
1934 McCoy Road
Orlando, FL 32822
Tel: 407-854-8771/8772
Fax: 407-854-8774
Toll Free: -800-758-5998

Portsmouth, VA VPC
3015 Airline Boulevard
Portsmouth, VA 23701
Tel: 757-465-4127
Fax: 757-465-3970
Toll Free: 800-810-7480

Richmond, CA VPC
1200 Wright Avenue
Richmond, CA 94804
Tel: 510-231-6831
Fax: 510-237-4046
Toll Free: 800-704-2444

San Diego VPC
4334 Sheridan Lane
San Diego, CA 92120
Tel: 619-563-6321
Fax: 619-563-6320
Toll Free: 877-344-8972

Seattle, WA VPC
2302 Ross Way
Tacoma, WA 98421
Tel: 253-272-1712
Fax: 253-272-2375
Toll Free: 800-597-1833

St. Louis, MO VPC
4236 Crescent Industrial Drive
Pontoon Beach, IL 62040
Tel : 618-931-2888
Fax: 618-931-2892
Toll Free: 800-275-3706

OCONUS
Operating hours are Monday through
Friday, excluding all federal, local,
and host-nation holidays. Arrive at
the VPC by 3:30 P.M. to ensure you
are processed on time. Hours of
operation are:

Benelux: (Chievres, Belgium/Schinnen,
   Netherlands) 8:00 A.M.–4:30 P.M.
England: 8:00 A.M.–4:30 P.M.
Germany: 8:00 A.M.–5:00 P.M.
Guam: 8:00 A.M.–4:00 P.M.
Hawaii: 8:00 A.M.–4:00 P.M. (for POV
   processing)
Alaska: 8:00 A.M.–5:00 P.M.
Italy: 8:30 A.M.–4:30 P.M.
Puerto Rico: 8:00 A.M.–4:00 P.M.
South Korea: 8:00 A.M.–5:00 P.M.
Turkey: 8:30 A.M.–4:30 P.M.
Spain: 9:00 A.M.–11:00 A.M.,
   11:00 A.M.–2:00 P.M., 2:00 P.M.–5:00 P.M.

BENELUX

Chievres, Belgium VPC
Transcar POV Shipping
Chievres Air Base
Building 46
Belgium
Tel: 32(0) 68665999
Fax: 32(0) 68665948
800: 00 800 87267227

Schinnen, Netherlands VPC
Transcar POV Shipping
Borgerweg 10
Building 27, Room 11
6365 CW-Schinnen, NL
Netherlands
Tel: 31(0) 464432851
Fax: 31(0) 464432735
800: 00 800 87267227

ENGLAND

Lakenheath/Mildenhall VPC
London Road Industrial Estate
40 Wimbledon Avenue
Brandon, Suffolk IP27, 0N7

Quality of Life VPC
RAF Fairford
Quality of Life VPC
Menwith Hill Station
Harrogate, Yorkshire

Quality of Life VPC
Joint Maritime Force
Raf JMF ST. Mawgan
Newquay, Cornwall

CONTACT TRANSCAR
Tel: 44(0) 1842813999
Fax: 44(0) 1842812981
800: 00 800 87267227
Tel: See Brandon VPC
Tel: 44 (0)1423 777887
Tel: 44 (0) 1637 853502

London VPC
RAF Fairford
For appointment: Contact Brandon
VPC

GERMANY

Baumholder VPC
Gebaeude 8716, Raum 1-3
Smith Barracks
Am Bahnof / Building 8716
55774 Baumholder, Germany
Tel: 49 6783 2455
Fax: 49 6783 3377
Toll Free: 00 800 87267227

Boeblingen VPC
Transcar POV Shipping
Panzer Kaserne
Building 2931
71032 Boeblingen, Germany
Tel: 49 7031 4
Fax: 49 7031 413408
DSN: 431-2617

Grafenwoehr VPC
U.S. Grafenwoehr Base
Saratoga Avenue/Building 515
92655 Grafenwoehr, Germany
Tel: 49 9641 8480
Fax: 49 9641 3597
Toll Free: 00 800 87267227

Kaiserslautern VPC
Kapaun Air Station
Building 2806
67661 Kaiserslautern, Germany
Tel: 49 631 98517
Fax: 49 631 98518
Toll Free: 00 800 87267227

Mannheim VPC
Taylor Barracks
Building 348
68309 Mannheim, Germany
Tel: 49 621 7140511
Fax: 49 621 7140711
Toll Free: 00 800 87267227

Schweinfurt VPC
Conn Barracks
Custer Street/Building 35
97421 Schweinfurt, Germany
Tel: 49 9721 803618
Fax: 49 6721 85224
Toll Free: 00 800 87267227

Spangdahlem VPC
Spangdahlem Air Base
Building 193A
54529 Spangdahlem, Germany
Tel: 49 6565 4484
Fax: 49 6565 4469
Toll Free: 00 800 87267227

Wiesbaden VPC
Transcar POV Shipping
Mainz Kastel Housing Area
Building 7513
55252 Mainz Kastel, Germany
Tel: 49 6134 69303
Fax: 49 6134 63579
Toll Free: 00 800 87267227

GUAM

Guam VPC
COMNAVMAR Naval Base
Building 3179
Santa Rita, Guam 96915
Tel: 671-339-2205
Fax: 671-564-2105
Toll Free: 877-716-7702

HAWAII

Honolulu VPC
Matson-Honolulu Terminal
Sand Island Parkway
Pier 51-B
Honolulu, HI 96820
Tel: 808 848 8383
Fax: 808 853 2116
800: 800 896 7745

ALASKA

Anchorage VPC
2945 Mountain View Drive
Anchorage, Alaska 99501
Tel: 907-297-1133
Fax: 907-297-1198
Toll Free: 866-848-7276

Fairbanks VPC
904 Aurora Drive
Fairbanks, Alaska 99701
Tel: 907-451-1753
Fax: 907-451-1826
Toll Free: 866-848-7277

ITALY

Aviano VPC
Transcar POV Shipping
Via Monte 20
Zona Industrial Area
33081 Aviano, Italy
Tel: 39(0) 434661419
Fax: 39(0) 434661420
Toll Free: 800 053388 (in Italy)

Sigonella VPC
Transcar POV Shipping
c/o Base Navale USA / NAS II
Strada Statale 417 Catania - Gela
95030 Piano d' Arci /Sigonella (CT)
Tel : 0039-095-86-5529
Fax: 0039- 434-661875
Toll Free: 800-053733
DSN: 624-5529

Livorno VPC
Transcar POV Shipping
Leghorn Army Depot
Camp Darby
Gate 27, Building 5130
SS 1 Aurelia
56018 Tirrenia/Pisa, Italy
Tel: 39(0) 50579920

Fax: 39(0) 5037649
DSN: 633-7059

Naples VPC
Vehicle Processing Center
c/o Naval Support Activity
Building 2081 Contrada Boscariello
81030 Gricignano di Aversa (CE)
Italy
Tel: 39-081-811-6521/6522
Fax: 39-081-811-6526
DSN: 625-4252

Vicenza VPC
Transcar POV Shipping
Via Strada Della Pelosa Building 970
Torri di Quartesolo
36040 Vicenza, Italy
Tel: 39(0) 44431898
Fax: 39(0) 444263168
DSN: 634-7760

PUERTO RICO

Puerto Rico VPC
Avenida J. F. Kennedy, Km 2.5
San Juan, Puerto Rico 00920
Tel: 787-792-1233
Fax: 787-781-0688
800: 888-872-6064

SOUTH KOREA

Pusan VPC
CLOSED JULY 2006
CONTACT SEOUL OR TAEGU VPC

Seoul VPC
Building C5721-A
34th Support Group, Yongson TMP
Seoul, Korea
Tel: 82 2 7916 7086 or 7088
DSN: 736 7086 or 7088
Fax: 82 2 7916 7091
DSN: 736 7091

Taegu VPC
20th Support Group
Building 1415
Camp Henry, Korea
Tel: 82 53 470 8112
Fax: 82 53 470 8113

TURKEY

Incirlik VPC
Yenimahalle 33 Sokak :31
TR-031340 Adana
Tel: 0090-322-332-7211
Fax: 0090 322 332 8921 or 7857
DSN: 679-9964
800: 0800- 521-1043

Izmir VPC
Hacilarkiri
Caddesi : 15/1
TR-35040 Borniva
Tel: 0090-232-478-2856
Fax: 0090 232-478-2859
Toll Free: 0800-479-7644

SPAIN

Rota VPC
Transportes Internacionales Ferris, S.A.
Avenida Crucero Baleares, :18
11520 Rota (Cadiz), Spain
Tel: 0034-956 -811044 / 0034
956 840185
Fax: 0034 956-815077
Toll Free: 0034-900-214304

Appendix L

Children's Clothing

CHILDREN'S SHOE SIZES

AGE	US	UK	EU
0–3 months	1–2	0–1	16–17
3–6 months	3	2	18
6–9 months	4	3	19
9–12 months	5	4	20
12–15 months	5½	4½	21
15–18 months	6	5	22
18–21 months	7	6	23
21–24 months	8	7	24
3 years	8½–9½	7½–8½	25–26
4 years	10	9	27
5 years	11	10	28
6 years	12	11	29
7 years	12½	11½	30
8 years	13–14	12–13	31–32
9 years	2	1	33
10 years	2½	1½	34
11 years	3½	2½	35
12 years	4½	3½	36
13 years	5	4	37
14 years	6–9	5–8	38

JUNIOR CLOTHING SIZES

US	UK	EUROPE	JAPAN
2	16/18	40/45	90 cm
4	20/22	50/55	100 cm
6	24/26	60/65	110 cm
8	28/30	70/75	120 cm
10	32/34	80/85	130 cm
12	38/38	90/95	140 cm

METRIC CONVERSION

Inches	22	24	26	28	30	32	34	36	38	40	42	44	46
Centimeters	56	61	66	71	76	81	86	91	97	102	107	112	117

Appendix M

Adult Clothing

MEN'S SHOE SIZES

US	EU	UK	JP (cm)
3–6½	36–39½	2–5½	21–24½
7–7½	40–40½	6–6½	25–25½
8–8½	41–41½	7–7½	26–26½
9–9½	42–42½	8–8½	27–27½
10–10½	43–43½	9–9½	28–28½
11–11½	44–44½	10–10½	29–29½
12–12½	45–45½	11–11½	30–30½
13–16	46–49	12–15	31–34

WOMEN'S SHOE SIZES

US	EU	UK	JP (cm)
4–5½	34–35½	1–1½	21–22½
6–6½	36–36½	3–3½	23–23½
7–7½	37–37½	4–4½	24–24½
8–8½	38–38½	5–5½	25–25½
9–9½	39–39½	6–6½	26–26½
10–10½	40–40½	7–7½	27–27½
11–11½	41–41½	8–8½	28–28½
12–14	42–44	9–11	29–31

MEN'S CLOTHING SIZES

SIZE	UK/US Waist	Italy	France	Shirts (collar) in.	Shirts (collar) cm.
XS	27–28	42	38		
S	29–30	44	40	14	36
M	31–32	46	42	14½–15	37–38
M	33–34	48	44	15½–15¾	39–40
L	35–36	50	46	16½–16¾	41–42
L	37–38	52	48	17½–17¾	43–44
XL	39–40	54	50	18½–18¾	45–46
XXL	41–42	56	52	19½–19¾	47–48

WOMEN'S CLOTHING SIZES

SIZE	Waist	US	Italy	France	UK	Japan
XXS	22–23	0	36	32	4	5
XS	24–25	2	38	34	6	7
S	26–27	4	40	36	8	9
S	28–29	6	42	38	10	11
M	30–31	8	44	40	12	13
M	32–33	10	46	42	14	15
L	34–35	12	48	44	16	17
XL	36–38	14–16	50–52	46–48	18–20	19–21

Glossary

20/20/15 Rule Allows ex-wives commissary, exchange and medical privileges if the marriage lasted for at least 20 years to a person who had 20 years of service creditable toward retirement and there was 15 years overlap between the marriage length and years of service.

Accompanied orders Orders authorizing family members to travel to a duty station with the servicemember.

Accompanied tour Tour of duty on which a servicemember is accompanied by his family.

Active duty Full-time duty in the active service of a uniformed service, including duty on the active list, full-time training duty, annual training duty, and attendance while in the active service at a school designated as a service school by law or by the secretary concerned.

Active duty for training (ADT) Full-time duty that reservists and guardsmen do. Includes annual training, military school attendance, and training exercises.

Active Guard and Reserve (AGR) Full-time reservists. They are considered reservists on active duty, not regular active duty.

Adjustable Rate Loan (ARM) A mortgage loan for which the interest rate is adjusted periodically based on prevailing rates.

Advance Basic Allowance for Housing A loan against the basic housing allowance.

Advance Leave Annual leave that is loaned against the balance for servicemembers who need to take leave but don't have enough.

Advance Overseas Housing Allowance (OHA) A loan granted against the housing allowance for overseas moves.

Advance Pay A loan granted against basic pay to help with the expenses of a Permanent Change of Station move.

Advanced Individual Training (AIT) The job training part of Basic Training in the Army.

AFSC Air Force Specialty Code (AFSC) Air Force term for a servicemember's specific military job.

Air Mobility Command (AMC) Air Force operation that flies servicemembers and their families to overseas duty stations.

Air Post Office (APO) A military address box assigned to an overseas unit. Mail to and from it is charged at the domestic rate.

Airman and Family Readiness Center *See* Army Community Services.

Alert The period of time during which servicemembers stand by in readiness for action.

Allotment Money sent directly from the paycheck to specific places and people to care for financial responsibilities.

Allowance A supplemental amount to basic pay allowed or granted for a specific purpose.

American Council on Education (ACE) An organization composed of over 1,800 accredited, degree-granting colleges, universities, and higher education–related associations.

American National Red Cross A humanitarian organization that provides emergency assistance, disaster relief, community services and education inside the U.S.

Annual Leave Vacation time accrued at the rate of 2.5 days for each month of active duty.

Appropriated funds Tax monies specifically designated by Congress to support base activities and salaries.

Armed Forces Radio and Television Service A military activity that provides radio and television services to overseas commands.

Armed Forces Recreation Centers DoD-operated recreational properties located all over the world.

Armed Services The Army, Navy, Air Force, Marine Corps, and Coast Guard.

Army Community Services (ACS) A family services program that assist military families in both everyday living and crisis situations.

Army Family Team Building On-base program designed for new Army spouses that cover subjects such as what is learned in basic training, acronyms, customs, socials, benefits, and places to go for help.

Arrears The state of being behind in payments.

Article 15 A nonjudicial punishment; one given via an administrator, not court-martial.

A-School A Navy term for technical training after boot camp.

Assumable loan A loan that may be passed on from a seller of a home to the buyer. The buyer "assumes" all outstanding payments.

AWOL Absent without leave. Being away from the duty station without proper authorization.

Barracks Living quarters for single servicemembers; called dormitories in the Air Force.

Base Location from which operations are conducted or supported. Also called garrison or post.

Basic Allowance for Housing (BAH) Money for housing expenses.

Basic Allowance for Housing Type II Money granted to Reservists entitled to a housing allowance when they are on active duty for less than 30 days.

Basic Allowance for Subsistence (BAS) Money for food given to married personnel, personnel living off base, and all officers.

Basic Pay A simple wage that covers a 24-hour, seven-day workweek.

Basic Training The initial process of transforming civilians into servicemembers, physically and behaviorally. It has two parts. The first is a general overview of the service; the second is specific job training.

BDU Battle dress uniform. Camouflage suits and boots.

Beneficiary One who benefits from the proceeds of a policy, gift, or inheritance.

Bond A long-term debt sold by companies to investors.

Bounced check Check that does not have enough deposited in the account to honor it, thus is returned to the person it was written to.

Branch 1. A functional job category to which Army officers are assigned. 2. A division of the military; the Army, Navy, and Air Force are separate branches.

Brat A term for someone who grew up while his or her parent or parents serve or served in the armed forces.

Brokerage house A company licensed to buy and sell securities. It is an intermediary between buyers and sellers.

Budget 1. A sum of money allocated for a specific purpose 2. A spending plan.

Cadet Army and Air Force term for a student at a service academy.

Calling Card A small, printed card with the holder's name and contact information. Can be a standard business card, used for leaving in trays at formal receptions.

Career Advancement Accounts (CAA) A demonstration project that helps military spouses gain the skills and credentials necessary to begin or advance their careers.

Career Field A functional job category to which Marine Corps officers are assigned.

Career Specialty A functional job category to which Air Force officers are assigned.

Cashiers check A paper that orders a sum of money, usually over $500, to be paid to someone else.

Casualty Any person who is lost to the organization by reasons of having been declared dead, missing, captured, interned, wounded, injured, or seriously ill.

Casualty Assistance Calls Officer (CACO) A Navy, Marines, and Coast Guard term for the person who assists survivors of servicemembers killed on active duty.

Casualty Assistance Officer (CAO) An Army term; *see* Casualty Assistance Calls Officer.

Casualty Assistance Representative (CAR) An Air Force term; *see* Casualty Assistance Calls Officer.

Catchment area Zip codes usually falling within a 40-mile radius of a facility.

Certificate of Deposit (CD) Financial instrument bought from a bank to obtain a higher interest rate than that available from regular savings accounts. Can be bought in different denominations and maturity dates.

Chain of command Organization of superiors and subordinates.

Change-of-command ceremony This is held to represent the passing of command from one commander to another.

Checking Account Money kept in a bank or savings and loan for safekeeping, and easily withdrawn by writing checks or using an ATM or debit card.

Child Development Center (CDC) On-base daycare center that cares for children from six weeks to 12 years old.

Civil servant Also called a public servant, this is an employee who works for a government department or agency.

Civil service Public sector (tax-funded) employment. May be federal, state, or local.

Civilian 1. A person not on active duty in a military, police, or fire-fighting force 2. An outsider.

Civilian personnel office (CPO) Office responsible for hiring civilian workers.

Clothing allowance Money given to enlisted servicemembers to maintain and replace uniforms.

CO Commanding officer. Officer in charge of a specific group or unit of personnel.

Coast Guard Work-Life Center *See* Army Community Services.

Coffee Social function primarily attended by officer spouses.

Collateral Property that is pledged to the lender in the event the loan is not paid off.

College Level Examination Program (CLEP) A series of tests in undergraduate college courses that provides students the opportunity to demonstrate college-level proficiency in the subject matter and receive college credit.

Color Guard A formal procession, typically composed of four servicemembers, who carry flags at events.

Combat 1. The engagement of warfare 2. A job field that includes specialties such as infantry, artillery, and Special Forces teams.

Combat Service Support A job field that provides administrative and logistical help to the combat forces such as supply, transportation, health care, and payroll.

Combat support A job field that provides operational help, such as military intelligence, security, and communications.

Combat-related Injury and Rehabilitation Pay (CIP) Money given for a portion of time that a servicemember spends in rehabilitation for wounds, injuries, and illness incurred from being in a combat operation or combat zone.

Command 1. Authority that a commander lawfully exercises over subordinates by virtue of rank or assignment. 2. Order given by a commander. 3. A unit, organization, or area under the authority of one individual.

Command Performance An event which a servicemember is required to attend.

Commissary On-base, tax-subsidized grocery store operated by the Defense Commissary Agency (DeCa).

Commission 1. To make ready for service, as to commission an aircraft or ship. 2. A written order bestowed by a sovereign government that gives a person rank and authority as an officer in the armed forces.

Commissioned Officer A person who holds a position of authority or command.

Common Access Card An ID card for military personnel which has the dual purpose of allowing electronic commerce, mess hall access, and other capabilities.

Community College of the Air Force (CCAF) An accredited institute of higher learning run by the Air Force.

COMPASS Program for Navy spouses; *see* Army Family Team Building.

Concurrent travel orders Orders permitting a servicemember and family to travel together to a new duty station.

Consignment The act of consigning, which is placing an item in a store but retaining ownership of it until it sells.

Consumables Allowance An annual allowance for consumable goods given to people stationed in some overseas locations.

Continental U.S. Cost-of-Living Allowance (ConUS) Money given to people living in areas where the cost of living is 8 percent or more above the national cost of living.

Continental United States (CONUS) The 48 contiguous states and the District of Columbia.

Continued Health Care Benefits Program (CHCBP) A premium-based health care program that bridges military health care benefits and a civilian health plan.

Convalescent (Sick) Leave Leave granted when the recipient is under special medical care or recovering from an operation.

Conventional loan Any mortgage loan other than VA or FHA.

Copayment See Cost share.

Cost share The portion of medical care a family member pays under Tricare. Also known as a copayment.

Cost-of-living allowance (COLA) Money to help pay living expenses at overseas duty stations.

Court-martial A military court. It oversees judicial punishments.

Credit 1. A loan 2. confidence in a borrower's intention and ability to repay; financial trustworthiness.

Credit Record A documentation of your credit activities.

Credit Union A bank that has an affiliation membership requirement.

Crossroads Air Force website that provides information on bases worldwide.

CSB/REDUX The Military Reform Act of 1986. It is a retired pay option. It comes with a Career Service Bonus.

Date of Entry into Military Service (DIEMS) The earliest date of enlistment, induction, or appointment in a regular or reserve component as a commissioned officer or enlisted member. It determines which of the three retired pay formulas a servicemember is eligible to use.

Date of Rank Date an officer entered the service.

Death Gratuity A one-time payment of $100,000 to the survivors of a servicemember killed on active duty.

Debit card A payment card that is linked to a customer's bank account, from which purchase costs are directly deducted, reducing the account balance.

Deductible Uninsured portion of an insurance policy; e.g., the first $200 of costs that the insured pays.

Defense Activity for Non-Traditional Educational Support (DANTES) Umbrella activity under which many educational programs operate.

Defense Eligibility Enrollment Reporting System (DEERS) List of all people eligible to use military health-care facilities or Tricare.

Defense Outplacement Referral System (DORS) National network that connects separating servicemembers and their spouses with private-sector employers.

Defined contribution plan A savings system where the amount of retirement income received depends on how much was contributed over the working years and the return that those contributions earned.

Delay enroute Leave for unforeseen delays during a PCS move.

Delayed Enlistment Program (DEP) The time period between the taking of the oath and the actual entrance into the military.

Department of Defense (DoD) Branch of government that runs the military services.

Department of Defense Educational Activity (DoDEA) A K-12 school system operated for military children. It consists of three separate systems: the Department of Defense Dependents Schools (DoDDS) Europe, DoDDS Pacific, and the Domestic Dependent Elementary and Secondary Schools (DDESS), which are Stateside.

Department of Veterans Affairs (VA) Agency that handles veterans' benefits and concerns.

Dependent Term for a person who receives all or some financial support from a servicemember.

Deployment The positioning of individuals or entire units in readiness for combat.

Depreciation The decrease in value of any property due to wear, tear, and/or time.

Diploma mill An institution of higher education that operates without supervision of a state or professional accrediting agency.

Direct commission Program that allows certain professionals to join the military without undergoing its standard training regimen. Typically reserved for medical, legal, engineering, or religious professionals.

Direct Hire Employees hired directly by an agency of DoD. These can be veterans or host citizens hired by the DoD to support DoD activities in their home countries.

Disabled Transition Assistance Program (DTAP) The portion of the Transition Assistance Program that assists servicemembers released due to disability issues.

Discharge The act of leaving military service in a manner that all legal ties with it are cut.

Dislocation Allowance Money given to help offset unreimbursable moving expenses.

Dividend Quarterly payment made to the holder of a stock or mutual fund.

Don't Ask, Don't Tell A Clinton-era policy that requires homosexuals or bisexuals not to engage in such activity on or off duty, nor to discuss it.

Dormitories An Air Force term; *see* barracks.

Dream Sheet Job and assignment preference worksheet.

Drill Training exercise for reserve members.

Duty Station Actual physical location where active-duty military personnel perform duty on a permanent basis.

Education Center On-base resource with personnel and information to help service families research and obtain their educational goals.

Emergency Leave Leave granted as annual, but can be used only for a family emergency.

Enlisted A person enrolled or conscripted into the military service. a servicemember who ranks below a commissioned officer.

Enlistment A voluntary entrance into military service under enlisted status. Also refers to a contractual period of time between enrollment and discharge.

Environmental and Moral Leave Leave provided to servicemembers and their families stationed in areas considered adverse or remote.

Equity The difference between the market value of a property and the claims held against it.

Exceptional Family Member Program (EFMP) A program that assists children with special physical or mental needs.

Excess Leave Leave without pay granted for emergencies or certain circumstances, such as job- or house-hunting, when the servicemember doesn't have enough paid leave accrued. It must be repaid either via cash or time worked.

Exchange (PX/AAFES/NEX/MCX) Post Exchange, Army and Air Force Exchange, Navy Exchange, Marine Corps Exchange. On base department store where household goods are sold.

Executive officer (XO) Second in command.

Executive Order (E.O.) 12721 A presidential action that enables certain eligible Foreign Service family members to receive a one-time, noncompetitive appointment to the Civil Service once they return to the U.S. from an overseas assignment.

Executor/executrix Person appointed to administer a deceased person's estate.

Expanded Legal Assistance Program Program under which servicemembers E-4 and below may have a military lawyer defend them, free of charge, in a civilian court.

ExpressScripts A Tricare benefit that sends prescription maintenance drugs to your home via a mail-order program.

Family care plan A formal document kept on file with commanding officers that describes contingency plans for minor children during deployment and field duties of a single servicemember or dual military couple.

Family member A servicemember's authorized benefits recipient.

Family Readiness Group (FRG) A spouse forum that is the official conduit for command information. It also serves social purposes.

Family separation allowance Money given to help pay for expenses caused by family separations.

Family Separation Housing Allowance This provides a dual housing allowance for servicemembers on unaccompanied tours overseas who are unable to get into government quarters but are still supporting a family stateside.

Family Subsistence Supplemental Allowance (FSSA) Money that increases the Basic Allowance for Subsistance for qualifying servicemembers, typically those with very large families.

Federal 1. A national, sovereign, central authority. Refers to the government of the United States 2. Refers to organizations funded or goods owned by this central authority, e.g., "the Federal Bureau of Investigation" or "federal property."

Federal Employees Health Benefits (FEHB) An insurance program for civilian government employees.

Federal Express (FedEx) A courier company that offers different mail services.

Fellowship A monetary award (scholarship) connected to working in a specific field, usually at the graduate or postgraduate level.

Feres Doctrine A 1950 Supreme Court ruling that prohibits servicemembers from suing the government for damages that occur incidental to service.

FHA loan A mortgage loan supported by the Federal Housing Administration and the Department of Housing and Urban Development.

FICA Federal Insurance Contributions Act tax. It is the Social Security deduction from the paycheck.

FICO score A number that sums up a person's creditworthiness, named for Fair Isaac, the company that developed it.

Field exercise A multitude of tasks done in a simulated war atmosphere.

Finance charge The cost of a loan. Consists of interest rate and possibly other fees.

Financial Industry Regulatory Authority (FINRA) Formerly called the National Association of Security Dealers (NASD). An industry organization that represents people and companies in the U.S. securities industry.

Fisher House A low-cost lodge near a military hospital that houses families visiting those hospitalized for serious injuries, operations, or treatment.

Fleet Post Office (FPO) *See* APO.

Float The time between deposit into a bank and when the funds actually clear.

Free Application for Federal Student Aid (FAFSA) A government form used to determine financial eligibility for student aid.

Functional category General term for a group of occupationally related jobs. Called branch in the Army, group in the Navy and Coast Guard, career field in the Marine Corps, and career specialty in the Air Force.

Funding fee A fee charged by law on VA loans.

Fund-raiser An activity designed to raise money for a specific goal.

Garnishment A court-ordered deduction from the paycheck, usually done for spousal or child support.

Garrison *See* Base.

General Equivalency Diploma (GED) A certificate that represents the equivalent of a high school diploma.

General Schedule (GS) A classification system of Federal government appropriated-fund jobs.

Gray Area Retiree A Guardsman or Reservist who has received a notification of eligibility for retirement but has not yet begun receiving retired pay.

Gross Domestic Product The total dollar value of all final goods and services produced in the country in a year.

Group A functional job category to which Navy and Coast Guard officers are assigned.

Hale and Farewell A social event where newcomers are greeted and outgoing members are wished well.

Handbook of Occupational Groups and Series Book that describes the education, experience, and combinations thereof needed for a Federal job.

Health Care Provider (HCP) The person or institution rendering medical services to a patient.

Heartlink Program for Air Force spouses; *see* Army Family Team Building.

High Year of Retention (HYR) The date by which a servicemember must make a certain rank or be forced out. It is the military's "up or out" policy.

High Year of Tenure (HYT) Navy and Air Force term for the time by which an enlisted person must reach a certain paygrade or not be allowed to reenlist.

Hop A flight on a military plane, or a military-chartered plane, taken for pleasure, not for transport, to an overseas duty station. Also called Space-A travel.

Hostile Fire/Imminent Danger Pay Money given for time spent in areas recognized as especially dangerous.

Household Goods Furniture and other personal goods shipped to a new duty station.

Identification card (ID) A small, laminated card with a bar code that contains a photo and identifying information of the holder. It is presented to receive military benefits.

Identity theft The act of fraudulently acquiring and using someone else's personal information, usually for purposes of financial gain.

Inactive National Guard (ING) Reservists who muster once a year with their unit.

Individual Ready Reserve (IRR) Units and individual members liable for duty in wartime or national emergency. These reservists are not in the selected reserve but are liable for mobilization.

Individual Retirement Account (IRA) A tax-deferred or tax free way of saving for retirement. There are regular and Roth IRAs.

Installment loan Borrowed money that is repaid in equal payments, or installments.

Interest rate A rate which is charged or paid for the use of money.

Internal Revenue Service The Federal agency that collects taxes and administers the tax code.

Interned Active duty military personnel who have been detained as the result of action of an unfriendly military or paramilitary force in a foreign country.

Involuntary Separation Pay Also called severance pay, this is given to servicemembers with over six years but less than twenty years, a good record, and an honorable discharge.

IRR reservists Has had military training and has some military obligation remaining, but is not affiliated with a drilling reserve unit. IRR personnel are in a non-drilling status and are available only for national emergency.

Job Fair Also called a Career Fair or Career Expo, it is an event where employers, recruiters, and schools meet with prospective job seekers.

Joint Chiefs of Staff Military advisory group to the president. The head of the Joint Chiefs of Staff is the highest link in the military chain of command.

Joint Federal Travel Regulations The rules that govern official travel and accommodations for all the military services.

Judge Advocate General (JAG) The military's equivalent of a law firm. Serves as legal advisor to the installation commander and provides advice and trial defense lawyers for servicemembers charged under the Uniform Code of Military Justice.

Judicial punishment A punishment administered through a court system.

Key Volunteer A volunteer, official liason between Marine Corps families and the command. Typically a senior enlisted spouse.

Keylogger A form of malware that records keystrokes.

Knowledge, Skills and Abilities form (KSA) A questionnaire that helps Federal employers match suitable applicants with available jobs. It supplements a resume in the hiring process.

Lease A contract agreement between tenant and the landlord, specifying rental conditions.

Leatherneck A nickname for Marines.

Leave 1.Vacation time, accrued at the rate of two-and-a-half calendar days for each month of active duty. 2. Time away from the service for nonvacation purpose, such as sickness.

Leave and Earnings Statement (LES) A monthly statement of a servicemember's earnings, deductions, leave balance, and other information.

Leave enroute Personal travel time during a PCS move.

Liberty Short amount of uncharged vacation time (usually a weekend). Also known as a pass.

Lien A legal claim or attachment against property as security for payment of an obligation.

Life insurance Protection against financial loss in case of the death of a breadwinner. Term and whole are the most common types.

Lifestyle Insights Networking Knowledge Skills (LINKS) Program for Marine Corps spouses; *see* Army Family Team Building.

Load Fee charged to mutual fund holders.

Locked Refers to a cell-phone that will only work with one service provicer; *see* unlocked.

Malware Malicious software (mal-ware); a computer program designed to steal information or install viruses.

Marine Corps Community Services *See* Army Community Services.

Medevac Medical evacuation. Air transport of people to medical facilities at another base.

Medicaid A government-funded program that provides medical expense coverage for eligible people under age 65 who are indigent and meet certain other criteria.

Medically necessary The frequency, extent, and types of services or supplies considered to be appropriate and accepted by qualified professionals as reasonable and adequate.

Medicare A government health insurance plan that provides hospital, medical, and surgical benefits for persons age 65 and older and people with certain disabilities. Medicare Part A provides basic hospital insurance and Medicare Part B provides benefits for physicians' professional services.

Midshipman A student at the Naval Academy.

Military Clause A condition in a rental lease that allows occupants to leave the premises with no repercussions in case of permanent change of station orders, deployment, or if the servicemember is killed or missing in action.

Military occupational specialty (MOS) A servicemember's specific job in the Army and Marine Corps.

Military One Source A comprehensive DoD family resource at http://www.military onesource.com.

Military Personnel and Civilian Employees' Claim Act (PCA) This is a payment statute that compensates for personal property that is lost, damaged, or destroyed incident to service.

Military Spouse Hiring Preference Part of the Military Family Act, a public law that gives worldwide employment preference to spouses of active-duty servicemembers who relocate to accompany their military sponsor on a Permanent Change of Station move.

Military Star Card A credit card issued by the Exchange for shopping there.

Military training Instruction to enhance combat readiness.

Military treatment facility (MTF) A military hospital or clinic.

Missing Active duty military personnel who are not present at their duty station due to apparent involuntary reasons and whose location is not known. Excluded are personnel who are in an absent-without-leave or deserter status, or those who have been dropped from the rolls of their military service.

Mobilization Assembling and organizing national resources in case of war or national emergency. Includes activating all or part of the reserve components.

Monetary Allowance in Lieu of Transportation (MALT) Reimbursement money given to families during a PCS move who drive instead of fly.

Money Market An account that merges many people's money to earn higher returns.

Money order A paper that orders a sum of money, usually under $500, to be paid to someone else.

Montgomery GI Bill Government program to help servicemembers pay for college tuition.

Morale, Well-being, and Recreation (MWR) Department that manages base leisure activities.

Mortgage A lien on a property or house that secures a loan and is paid in installments over a set period of time.

Move-In Housing Allowance (MIHA) Money given for overseas moves only to help defray the costs of furnishing an unfurnished rental apartment.

Mutual fund Financial instrument bought for investment purposes; consists of a large pool of money deposited from many different people. Grouped into three load types: no-load, low-load, and loaded.

myPay A feature that allows viewing of the Leaving and Earning Statement and other details online (https://mypay.dfas.mil/mypay.aspx).

National Military Family Association (NMFA) A nonprofit private association dedicated to improving the quality of life for military families.

Navy Family Service Center *See* Army Community Services.

NCO Noncommissioned officer. Enlisted servicemember above the rank of E-4.

NCOIC Noncommissioned officer in charge. NCO in charge of a particular unit or activity.

Need to know Security procedures that require the recipients of classified information to prove that they need the information in order to perform their jobs.

Network provider A credentialed health-care provider contracted to render services to Tricare beneficiaries.

Nonappropriated funds (NAF) 1. A classification of government, non-taxpayer funded jobs. 2. Money generated by military and civilian personnel and their families that supplements taxpayer funds to provide morale-building, religious, educational and recreational programs on military bases.

Non-Availability Statement (NAS) A certification from a military hospital stating that it cannot provide the required care.

Noncompetitive appointment This is a job offered directly to an applicant without requiring him to go through the standard competition process against other eligible candidates.

Nonconcurrent travel orders Orders that do not permit a servicemember and his family to travel together to a new duty station.

Nonjudicial punishment A limited punishment awarded for minor disciplinary offenses by a commanding officer or officer in charge to members of his command.

Non-Temporary Storage (NTS) Also called extended or permanent storage, long-term household goods storage.

Notification of Eligibility (NOE) Paper received by reservists informing them that they have completed 20 years of military service. Also known as the "20-year letter."

OCC Officer Candidate Class Marine Corps term for a program that enables enlisted servicemembers to become officers.

Officer A commissioned or warrant officer.

Officer Candidate School (OCS) Army and Navy term for a leadership program that trains enlisted personnel to become officers.

Officer in charge (OIC) The officer responsible with the command, organization, and management of a unit.

Officer of the Deck (OOD) Represents the ship's captain and greets guests as they arrive on the quarterdeck.

Officer Training School (OTS) Air Force term for a program that enables enlisted service-members to become officers.

Ombudsman A volunteer, official liaison between Navy and Coast Guard families and the command. Typically a senior enlisted spouse.

On the economy Goods and services bought from local civilian vendors rather than at military facilities.

One-Stop Career Center Department of Labor–sponsored website that offers career resources and workforce information to job seekers, students, businesses, and workforce professionals.

Optional Form OP-612 A form that may be submitted in lieu of a resume when applying for a Federal job.

Outside the Continental United States (OCONUS) Overseas duty stations, including Alaska and Hawaii.

Overseas housing allowance (OHA) Money given to offset the higher cost of living at some overseas duty locations.

Pass *See* Liberty.

Passport An internationally recognized travel document that verifies the bearer's identity and nationality.

Patriot Express A pilot program run by the Small Business Administration that provides loans or loan guarantees to start or expand a small business.

Pawn shop A business which offers loans using the the borrower's personal property as collateral.

Pay grade 1. Military rank 2. The point on a graded pay structure where jobs of a similar size or value are placed.

Payday loan A short, uncollateralized, high-interest loan.

Pell Grant A federal need-based monetary award, usually for students who haven't yet earned a bachelor's or graduate degree.

Per Diem Daily expense allowance for food and lodging for each day of authorized travel during a PCS move.

Permanent change of station (PCS) Relocation from one permanent duty station to another.

Permissive Temporary Duty Assignment (PTDY) Leave granted when a servicemember wants to attend a conference or class that the military won't pay for, but which benefits him professionally, in turn, benefiting the military.

Personally procured transportation (PPT) Self-help move in which a servicemember packs and moves himself instead of having a government-hired mover do it for him.

Phishing Pretending to be a trustworthy source for purposes of fraudulently obtaining information.

Point of contact (POC) Person to call for more information.

Port call Place and date a servicemember reports for transportation to an overseas duty assignment.

Post *See* Base.

Posting of the Colors A tradition performed at certain events where flags are carried in a procession by a color guard, and then posted (placed) in a certain location.

Power of attorney A document that authorizes a person to act on behalf of someone else. There are general and specialized ones.

Premium Monthly insurance payment.

Primary care manager (PCM) A physician or other health-care provider who assumes primary responsibility for arranging and coordinating a beneficiary's total health needs.

Private Mortgage Insurance (PMI) A type of insurance which protects the lender in the event the borrower defaults on the loan.

Proceed time A leave of absence of up to seven days at both the old and new duty stations to process in and out.

Professional Books, Papers, and Equipment (PBPE) A moving allowance for items required to perform official duties.

Promotion Advancement to a higher rank or pay grade.

Prospectus A pamphlet or brochure that provides information about a mutual fund or stock.

Protocol Etiquette for military affairs.

Public and Community Service (PACS) National network that connects separating service-members and their spouses with public and community service employers.

Quarterdeck The area of the ship where official and ceremonial functions are held while the ship is in port. It is considered the ship's "seat of authority."

Quarters On-base government housing.

Rank A relative standing or position; a hierarchical arrangement. It is called "rate" in the Coast Guard.

Rate Navy and Coast Guard term; *see* rank.

Rating A servicemember's specific job in the Navy and Coast Guard.

Ready Reserve Consists of the Selected Reserve, Individual Ready Reserve (IRR), and Inactive National Guard (ING).

Receiving Line A line at a formal social event that that permits the host and hostess to personally welcome the guests into the reception.

Reception A party typically held for holidays, in honor of someone's promotion or retirement, or for special occasions, such as the christening or commissioning of a ship.

Remote tour A duty assignment in an area that lacks standard family supports, hence is unaccompanied.

Renter's Insurance Also called a tenant's policy, this protects the personal property of those living in rental houses and apartments.

Rent-to-Own (RTO) A type of business which rents items that will eventually be owned by the renter when the rental period is over.

Reserve Members of the military services who are not in active service but are subject to call to active duty.

Reserve components Army National Guard of the United States, Army Reserve, Naval Reserve, Air National Guard of the United States, Air Force Reserve, and Coast Guard Reserve. In each component there are three categories: ready reserve, standby reserve, and retired reserve.

Reserve Officers Training Corps (ROTC) A college leadership program that prepares graduates to enter the military as officers.

Resume A document that describes skills and experiences in a manner that allows an employer to evaluate an applicant's suitability for a specific job.

Resumix An automated resume-scanning system that uses optical character recognition software, imaging technologies, and a skill-extraction system to read resumes.

Retainer pay A Navy and Marine Corps term; *see* retired pay.

Retention Control Point (RCP) Army term; *see* High Year of Tenure.

Retired pay A lifetime, inflation-protected annuity to those who complete at least 20 years of active duty.

Retired reserve Reservists who have attained retirement through their reserve service. Can be ordered to active duty only if the secretary of their branch of service decides that there are not enough qualified personnel to meet mobilization requirements.

Retired reservists Reservists who have already attained military retirement but have not yet reached age 60, have not chosen to be discharged, and can be called to duty if there is a need and there are not enough ready reservists.

Retreat Also called evening colors, the evening lowering and folding of the flag into a star-topped triangle, signaling the end of the day. It is accompanied by a bugle call.

Reveille Also called morning colors, the name of the bugle call that accompanies the daily ritual of raising the American flag, signaling the start of the day.

Revolving loan A loan in which you have continuous access to non-collateralized credit, up to a set amount.

Saber Drawn sword.

Saber Arch A sword ceremony performed at the military weddings of commissioned, warrant, and noncommissioned officers.

Salute A form of greeting between servicemembers.

Sanctuary The time period in a servicemember's career where enough creditable service to be within two years of retirement eligibility has been earned, hence he may not be easily involuntarily separated.

Savings Account Also called a passbook account, this is a liquid account that provides insurance in case of bank insolvency.

Savings and Loan Depository financial institution that obtains most of its deposits from consumers and holds the majority of its assets as home mortgage loans.

Savings Deposit Program (SDP) A program that allows servicemembers deployed at least 30 consecutive days to contribute an amount up to the total monthly pay and allowances into an account that pays 10 percent interest.

Schedule A Handicapped Appointment A noncompetitive, direct-hire status for people with cognitive disabilities who meet the eligibility requirements.

Scholarship A merit-based monetary award provided to a student for pursuing educational goals.

Scholastic Aptitude Test (SAT) A standardized test for college admission.

Secured Credit Card A credit card with an amount predeposited on it by the holder.

Securities General term for a financial instrument, e.g., stock, bond, certificate of deposit, mutual fund.

Selected reserve Part of the ready reserve. Provides trained units and personnel for the "total force" concept.

Selected reservist Available for immediate mobilization. They actively drill, are eligible for promotion, collect pay and benefits, and accumulate points toward retirement.

Separation 1. Time away from the family. 2. Term for the act of leaving military service.

Service Academy College run by the Defense Department to prepare graduates to become military officers. They are: the U.S. Military Academy at West Point, NY; the U.S. Naval Academy in Annapolis, MD; the U.S. Air Force Academy in Colorado Springs, CO; and the U.S. Coast Guard Academy in New London, CT.

Servicemember A member of the Armed Forces.

Servicemembers Opportunity Colleges (SOC) A service-wide network of accredited colleges and universities that contract with the Department of Defense to offer on-base degree programs. It includes SOCAD for the Army, SOCNAV for the Navy, SOCMAR for the Marine Corps, SOCCOAST for the Coast Guard, and SOCGuard for the Army National Guard.

Servicemen's Civil Relief Act (SCRA) A law that gives servicemembers certain financial protections when they are deployed or called to active duty.

Servicemen's Group Life Insurance (SGLI) Up to $400,000 of coverage that can be purchased by active-duty personnel.

SIM card A small chip inserted into a cell phone, which contains the phone number and any additional services subscribed to.

Social Security Retirement and disability programs established under the federal Social Security Act or the Railroad Retirement Act.

Sovereign An entity with the right and power of autonomous self-government.

Space-Available Travel. *See* Hop.

Special Pay An addition to basic pay that compensates for critical skills and unique hardships. Also takes the form of reenlistment bonuses.

Special-Leave Accrual (SLA) Type of leave that accrues when a servicemember is stationed in an area which entitles him to hostile fire/imminent danger pay.

Spending Journal A record of all purchases for the purpose of financial management.

Sponsor 1. The active-duty servicemember. 2. A servicemember assigned to help a newcomer and family in-process and settle into a new duty station.

Spouse Telework Employment Program (STEP) A partnership among six federal agencies to improve military spouses' access to remote training and private-sector telework opportunities.

Spouses to Teachers A program that helps spouses of active duty and reservists become public school teachers.

Spyware A form of malware that performs tasks like browser hijacking, keylogging, and recording/sending web-browsing habits to a third party, all of which will slow down a computer.

Standby reservists Selected and individual Ready Reservists are called when there are not enough qualified members in the Ready Reserve to fulfill mobilization requirements.

Status of Forces Agreement (SOFA) This is a contract between the U.S. government and the government of the country hosting its base.

Stock A fractional share in a company.

Stock market A giant market in which shares are bought and sold.

Stop-loss A temporary hold on the ability of military personnel to leave the service.

Survivor 1. The family members of a servicemember killed on active duty who qualify for benefits. 2. A status that determines Tricare premium costs. *See* transitional survivor.

Survivor Benefit Plan An insurance plan designed to provide income for a retiree's wife, kids, or insurable interest.

Survivors' and Dependents' Educational Assistance Program (DEA) An educational assistance program for qualifying spouse and children of living veterans.

TAD Temporary additional duty. Navy and Marine Corps term for time spent away from the permanent duty station.

Tea *See* Coffee.

Technical School Also called Tech School, it's the job training part of Basic Training in the Air Force.

Temporary duty (TDY) Army and Air Force term for time spent away from the permanent duty station.

Temporary Employment Agency Also called Temporary Labor Agency, it is an employment services office that places various types of workers with companies for set periods of time.

Temporary Lodging Allowance (TLA) Money given to help offset up to 60 days of temporary living expenses on overseas moves.

Temporary Lodging Entitlement (TLE) Money given to help defray up to 10 days' living expenses during CONUS moves, when a family occupies temporary lodging.

Term Life Insurance This protects the beneficiary for a limited period and expires without maturity value if the insured survives the period specified in the policy. Types are level and decreasing.

Terminal Leave Leave granted when discharged or retiring.

Theater Geographical area outside the continental United States for which a commander is assigned military responsibility.

Thrift Savings Plan (TSP) A defined contribution plan offered by the Federal government that has savings and tax benefits.

Thrift Shop A resale shop for clothes and household items sold on consignment.

Total Force Term given to describe the combined strength of Active Duty, Reserve and National Guard personnel.

Transition Assistance Program (TAP) A three-day workshop of services to help service-members who are within 180 days of separation or retirement and their spouses' transition to the civilian world.

Transitional Assistance Management Program (TAMP) 180 days of transitional health care benefits to service families beginning on the separation date.

Transitional Survivor A temporary status for the survivors of a servicemember killed on active duty as it applies to Tricare premium costs.

Travelers Check A preprinted, fixed-amount check that is bought at a bank, typically for 1 percent of the face value.

Treasury bonds Debt obligations of the U.S. government. Choices are Series EE, HH, and I.

Tricare Medical health-care program used by military families. Options include Prime, Extra, Standard, Remote, Plus, Echo, Reserve Select, and Reserve Family Demonstration Project, Tricare Prime Overseas, Tricare Standard Overseas, Tricare Global Remote Overseas, and Tricare for Life.

Troops Collective term for uniformed military personnel (usually not applied to naval personnel afloat).

Troops to Teachers A program that helps former servicemembers become public school teachers.

Tuition A fee paid for instruction (usually higher education).

Twenty-Year Letter *See* Notification of Eligibility.

UCMJ (Uniform Code of Military Justice) Set of federal laws that defines what actions are crimes in the military.

Unaccompanied Baggage Also called hold, this is a small shipment sent to the new duty station ahead of household goods to facilitate basic housekeeping upon arrival.

Unaccompanied Orders Orders that authorize the servicemember only to travel to a duty station.

Unaccompanied Tour Tour of duty a servicemember does unaccompanied by his family; *see* Remote.

Under Arms A color guard that carries rifles.

Unemployment benefits Monetary payments for a specific period of time or until the worker finds a new job.

Uniformed Services The Army, Navy, Air Force, Marine Corps, Coast Guard, National Oceanic and Atmospheric Administration, and the U.S. Public Health Service.

Uniformed Services Employment and Reemployment Rights Act (USERRA) A law that prohibits employers from discriminating or retaliating against any employee or applicant because of the his or her military service.

United Concordia The provider of the Tricare Dental Plan.

United Services Organization (USO) A private, non-profit organization that provides entertainment to the troops and morale-building services and activities to them and their families.

Unlocked Refers to a cell phone that can work with any service provider; *see* locked.

USAJobs The official Federal government jobs website (*http://www.usajobs.opm.gov/*).

VA loan Government-backed mortgage loan supported by the Department of Veterans Affairs.

Variable housing allowance (VHA) Money given to servicemembers not living in quarters to help offset the price of housing in high-cost areas.

Veterans Educational Assistance Program (VEAP) Program to help servicemembers pay for college tuition.

Veterans Group Life Insurance (VGLI) Renewable term life insurance that servicemembers may purchase upon release from active duty.

Veterans Readjustment Appointment A special authority by which Federal agencies may appoint an eligible veteran without nonveteran competition.

Veterans' Recruitment Act (VRA) Allows certain veterans to be appointed noncompetitively to Federal jobs.

Vocational Rehabilitation and Employment Program A VA program that provides vocational rehabilitation services to veterans with military-related disabilities.

Voice over Internet Protocol (VoIP) Also called IP Telephony, this is the transmission of voice traffic over computers.

Wage System A classification system of government trades, craft, and labor positions. See *http://www.opm.gov/fedclass/html/fwseries.asp* for a list of such jobs.

Warrant An official document bestowed by a military branch, assigning the holder specific duties and responsibilities.

Warrant Officer (WO) A person who holds a commission or warrant in a warrant officer grade. Ranks in between enlisted and officer personnel. WOs have a high degree of specialization in a particular field instead of the more general assignment pattern of other commissioned officers.

Weight allowance A maximum weight that may be moved and/or stored at government expense, based on rank.

Weighted Airman Promotion System (WAPS) The Air Force's promotion evaluation system for enlisted personnel between grades E-5 and E-7.

Welcome packet Folder of information about a duty station. Includes emergency and convenience telephone numbers; local and military services available; recreational facilities; exchange, commissary, and hospital hours; and other useful information.

Wetting Down Navy promotion party.

Whole Life Insurance Also called permanent, it protects the beneficiary over the course of his/her entire life, as long as the premiums are paid.

Will A legal document that describes what should be done with the deceased's property and who is to be the guardian of minor children.

Women, Infant and Children's Program (WIC) Nutrition program run by the Department of Agriculture that provides coupons to qualifying families that are redeemable for healthy foods at grocery stores and the commissary.

Wounded Warrior A servicemember who was severely injured in the line of duty.

Zone of consideration The time period during which officers whose dates of rank are the same as, one year earlier than, or one year later than the date announced by the headquarters, are considered for promotion.

Index

Page numbers in italics indicate sidebars, tables and charts.